Wellington's Despatches & Letters

The Duke of Wellington on Copenhagen

Wellington's Despatches & Letters

A Selection from The Peninsular War & Waterloo Campaign, 1808-1815

ILLUSTRATED WITH MAPS

Walter Wood

and

Charles Walker Robinson

LEONAUR

Wellington's Despatches & Letters
A Selection from The Peninsular War & Waterloo Campaign, 1808-1815
ILLUSTRATED *WITH MAPS*
by Walter Wood and Charles Walker Robinson

FIRST EDITION

Leonaur is an imprint of Oakpast Ltd

ISBN: 978-1-917666-50-3 (hardcover)
ISBN: 978-1-917666-51-0 (softcover)

http://www.leonaur.com

Publisher's Notes

Contents

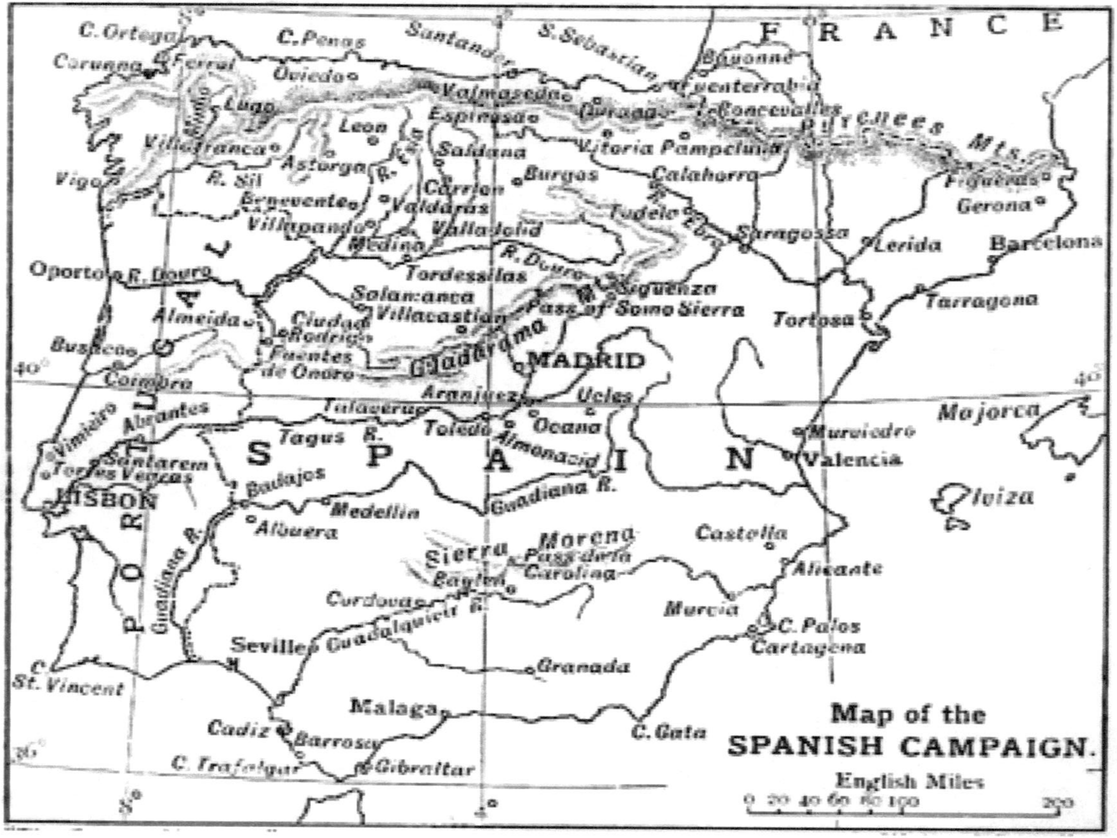

Map of the
SPANISH CAMPAIGN.

Campaign in the Peninsula

In the spring of 1808 a force was assembled at Cork, with a view, as it was supposed, to some of the Spanish colonies of South America; but from the extraordinary changes which had taken place towards the latter end of 1807 and the beginning of 1808, in the affairs of Spain and Portugal, by the French intervention, or rather invasion, of those countries, and the consequent national appeals to Great Britain for aid to rescue them from this flagrant usurpation of Bonaparte, new fields presented themselves, in which the palm of victory was to be disputed with the conquerors of Europe.

The British Army was now successfully to emulate the splendid fame of the navy; and during the seven following years, by its discipline and courage under the great general who commanded it in the Peninsula, its own former proud days of Crecy, Poictiers, Agincourt, Blenheim, Ramillies, and Malplaquet, (see table following), were to be eclipsed by the still prouder successes which now annually, (see table following), followed, to be finally crowned by the most triumphant and decisive victory gained in modern times, at the great Battle of Waterloo.

Crecy	- 1346	Agincourt	- 1415	Ramillies	- 1706
Poictiers	- 1356	Blenheim	- 1704	Malplaquet	1709
1. Vimeiro	- 1808	6. Ciudad Rodrigo	- 1812	11. Nivelle	- 1813
2. Oporto	- 1809	7. Badajoz	- 1812	12. Nive -	- 1813
3. Talavera	- 1809	8. Salamanca	1812	13. Orthez	- 1814
4. Busaco	- 1810	9. Vittoria	- 1813	14. Toulouse	- 1814
5. Fuentes de Oñoro	- 1811	10. Sorauren	- 1813	15. WATERLOO	1815

★★★★★★★★★★

'Peninsula'heads the list of British military battle-honours, being borne by no fewer than 71 regiments—20 cavalry and 51 infantry. Of the Peninsular honours 'Vittoria'is highest, being borne by 44 regiments—8 cavalry and 36 infantry. Thirty-eight regiments have Waterloo also an honour—15 cavalry and 23 infantry.—W. W.

His Royal Highness the Commander-in-Chief to Lieutenant-General the Hon. Sir A. Wellesley, K.B.

(*Sir A. Wellesley had been promoted to the rank of Lieutenant. General on April 25, 1808.*)

'Horse Guards,
June 14, 1808.

'His Majesty having been graciously pleased to appoint you to the command of a detachment of his army, to be employed upon a particular service, I have to desire that you will be pleased to take the earliest opportunity to assume the command of this force, and carry into effect such instructions as you may receive from His Majesty's Ministers. . . '

Viscount Castlereagh, Secretary of State, to Lieutenant-General the Hon. Sir A. Wellesley, K.B.

'Downing Street,
'June 30, 1808.

'The occupation of Spain and Portugal by the troops of France, and the entire usurpation of their respective Governments by that Power, has determined His Majesty to direct a corps of his troops, as stated in the margin, to be prepared for service, to be employed, under your orders, in counteracting the designs of the enemy, and in affording to the Spanish and Portuguese nations every possible aid in throwing off the yoke of France. . ..

'You are authorised to give the most distinct assurances to the Spanish and Portuguese people, that His Majesty, in sending a force to their assistance, has no other object in view than to afford them the most unqualified and disinterested support; and in any arrangements that you may be called upon to make with either nation, in the persecution of the common cause, you will act with the utmost liberality and confidence, and upon the principle that His Majesty's endeavours are to be directed to aid the people of Spain and Portugal in restoring and maintaining against France the independence and integrity of their respective monarchies.

'In the rapid succession in which events must be expected to follow each other, situated as Spain and Portugal now are, much must be left to your judgment and decision on the spot....

'You will, however, impress upon the minds of persons in authority that, consistently with the effectual assertion of their independence, they cannot possibly acknowledge the King or Prince of Asturias as, at present, possessing any authority whatever, or consider any act done by them as valid until they return within the country, and become absolutely free agents. That they never can be considered free so long as they shall be prevailed on to acquiesce in the continuance of French troops either in Spain or Portugal.

'The entire and absolute evacuation of the Peninsula, by the troops of France, being, after what has lately passed, the only security for Spanish independence, and the only basis upon which the Spanish nation should be prevailed upon to treat or to lay down their arms.'

To Viscount Castlereagh, Secretary of State.

'Cove,
'July 10, 1808.

'The wind is still contrary, but we hope it will change so as to sail this evening. We are unmoored, and shall not wait one moment after the wind may be fair.

'I see that people in England complain of the delay which has taken place in the sailing of the expedition; but, in fact, none has taken place; and even if all had been on board, we could not have sailed before this day. . . .'

THE BRITISH FORCE.

'Horse Guards,
'July 20, 1808.

'*List of the Several Corps, General and Staff Officers, composing a Large Division of His Majesty's Army, to be employed upon a Particular Service.*

'His Majesty has been pleased to direct that the undermentioned corps should be formed into one army. . . . (These were Sir John Moore's corps of 11,253; Major-General Spencer's corps, 4,793; Sir Arthur Wellesley's corps, 9,280; and a force embarking of 4,803—in all 30,129.—W. W.)

'His Majesty has further been pleased to direct that Lieutenant-General Sir Hew Dalrymple shall have the chief command thereof, and that Lieutenant-General Sir Harry Burrard be second in command, when the Staff of this army will consist as follows, *viz.*:

Lieutenant-General Sir Hew Dalrymple, Commander of the Forces.

Lieutenant-General Sir Harry Burrard, second in command.

Lieutenant-Generals Sir John Moore, the Hon. John Hope, Mackenzie Fraser, Lord Paget, Sir Arthur Wellesley.

Major-Generals J. Murray, Lord W. Bentinck, Hon. Edward Paget, Spencer, Hill, Ferguson.

Brigadier-Generals Acland, Nightingall, R. Stewart, the Hon. C. Stewart, H. Fane, R. Anstruther, Catlin Craufurd.

Brigadier-General H. Clinton, 1st Foot Guards, Acting Adjutant-General.

Lieutenant-Colonel Murray, 3rd Foot Guards, Acting Quartermaster-General.

Brevet Lieutenant-Colonel Torrens, 89th Foot, Military Secretary.'

Arrival off Oporto.

To Viscount Castlereagh.

'H.M.S. *Crocodile*, off Oporto,
'July 25, 1808.

'I avail myself of the opportunity of the return of the *Peacock* to England to inform you that I sailed from Coruna, as I told you I should, on the night of the 21st, and joined the fleet the next day, and arrived here yesterday in the *Crocodile*. The fleet are now coming on. (The *Crocodile* was commanded by the Hon. G. Cadogan, afterwards Earl Cadogan.)

'All the provinces to the north of the Tagus, with the exception of the country immediately about Lisbon, are in a state of insurrection against the French, and the people are ready and desirous to take arms; but, unfortunately, there are none in the country—indeed, I may say, none to arm the troops which the Bishop of Oporto and the *Junta* of this place have assembled. They have at present a corps of about 5,000 men, regular troops and militia, including 300 cavalry at Coimbra, armed with 1,000 muskets, got from the fleet, fowling-pieces, etc., and 12,000 peasantry, mostly unarmed, I believe.

'The regular troops are composed of detachments of different corps, and cannot in any respect be deemed an efficient force. Besides these, there are 300 Spanish infantry, about 1,500 regular Portuguese infantry, and some militia volunteers and peasantry here....

'The French corps is concentrated at or about Lisbon, and is said to consist of from 13,000 to 14,000 men. Sir Charles Cotton says they are adding to the fortifications of the town, of a citadel within the town, and of Fort St. Julian.

'The measures to be adopted for this country are to supply it with arms and money. I saw a statement last night, from which it appears that they could get together 38,000 men with ease, if they had arms or money to pay them. If I should find the troops at Coimbra to be worth it, I propose to arm them.'

Bonaparte's Strength.

To Major-General Spencer.

'H.M.S. *Crocodile*, off the Tagus,
'July 26, 1808.

'I think there is reason to believe that Bonaparte is not now very strong in Spain, and that he has not at his command the means of reinforcing his troops sufficiently to strike any blow which can have a permanent effect. . . .'

Memorandum for Disembarkation.

'July 29, 1808.

'In the event of a landing being determined upon in Mondego Bay, a signal will be made to Captain Malcolm, when it will be settled at what period it may be proper to move the horse ships, and the ships having the ordnance on board, into the river.

'The infantry will be directed to be landed from the transports in the roads, and to be rowed in the boats up the river, and landed on the south bank of it; General Fane's brigade first, excepting the Veteran battalion, which is to remain on board; then General Ferguson's; then General Craufurd's. . . .

'The men to land, each with one shirt and one pair of shoes, besides those on them, combs, razor, and a brush, which are to be packed up in their greatcoats. The knapsacks to be left in the transports, and the baggage of the officers, excepting such light articles as are necessary for them. A careful sergeant to be left in the headquarter ship of each regiment, and a careful private man in each of the other ships, in charge of the baggage; and each officer who shall leave any baggage in a transport must take care to have his name marked on each package, and each numbered, and give a list of what he leaves to the soldier in charge of the baggage, in order that he may get what he may require.

'The men will land with three days' bread and two days' meat, cooked.

'The commanding officer of artillery is to land the three brigades of artillery, each with half the usual proportion of ammunition, the forge cart, etc. He will also land 500,000 rounds of musket ammunition for the use of the troops, for which carriage will be provided.

'Each soldier will have with him three good flints.

'Besides the bread above directed to be landed with the soldiers, three days' bread to be packed up in bags, containing 100 pounds each, on board each of the transports, for the number of soldiers who shall be disembarked from it. . .'

PORTUGUESE TROOPS.

To Viscount Castlereagh.

'H.M.S. *Donegal*,
'August 1, 1808.

'. . . My opinion is that Great Britain ought to raise, organise, and pay an army in Portugal, consisting of 30,000 Portuguese troops, which might be easily raised at an early period, and 20,000 British, including 4,000 or 5,000 cavalry. This army might operate on the frontiers of Portugal in Spanish Estremadura, and it would serve as the link between the kingdoms of Galicia and Andalusia. It would give Great Britain the preponderance in the conduct of the war in the Peninsula; and whatever might be the result of the Spanish exertions, Portugal would be saved from the French grasp. You know best whether you could bear the expense, or what part of it the Portuguese Government would or could defray. But if you should adopt this plan, you must send everything from England—arms, ammunition, clothing, and accoutrements, ordnance, flour, oats, etc. . . .'

MEMORANDUM FOR THE COMMISSARY-GENERAL.

'H.M.S. *Donegal*,
'August 1, 1808.

'*1st.* The troops will land with four days' bread and two days' meat; and it will be necessary to keep up that supply at the village of Lavaos, so that, when the army shall march, the troops may carry, each man, four days' bread.

'*2nd.* Besides this quantity of bread to be carried by the men themselves, a quantity, equal to three days' consumption for 10,000 men, must be carried, if possible, on the backs of mules—*viz.*, two bags, or 224 pounds, on each mule. This will require 130 mules.

'*3rd.* Besides these seven days' bread to move with the troops, the Lieutenant-General desires that ten days' bread, five days' meat, and ten days' spirits, for 10,000 men, should move from Lavaos about the same time, by the carts of the country, to be formed into a depot about seventy miles in advance. This will require:

	Carts.
Bread	170
Meat	100
Spirits	37
Total	307

These carts must be levied, and will be relieved at Leyria.

'*4th*. The Medical Department will require two carts to march with the army, carrying twenty-four bearers for wounded men, a case of utensils, and a medicine-chest.

'*5th*. The artillery will require, to move with the army, 250 mules, each to carry 2,000 rounds of musket ammunition.

'*6th*. The Quartermaster-General's Department will require thirty mules to carry entrenching tools.

'*7th*. The Commissary-General will make arrangements for supplying the troops at Lavaos with bread, meat, spirits, and wood.

'*8th*. The Commissary-General will see in the General Orders to what day the troops, as they disembark, will have bread and meat, and he will provide accordingly for their subsistence.

'*9th*. The horses will land, each with three days' forage and oats. Provision must be made for them after the 3rd instant; but as the demand must be small, it is concluded that the country will experience no difficulty in supplying their wants, and therefore no provision is made for carrying forward forage or oats.

'*10th*. The muleteers and carmen are to be provisioned from this date, and their cattle foraged.

'*11th*. Bread, etc., to be handed from the ships accordingly.

'A. W.'

Proclamation

By the Commanders-in-Chief of His Britannic Majesty's Land and Sea Forces, employed to assist the Loyal Inhabitants of the Kingdom of Portugal.

'People of Portugal.

'The time has arrived to rescue your country, and restore the government to your lawful prince.

'His Britannic Majesty, our most gracious King and master, has, in compliance with the wishes and ardent supplications for succour from all parts of Portugal, sent to your aid a British Army, directed to co-operate with his fleet, already on your coast.

'The English soldiers who land upon your shore do so with every sentiment of friendship, faith, and honour.

'The glorious struggle in which you are engaged is for all that is dear to man—the protection of your wives and children; the restoration of your lawful prince; the independence—nay, the very existence—of your kingdom; and for the preservation of your holy religion. Objects like these can only be obtained by distinguished examples of fortitude and constancy.

'The noble struggle against the tyranny and usurpation of France will be jointly maintained by Portugal, Spain, and England; and in contributing to the success of a cause so just and glorious, the views of His Britannic Majesty are the same as those by which you are yourselves animated.

'Arthur Wellesley.
'Charles Cotton.

'Lavaos, August 2, 1808.'

Inefficient Commissariat.

To Viscount Castlereagh.

'Lavaos,
'August 8, 1808.

'My despatch contains the fullest information upon every subject, and I have nothing to add to it. I have had the greatest difficulty in organising my commissariat for the march, and that department is very incompetent, notwithstanding the arrangements which I made with Huskisson upon the subject. This department deserves your serious attention. The existence of the army depends upon it, and yet the people who manage it are incapable of managing anything out of a counting-house.

'I shall be obliged to leave Spencer's guns behind for want of means of moving them, and I should have been obliged to leave my own, if it were not for the horses of the Irish Commissariat. Let nobody ever prevail upon you to send a corps to any part of Europe without horses to draw their guns. It is not true that horses lose their condition at sea.'

Early Obstacles.

To Lieutenant-General Sir H. Burrard, Bart.

'Leyria,
'August 11, 1808.

'In my official letters of the 8th and 10th I have apprised you of the state of the war in this country and in Spain, and I shall adopt this mode of communicating to you what I know of the resources of this country, and those matters of which it will be convenient to you to be apprised in the operations which you will have to conduct.

'In the first place, in the present season of the year, you cannot depend upon the country for bread. Portugal never fed itself during more than seven months out of twelve. The common consumption of the country is Indian corn; and the little which there is in the country cannot be ground at this season of the year, as the mills are generally turned by water, and there is now no water in the mill streams; you must therefore depend upon your transports for bread. Wine and beef you will get in the country; and in a short time, straw and Indian corn, or barley, for your horses; but the supply of these articles will not last long: this, however, is a consideration for a future period....

'As for mules for carriage, I am afraid you will get none, for I believe my corps has swept the country very handsomely of this animal. You must therefore depend for the carriage of your bread upon the carts of the country, drawn by bullocks; each of these will carry about 600 pounds, and will travel in a day about twelve miles; but I do not believe that any power that you could exert over them, particularly when they shall have already made an exertion against the enemy, by the assistance which they have given to me, would induce the owners of the carts to go from their homes a greater distance than to the nearest place where you could get carts to relieve them....

'With a view, therefore, to your first operation in Portugal, which I will suppose to be to march to Santarem, I would recommend to you to form a magazine of ten days' bread and five days' meat, in case of accidents, at Leyria; and then to keep that quantity up or to increase it as you may find it convenient for your purposes at Santarem. You will probably find it convenient to increase it, in which you will experience no difficulty.

'You will find the people of this country well-disposed to assist you with everything in their power, but they have very little in their power, and they have been terribly plundered by the French. . . . '

To General Freire, commanding the Portuguese Army.

Calvario,
'August 13, 1808.

'Lieutenant-Colonel Trant informed me this morning of the distress which your troops were likely to suffer from want of bread, and he earnestly urged me, on the part of Your Excellency, to issue bread to the Portuguese troops from the British Commissariat....

'I am really much concerned that Your Excellency's troops should suffer any distress, but you must be aware that the arrangements for providing for them have not fallen upon me; and that I have not required a greater proportion of the resources of the country (particularly not bread) than is necessary for those of His Majesty; and I trust that Your Excellency will see the propriety of adopting some arrangement which will provide effectually for the subsistence of the army which you will march to Lisbon; at the same time, that you will allow His Majesty's troops to enjoy such of the resources of the country as I have above mentioned, which they require. . . .'

The Battle of Roleia.

To Viscount Castlereagh,

'Caldas,
'August 16, 1808.

'. . . . I marched from Leyria on the 13th, and arrived at Alcobaça on the 14th, which place the enemy had abandoned in the preceding night; and I arrived here yesterday. The enemy, about 4,000 in number, were posted about ten miles from hence, at Roliça; and they occupied Obidos, about three miles from hence, with their advanced posts. As the possession of this last village was important to our future operations, I determined to occupy it, and as soon as the British infantry arrived upon the ground, I directed that it might be occupied by a detachment consisting of four companies of riflemen of the 60th and 95th Regiments.

'The enemy, consisting of a small picket of infantry and a few cavalry, made a trifling resistance and retired; but they were followed by a detachment of our riflemen to the distance of three miles from Obidos. The riflemen were there attacked by a superior body of the enemy, who attempted to cut them off from the main body of the detachment to which they belonged, which had now advanced to their support; larger bodies of the enemy appeared on both the flanks of the detachments, and it was with difficulty that Major-General Spencer, who had gone out to Obidos when he heard that the riflemen had advanced in pursuit of the enemy, was enabled to effect their retreat to that village. They have since remained in possession of it, and the enemy have retired entirely from the neighbourhood.

'In this little affair of the advanced post, which was occasioned solely by the eagerness of the troops in pursuit of the enemy, I am concerned to add that Lieutenant Bunbury, of the 2nd Battalion 95th Regiment, was killed, and the Hon. Captain Pakenham wounded, but slightly; and we have lost some men, of whose numbers I have not received the returns. . . .'

★★★★★★★★★★

The 60th is now the King's Royal Rifle Corps, and the 95th is the Rifle Brigade. The sixteen Peninsular honours which the King's Royal Rifle Corps possess were won by the famous 5th or Jager Battalion—foreigners, mostly Germans, in British pay. The Rifle Brigade has been from its origin in 1800 composed entirely of British troops. These two bodies of riflemen fired the opening shots of the war.—W. W.

★★★★★★★★★★

To Viscount Castlereagh.

'Caldas,
'August 16, 1808.

'. . We are going on as well as possible—the army in high order and in great spirits. We make long marches, to which they are becoming accustomed; and I make no doubt they will be equal to anything when we shall reach Lisbon. I have every hope of success....

'Our artillery horses are not what we ought to have. They have great merit in their way as cast horses of dragoons, and Irish cart horses, bought for £12 each! but not fit for an army, that, to be successful and carry things with a high hand, ought to be able to move.'

To Viscount Castlereagh.

'Villa Verde,
'August 17, 1808.

'The French General Laborde having continued in his position at Roliça, since my arrival at Caldas on the 15th instant, I determined to attack him in it this morning. Roliça is situated on an eminence, having a plain in its front, at the end of a valley, which commences at Caldas, and is closed to the southward by mountains which join the hills forming the valley on the left.

'Looking from Caldas, in the centre of the valley and about eight miles from Roliça, is the town and the old Moorish fort of Obidos, from whence the enemy's pickets had been driven on the 15th; and from that time he had posts in the hills on both sides of the valley, as well as in the plain in front of his army, which was posted on the heights in front of Roliça, its right resting upon the hills, its left upon an eminence on which was a windmill, and the whole covering four or five passes into the mountains on his rear.

'I have reason to believe that his force consisted of at least 6,000 men, of which about 500 were cavalry, with five pieces of cannon; and there was some reason to believe that General Loison, who was at Rio Mayor yesterday, would join General Laborde by his right in the course of the night.

'The plan of attack was formed accordingly, and the army, having broken up from Caldas this morning, was formed into three columns. The right, consisting of 1,200 Portuguese infantry, fifty Portuguese cavalry, destined to turn the enemy's left, and penetrate into the mountains in his rear. The left, consisting of Major-General Ferguson's and Brigader-General Bowes's brigade of infantry, three companies of riflemen, a brigade of light artillery, and twenty British and twenty Portuguese cavalry, was destined, under the command of Major-General Ferguson, to ascend the hills at Obidos, to turn all the enemy's posts on the left of the valley, as well as the right of his post at ça.

'This corps was also destined to watch the motions of General Loison on the enemy's right, who, I had heard, had moved from Rio Mayor towards Alcoentre last night. The centre column, consisting of Major-General Hill's, Brigadier-General Nightingall's, Brigadier-General C. Craufurd's, and Brigadier-General Fane's brigades (with the exception of the riflemen detached with Major-General Ferguson), and 400 Portuguese light infantry, the British and Portuguese cavalry, a brigade of 9-pounders, and a brigade of 6-pounders, was destined to attack General Laborde's position in the front.

'The columns being formed, the troops moved from Obidos about seven o'clock in the morning. Brigadier-General Fane's riflemen were immediately detached into the hills on the left of the valley, to keep up the communication between the centre and left columns, and to protect the march of the former along the valley, and the enemy's posts were successively driven in.

'Major-General Hill's brigade, formed in three columns of battalions, moved on the right of the valley, supported by the cavalry, in order to attack the enemy's left; and Brigadier-Generals Nightingall and Craufurd moved with the artillery along the highroad, until at length the former formed in the plain immediately in the enemy's front, supported by the light infantry companies, and the 45th Regiment of Brigadier-General Craufurd's brigade; while the two other regiments of this brigade (the 50th and 91st), and half of the 9-pounder brigade, were kept up as a reserve in the rear.

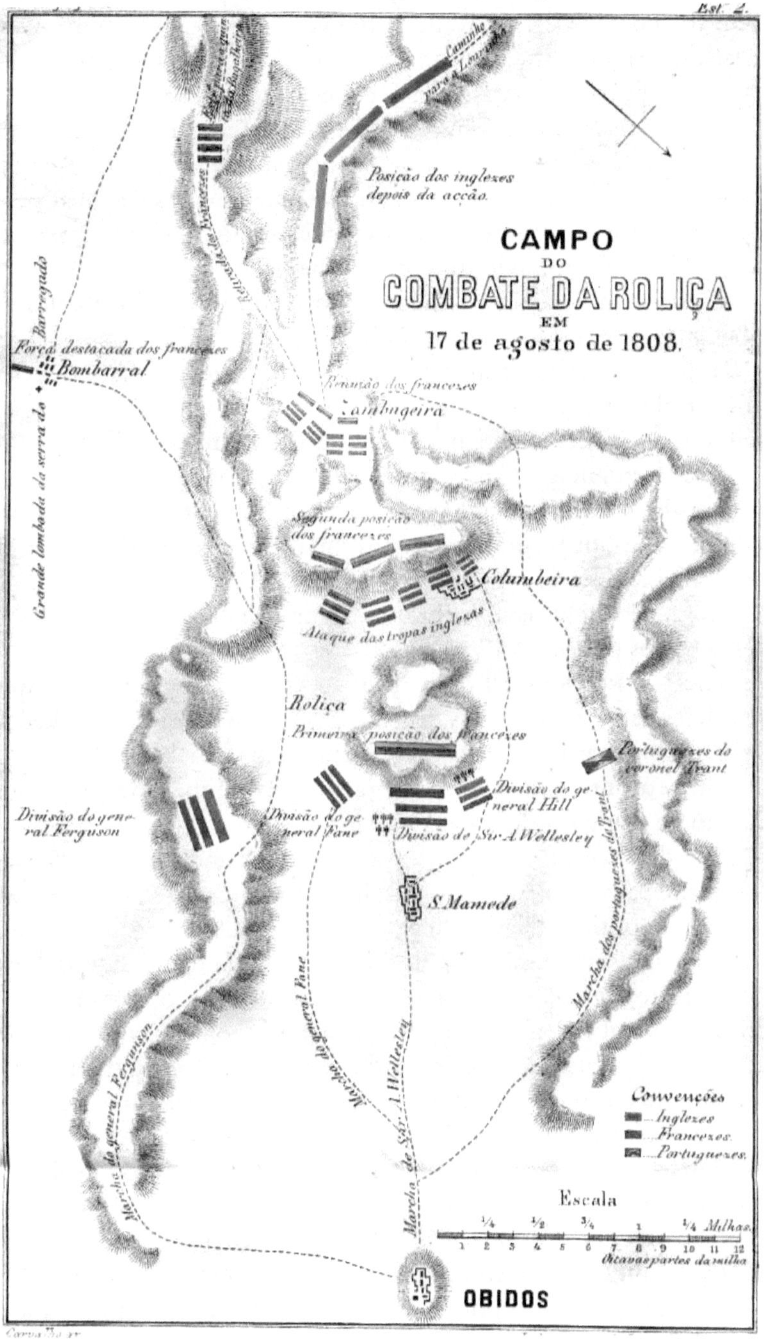
CAMPO
DO
COMBATE DA ROLIÇA
EM
17 de agosto de 1808.
Posição dos inglezes
depois da acção.
Barregudo
Força destacada dos francezes
Bombarral
Grande lombada da serra do
Retirada dos francezes
Reunião dos francezes
Zambugeira
Segunda posição
dos francezes
Columbeira
Ataque das tropas inglezas
Roliça
Primeira posição dos francezes
Portuguezes do
coronel Trant
Divisão do ge-
neral Hill
Divisão do gene-
ral Ferguson
Divisão do ge-
neral Fane
Divisão de Sir A. Wellesley
S. Mamede
Marcha dos portuguezes de Trant
Marcha do general Fane
Marcha de Sir A. Wellesley
Marcha do general Ferguson
Convenções
Inglezes
Francezes
Portuguezes
Escala
1/4 1/2 3/4 1 1/4 Milhas
1 2 3 4 5 6 7 8 9 10 11 12
Oitavas partes da milha
OBIDOS

'Major-General Hill and Brigadier-General Nightingall advanced upon the enemy's position, and at the same moment Brigadier-General Fane's riflemen were in the hills on his right, the Portuguese in a village upon his left, and Major-General Ferguson's column was descending from the heights into the plain. From this situation the enemy retired by the passes into the mountains with the utmost regularity and the greatest celerity; and notwithstanding the rapid advance of the British infantry, the want of a sufficient body of cavalry was the cause of his suffering but little loss on the plain.

'It was then necessary to make a disposition to attack the formidable position which he had taken up.

'Brigadier-General Fane's riflemen were already in the mountains on his right, and no time was lost in attacking the different passes, as well to support the riflemen as to defeat the enemy completely.

'The Portuguese infantry were ordered to move up a pass on the right of the whole. The light companies of Major-General Hill's brigade, and the 5th Regiment, moved up a pass next on the right; and the 29th Regiment, supported by the 9th Regiment, under Brigadier-General Nightingall, a third pass; and the 45th and 82nd Regiments, passes on the left.

'These passes were all difficult of access, and some of them were well defended by the enemy, particularly that which was attacked by the 29th and 9th Regiments. These regiments attacked with the utmost impetuosity, and reached the enemy before those whose attacks were to be made on their flanks.

'The defence of the enemy was desperate; and it was in this attack principally that we sustained the loss which we have to lament, particularly of that gallant officer, the Hon. Lieutenant-Colonel Lake, who distinguished himself upon this occasion. The enemy was, however, driven from all the positions he had taken in the passes of the mountains, and our troops were advanced in the plains on their tops. For a considerable length of time the 29th and 9th Regiments alone were advanced to this point, with Brigadier-General Fane's riflemen at a distance on the left, and they were afterwards supported by the 5th Regiment, and by the light companies of Major-General Hill's brigade, which had come upon their right, and by the other troops ordered to ascend the mountains, who came up by degrees.

'The enemy here made three most gallant attacks upon the 29th and 9th Regiments, supported as I have above stated, with a view to cover the retreat of his defeated army, in all of which he was, however, repulsed; but he succeeded in effecting his retreat in good order, owing principally to my want of cavalry, and, secondly, to the difficulty of bringing up the passes of the mountains, with celerity, a sufficient number of troops and of cannon to support those which had first ascended. The loss of the enemy has, however, been very great, and he left three pieces of cannon in our hands.

'I cannot sufficiently applaud the conduct of the troops throughout this action. The enemy's positions were formidable, and he took them up with his usual ability and celerity, and defended them most gallantly.

'But I must observe that, although we had such a superiority of numbers employed in the operations of this day, the troops actually engaged in the heat of the action were, from unavoidable circumstances, only the 5th, 9th, 29th, the riflemen of the 95th and 60th, and the flank companies of Major-General Hill's brigade, being a number by no means equal to that of the enemy. Their conduct, therefore, deserves the highest commendation. . . .

'I have the honour to enclose herewith a return of killed, wounded, and missing.'

	Officers.	Non-commissioned Officers and Drummers.	Rank and File.	Horses.	Total Loss of Officers, Non-commissioned Officers, and Rank and File.
Killed - -	4	3	63	1	70
Wounded -	20	20	295	2	335
Missing -	4	2	68	...	74

To Viscount Castlereagh.

'Lourinha,
'August 18, 1808.

'My despatch of yesterday and of this day will inform you of the state of affairs here. I never saw such desperate fighting as in the attack of the pass by Lake, and in the three attacks by the French on our troops in the mountains. These attacks were made in their best style, and our troops defended themselves capitally; and if the difficulties of the ground had not prevented me from bringing up a sufficient number of the troops and of cannon, we should have taken the whole army.

'They say that the French lost 1,500 men, which is a large amount; but I think they had more than 6,000 men in the action. . . .'

The Battle of Vimeiro.

To Lieutenant-General Burrard.

'Vimeiro,
'August 21, 1808.

'I have the honour to inform you that the enemy attacked us in our position at Vimeiro this morning.

'The village of Vimeiro stands in a valley, through which runs the River Maceira; at the back, and to the westward and northward of this village, is a mountain, the western point of which touches the sea, and the eastern is separated by a deep ravine from the heights, over which passes the road which leads from Lourinha, and the northward to Vimeiro. The greater part of the infantry—the 1st, 2nd, 3rd, 4th, 5th, and 8th Brigades—were posted on this mountain, with eight pieces of artillery, Major-General Hill's brigade being on the right, and Major-General Ferguson's on the left, having one battalion on the heights separated from the mountain.

'On the eastern and southern side of the town is a mill, which is entirely commanded, particularly on its right, by the mountain to the westward of the town, and commanding all the ground in the neighbourhood to the southward and eastward, on which Brigadier-General Fane was posted with his riflemen and the 50th Regiment, and Brigadier-General Anstruther with his brigade, with half a brigade of 6-pounders and half a brigade of 9-pounders, which had been ordered to the position in the course of last night. The ground over which passes the road from Lourinha commanded the left of this height, and it had not been occupied, excepting by a picket, as the camp had been taken up only for one night, and there was no water in the neighbourhood of this height.

'The cavalry and the reserve of artillery were in the valley, between the hills on which the infantry stood, both flanking and supporting Brigadier-General Fane's advanced-guard.

'The enemy first appeared about eight o'clock in the morning, in large bodies of cavalry on our left, upon the heights on the road to Lourinha; and it was soon obvious that the attack would be made upon our advanced-guard and the left of our position; and Major-General Ferguson's brigade was immediately moved across the ravine to the heights on the road to Lourinha, with three pieces of cannon; he was followed successively by Brigadier-General Nightingall, with his brigade and three pieces of cannon, Brigadier-General Acland and his brigade, and Brigadier-General Bowes with his brigade.

'These troops were formed (Major-General Ferguson's brigade in the first line, Brigadier-General Nightingall's in the second, and Brigadier-General Bowes's and Acland's in columns in the rear) on those heights, with their right upon the valley which leads into Vimeiro, and their left upon the other ravine, which separates these heights from the range which terminates at the landing-place at Maceira. On the last-mentioned heights the Portuguese troops, which had been in the bottom near Vimeiro, were posted in the first instance, and they were supported by Brigadier-General C. Craufurd's brigade.

'The troops of the advanced-guard, on the heights to the southward and eastward of the town, were deemed sufficient for its defence, and Major-General Hill was moved to the centre of the mountain, on which the great body of the infantry had been posted, as a support to these troops, and as a reserve to the whole army; in addition to this support, these troops had that of the cavalry in the rear of their right.

'The enemy's attack began in several columns upon the whole of the troops on this height; on the left they advanced, notwithstanding the fire of the riflemen close to the 50th Regiment, and they were checked and driven back only by the bayonets of that corps. The 2nd Battalion 43rd Regiment was likewise closely engaged with them in the road which leads into Vimeiro, a part of that corps having been ordered into the churchyard to prevent them from penetrating into the town. On the right of the position, they were repulsed by the bayonets of the 97th Regiment, which corps was successfully supported by the 2nd Battalion 52nd, which, by an advance in column, took the enemy in flank.

'Besides this opposition given to the attack of the enemy on the advanced-guard by their own exertions, they were attacked in flank by Brigadier-General Acland's brigade in its advance to its position on the heights on the left, and a cannonade was kept up on the flank of the enemy's columns by the artillery on those heights.

'At length, after a most desperate contest, the enemy was driven back in confusion from this attack, with the loss of seven pieces of cannon, many prisoners, and a great number of officers and soldiers killed and wounded. He was pursued by a detachment of the 20th Light Dragoons, but the enemy's cavalry were so much superior in numbers that this detachment has suffered much, and Lieutenant-Colonel Taylor was unfortunately killed.

'Nearly at the same time the enemy's attack commenced upon the heights on the road to Lourinha: this attack was supported by a large

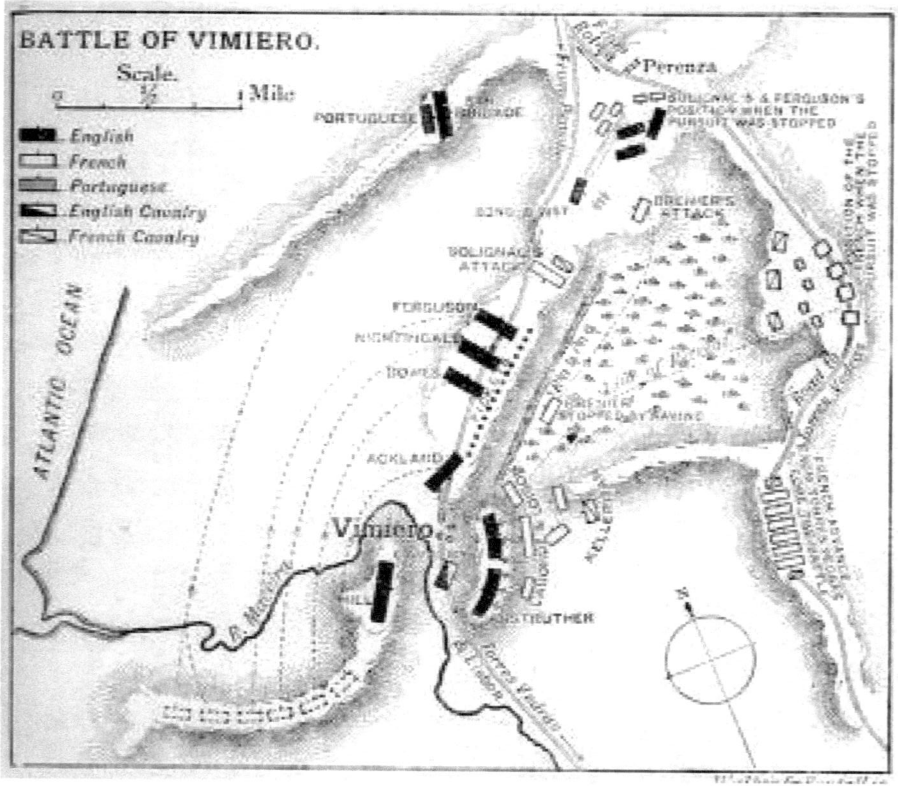
BATTLE OF VIMIERO.
Scale.
0
½
1 Mile
English
French
Portuguese
English Cavalry
French Cavalry
ATLANTIC OCEAN
PORTUGUESE
Perenza
BOLIGNAC'S & FERGUSON'S POSITION WHEN THE PURSUIT WAS STOPPED
POSITION OF THE FRENCH WHEN THE PURSUIT WAS STOPPED
BRENIER'S ATTACK
BOLIGNAC'S ATTACK
FERGUSON
NIGHTINGALE
BOWES
ACKLAND
BRENIER STOPPED BY RAVINE
Vimiero
HILL
ANSTRUTHER
KELLERMAN
FRENCH ADVANCE FROM TORRES VEDRAS CONE THE BATTLE
R. Maceira
Torres Vedras
N

body of cavalry, and was made with the usual impetuosity of French troops. It was received with steadiness by Major-General Ferguson's brigade, consisting of the 36th, 40th, and 71st Regiments, and these corps charged as soon as the enemy approached them, who gave way, and they continued to advance upon him, supported by the 82nd, one of the corps of Brigadier-General Nightingall's brigade, which, as the ground extended, afterwards formed a part of the first line by the 29th Regiment, and by Brigadier-General Bowes's and Acland's brigades; whilst Brigadier General C. Craufurd's brigade and the Portuguese troops, in two lines, advanced along the height on the left. In the advance of Major-General Ferguson's brigade, six pieces of cannon were taken from the enemy, with many prisoners, and vast numbers were killed and wounded.

'The enemy afterwards made an attempt to recover part of his artillery by attacking the 71st and 82nd Regiments, which were halted in a valley in which it had been taken. These regiments retired from the low grounds in the valley to the heights, where they halted, faced about, and fired, and advanced upon the enemy, who had by that time arrived in the low ground, and they thus obliged him again to retire with great loss.

'In this action, in which the whole of the French force in Portugal was employed, under the command of the Duc D'Abrantes in person, in which the enemy was certainly superior in cavalry and artillery, and in which not more than half of the British Army was actually engaged, he has sustained a signal defeat, and has lost thirteen pieces of cannon, twenty-three ammunition waggons, with powder, shells, stores of all descriptions, and 20,000 rounds of musket ammunition. One general officer has been wounded (Brenier) and taken prisoner, and a great many officers and soldiers have been killed, wounded, and taken.

'The valour and discipline of His Majesty's troops have been conspicuous upon this occasion, as you, who witnessed the greatest part of the action, must have observed.

'In mentioning Colonel Burne and the 36th Regiment, (now the 2nd Battalion the Worcestershire Regiment.—W. W.), upon this occasion, I cannot avoid adding that the regular and orderly conduct of this corps throughout the service, and their gallantry and discipline in action, have been conspicuous.

'I must take this opportunity of acknowledging my obligations to the general and staff officers of the army. . .'

Return of the of Killed, Wounded, and Missing of the Army under the Command of Lieutenant-General the Hon. Sir Arthur Wellesley, K.B., on August 21, 1808.

	Officers.	Non-commissioned Officers and Drummers.	Rank and File.	Horses.	Total Loss of Officers, Non-commissioned Officers, and Rank and File.
Killed -	4	3	128	30	135
Wounded -	37	31	466	12	534
Missing -	2	3	46	1	51

Return of Ordnance and Ammunition taken in the Action of August 21, 1808.

'One 6-pounder four 4-pounders, three 2-pounders, six 5½-inch howitzers, two ammunition waggons, twenty-one Portuguese ammunition cars, forty horses, four mules.

'The above is only the number already arrived in the park, but from several accounts there are eight more taken from the enemy The ammunition waggons and cars contain a portion of powder, shells, and stores of all descriptions, and about 20,000 rounds of musket ammunition.

'William Robe, Lieutenant-Colonel,
commanding Royal Artillery.

To Viscount Castlereagh.

'Vimeiro,
'August 22, 1808.

'After I wrote to you yesterday morning, we were attacked by the whole of the French Army, Sir Harry Burrard being still on board ship, and I gained a complete victory. It was impossible for troops to behave better than ours did, only wanted a few hundred more cavalry to annihilate the French Army.

'I have sent my report upon this action to Sir Harry Burrard, who will send it home. You will see in it that I have mentioned Colonel Burne, of the 36th Regiment in a very particular manner, and I assure you that there is nothing that will give me so much satisfaction as to learn that something has been done for this old and meritorious soldier. (This officer was shortly afterwards rewarded by the government of Carlisle being conferred on him.) The 36th Regiment are an example to this army.

'Sir Harry did not land till late in the day in the midst of the attack, and he desired me to continue my own operations; and as far as I am personally concerned in the action, I was amply rewarded for any disappointment I might have felt in not having had an opportunity of bringing the service to a close, by the satisfaction expressed by the army that the second and more important victory had been gained by their old general.

'I have also the pleasure to add that it has had more effect than all the arguments I could use to induce the general to move on, and I believe he will march tomorrow.

'Indeed, if he does not, we shall be poisoned here by the stench of the dead and wounded; or we shall starve, everything in the neighbourhood being already eaten up.'

To Captain Pulteney Malcolm, H.M.S. 'Donegal'.

'Ramalhal,
'August 23, 1808.

'Torrens wrote to you on the night of the 21st to apprise you of the complete victory which we had gained, one of the consequences of which has been a suspension of arms between the French and us, preparatory to the evacuation of the country by them, the conditions of which I signed last night.

'Although I signed these conditions, I beg that you will not believe that I entirely approve of the manner in which the instrument is worded.

'You will receive a public letter from me upon this subject this day, in which I have requested you to bring the whole of your fleet of transports to the mouth of the Tagus, with the exception of the horse ships, which are to go to England.

'*P.S.*—It would be very convenient to us if you would communicate with Captain Bligh as you pass by. I shall be much obliged to you if you will have another cask of my claret broken up and put in chests such as the last, and leave one of them with Bligh for me.'

PRAISE OF NAVAL OFFICERS.

To Lord Mulgrave, First Lord of the Admiralty.

'Ramalhal,
'August 26, 1808.

'As my command is at an end, I hope I may be permitted to trouble you with a few lines on the co-operation which I have received from the navy. I have long been in the habits of friendship and intimacy with Captain Malcolm, of the *Donegal*; but it is impossible for me to describe the zeal, the ardour, and the kindness with which he entered into all my views; and the whole army will bear testimony to the exertions which he and all the officers of the navy acting under him made to provide for their convenience on the passage, to land them with celerity, and to provide for all their necessities and comforts when they were on shore.

'His views in all these respects were fully carried into execution by Captain Adam, of the *Resistance*, and Captain Cadogan, of the *Crocodile*; and, after our arrival on the coast of Portugal, by Captain Bligh, of the *Alfred*, from whom we received some most essential assistance. There were other captains of the navy with whom we have had at different times occasion to communicate, and I must say that the same desire to render us every assistance in their power has animated them all; which I attribute in a great degree to the disposition which, throughout the service, has been manifested by Captain Malcolm, who was principally charged with its conduct.

'I also beg leave to recommend to Your Lordship's favour and protection Lieutenant Fleetwood, the agent of transports, who superintended the fleet in which the army under my command was embarked. He is the most active, intelligent, and zealous of all the officers that I have seen in that line of the naval profession, and he really deserves promotion.

'If his services should be continued in the transport line of the profession, benefit will be derived from his promotion, as his sphere will be enlarged, and the armies to which he may be attached in future will not suffer the inconvenience which that under my command did, of having him superseded by an officer without any of his qualifications, in the midst of the service. I have to add that Captain Malcolm is equally satisfied with Lieutenant Fleetwood.'

WELLESLEY DESIRES TO QUIT THE ARMY.

To Viscount Castlereagh.

'Camp North of Torres Vedras,
'August 30, 1808.

'...I assure you, my dear Lord, matters are not prospering here, and I feel an earnest desire to quit the army.

'I have been too successful with this army ever to serve with it in a subordinate situation, with satisfaction to the person who shall command it, and of course not to myself. However, I shall do whatever the Government may wish.'

Suspension of Hostilities.

To Charles Stewart, Esq.

'Sobral,
'September 1, 1808.

'In the last letter which I wrote to you I believe I informed you of our actions on August 17 and 21; and that the Commander-in-Chief had agreed to a suspension of hostilities with the French, with a view to the settlement of a Convention for their entire evacuation of Portugal.

'. . . The agreement for the suspension of hostilities, concluded on the night of August 22, ended in a Convention for the evacuation of Portugal by the French, signed on the 30th of that month. As far as I have learnt, the Convention contains nothing material, excepting that the French are to be taken to a port in France, that they are to embark within seven days; that till they are embarked they are to remain in possession of Lisbon and a circuit of two leagues; and we are to have Fort St. Julian, Cascaes, and all the forts on the coast and in the interior, upon the ratification of the Convention.

'They are to give up the Spanish prisoners on the General, engaging to use his good offices that Frenchmen taken in Spain, not having engaged in hostilities, should likewise be released.

'There is nothing else in the Convention that I have heard of that is of any importance. The Russians, Danes, etc., are left at our mercy.

'As far as I have any knowledge of them, I have many objections both to the agreement for suspending hostilities, and to the Convention for the evacuation of Portugal by the French. I approve, however, of the principal point in the latter, *viz.*, to allow them to evacuate; and it is useless to trouble you with my objections to the mode in which that point has been brought about. . . .'

A Frank Letter to Sir John Moore.

To Lieutenant-General Sir John Moore, K.B.

'Lumiar,
'September 17, 1808.

'I write to you on the subject to which this letter relates with the same freedom with which I hope you would write to me on any point in which you might think the public interests concerned.

'It appears to me to be quite impossible that we can go on as we are now constituted; the commander-in-chief must be changed, and the country and the army naturally turn their eyes to you as their commander. I understand, however, that you have lately had some unpleasant discussions with the King's Ministers, the effect of which might be to prevent the adoption of an arrangement for the command of this army, which, in my opinion, would be the best, and would enable you to render those services at this moment for which you are peculiarly qualified. . . .

'In these times, my dear General, a man like you should not preclude himself from rendering the services of which he is capable by any idle point of form. Circumstances may have occurred, and might have justified the discussions to which I have referred; but none can justify the continuance of the temper in which they are carried on; and yet, till there is evidence that it is changed, it appears to be impossible for the King's Ministers to employ you in the high situation for which you are the most fit, because during the continuance of this temper of mind there can be no cordial or confidential intercourse.

'In writing thus much I have perhaps gone too far, and have taken the permission for which it was the intention of this letter to ask; but I shall send it, as it may be convenient for you to be apprised of the view which I have already taken of these discussions, as far as I have any knowledge of them, in deciding whether you will allow me to talk to you any further about them.

'If you should do so, it would probably be most convenient to us both to meet at Lisbon, or I can go over to you, if that should suit you better.'

Wellington and Sir Hew Dalrymple.

To Lieutenant-Colonel Murray, Quartermaster-General.

'Lisbon,
'September 19, 1808.

'I am going tomorrow, and I regret that it was so late when I reached headquarters yesterday that I could not endeavour to find you before I came away.

'I do not conceal from you that I am not quite satisfied with our situation; but nothing should have induced me to go away if I had thought there was the smallest prospect of early active employment for the army. . . .

'In regard to matters personal to myself, I shall not enter into them; I wish that Sir Hew had given me credit for a sincere desire to forward his views, whatever they might be; and I think I could have been of as much use to him as I believe I have been to other officers under whose orders I have served. He is the only one of whom I have not been the right hand for some years past; and at the same time, I must say that I felt the same inclination to serve him that I had to serve the others. . . .'

The Convention of Cintra.

To Viscount Castlereagh.

'London,
'October 6, 1808.

'I have the honour to inform Your Lordship that I arrived in London this day, by leave of the Commander of the Forces in Portugal; and having seen a copy of his Excellency's letter to Your Lordship, dated at Cintra, September 3, in which it would appear, from an inaccuracy of expression, that I had agreed upon and signed certain articles "for the suspension of hostilities on the 22nd of August,"

'I beg leave to inform Your Lordship that I did not negotiate that agreement; that it was negotiated and settled by His Excellency in person, with General Kellermann, in the presence of Lieutenant-General Sir Harry Burrard and myself, and that I signed it by His Excellency's desire. But I could not consider myself responsible in any degree for the terms in which it was framed, or for any of its provisions. . . .'

****

The inquiry into the Convention (commonly called the Convention of Cintra, although framed and signed at Lisbon) was held at the Royal College at Chelsea, from November 14 to December 27, 1808.

****

Viscount Castlereagh to H.R.H. the Commander-in-Chief.

'Downing Street,
'October 29, 1808.

'I am to signify to your Royal Highness His Majesty's pleasure, that a full investigation by a Court of Inquiry should be made as soon as possible into the late Armistice and Convention concluded in Portugal, and into all the circumstance connected therewith.

'It is considered, from the nature of the transaction, that the proceeding by a Court of Inquiry, in the first instance, will best bring before His Majesty a full explanation of all the considerations and causes which may have influenced the conclusion of the said Armistice and Convention, and ultimately lead to a just judgment thereupon. . . .'

Report.

'May it please Your Majesty,

'We, the underwritten general officers of the army, in obedience to Your Majesty's warrant, which bears date November 1, 1808, commanding us strictly to examine and inquire into the conditions of a suspension of arms, concluded on August 22, 1808, between Your Majesty's army in Portugal and the French force in that country; and also into a definitive Convention, concluded with the French General commanding on August 31 following, etc., etc.; most humbly report to Your Majesty that it appears that the operations of the army under Sir Arthur Wellesley, from his landing in Mondego Bay, August 1, until the conclusion of the action at Vimeiro, August 21, were highly honourable and successful, and such as might be expected from a distinguished general at the head of a British Army of 13,000 men, augmented on the 20th and 21st to 17,000, deriving only some small aid from a Portuguese corps (1,600 men), and against whom an enemy not exceeding 14,000 men in the field was opposed; and this before the arrival of a very considerable reinforcement from England under Lieutenant-General Sir John Moore, which, however, did arrive; and join the army from August 25 to 30.

'It appears a point on which no evidence adduced can enable the Board to pronounce with confidence, whether or not a pursuit after the battle of the 21st could have been efficacious; nor can the Board feel competent to determine on the expedition of a forward movement to Torres Vedras, when Sir Harry Burrard has stated weighty considerations against such a measure.

'Further it is to be observed, that so many collateral circumstances could not be known in the moment of the enemy's repulse as afterwards became clear to the army, and have been represented to the Board.

'And considering the extraordinary circumstances under which two new commanding generals arrived from the ocean and joined, the army (the one during, and the other immediately after, a battle, and those successively superseding each other, and both the original commander, within the space of twenty-four hours), it is not surprising that the army was not carried forward until the second day after the action, from the necessity of the generals being acquainted with the actual state of things and of their army, and proceeding accordingly.

'It appears that the Convention of Cintra, in its progress and conclusion, or at least all the principal articles of it, were not objected to by the five distinguished lieutenant-generals of that army; and other general officers who were on that service, whom we have had an opportunity to examine, have also concurred in the great advantages that were immediately gained to the country of Portugal, to the army and navy, and to the general service, by the conclusion of the Convention at that time.

'On a consideration of all circumstances, as set forth in this report, we most humbly submit our opinion that no further military proceeding is necessary on, the subject; because, howsoever some of us may differ in our sentiments respecting the fitness of the Convention in the relative situation of the two armies, it is our unanimous declaration, that unquestionable zeal and firmness appear throughout to have been exhibited by Lieutenant-Generals Sir Hew Dalrymple, Sir Harry Burrard, and Sir Arthur Wellesley, as well as that the ardour and gallantry of the rest of the officers and soldiers on every occasion during this expedition have done honour to the troops, and reflected lustre on Your Majesty's arms.'

Viscount Castlereagh to H.R.H. the Commander-in-Chief.

'Downing Street,
'January 18, 1809.

'The King has taken into his consideration the report of the Board of Inquiry, together with the documents and opinions thereunto annexed.

'While His Majesty adopts the unanimous opinion of the Board, that no further military proceeding is necessary to be had upon the transactions referred to their investigation, His Majesty does not intend thereby to convey any expression of His Majesty's satisfaction at the terms and conditions of the Armistice or Convention.

'When those instruments were first laid before His Majesty, the King, reserving for investigation those parts of the definitive Convention in which His Majesty's immediate interests were concerned, caused it to be signified to Sir Hew Dalrymple, by His Majesty's Secretary of State, that His Majesty, nevertheless, felt himself compelled at once to express his disapprobation of those articles in which stipulations were made directly affecting the interests or feelings of the Spanish and Portuguese nations.

'At the close of the inquiry, the King (abstaining from any observations upon other parts of the Convention) repeats his disapprobation of those articles, His Majesty deeming it necessary that his sentiments should be clearly understood, as to the impropriety and danger of the unauthorised admission into military Conventions of articles of such a description, which, especially when incautiously framed, may lead to the most injurious consequences.

'His Majesty cannot forbear further to observe, that Lieutenant-General Sir Hew Dalrymple's delaying to transmit, for his information, the Armistice concluded on August 22, until September 4, when he at the same time transmitted the ratified Convention, was calculated to produce great public inconvenience, and that such public inconvenience did, in fact, result therefrom.'

****

Sir Arthur Wellesley, on his return from Portugal after the Battle of Vimeiro, had resumed the duties of his office as Chief Secretary for Ireland; and the Court of Inquiry having concluded, he proceeded in the month of December to Dublin.

Parliament having reassembled in January, 1809, he returned to London to attend the House of Commons; and on January 27, when in his place, he received the thanks of the House for his conduct at the Battle of Vimeiro, by the Speaker.

According to the stipulations of the Convention of Cintra, the French Army under General Junot was embarked in British vessels, and landed at La Rochelle in October, 1808.

****

It was erroneously called the 'Convention of Cintra,' from that document having been forwarded by Lieutenant-General Sir Hew Dalrymple to the Secretary of State in a despatch dated Cintra, September 3, 1808. The error, however, having become habitual, it has been retained.

****

The British Army being thus left disposable for other services, the greater part of it was detached into Castille, under the command of Lieutenant-General Sir John Moore, and was joined on the Duero in December by an additional force from England, which had landed at Coruna.

In the month of November, the French armies having been greatly reinforced, and the Spaniards having been successively defeated at Tudela and in other battles, the city of Madrid fell again into the hands of the enemy. Buonaparte, who had arrived to superintend in person the operations in Spain, directed, in the month of December, a combined movement of several corps, under the command of Marshal Soult, against the army under Sir John Moore, which consequently retreated into Galicia; and a battle took place on January 16, 1809, at Coruña, where Sir John Moore was killed in the hour of victory.

In the meantime, Lieutenant-General Sir John Cradock, (afterwards General Lord Howden, G.C.B.), had been appointed to the command of the British troops remaining in Portugal; and that country, after the Battle of Coruña, again became the seat of active military operations.

Marshal Soult having invaded its northern provinces from Galicia, and taken possession of Oporto on March 29, 1809. Lisbon was consequently thrown into alarm; and the Regency having urgently implored the aid and protection of the British nation, reinforcements were directed to be embarked, and Lieutenant-General Sir Arthur Wellesley, having resigned the office of Chief Secretary in Ireland and his seat in Parliament, was again sent to command in Portugal.

****

BACK TO PORTUGAL.

To Viscount Castlereagh.

'Lisbon,
'April 27, 1809.

'I arrived here on the 22nd instant, and having communicated with Lieutenant-General Sir John Cradock to put me in orders on the 25th, I have assumed the command of the army.

'The whole of the British Army in Portugal are assembled at Leyria and Alcobaca, with the exception of the 2nd Battalion 30th Regiment, in garrison at Lisbon; of the 16th Light Dragoons, on its march to join the army; and of the 2nd Battalion 24th Regiment, the 3rd Dragoon Guards, and the 4th Dragoons, just landed...'

ADVERSE CRITICISM.

To Marshal Beresford.

'Coimbra,
'May 6, 1809, 1.30 p.m.

'...Your troops made but a bad figure this morning at the review. The battalions very weak, not more than 300 men; the body of men, particularly of the —— Regiment, very bad; and the officers worse than anything I have seen....'

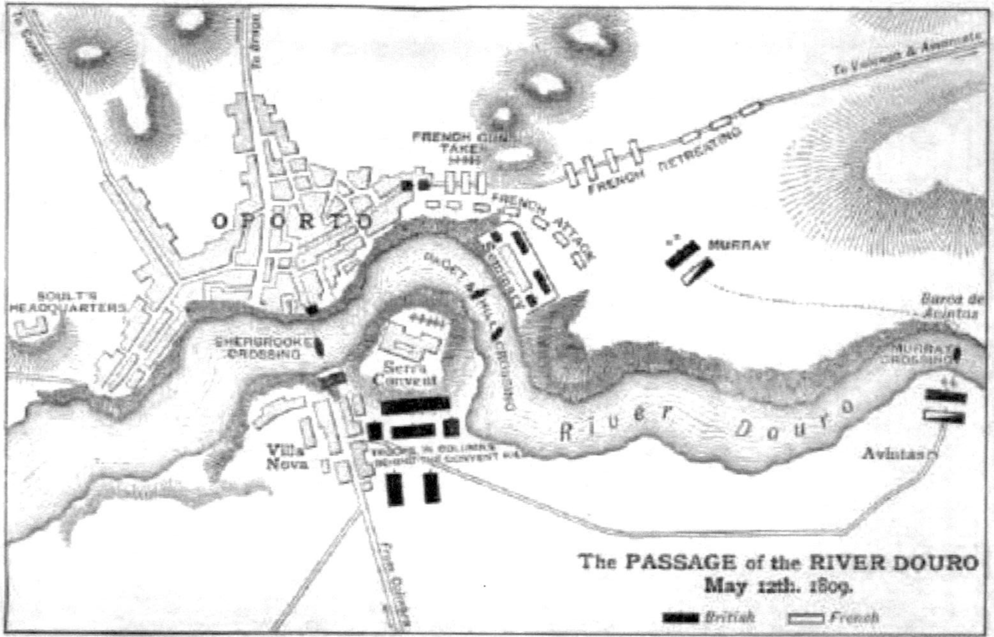

The PASSAGE of the RIVER DOURO
May 12th. 1809.

Walker & Boutall sc.

A Plot to seize Marshal Soult.

To Viscount Castlereagh.

'Lisbon,
'April 27, 1809.

'I have but little to add to my public despatches of this date. I fully believe in the intentions of the French officers to revolt. The existence of this intention is confirmed by the recollection of what dropped from nearly every individual of the French Army with whom I conversed when I was in this country last year, and it is highly probable on other grounds. I doubt, however, whether it will be quite so easy to carry their intentions successfully into execution as their emissary appears to imagine. . . .

'It is, however, very certain that the successful revolt of one French Army would have a great effect, particularly in this part of the world; and would probably do more for Spain than Spain would ever do for itself.

'In case there should be an opportunity, I should not wait for a revolt, but shall try my own means of subduing Soult.

'If this army should revolt, or, indeed, at all events, I anxiously recommend to you to set all your emissaries to work in France. I have no doubt of the detestation of Buonaparte by the people of that country. .'

To Viscount Castlereagh.

'Coimbra,
'May 7, 1809.

'I met last night ——, for the first time since I had seen him at Lisbon.

'He told me that the French Army was at this time divided into two parties—one, which intended to seize Soult at all events, and to carry into execution the plan he had before communicated to me; the other, consisting of ——, ——, and even those connected with Buonaparte, who were determined to seize Soult if he should declare himself King of Portugal, of which he has manifested an intention. This latter party would then lead the army into France, where it is understood that Buonaparte wishes to have it. But —— thinks that if Soult was once seized, everything would go on as *his* friends wished. . .

'I firmly believe what he says respecting the prevailing discontent, and I think it not improbable that ——, and others attached to Buonaparte, aware of it, and apprehensive of its effects, would turn it so far to account of Buonaparte as to induce the army to seize their general, for being guilty of an ambitious abuse of his authority and disobedience of the orders of the emperor. And if they are really in a scrape, which I acknowledge I doubt, they would make use of this act, if possible, to induce us to allow them to go away. . . .'

The Battle of Oporto.

To Viscount Castlereagh.

'Oporto,
'May 12, 1809.

'I had the honour to apprise Your Lordship on the 7th instant that I intended that the army should march on the 9th from Coimbra, to dispossess the enemy of Oporto.

'The advanced-guard and the cavalry had marched on the 7th, and the whole had halted on the 8th, to afford time for Marshal Beresford with his corps to arrive upon the upper Douro.

'The infantry of the army was formed into three divisions for this expedition, of which two, the advanced-guard, consisting of the King's German Legion, and Brigadier-General R. Stewart's brigade, with a brigade of 6-pounders, and a brigade of 3-pounders, under Lieutenant-General Paget; and the cavalry under Lieutenant-General Payne; and the brigade of Guards, Brigadier-General Campbell's and Brigadier-General Sontag's brigades of infantry, with a brigade of 6-pounders, under Lieutenant-General Sherbrooke, moved by the highroad from Coimbra to Oporto; and one, composed of Major-General Hill's and Brigadier-General Cameron's brigades of infantry, and a brigade of 6-pounders, under the command of Major-General Hill, by the road from Coimbra to Aveiro.

'On the 10th in the morning, before daylight, the cavalry and advanced-guard crossed the Vouga, with the intention to surprise and cut off four regiments of French cavalry, and a battalion of infantry and artillery, cantoned in Albergaria Nova and the neighbouring villages, about eight miles from that river, in the last of which we failed; but the superiority of the British cavalry was evident throughout the day.

'We took some prisoners and their cannon from them; and the advanced-guard took up the position of Oliveira.

'On the same day Major-General Hill, who had embarked at Aveiro on the evening of the 9th, arrived at Ovar, in the rear of the enemy's right; and the head of Lieutenant-General Sherbrooke's division passed the Vouga on the same evening.

'On the 11th the advanced-guard and cavalry continued to move on the highroad towards Oporto, with Major-General Hill's division in a parallel road which leads to Oporto from Ovar.

'On the arrival of the advanced-guard at Vendas Novas, between Souto Redondo and Grijo, they fell in with the outposts of the enemy's advanced-guard, which were immediately driven in; and shortly afterwards we discovered the enemy's advanced-guard, consisting of about 4,000 infantry and some squadrons of cavalry, strongly posted on the heights above Grijo, their front being covered by woods and broken ground.

'The enemy's left flank was turned by a movement well executed by Major-General Murray, with Brigadier-General Langworth's brigade of the King's German Legion; while the 16th Portuguese Regiment of Brigadier-General Richard Stewart's brigade attacked their right, and the riflemen of the 95th, and the flank companies of the 29th, 43rd, and 52nd of the same brigade, under Major Way, attacked the infantry in the woods and village in their centre.

'These attacks soon obliged the enemy to give way, and Brigadier-General the Hon. Charles Stewart led two squadrons of the 16th and 20th Dragoons, under the command of Major Blake, in pursuit of the enemy, and destroyed many and took several prisoners.

'On the night of the 11th the enemy crossed the Douro, and destroyed the bridge over that river.

'It was important, with a view to the operations of Marshal Beresford, that I should cross the Douro immediately; and I had sent Major-General Murray in the morning with a battalion of the King's German Legion, a squadron of cavalry, and two 6-pounders, to endeavour to collect boats, and, if possible, to cross the river at Avintas, about four miles above Oporto; and I had as many boats as could be collected brought to the ferry, immediately above the towns of Oporto and Villa Nova.

'The ground on the right bank of the river at this ferry is protected and commanded by the fire of cannon, placed on the height of the Serra Convent at Villa Nova; and there appeared to be a good position for our troops on the opposite side of the river, till they should be collected in sufficient numbers.

'The enemy took no notice of our collection of boats, or of the embarkation of the troops, till after the first battalion (the Buffs) were landed, (the Buffs particularly distinguished themselves, the first of their Peninsular honours is 'Douro.'—W. W.), and had taken up their position, under the command of Lieutenant-General Paget, on the opposite side of the river.

'They then commenced an attack upon them with a large body of cavalry, infantry, and artillery, under the command of Marshal Soult, which that corps most gallantly sustained till supported successively by the 48th and 66th Regiments, belonging to Major-General Hill's brigade, and a Portuguese battalion, and afterwards by the first battalion of detachments belonging to Brigadier-General Richard Stewart's brigade.

'Lieutenant-General Paget was unfortunately wounded soon after the attack commenced, when the command of these gallant troops devolved upon Major-General Hill.

'Although the French made repeated attacks upon them, they made no impression; and at last, Major-General Murray having appeared on the enemy's left flank on his march from Avintas, where he had crossed; and Lieutenant-General Sherbrooke, who by this time had availed himself of the enemy's weakness in the town of Oporto, and had crossed the Douro at the ferry between the towns of Villa Nova and Oporto, having appeared upon their right with the brigade of Guards and the 29th Regiment; the whole retired in the utmost confusion towards Amarante, leaving behind them five pieces of cannon, eight ammunition tumbrils, and many prisoners.

'The enemy's loss in killed and wounded in this action has been very large, and they have left behind them in Oporto 700 sick and wounded.

'Brigadier-General the Hon. Charles Stewart then directed a charge by a squadron of the 14th Dragoons, under the command of Major Hervey, who made a successful attack on the enemy's rear-guard.

'In the different actions with the enemy, of which I have above given Your Lordship an account, we have lost some, and the immediate services of other valuable officers and soldiers. . . .

'I cannot say too much in favour of the officers and troops. They have marched in four days over eighty miles of most difficult country, have gained many important positions, and have engaged and defeated three different bodies of the enemy's troops. . . .'

Return of Ordnance captured on May 12, 1809.

Ten 12-pounders, twelve 8-pounders, eighteen 4-pounders, sixteen 3-pounders, two howitzers.

Abstract of the Killed, Wounded, and Missing in the Army under the Command of Lieutenant-General the Right Hon. Sir A. Wellesley, K.B., in Action with the French Army under the Command of Marshal Soult, on March 10, 11, 12, 1809.

	Officers.	Sergeants.	Rank and File.	Horses.	Total Loss of Officers, Non-commissioned Officers, and Rank and File.
Killed - -	1	—	42	—	43
Wounded - -	17	1	150	—	168
Missing - -	—	—	17	—	17

The French Sick and Wounded.

To Marshal Soult

'Oporto,
'*Ce 12 Mai*, 1809.

'Vous savez que vous avez laissé dans cette ville un grand nombre de malades et de blessés, dont vous pouvez etre sur qne je prendrai le plus grand soin, et qu'autant que je le pourrai, personne ne leur fera du mal. Mais vous avez oublié de laisser avec eux des Officiers de Santé pour les soigner. Je ne crois pas qu'on doive se fier aux Officiers de Santé de la ville d'Oporto; et je vous previens que je n'ai pas un plus grand nombre d'Officiers de Sante, qu'il ne me faut pour le service des troupes qui sont sous mes ordres.

'Je vous prie donc d'en envoyer ici un nombre suffisant pour le soin de tous les malades et blessés de l'armée Française que vous avez laissés ici, et je vous promets que quand ils auront guéri les malades, ils vous seront renvoyés.

'Vous avez quelques officiers et soldats de l'armée Anglaise, prisonniers de guerre, et je serai bien aise d'établir avec vous un cartel d'échange pour ceux de l'armée Française que j'ai en mon pouvoir.'

(On leaving Eton, Wellington went to Brussels and Angers, where he gained a knowledge of French, which in after years proved very useful.—W.W.)

Proclamation.

'Arthur Wellesley, Commander of the British Army in Portugal, and Marshal-General of the Armies of H.R.H. the Prince Regent.

'Inhabitants of Oporto—The French troops having been expelled from this town by the superior gallantry and discipline of the army under my command, I call upon the inhabitants of Oporto to be merciful to the wounded and prisoners. By the laws of war, they are entitled to my protection, which I am determined to afford them;

and it will be worthy of the generosity and bravery of the Portuguese nation not to revenge the injuries which have been done to them on these unfortunate persons, who can only be considered as instruments in the hands of the more powerful, who are still in arms against us.

'I therefore call upon the inhabitants of this town to remain peaceably in their dwellings. I forbid all persons not military to appear in the streets with arms; and I give notice that I shall consider any person who shall injure any of the wounded or of the prisoners as guilty of the breach of my orders . . . .'

A Terrible Retreat.

To Viscount Castlereagh.

'Montealegre,
'May 18, 1809.

'I arrived at Braga on the 15th (General Murray being at Guimaraens, and the enemy about fifteen miles in our front), and at Salamonde on the 16th.

'We had there an affair with their rearguard. The Guards, under Lieutenant-General Sherbrooke and Brigadier-General Campbell, attacked their position, and having turned their left flank by the heights, they abandoned it, leaving a gun and some prisoners behind them. This attack was necessarily made at a late hour in the evening.

'On the 17th we moved to Ruivaes (waiting to see whether the enemy would turn upon Chaves, or continue his retreat upon Montealegre), and on the 18th to this place. . . .

'The enemy commenced this retreat, as I have informed Your Lordship, by destroying a great proportion of his guns and ammunition. He afterwards destroyed the remainder of both and a great proportion of his baggage, and kept nothing excepting what the soldiers or a few mules could carry. He has left behind him his sick and wounded; and the road from Penafiel to Montealegre is strewed with the carcases of horses and mules, and of French soldiers, who were put to death by the peasantry before our advanced-guard could save them.

'This last circumstance is the natural effect of the species of warfare which the enemy have carried on in this country.

'Their soldiers have plundered and murdered the peasantry at their pleasure; and I have seen many persons hanging in the trees by the sides of the road, executed for no reason that I could learn, excepting that they have not been friendly to the French invasion and usurpation of the government of their country; and the route of their column on their retreat could be traced by the smoke of the villages to which they set fire.

'We have taken about 500 prisoners. Upon the whole, the enemy has not lost less than a fourth of his army, and all his artillery and equipments, since we attacked him on the Vouga.

'I hope Your Lordship will believe that no measure which I could take was omitted to intercept the enemy's retreat. It is obvious, however, that if an army throws away all its cannon, equipments, and baggage, and everything which can strengthen it, and can enable it to act together as a body; and abandons all those who are entitled to its protection, but add to its weight and impede its progress; it must be able to march by roads through which it cannot be followed, with any prospect of being overtaken, by an army which has not made the same sacrifices.

'It is impossible to say too much of the exertions of the troops. The weather has been very bad indeed. Since the 13th the rain has been constant, and the roads in this difficult country almost impracticable...'

English-Portuguese Officers.

To the Right Hon. J. Villiers.

'Ruivaes,
'May 19, 1809.

'...The question of rank between the English and English-Portuguese officers is one of a very delicate nature, and it arises entirely out of the practice of giving to officers going into the Portuguese service a step of Portuguese rank beyond that which they held in the service of the King.

'The officers in the two services must rank according to the dates of their respective commissions; but English officers taking temporary Portuguese commissions must rank, in respect to British officers, according to the date of the commission which they hold in the service of His Majesty. In future, I recommend that they should serve in the Portuguese Army with the same rank as they have in that of the King. It is my opinion, the situation of these officers having advanced, Portuguese rank will be an anomaly, but that cannot be helped.

'I wish to God that Beresford would resign his English Lieutenant-General's rank. It is inconceivable the embarrassment and ill-blood which it occasions. It does him no good; and if the army was not most successful, this very circumstance would probably bring us to a standstill.'

Salvage.

To the Right Hon. J. Villiers.

'Oporto,
'May 23, 1809,

'. . . Upon the capture of Oporto, we found here several English, some Danish, Swedish, and one or two French vessels, and a considerable quantity of property, some of which had been loaded in these ships; and another part, principally cotton, which the French had bought in different parts of the country, and had collected here in charge of the French Consul. . . .

'The most valuable part of this property is 3,000 tons of wine, belonging, I believe, to the English merchants; upon which the admiral, on the notion that all the property at Oporto is liable to be considered and dealt with by the rules of prize, thinks us entitled to salvage. My opinion is that, if we are entitled to it at all, we are entitled to the whole of the property; but the doubt which I entertain is, whether we have a right to any part of this property; and upon this doubt I wish to have your opinion. . . .'

Lenient Treatment of a Marquis.

To Brigadier-General Alexander Campbell.

'Oporto,
'May 24, 1809.

'The Adjutant-General has communicated to me your letter of the 23rd instant, reporting the conduct of Captain the Marquis —— in absenting himself from his battalion without leave on the 15th instant, and that you had put him in arrest. 'I observe from the date that this offence was aggravated by being committed at a moment when the troops were in march in pursuit of the enemy. I am not disposed, however, to carry matters to extremities with the marquis; and I beg that you will call him and the officers of the regiment to which he belongs before you, and point out to him the extreme impropriety of his conduct. . . .

'You will tell the marquis that I hope that the lenity with which his fault has been treated upon this occasion will induce him to be more attentive to his duty; and that I expect from him exertions in the cause of his country, patience to bear the hardships of a military life, and submission to the rules of military discipline and subordination, in proportion as his rank, station, and fortune are superior to those of others of his countrymen in the service. You will then release the marquis from his arrest.'

Plundering.

To the Right Hon. J. Villiers.

'Coimbra,
'May 31, 1809.

'I have long been of opinion that a British Army could bear neither success nor failure, and I have had manifest proofs of the truth of this opinion in the first of its branches in the recent conduct of the soldiers of this army. They have plundered the country most terribly, which has given me the greatest concern. The Town Major of Lisbon, if he has the orders, will show you, if you wish to read them, those that I have given out upon this subject.

'They have plundered the people of bullocks, among other property, for what reason I am sure I do not know, except it be, as I understand is their practice, to sell them to the people again. I shall be very much obliged to you if you will mention this practice to the Ministers of the Regency, and beg them to issue a proclamation forbidding the people, in the most positive terms, to purchase anything from the soldiers of the British Army. . .'

Prisoners of War.

To Lieutenant-Colonel Trant.

'Thomar,
'June 7, 1809.

'I think it probable that the admiral will immediately require all the cavalry ships which he has lately sent to Oporto, to receive the prisoners of war to send to England without loss of time, in the shape of cavalry ships. You will, therefore, immediately discontinue your alteration of those ships, if you should have continued them after the receipt of Colonel Murray's letter upon this subject.

'I have requested the admiral to send you directions either to embark the prisoners in the cavalry ships, or not, as he may think proper, supposing that he should wish to send to England immediately the cavalry ships destined to convey the prisoners. You will, therefore, have the prisoners in readiness to embark in store-ships at a moment's notice if the admiral should desire it, and, at all events, the ships in readiness to sail.

'You will understand, however, that the prisoners must not be unreasonably crowded in these ships, and you will report to me what number will remain at Oporto, after you shall have sent those whom the admiral may require you to send in the cavalry ships.'

Hospital Stoppages.

To the Right Hon. the Secretary at War.

'Thomar,
'June 7, 1809.

'I had the honour of receiving your letter of May 4 this morning, and I beg to inform you that it has been the practice hitherto in this army to make the soldiers pay tenpence *per diem* when in hospital, leaving to them a residue of twopence *per diem*, and to other ranks a proportionate sum. I have ordered that from the 25th instant, inclusive, the hospital stoppage shall be for all ranks ninepence, leaving for each rank the daily net sum stated in the enclosure No. I. of your letter. I shall be obliged to you if you will let me know whether it is your intention that the directions contained in your letter of May 4 should have a retrospect; and if so, from what period. The soldiers in Portugal receive a full ration from the commissariat, and of course are liable to a daily deduction from their pay each of sixpence.'

The Army Head over Ears in Debt.

To the Right Hon. J. Villiers.

'Abrantes,
'June 11, 1809.

'... The ball is now at my foot, and I hope I shall have strength enough to give it a good kick. I should begin immediately, but I cannot venture to stir without money. The army is two months in arrears, we are overhead and ears in debt everywhere, and I cannot venture into Spain without paying what we owe, at least in this neighbourhood, and giving a little money to the troops ...'

An Obstinate Spanish General.

To the Right Hon. J. H. Frere.

'Abrantes,
'June 13, 1809.

'I send you copies of the letters I have received from the Spanish headquarters, and of those which I have written to General Cuesta and Colonel Bourke this day.

'Colonel Bourke's letter explains so fully the situation of Cuesta's army, and my letter to him is so explicit upon the dangers of his position; the small chance there is that I shall be able to serve him, unless he should take up a strong position till I can come to his assistance; and upon the advantages of the operation which I had proposed; that

I do not think it necessary to trouble you further upon the subject.

'I can only say that the obstinacy of this old gentleman is throwing out of our hands the finest game that any armies ever had; and that we shall repent that we did not cut off Victor when we shall have to beat the French upon the Ebro. With such a letter, however, as Colonel Bourke's before me, I could not but yield the point to General Cuesta, which I hope will convince the Spanish Government of my sincere desire to be of service to them.'

To Viscount Castlereagh.

'Abrantes,
'June 17, 1809.

'. . . . My correspondence with General Cuesta has been a very curious one, and proves him to be as obstinate as any gentleman at the head of any army need be. . . .'

Disorderly Regiments.

To Colonel Donkin.

(*Afterwards Lieutenant-General Sir Rufane Donkin, K.C.B.*)

'Abrantes,
'June 16, 1809.

'. . . .'I trouble you now upon a subject which has given me the greatest pain—I mean the accounts which I receive from all quarters of the disorders committed by, and the general irregularity of, the —— and —— Regiments. I have ordered a provost to Castello Branco to put himself under your orders, and I hope you will not fail to make use of him.

'I beg that on the receipt of this letter you will call on the commanding officers of the —— and —— Regiments, and apprise them of the concern with which I have heard these reports of their regiments; and of my determination, if I should hear any more of them, to send their regiments into garrison, and to report them to His Majesty as unfit for service in the field, on account of irregularity of conduct and disorder.

'I desire that upon the receipt of this letter the —— and —— Regiments may be hutted outside of the town of Castello Branco, if there should be wood in the neighbourhood, not fruit-trees, and the rolls to be called every hour, from sunrise till eight in the evening, all officers, as well as soldiers, to attend.

'The number of men absent from these regiments in consequence of their late marches is scandalous, and I desire that an officer from each of them may go back immediately the whole road by which the brigade has moved since May 5, in search of the missing men. Those missing on the late march and ground between Guarda and Castello Branco must be sent on immediately to Castello Branco; and those missing on the former march must be collected at Guarda, and afterwards brought up by the officers to the regiment when they shall return through that town.

'I beg to have reports from you of the state of the arms, ammunition, etc., of these regiments, and to hear whether the roll-calls above ordered are regular, and are attended by all the officers. Non-commissioned officers and soldiers absent must be punished. I beg to know whether the brigade has received all the orders.'

To Viscount Castlereagh.

'Abrantes,
'June 17, 1809.

'I cannot, with propriety, omit to draw your attention again to the state of discipline of the army, which is a subject of serious concern to me, and well deserves the consideration of His Majesty's Ministers.

'It is impossible to describe to you the irregularities and outrages committed by the troops. They are never out of the sight of their officers, I may almost say never out of the sight of the commanding officers of their regiments, and the general officers of the army, that outrages are not committed; and notwithstanding the pains which I take, of which there will be ample evidence in my orderly books, not a post or a courier comes in, not an officer arrives from the rear of the army, that does not bring me accounts of outrages committed by the soldiers who have been left behind on the march, having been sick, or having straggled from their regiments, or who have been left in hospitals.

'We have a provost marshal, and no less than four assistants. I never allow a man to march with the baggage. I never leave a hospital without a number of officers and non-commanding officers proportionable to the number of soldiers; and never allow a detachment to march, unless under the command of an officer; and yet there is not an outrage of any description, which has not been committed on a people who have uniformly received us as friends, by soldiers who never yet, for one moment, suffered the slightest want or the smallest privation.

'In the first place, I am convinced that the law is not strong enough to maintain discipline in an army upon service. It is most difficult to convict any prisoner before a regimental court-martial, for I am sorry to say that soldiers have little regard to the oath administered to them; and the officers who are sworn "well and truly to try and determine, *according to the evidence*, the matter before them," have too much regard to the strict letter of that administered to them. This oath, to the members of a regimental court-martial, has altered the principle of the proceedings of that tribunal. It is no longer a court of honour, at the hands of which a soldier was certain of receiving punishment if he deserved it; but it is a court of law, whose decisions are to be formed according to the evidence, principally of those on whose actions it is constituted as a restraint.

'But, admitting the regimental or detachment court-martial, as now constituted, to be a control upon the soldiers equally efficient with that which existed under the old constitution of a court-martial, which my experience tells me it is not, I should wish to know whether any British Army (this army in particular, which is composed of second battalions, and therefore but ill provided with officers) can afford to leave with every hospital, or with every detachment, two captains and four subalterns, in order to be enabled to hold a detachment court-martial.

'The law in this respect ought to be amended; and when the army is on service in a foreign country, any one, two, or three officers ought to have the power of trying criminals, and punishing them *instanter*; taking down all proceedings in writing, and reporting them for the information of the commander-in-chief on their joining the army.

'Besides this improvement of the law, there ought to be in the British Army a regular provost establishment, of which a proportion should be attached to every army sent abroad. All the foreign armies have such an establishment: the French *gendarmerie nationale*, to the amount of thirty or forty with each of their corps; the Spaniards their *policia militar*, to a still larger amount; while we, who require such an aid more, I am sorry to say, than any of the other nations of Europe, have nothing of the kind, excepting a few sergeants, who are taken from the line for the occasion, and who are probably not very fit for the duties which they are to perform.

'The authority and duties of the provost ought, in some manner, to be recognised by the law. By the custom of British armies, the provost has been in the habit of punishing on the spot (even with death, under the orders of the commander-in-chief) soldiers found in the act of disobedience of orders, of plunder, or of outrage.

'There is no authority for this practice excepting custom, which I conceive would hardly warrant it; and yet I declare that I do not know in what manner the army is to be commanded at all, unless the practice is not only continued, but an additional number of provosts appointed.

'There is another branch of this subject which deserves serious consideration. We all know that the discipline and regularity of all armies must depend upon the diligence of the regimental officers, particularly the subalterns. I may order what I please; but if they do not execute what I order, or if they execute with negligence, I cannot expect that British soldiers will be orderly or regular.

'There are two incitements to men of this description to do their duty as they ought—the fear of punishment, and the hope of reward.

'As for the first, it cannot be given individually; for I believe I should find it very difficult to convict any officer of doing this description of duty with negligence, more particularly as he is to be tried by others probably guilty of the same offence. But these evils of which I complain are committed by whole corps; and the only way in which they can be punished is by disgracing them, by sending them into garrison and reporting them to His Majesty. I may and shall do this by one or two battalions, but I cannot venture to do it by more; and then there is an end to the fear of this punishment, even if those who received it were considered in England as disgraced persons rather than martyrs.

'As for the other incitement to officers to do their duty zealously, there is no such thing. We who command the armies of the country, and who are expected to make exertions greater than those made by the French Armies—to march, to fight, and to keep our troops in health and in discipline—have not the power of rewarding, or promising a reward for a single officer of the army; and we deceive ourselves, and those who are placed under us, if we imagine we have that power, or if we hold out to them that they shall derive any advantage from the exertion of it in their favour.

'You will say, probably, in answer to all this, that British armies have been in the field before, and that these complaints, at least to the same extent, have not existed; to which I answer—first, that the armies are now larger, their operations more extended, and the exertions required greater than they were in former periods; and that the mode of carrying on war is different from what it was. Secondly, that our law, instead of being strong in proportion to the temptation and means for indiscipline and irregularity, has been weakened; and that we have not adopted the additional means of restraint and punishment practised by other nations, and our enemies, although we have imitated them in those particulars which have increased and aggravated our irregularities. And, finally, that it is only within late years that the commanders-in-chief abroad have been deprived of all patronage, and of course of all power of incitement to the officers under their command.

'It may be supposed that I wish for this patronage to gratify my own favourites; but I declare most solemnly that, if I had it tomorrow, there is not a soul in the army whom I should wish to promote, excepting for services performed.

'I have thought it proper to draw your attention to these subjects, which I assure you deserve the serious consideration of the King's Ministers.

'We are an excellent army on parade, an excellent one to fight; but we are worse than an enemy in a country; and take my word for it that either defeat or success would dissolve us.'

Shot in a Duel.

To the Right Hon. John Villiers.

'Abrantes,
'June 23, 1809.

'I am sorry to have to inform you that Lieutenant B——, of the 66th, was shot in a duel some days ago, as is supposed, by Lieutenant D——, of the same regiment. I enclose you the report of persons who viewed the body of Lieutenant B—— after he was dead, and the proceedings of a court of inquiry into the circumstances which occasioned the duel. Captain M——, Lieutenant D——, etc., are now in arrest; and if the Government of the country think proper to order that they should be tried by the tribunal of the country, they shall be given up: if not, I shall give directions that they may be tried by a general court-martial.'

Welcome Ships.

To the Right Hon. John Villiers.

'Castello Branco,
'June 30, 1809.

'I arrived here this day, and shall go on the day after tomorrow. I find that £225,000 have arrived in the *Rosamond* and the *Niobe*. I have desired that £80,000 of this sum be paid to you in the proportions of gold and dollars as they are in the military chest at present. I have allotted £50,000 to pay part of our debts in the north; £60,000 to be sent to us into Spain, in Spanish *doubloons*; and £35,000 to remain in the chest in Lisbon.'

'Horrible Abuses and Hardships.'

To the Right Hon. John Villiers.

'Plasencia,
'July 9, 1809.

'I have received your letter of the 5th, and I am perfectly satisfied with any notice taken by the Government of the present acts of enmity committed by the people of Portugal on the troops, which I fear that the latter deserve but too well.

'We must have some general rule of proceeding in cases of criminal outrages by British officers and soldiers, by which the individuals guilty of them may be brought to early punishment. As matters are now conducted, the Government and I stand complimenting each other, while no notice is taken of the murderer; and the example of his early trial and punishment is lost to the troops.

'The artilleryman who has committed the murder at Cascaes must be tried according to the laws of the country, or for a military offence under the Articles of War. My opinion is that he, and all guilty of similar offences, ought to be tried (I mean tried in earnest, and not as the officers of the ——th were tried) according to the laws of the country; but if the Government prefer that we should take cognisance of these offences, as being of a military nature, we will do so at once in every case; but they must assist us in obliging the witnesses to come forward and give their testimony on oath, to which I find they have great objections. . . .

'I shall most readily come into any measure proposed by Government to remedy the horrible abuses and hardships now existing, and occasioned entirely by the mode in which carts are taken for the service of the British Army. . . .'

Soldier Servants.

To Marshal Beresford.

'Plasencia,
'July 13, 1809.

'. . . I am sorry that I cannot allow any officers to take soldiers as servants from the British regiments in this army. . . .'

Striking Officers.

To Major-General Mackenzie, President of a General Court-martial.

'Plasencia,
'July 16, 1809.

'I have perused the proceedings and sentence of the general court-martial, on the trial of ——, private in the ——Regiment, for striking Ensign ——, of the —— Regiment, and I am concerned that I cannot agree in opinion with the general court-martial in respect to their sentence, and that I must request them to revise it.

'There appears to be no doubt of the guilt of the prisoner ——; and the question remains for consideration whether any circumstances have appeared upon the trial which ought to prevent the court from passing upon —— the sentence of death. . . .

'I am the more anxious that the general court-martial should revise their sentence upon this occasion, because I am concerned to state that several instances have occurred lately of soldiers having struck officers and non-commissioned officers in the execution of their duty.'

Spanish Selfishness.

To the Right Hon. J. H. Frere.

'Talavera de la Reyna,
'July 24, 1809.

'It is ridiculous to pretend that the country cannot supply our wants. The French Army is well fed, and the soldiers who are taken in good, health, and well supplied with bread, of which, indeed, they left a small magazine behind them. . . .

'The Spanish Army has plenty of everything, and we alone, upon whom everything depends, are actually starving.

'I am aware of the important consequences which must attend the step which I shall take in withdrawing from Spain. It is certain that the people of England will never hear of another army entering Spain after they shall have received the accounts of the treatment we have met with; and it is equally certain that without the assistance, the example, and the countenance of a British Army the Spanish Armies, however brave, will never effect their object.

'But no man can see his army perish by want without feeling for them, and most particularly must he feel for them when he knows that they have been brought into the country in which this want is felt by his own act, and on his own responsibility, and not by orders from any superior authority. . .

THE BATTLE OF TALAVERA.

To Viscount Castlereagh.

'Talavera de la Reyna,
'July 29, 1809.

'General Cuesta followed the enemy's march with his army from the Alberche, on the morning of the 24th, as far as Sta. Olalla, and pushed forward his advanced-guard as far as Torrijos. For the reasons stated to Your Lordship in my despatch of the 24th, I moved only two divisions of infantry and a brigade of cavalry across the Alberche to Cazalegas, under the command of Lieutenant-General Sherbrooke, with a view to keep up the communication between General Cuesta and me, and with Sir Robert Wilson's corps at Escalona.

'It appears that General Venegas had not carried into execution that part of the plan of operations which related to his corps, and that he was still at Daymiel, in La Mancha; and the enemy, in the course of the 24th, 25th, and 26th, collected all his forces in this part of Spain, between Torrijos and Toledo, leaving but a small corps of 2,000 men in that place.

'This united army thus consisted of the corps of Marshal Victor, of that of General Sebastiani, and of 7,000 or 8,000 men, the guards of Joseph Buonaparte, and the garrison of Madrid; and it was commanded by Joseph Buonaparte, aided by Marshals Jourdan and Victor, and by General Sebastiani.

'On the 26th General Cuesta's advanced-guard was attacked near Torrijos and obliged to fall back; and the General retired with his army on that day to the left bank of the Alberche, General Sherbrooke continuing at Cazalegas, and the enemy at Sta. Olalla.

'It was then obvious that the enemy intended to try the result of a general action, for which the best position appeared to be in the neighbourhood of Talavera, and General Cuesta having consented to take up this position on the morning of the 27th, I ordered General Sherbrooke to retire with his corps to its station in the line, leaving General Mackenzie with a division of infantry and a brigade of cavalry as an advanced-post in the wood, on the right of the Alberche, which covered our left flank.

'The position taken up by the troops at Talavera extended rather more than two miles: the ground was open upon the left, where the British Army was stationed, and it was commanded by a height, on which was placed in echelon, as the second line, a division of infantry under the orders of Major-General Hill.

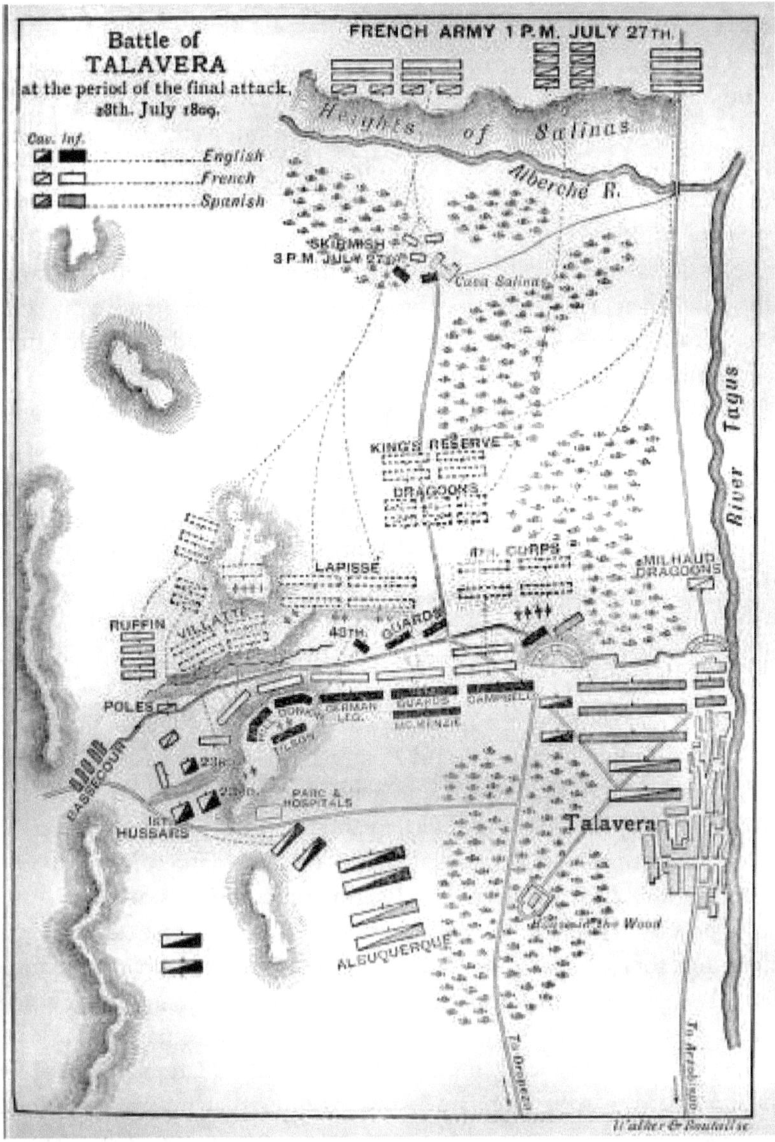

Battle of
TALAVERA
at the period of the final attack,
28th. July 1809.
Cav. Inf.
English
French
Spanish
FRENCH ARMY 1 P.M. JULY 27TH.
Heights of Salinas
Alberche R.
SKIRMISH
3 P.M. JULY 27TH.
Casa Salinas
KING'S RESERVE
DRAGOONS
LAPISSE
4TH. CORPS
MILHAUD
DRAGOONS
RUFFIN
VILLATTE
48TH.
GUARDS
POLES
GERMAN LEG.
GUARDS
CAMPBELL
MC.KENZIE
TILSON
23RD.
CASSECOUR
PARC &
HOSPITALS
1ST.
HUSSARS
Talavera
ALBUQUERQUE
River Tagus
To Oropeza
To Arzobispo
Walker & Boutall sc.

'There was a valley between the height and a range of mountains still farther upon the left, which valley was not at first occupied, as it was commanded by the height before mentioned; and the range of mountains appeared too distant to have any influence on the expected action.

'The right, consisting of Spanish troops, extended immediately in front of the town of Talavera, down to the Tagus. This part of the ground was covered by olive-trees, and much intersected by banks and ditches. The highroad leading from the bridge over the Alberche was defended by a heavy battery in front of a church, which was occupied by Spanish infantry.

'All the avenues of the town were defended in a similar manner. The town was occupied, and the remainder of the; Spanish infantry was formed in two lines behind the banks on the road which led from the town and the right to the left of our position.

'In the centre, between the two armies, there was a commanding spot of ground, on which we had commenced to construct a redoubt, with some open ground in its rear. Brigadier-General Alexander Campbell was posted at this spot with a division of infantry, supported in his rear by General Cotton's brigade of dragoons and some Spanish cavalry.

'At about two o'clock on the 27th the enemy appeared in strength on the left bank of the Alberche, and manifested an intention to attack General Mackenzie's division. The attack was made before they could be withdrawn; but the troops, consisting of General Mackenzie's and Colonel Donkin's brigades, and General Anson's brigade of cavalry, and supported by General Payne with the other four regiments of cavalry in the plain between Talavera and the wood, withdrew in good order, but with some loss, particularly by the 2nd Battalion 87th Regiment and the 2nd Battalion 31st Regiment in the wood.

'Upon this occasion the steadiness and discipline of the 45th Regiment and the 5th Battalion 60th Regiment were conspicuous, and I had particular reason for being satisfied with the manner in which Major-General Mackenzie withdrew this advanced-guard.

'As the day advanced, the enemy appeared in larger numbers on the right of the Alberche, and it was obvious that he was advancing to a general attack upon the combined armies. General Mackenzie continued to fall back gradually upon the left of the position of the combined armies, where he was placed in the second line in the rear of the Guards, Colonel Donkin being placed in the same situation farther upon the left, in the rear of the King's German Legion.

'The enemy immediately commenced his attack, in the dusk of the evening, by a cannonade upon the left of our position, and by an attempt with his cavalry to overthrow the Spanish infantry, posted, as I have before stated, on the right. This attempt entirely failed.

'Early in the night he pushed a division along the valley on the left of the height occupied by General Hill, of which he gained a momentary possession; but Major-General Hill attacked it instantly with the bayonet, and regained it.

'This attack was repeated in the night, but failed; and again, at daylight on the morning of the 28th, by two divisions of infantry, and was repulsed by Major-General Hill.

'Major-General Hill has reported to me, in a particular manner, the conduct of the 29th Regiment, and of the 1st Battalion 48th Regiment, in these different affairs, as well as that of Major-General Tilson and Brigadier-General R. Stewart.

'We lost many brave officers and soldiers in the defence of this important point in our position; among others, I cannot avoid mentioning Brigade-Major Fordyce and Brigade-Major Gardner, and Major-General Hill was himself wounded, but I am happy to say, but slightly.

'The defeat of this attempt was followed about noon by a general attack with the enemy's whole force upon the whole of that part of the position occupied by the British Army.

'In consequence of the repeated attempts upon the height upon our left, by the valley, I had placed two brigades of British cavalry in that valley, supported in the rear by the Duque de Alburquerque's division of Spanish cavalry.

'The enemy then placed light infantry in the range of mountains on the left of the valley, which were opposed by a division of Spanish infantry, under Lieutenant-General Bassecourt.

'The general attack began by the march of several columns of infantry into the valley, with a view to attack the height occupied by Major-General Hill. These columns were immediately charged by the 1st German Hussars and 23rd Light Dragoons, under Brigadier-General Anson, directed by Lieutenant-General Payne, and supported by Brigadier-General Fane's brigade of heavy cavalry; and although the 23rd Dragoons suffered considerable loss, the charge had the effect of preventing the execution of that part of the enemy's plan.

'At the same time, he directed an attack upon Brigadier-General Alexander Campbell's position in the centre of the combined armies, and on the right of the British.

'This attack was most successfully repulsed by Brigadier-General Campbell, supported by the King's regiment of Spanish cavalry and two battalions of Spanish infantry, and Brigadier-General Campbell took the enemy's cannon.

'The brigadier-general mentions particularly the conduct of the 97th, the 2nd Battalion 7th, and of the 2nd Battalion of the 53rd Regiment; and I was highly satisfied with the manner in which this part of the position was defended.

'An attack was also made at the same time upon Lieutenant-General Sherbrooke's division, which was in the left and centre of the first line of the British Army. This attack was most gallantly repulsed by a charge with bayonets by the whole division; but the brigade of Guards, which were on the right, having advanced too far, they were exposed on their left flank to the fire of the enemy's batteries, and of their retiring columns, and the division was obliged to retire towards the original position, under cover of the second line of General Cotton's brigade of cavalry, which I moved from the centre, and of the 1st Battalion 48th Regiment.

'I had moved this last regiment from its position on the heights as soon as I observed the advance of the Guards, and it was formed in the plain, and advanced upon the enemy, and covered the formation of Lieutenant-General Sherbrooke's division.

'Shortly after the repulse of this general attack, in which, apparently, all the enemy's troops were employed, he commenced his retreat across the Alberche, which was conducted in the most regular order, and was effected during the night, leaving in our hands twenty pieces of cannon, ammunition, tumbrils, and some prisoners.

'Your Lordship will observe, by the enclosed return, the great loss which we have sustained of valuable officers and soldiers in this long and hard-fought action with more than double our numbers. That of the enemy has been much greater.

'I have been informed that entire brigades of infantry have been destroyed; and, indeed, the battalions which retreated were much reduced in numbers.

'I have particularly to lament the loss of Major-General Mackenzie, who had distinguished himself on the 27th, and of Brigadier-General Langwerth, of the King's German Legion, and of Brigade-Major Beckett of the Guards.

'Your Lordship will observe that the attacks of the enemy were principally, if not entirely, directed against the British troops. The Spanish Commander-in-Chief, his officers and troops, manifested every disposition to render us assistance, and those of them who were engaged did their duty; but the ground which they occupied was so important, and its front at the same time so difficult, that I did not think it proper to urge them to make any movement on the left of the enemy while he was engaged with us.

'I have reason to be satisfied with the conduct of all the officers and troops. I am much indebted to Lieutenant-General Sherbrooke for the assistance I received from him, and for the manner in which he led on his division to the charge with bayonets; to Lieutenant-General Payne and the cavalry, particularly Brigadier-General Anson's brigade; to Major-Generals Hill and Tilson, Brigadier-Generals Alexander Campbell, Richard Stewart, and Cameron, and to the divisions and brigades of infantry under their command respectively, particularly to the 29th Regiment, commanded by Colonel White; to the 1st Battalion 48th, commanded by Colonel Donellan, afterwards, when that officer was wounded, by Major Middlemore; to the 2nd Battalion 7th, commanded by Lieutenant-Colonel Sir W. Myers; to the 2nd Battalion 53rd, commanded by Lieutenant-Colonel Bingham; to the 97th, commanded by Colonel Lyon; to the 1st Battalion of detachments, commanded by Lieutenant-Colonel Bunbury; to the 2nd Battalion 30th, commanded by Major Watson; the 45th, commanded by Lieutenant-Colonel Guard; and to the 5th Battalion 60th, commanded by Major Davy.

'The advance of the brigade of Guards was most gallantly conducted by Brigadier-General H. Campbell; and, when necessary, that brigade retired and formed again in the best order.

'The artillery, under Brigadier-General Howorth, was also throughout these days of the greatest service; and I had every reason to be satisfied with the assistance I received from the Chief Engineer, Lieutenant-Colonel Fletcher; the Adjutant-General, Brigadier-General the Hon C. Stewart; the Quartermaster-General, Colonel Murray; and the officers of those departments respectively; and from Lieutenant-Colonel Bathurst and the officers of my personal staff.

'I also received much assistance from Colonel O'Lalor, of the Spanish service, and from Brigadier-General Whittingham, who was wounded in bringing up the two Spanish battalions to the assistance of Brigadier-General Alexander Campbell.'

Return of Ordnance captured from the Enemy at the Battle of Talavera de la Reyna.

15 pieces of cannon of various calibre.
2 howitzers.
2 tumbrils, with ammunition complete.

Return of the Numbers of Killed, Wounded, and Missing of the Army under the Command of Lieutenant-General the Hon. Sir Arthur Wellesley, K.B., in Action with the French Army commanded by King Joseph Buonaparte in Person, at Talavera de la Reyna, on July 27, 28, 1809.

	Officers.	Sergeants.	Rank and File.	Horses.	Total Loss of Officers, Non-commissioned Officers, and Rank and File.
Killed	40	28	789	211	857
Wounded	195	165	3,553	71	3,913
Missing	9	15	629	159	653

MEMORANDUM UPON THE BATTLE OF TALAVERA.

'The position was well calculated for the troops which were to occupy it. The ground in front of the British Army was open, that in front of the Spanish Army covered with olive-trees, intersected by roads, ditches, etc. The Spanish infantry was posted behind the bank of the road leading from Talavera to the left of the position.

'The German Legion were on the left of the position in the first line. I had intended this part for the Guards; but I was unfortunately out, employed in bringing in General Mackenzie's advanced-guard, when the troops took up their ground. The 5th and 7th Battalions of the legion did not stand their ground on the evening, and in the beginning of the night of the 27th, which was the cause of the momentary loss of the height in the second line.

'General Sherbrooke moved his division, which was the left of the first line, to support General Hill's attack, in order to regain the height; and it was difficult to resume in the night the exact position which had been first marked out; and in fact, on account of these circumstances, we had not that precise position till after the enemy's attack upon the height at daylight in the morning had been repulsed.

'The advance of the Guards to the extent to which it was carried was nearly fatal to us, and the battle was certainly saved by the advance, position, and steady conduct of the 48th Regiment, (now the 1st Battalion Northamptonshire Regiment.—W.W.), upon which

General Sherbrooke's division formed again.

'The ground in front of the Spanish troops would not have been unfavourable to an attack upon the enemy's flank, while they were engaged with us, as there were broad roads leading from Talavera and different points of their position, in a direct line to the front, as well as diagonally to the left. But the Spanish troops are not in a state of discipline to attempt a manoeuvre in olive grounds, etc., and if they had got into confusion all would have been lost.

'Arthur Wellesley.'

To the Right Hon. John Villiers.

'Talavera de la Reyna,
'July 29, 1809.

'The enemy, having collected all the troops he had in this part of Spain, attacked us here on the 27th. The battle lasted till yesterday evening, when we beat him in all parts of our line; and he retreated in the evening and night, leaving in our hands twenty pieces of cannon, ammunition, waggons, prisoners, etc. The battle was a most desperate one. Our loss has been very great, that of the enemy larger. The attack was made principally upon the British, who were on the left; and we had about two to one against us—fearful odds! but we maintained all our positions, and gave the enemy a terrible beating.

'The Spanish troops that were engaged behaved well; but there were very few of them engaged, as the attack was made upon us. . . .'

To the Right Hon. J. H. Frere.

'Talavera de la Reyna,
'July 29, 1809.

'I have to inform you that the enemy, having collected all their forces in this part of Spain, made an attack upon the combined armies on the day before yesterday, which lasted till a late hour yesterday. Their principal efforts were directed against the British troops, which were upon the left of our position; but they were repulsed in all their attacks with considerable loss, and they retreated during the night, leaving in our hands twenty pieces of cannon, some ammunition, tumbrils, prisoners, etc.

'Our loss has been very large indeed, as may well be imagined, considering that, during two days and a night, we were attacked by a body of French troops of more than double our strength.

'But a reinforcement of 3,000 men has joined the army this morning, which will, I hope, make up in some degree for our loss of men;

that of officers is, I am afraid, irreparable.

'I am well satisfied with the conduct of the Spanish officers and troops who had an opportunity of assisting us.'

Plain Words to a Don.

To the Right Hon. J. H. Frere,

'Talavera de la Reyna,
'July 31, 1809.

'I have the honour to enclose the copy of a letter which I have received from Don Martin de Garay, upon which I request of you to convey to him the following observations. . . .

'It is not a difficult matter for a gentleman in the situation of Don Martin de Garay to sit down in his cabinet and write his ideas of the glory which would result from driving the French through the Pyrenees; and I believe there is no man in Spain who has risked so much, or who has sacrificed so much, to effect that object as I have.

'But I wish that Don Martin de Garay, or the gentlemen of the Junta, before they blame me for not doing more, or impute to me beforehand the probable consequences of the blunders or the indiscretion of others, would either come or send here somebody to satisfy the wants of our half-starved army, which, although they have been engaged for two days, and have defeated twice their numbers, in the service of Spain, have not bread to eat. It is positively a fact that, during the last seven days, the British Army have not received one third of their provisions; that at this moment there are nearly 4,000 wounded soldiers dying in the hospital in this town from want of common assistance and necessaries, which any other country in the world would have given even to its enemies; and that I can get no assistance of any description from the country. I cannot prevail upon them even to bury the dead carcases in the neighbourhood, the stench of which will destroy themselves as well as us.

'I cannot avoid feeling these circumstances; and the *Junta* must see that, unless they and the country make a great exertion to support and supply the armies, to which the invariable attention and the exertion of every man and the labour of every beast in the country ought to be directed, the bravery of the soldiers, their losses and their success, will only make matters worse and increase our embarrassment and distress.

'I positively will not move—nay, more, I will disperse my army—till I am supplied with provisions and means of transport as I ought to be.'

More Complaints.

To Major-General O'Donoju.

'Talavera de la Reyna,
'August 1, 1809.

'. . . During the action of the 28th many of the horses of our dragoons and of the artillery strayed, and were taken possession of by the stragglers from the Spanish Army who were in the rear of the town. I see English horses, with short tails, in possession of many of the Spanish troops; and I shall be very much obliged to you if you will urge General Cuesta to give an order that all persons having in their possession English horses, or horse appointments, such as saddles, bridles, etc., should take them to the English cavalry lines forthwith.

'I also understand that on the morning of the 29th, when our officers and soldiers were engaged in collecting the wounded and in burying the dead, the arms and accoutrements of both were collected and carried away by the Spanish troops.

'The consequence is that, as our soldiers recover in the hospital, we shall have no arms or accoutrements for them. I shall be very much obliged to General Cuesta if he will give orders that all English arms and accoutrements of infantry may be lodged at the convent of San Geronimo.

'We are much in want of medical assistance for the attendance of the wounded in the hospital; and I have been obliged to send there all those who ought properly to do duty with the regiments in the field. This cripples our operations much.'

'Horribly distressed for Provisions.'

To Viscount Castlereagh.

'Talavera de la Reyna,
'August 1, 1809.

' . . . We are miserably supplied with provisions, and I do not know how to remedy this evil. The Spanish armies are now so numerous that they eat up the whole country. They have no magazines, nor have we, nor can we collect any; and there is a scramble for everything.

'I think the battle of the 28th is likely to be of great use to the Spaniards; but I do not think them yet in a state of discipline to contend with the French; and I prefer infinitely to endeavour to remove the enemy from this part of Spain by manoeuvre to the trial of another pitched battle.'

To Marshal Beresford.

'Oropesa,
'August 3, 1809.

'. . . We are miserably off for provisions, and it is possible that I may be obliged to halt a day, to endeavour to procure a day's bread for the men. . . .'

To the Right Hon. J. H. Frere.

'Oropesa,
'August 3, 1809.

'In the meantime, with all these movements, we are horribly distressed for provisions. The soldiers seldom get enough to eat, and what they do get is delivered to them half mouldy, and at hours at which they ought to be at rest.'

To the Right Hon. J. H. Frere.

'Puente del Arzobispo,
'August 4, 1809.

'. . . In order that these operations and battles should be successful, it was necessary that the marches to be made should be long, and made with great celerity. I am sorry to say that, from the want of food, the troops are now unequal to either the one or the other; and it is more than probable that Victor would have been upon our backs before the first action between Soult and me could have been concluded. . .'

CHASING SOULT.

To His Grace the Duke of Richmond.

'Oporto,
'May 22, 1809.

'I have just returned from the most active and severe service. I have been on the pursuit, or rather chase, of Soult out of Portugal. We should have taken him if Silveira had been one or two hours earlier at the bridge of Melgaço, or if the captain of militia of the province had allowed the peasants, as they wished, to destroy it.

'We should have taken his rear-guard on the 16th, if we had had a quarter of an hour's more daylight; but in the dark our light infantry pursued by the road to Ruivaes instead of by that of Melgaço. But as it is, I think the chase out of Portugal is a *pendant* for the retreat to Coruña. It answers completely in weather; it has rained in torrents since the 12th. . . .'

Wellington's Escape at Talavera.

To the Duke of Richmond.

'Talavera de la Reyna,
'July 29, 1809.

'You will see the account of the great battle we fought yesterday. Our loss is terribly great. Your nephew is safe. His horse was shot under him on the 27th. Almost all my staff are either hit or have lost their horses, and how I have escaped unhurt I cannot tell. I was hit in the shoulder at the end of the action, but not hurt, and my coat shot through. . .'

Dire Effects of Starvation.

To the Duke of Richmond.

'Truxillo,
'August 21, 1809.

'Starvation has produced such dire effects upon the army, we have suffered so much, and have received so little assistance from the Spaniards, that I am at last compelled to move back into Portugal to look for subsistence. There is no enemy in our front of any consequence: Ney is gone back into Castille; Soult is at Plasencia; Mortier at Oropesa, Arzobispo, and Navalmoral; Victor's corps is divided, being half of it at Talavera, and half in La Mancha with Sebastiani. They cannot say we were compelled to go, therefore, by the enemy, but by a necessity created by the neglect of the Spaniards of our wants.'

To His Excellency Marquis Wellesley, K.P.

'Deleytosa,
'August 8, 1809.

'. . . . I wish I could see you, or could send somebody to you; but we are in such a situation that I cannot go to you myself, and I cannot spare the only one or two people, to converse with whom would be of any use to you. I think, therefore, that the best thing you can do is to send somebody to me as soon as you can—that is to say, if I remain in Spain, which I declare I believe to be almost impossible, notwithstanding that I see all the consequences of withdrawing. But a starving army is actually worse than none. The soldiers lose their discipline and their spirit. They plunder even in the presence of their officers. The officers are discontented, and are almost as bad as the men; and with the army which a fortnight ago beat double their numbers, I should now hesitate to meet a French corps of half their strength, . .'

To Captain-General Don Gregorio Cuesta.

'Deleytosa,
'August 11, 1809.

'I have had the honour of receiving Your Excellency's letter of the 10th instant, and I am concerned that you should conceive that you have any reason to complain of the conduct of the British troops; but when troops are starving, which those under my command have been, as I have repeatedly told Your Excellency since I joined you on the 22nd of last month, and particularly had no bread whatever from the 3rd to the 8th instant, it is not astonishing that they should go to the villages, and even to the mountains, and look for food where they think they can get it.

'The complaints of the inhabitants, however, should not have been confined to the conduct of the British troops; in this very village I have seen the Spanish soldiers, who ought to have been elsewhere, take the doors off the houses which were locked up, in order that they might plunder the houses, and they afterwards burnt the doors. I absolutely and positively deny the assertion that anything going to the Spanish Army has been stopped by the British troops or Commissaries.

'. . . I also declare to Your Excellency most positively, on the honour of a gentleman, that the British Army has received no provisions since it has been at Deleytosa, excepting some sent from Truxillo, by Señor Lozano de Torres; and I call upon the gentleman who has informed his friend that biscuit addressed to the Spanish Army has been taken by my Commissaries to prove the truth of his assertion. . . .

'In regard to the assertion in Your Excellency's letter that the British troops sell their bread to the Spanish soldiers, it is beneath the dignity of Your Excellency's situation and character to notice such things, or for me to reply to them. I must observe, however, that the British troops could not sell that which they had not, and that the reverse of the statement of Your Excellency upon this subject is the fact, at the time the armies were at Talavera, as I have myself witnessed frequently in the street of that town.'

To the Right Hon. J. Villiers.

'Jaraicejo,
'August 12, 1809.

'We are starving, and are ill-treated by the Spaniards in every way: but more of this hereafter. There is not a man in the army who does not wish to return to Portugal.'

Starved out of Spain.

To Marshal Beresford.

'Jaraicejo,
'August 19, 1809.

'. . . . After having made an effort to maintain myself here, I find it quite impossible. We are starving, our men falling sick, and we have nothing to give them in the way of comfort for their recovery; and our horses are dying by hundreds in the week. We have not had a full ration of provisions ever since the 22nd of the last month; and I am convinced that in that time the men have not received ten days' bread, and the horses not three regular deliveries of barley. We have no means of transport, and I shall be obliged to leave my ammunition on the ground, on quitting this place. We now want 1,800 horses to complete the cavalry, and 200 or 300 for the artillery.

'Under these circumstances, and seeing no prospect of an amelioration of our situation, which gets worse and worse every day, I have determined to withdraw towards the frontiers of Portugal, and I shall begin my march tomorrow. . . . .'

To His Excellency General Eguia.

'Jaraicejo,
'August 19, 1809.

'I have had the honour of receiving Your Excellency's letter of this day's date, and I feel much concerned that anything should have occurred to induce Your Excellency to express a doubt of the truth of what I have written to you. As, however, Your Excellency entertains that doubt, any further correspondence between us appears unnecessary; and, accordingly, this is the last letter which I shall have the honour of addressing to you.

'Although Your Excellency has expressed a doubt of the truth of what I have written to you, I entertain none of what Your Excellency has written to me; and I am well convinced that Your Excellency has given orders, and that all the contents of the magazine at Truxillo will be given to the British troops, even though the Spanish troops should want food. But, notwithstanding these orders, and an obedience to them, the British troops are still in want. Yesterday they received but one third of a ration, and that was in flour; this day they received only half a ration, likewise in flour. Whatever Your Excellency may think of the truth or falsehood of my assertion, I repeat that want and the apprehension of its further consequences, are the only reasons for my quitting Spain. . .'

To Viscount Castlereagh.

'Truxillo,
'August 21, 1809.

'. . . In my former despatches I have informed Your Lordship of our distress for the want of provisions and means of transport. These wants, which were the first cause of the loss of many advantages after July 22, which were made known to the Government, and were actually known by them on the 20th of last month, still exist in an aggravated degree, and have produced all the evil effects upon the health and efficiency of the army which might have been expected from them.

'Since the 22nd of last month, when the Spanish and British Armies joined, the troops have not received ten days' bread; on some days they have received nothing, and for many days together only meat, without salt; frequently flour instead of bread, and scarcely ever more than one-third, or at most half, of a ration. The cavalry and the horses of the army have not received, in the same time, three regular deliveries of forage, particularly of barley, the only wholesome subsistence for a horse in this country; and the horses have been kept alive by what they could pick up for themselves, for which they have frequently been obliged to go from twelve to twenty miles' distance, particularly lately.

'During a great part of this time, at least till the 4th or 5th of this month, I know that the Spanish Army received their regular rations daily. After they lost the bridge of Arzobispo, I believe they were in want for some days; but since they have come through the passes of the mountains I know, from the best authority, that of General Eguia, that the Spanish cavalry have been supplied daily with at least half a ration of barley, and I believe the troops have received their regular allowance of bread.

'The consequence of these privations upon the British Army has been the loss of many horses of the cavalry and artillery. We lost 100 in the cavalry last week; and we now want 1,000 horses to complete the six regiments of dragoons, besides about 700 that are sick, and will probably be fit for service only after a considerable period of rest and good food. The horses of the artillery are also much diminished in numbers, and are scarcely able to draw the guns.

'The sickness of the army, from the same cause, has increased considerably, particularly among the officers, who have fared no better than the soldiers, and have had nothing but water to drink, and frequently nothing but meat without salt to eat, and seldom any bread, for the last month.

'Indeed, there are few, if any, officers or soldiers of the army who, although doing their duty, are not more or less affected by dysentery, and the whole lie out, and nothing can be got for them in this part of the country.

'To these circumstances I must add that I have not been able to procure means of transport of any description since my arrival in Spain. I was obliged to employ the largest proportion of the carts in the army, whether they carried money or ammunition, to convey the wounded soldiers to the hospital at Elvas; and the ammunition which was laid down at Mesa de Ibor and Deleytosa was delivered to the Spanish General. The few carts which remained in the army were required to move the sick we have at present, and I have been obliged to leave behind me the remainder of the reserve ammunition, which I have also given to the Spanish troops; and if I had waited longer, I should not have been able to move at all without leaving the sick behind. . .'

Refusal to divide the British Army.

To Viscount Castlereagh.

'Deleytosa,
'August 8, 1809.

'. . . . General Cuesta proposed that half of the army should move to the rear to oppose the enemy, while the other half should maintain the post at Talavera. My answer was that, if by half the army he meant half of each army, I could only answer that I was ready either to go or to stay with the whole British Army, but that I could not divide it. He then desired me to choose whether I would go or stay, and I preferred to go, from thinking that the British troops were most likely to do the business effectually, and without contest; and from being of opinion that to open the communication through Plasencia was more important to us than to the Spanish Army, although very important to them. With this decision General Cuesta appeared perfectly satisfied. . . .'

Cowardice of Spanish Troops.

To Marquis Wellesley.,

'Merida,
'August 24, 1809.

' . . . . I come now to another topic, which is one of serious consideration, and has considerable weight in my judgment upon this whole subject, and that is the frequent, I ought to say constant, and shameful misbehaviour of the Spanish troops before the enemy. We in England never hear of their defeats and flights; but I have heard of Spanish officers telling of nineteen and twenty actions of the description of that at the bridge of Arzobispo, an account of which has, I believe, never been published.

'In the Battle of Talavera, in which the Spanish Army, with very trifling exceptions, was not engaged, whole corps threw away their arms, and ran off *in my presence*, when they were neither attacked nor threatened with an attack, but frightened, I believe, by their own fire.

'I refer Your Excellency for evidence upon this subject to General Cuesta's orders, in which, after extolling the gallantry of his army in general, he declares his intention to decimate the runaways, an intention which he afterwards carried into execution.

'When these dastardly soldiers run away, they plunder everything they meet; and in their flight from Talavera, they plundered the baggage of the British Army, which was at the moment bravely engaged in their cause. . . .'

To Viscount Castlereagh.

'Merida,
'August 25, 1809.

'. . . I come now to the description of the troops, and here I am sorry to say that our allies fail us still more than they do in numbers and composition.

'The Spanish cavalry are, I believe, nearly entirely without discipline. They are in general well clothed, armed and accoutred, and remarkably well mounted, and their horses are in good condition—I mean those of Eguia's army, which I have seen. But I have never heard anybody pretend that in any one instance they have behaved as soldiers ought to do in presence of an enemy. They make no scruple of running off, and after an action are to be found in every village, and every shady bottom within fifty miles of the field of battle.

'The Spanish artillery are, as far as I have seen of them, entirely unexceptionable, and the Portuguese artillery excellent.

'In respect to the great body of all armies—I mean the infantry—it is lamentable to see how bad that of the Spaniards is, and how unequal to a contest with the French. They are armed, I believe, well; they are badly accoutred, not having the means of saving their ammunition from the rain; not clothed in some instances at all, in others clothed in such a manner as to make them look like peasants, which ought of all things to be avoided; and their discipline appears to me to be confined to placing them in the ranks, three deep at very close order, and to the manual exercise.

'It is impossible to calculate upon any operation with these troops. It is said that sometimes they behave well; though I acknowledge that I have never seen them behave otherwise than ill. Bassecourt's corps, which was supposed to be the best in Cuesta's army, and was engaged on our left in the mountains, at the Battle of Talavera, was kept in check throughout the day by one French battalion; this corps has since run away from the bridge of Arzobispo, leaving its guns; and many of the men, according to the usual Spanish custom, throwing away their arms, accoutrements and clothing.

'It is a curious circumstance respecting this affair at Arzobispo (in which Soult writes that the French took thirty pieces of cannon), that the Spaniards ran off in such a hurry that they left their cannon loaded and unspiked; and that the French, although they drove the Spaniards from the bridge, did not think themselves strong enough to push after them; and Colonel Waters, whom I sent in with a flag of truce on the 10th, relating to our wounded, found the cannon on the road, abandoned by the one party, and not taken possession of, and probably not known of, by the other.

'This practice of running away, and throwing off arms, accoutrements, and clothing, is fatal to everything, excepting a re-assembly of the men in a state of nature, who as regularly perform the same manoeuvre the next time an occasion offers. Nearly 2,000 ran off on the evening of the 27th from the Battle of Talavera (not 100 yards from the place where I was standing), who were neither attacked nor threatened with an attack, and who were frightened only by the noise of their own fire: they left their arms and accoutrements on the ground, their officers went with them; and they, and the fugitive cavalry, plundered the baggage of the British Army which had been sent to the rear. Many others went whom I did not see.

'Nothing can be worse than the officers of the Spanish Army; and it is extraordinary that when a nation has devoted itself to war, as this nation has, by the measures it has adopted in the last two years, so little progress has been made in any one branch of the military profession by any individual, and that the business of an army should be so little understood. They are really children in the art of war, and I cannot say that they do anything as it ought to be done, with the exception of running, away and assembling again in a state of nature.

'I really believe that much of this deficiency of numbers, composition, discipline, and efficiency, is to be attributed to the existing government of Spain. They have attempted to govern the kingdom in a state of revolution, by an adherence to old rules and systems, and with the aid of what is called enthusiasm; and this last is, in fact, no aid to accomplish anything, and is only an excuse for the irregularity with which everything is done, and for the want of discipline and subordination of the armies. . . .

'I now come to another branch of the subject, which is Portugal itself. I have not got from Beresford his report upon the present and the probable future state of the Portuguese Army; and therefore, I should wish to be understood as writing, upon this part of the subject, liable to corrections from him.'

Portuguese Troops.

'My opinion is, and always has been, that the mode of applying the services of the English officers to the Portuguese Army has been erroneous. I think that Beresford ought to have had the temporary assistance of the ablest officers the British service could afford, that these officers ought not to have been posted to regiments in the Portuguese Army, but under the title of Adjutants to the Field-Marshal, or any other, they ought to have superintended discipline, military movements, and arrangements of all descriptions, wherever they might be: fewer officers would then have answered his purpose, and every one given to him would have been useful; whereas many (all in the inferior ranks) are under existing arrangements useless.

'Besides this, the selection of officers sent out to Portugal for this service has been unlucky, and the decision on the questions which I sent to England on June 7, has been made without reference to circumstances or to the feelings or opinions of the individuals on whom it was to operate, and, just like every other decision I have ever seen from the same quarter, as if men were stocks and stones.

'To this, add that rank (Portuguese rank, I mean) has been given in the most capricious manner. In some instances, a man not in the army at all is made a Brigadier-General; in others, another who was the senior of the Brigadier-General when both were in the army is a Lieutenant-Colonel; then a junior Lieutenant-Colonel is made a Brigadier-General, his senior a Colonel, and his senior a junior Colonel; and there are instances of juniors being preferred to seniors in every rank; in short, the Prince Regent of Portugal is a despotic prince, and his commissions have been given to British officers and subjects in the most arbitrary manner at the Horse Guards; and the answer to all these complaints at the Horse Guards must be uniform, nobody has any right to complain; the Prince Regent has a right to give to anybody any commission he pleases, bearing any date he chooses to assign to it. The officers of this army have to a man quitted the Portuguese service, as I said they would, and there is not an officer who has joined it from England who would not quit it if we would allow him; but here we keep them: so much for that arrangement.

'The subject upon which particularly I wished Beresford to report was the state of the Portuguese Army in respect to its numbers. The troops have lately deserted to an alarming degree, and, in fact, none of the regiments are complete. The Portuguese Army is recruited by conscription constitutionally, very much in the same manner with the French Army; but then it must be recollected that, for the last fifty years nearly, the troops have never left their province, and scarcely ever their native town; and their discipline, and the labours and exertion required from them, were nothing.

'Things are much altered lately, and, notwithstanding that the pay has been increased, I fear that the animal is not of the description to bear up against what is required of him, and he deserts most terribly...'

Soldiers and Religious Worship.

To the Right Hon. John Villiers.

'Badajoz,
'September 8, 1809.

'The soldiers of the army have permission to go to Mass, so far as this: they are forbidden to go into the churches during the performance of Divine service, unless they go to assist in the performance of the service. I could not do more, for, in point of fact, soldiers cannot by law attend the celebration of Mass, excepting in Ireland. The thing now stands exactly as it ought; any man may go to Mass who chooses, and nobody makes any inquiry about it. The consequence is that nobody goes to Mass, and although we have whole regiments of Irishmen, and of course Roman Catholics, I have not seen one soldier perform any one act of religious worship in these Catholic countries, excepting making the sign of the cross to induce the people of the country to give them wine.

'Although, as you will observe, I have no objection, and they may go to Mass if they choose it, I have great objections to the inquiries and interference of the priests of the country to induce them to go to Mass. The orders were calculated to prevent all intrigue and interference of that description; and I was very certain that, when the Irish soldiers were left to themselves either to go or not, they would do as their comrades did, and not one of them would be seen in a church.

'I think it best that you should avoid having any further discussion with the priests on this subject; but if you should have any, it would be best that you should tell them what our law is, and what the order of this army.

'Prudence may then induce them to refrain from taking any steps to induce the Roman Catholic soldiers to attend Mass; but if it should not, and their conduct should be guided by religious zeal, I acknowledge that, however indifferent I should have been at seeing the soldiers flock to the churches under my orders, I should not be very well satisfied to see them filled by the influence of the priests, taking advantage of the mildness and toleration which is the spirit of that order. . . .'

Withholding the Death Punishment.

'It is a curious circumstance, that notwithstanding I have been aware of the necessity, and have determined to execute any man found guilty or in the act of plunder, I have not yet executed one; although I really believe that more plunder and outrage have been committed by this army than by any other that ever was in the field: to this add, that I have not less than seven or eight provosts, other armies having usually two. . .'

Women and Children's Rations.

To Colonel Peacocks.

'Badajoz,
'September 12, 1809.

'. . . . The women and children of the officers and soldiers of the army are entitled, the former each to half a ration, the latter to a quarter of a ration daily; and I see no objection to extending these allowances to the wives and children of clerks and others employed in the public departments, provided they are English born. If the clerk be Portuguese, it may be very necessary and proper to give him his rations, but it cannot be necessary to his wife and children, and I desire that this practice may be discontinued.

'I conclude that the rations drawn by the lady, to whom you refer as an officer's wife, are for the wives of other officers or soldiers, and if so, they are perfectly regular; if not, they must be discontinued; and, at all events, forage must not be allowed to the horse of an officer's lady residing at Lisbon.

'I beg that you will understand that I am desirous of giving to the wives of the officers and soldiers of the army every indulgence to the fullest extent allowed by His Majesty's regulations; but I can suffer no abuse, and every appearance of abuse must be checked immediately.

'The officers of the army are allowed to draw rations in the field for servants not soldiers, paying for the same; and I conceive the same indulgence may be extended to their families residing at Lisbon for English servants, but not for Portuguese.'

Praise for the 29th Regiment.

To Viscount Castlereagh.

'Badajoz,
'September 12, 1809.

'I wish very much that some measures could be adopted to get some recruits for the 29th Regiment. It is the best regiment in this army, has admirable internal system, and excellent non-commissioned officers; but for the want of a second battalion, and somebody to attend to its recruiting, it is much reduced in numbers, by losses in the action of Roliça and Vimeiro, in the expedition to the north of Portugal and at Talavera. . . .'

★★★★★★★★★★

Now the 1st Battalion the Worcestershire Regiment. The 29th bore the brunt of the fight at Roliça, and was the last regiment of the famous Peninsular Army to retain the pigtail and hair-powder.—W.W.

★★★★★★★★★★

First Use of the Name 'Wellington.'

To the Right Hon. John Villiers.

'Badajoz,
'September 16, 1809.

'My dear Villiers,

'. . . The sum of money received in the last month of August for bills, and in all modes, amounts to £158,000, of which sum the fifth, or about £32,000, are at your disposal, at the Commissary General's officer. Of this sum you have already, I understand, received a part. This sum of £158,000 is exclusive of the money arrived in the Fylla, amounting to £150,000 and more, the silver belonging, I understand, exclusively to the Portuguese Government.

'Believe me, etc.,

'Wellington.

'This is the first time I have signed my new name. Would the Regency give me leave to have a *Chasse* at Villa Viçosa?'

The Care of Kettles.

To Brigadier-General Robert Craufurd.

'Badajoz,
'September 29, 1809.

'I have been for some time very anxious respecting a part of what forms the subject of your letter of the 26th—I mean the camp kettles; and I am much obliged to you for your opinions on the subject. Faulty as is the existing mode of carrying the camp kettles, it is more efficient than that of which it is the substitute in this country.

'There is much to be said on both sides of the question respecting the description of kettle which the soldiers ought to have, and as the iron kettle is the best for cooking, and lasts longest, and, moreover, as the use of that description and size of kettle requires the employment of fewest men in cooking, the choice between them resolves itself into this point, which is most likely to be carried with certainty, so as to give the soldier at all times the use of a kettle. . . .

'Upon the whole, therefore, I prefer the iron kettles to the tin for general purposes; but I have no objection to try the latter in some of our best regiments, in order to see how the experiment may answer. . .'

The 1st Dragoons.

To Lieutenant-General Payne.

'Lisbon,
'October 11, 1809.

'I arrived here yesterday, and I saw the 1st Dragoons in the streets, and I think that in my life I have never seen a finer regiment. They were very strong, the horses in very good condition, and the regiment apparently in high order.'

German Deserters from the French Service.

Memorandum.

'*According to the desire expressed by Mr. Villiers, I proceed to give my opinion on the points referred to in his despatch to the Secretary of State, dated October 2, 1809.*

'October 11, 1809.

'. . . I rather believe Mr. Villiers is misinformed respecting the desertion of the German troops in the French service; they do desert, certainly, when the British Army is near them, and so do the French, but not in the numbers supposed. I believe, however, that they would desert in greater numbers if the Spanish peasants did not murder everything in the shape of a French soldier found at any distance from the lines; and General Cuesta had already adopted measures to encourage desertion, by preventing these murders, by offering and giving a reward for every soldier belonging to the enemy brought in alive. . . .'

To the Earl of Liverpool.

'Badajoz,
'November 27, 1809.

'I have had the honour of receiving Your Lordship's letter of the 2nd instant, in which you have enclosed the copy of one from Mr. Villiers; and in case I should have any opportunity of communicating with the German corps in the service of the enemy, I shall attend to Your Lordship's instructions.

'It is impossible for me to say what number of Germans were enlisted at Oporto and Ciudad Rodrigo from the enemy's troops, because I did not command His Majesty's troops in this country at the time; but I did in the months of July and August last, and I have no recollection of the arrival of any German deserters from the Escurial, much less of 160. Neither do I recollect the circumstance of a battalion being in treaty to join us, when the British Army was in the neighbourhood of that of the enemy in July and August.

'The German troops were at and in the neighbourhood of Toledo, with few exceptions; some few then deserted, but not in such numbers as to deserve serious attention; and adverting to the encouragement they had from the Commander-in-Chief of the Spanish Army, and to the facilities afforded to them by our neighbourhood and their own position, I was rather inclined to be of opinion that as a body, or even in very large numbers, they were not desirous of quitting the French service.

'At the same time, the commanding officers of the German regiments in the British service were not anxious to receive them as recruits, in which they were not wrong, as most of the few they did receive have since deserted from them; and, upon the whole, I did not think there was any ground for a belief that any measures which I might adopt to encourage or facilitate desertion from the enemy's

German troops would have an effect at all proportionate to the expense of them.'

Officer's Unbecoming Conduct.

To Brigadier -General Slade, President of a General Court-martial.

'Lisbon,
'October 12, 1809.

'I have perused the proceedings of the general court-martial, of which you are President, on the trial of Lieutenant ——, of the —— Regiment, for, "most unofficerlike and ungentlemanlike conduct, in being concerned in an affray which took place in the city of Lisbon on the night of the 3rd of March last, 1809," of which crime the court have honourably acquitted him; and I request you to reassemble the general court-martial, and to desire them to revise this sentence.

'It appears that the affray in which the court have found that Lieutenant —— was concerned originated in a brothel, in which Lieutenant —— was with other officers; and although his conduct in the affray might have been distinguished by his activity to quell it, and merits the acquittal which the court have sentenced, I should not do my duty by them or by His Majesty, who has entrusted me with the power of confirming their sentence, if I did not draw their attention to the use of the term *honourably*, which it contains.

'It is difficult and needless at present to define in what cases an honourable acquittal by a court-martial is peculiarly applicable; but it must appear to all persons to be objectionable in a case in which any part of the transaction, which has been the subject of investigation before the court-martial, is disgraceful to the character of the party under trial.

'A sentence of honourable acquittal by a court-martial should be considered by the officers and soldiers of the army as a subject of exultation; but no man can exult in the termination of any transaction a part of which has been disgraceful to him; and although such a transaction may be terminated by an *honourable* acquittal by a court-martial, it cannot be mentioned to the party without offence, or without exciting feelings of disgust in others: these are not the feelings which ought to be excited by the recollection and mention of a sentence of honourable acquittal.

'I believe that there is no officer upon the general court-martial who wishes to connect the term honour with the act of going to a brothel; the common practice forbids it, and there is no man who, unfortunately, commits this act who does not endeavour to conceal it from the world and his friends. But the honourable acquittal of Lieutenant ——, as recorded in this sentence, which states that he was concerned in an affray which is known to have originated in a brothel, will have the effect of connecting with the act of going to a brothel the honourable distinction which it is in the power of a court-martial to bestow on those brought before them on charges of a very different nature, by the sentence which it may pass upon them.

'I therefore anxiously recommend to the general court-martial to omit the word *honourably* in their sentence.'

Officers' Misbehaviour in Theatres.

To Colonel Peacocke.

'Lisbon,
'October 26, 1809.

'I am concerned to be obliged to inform you that it has been mentioned to me that the British officers who are in Lisbon are in the habit of going to the theatres, where some of them conduct themselves in a very improper manner, much to the annoyance of the public, and to the injury of the proprietors and of the performers. I cannot conceive for what reason the officers of the British Army should conduct themselves at Lisbon in a manner which would not be permitted in their own country, is contrary to rule and custom in this country, and is permitted in none when there is any regulation or decency of behaviour.

'The officers commanding regiments and the superior officers must take measures to prevent a repetition of the conduct adverted to, and of the consequent complaints which I have received; or I must take measures which shall effectually prevent the character of the army and of the British nation from suffering by the misconduct of a few.

'The officers of the army can have nothing to do behind the scenes, and it is very improper that they should appear upon the stage during the performance. They must be aware that the English public would not bear either the one or the other, and I see no reason why the Portuguese public should be worse treated.

'I have been concerned to see officers in uniform, with their hats on, upon the stage during the performance, and to hear of the riots and outrages which some of them have committed behind the scenes; and I can only repeat that, if this conduct should be continued, I shall be under the necessity of adopting measures to prevent it, for the credit of the army and of the country.

'I beg you to communicate this letter to the commanding officers of the regiments in the garrison of Lisbon, and to the commanding officer of the detachments of convalescents, and desire them to communicate its contents to the officers under their command respectively.

'Indeed, officers who are absent from their duty on account of sickness might as well not go to the playhouse, or at all events upon the stage and behind the scenes. I beg you also to take such measures as may appear to you to be necessary to prevent a repetition of this conduct.'

Cartel of Exchange.

'Headquarters of the British Army,

'October 20, 1809.

'Cartel of exchange between Lieutenant Cameron of the 79th Regiment, taken by the French Army at Talavera (and sent into the British Army, on a cartel of exchange with Lieutenant de Turenne, *Aide-de-Camp* to General Kellermann), and Lieutenant Louis Vernon de Farincourt, of the and Light Infantry of the French Army, taken by the Portuguese Army at Chaves, and now in confinement at Lisbon.

'The above-mentioned exchange with Lieutenant de Turenne not taking effect, Lieutenant Cameron of the 79th is exchanged for Lieutenant Louis Vernon de Farincourt. In consequence thereof, Lieutenant Louis Vernon de Farincourt is authorised to join the French Army; and all officers commanding English, Portuguese, and Spanish troops are requested to allow him to pass to the French Army without molestation.

'Lieutenant Vernon de Farincourt will show this cartel of exchange to the Commander-in-Chief of the French Army.

'Wellington.'

The Talavera Club.

To the Right Hon. John Villiers.

'Badajoz,
'November 20, 1809.

'. . . In respect to the Talavera Club, before I consent to belong to it, I must see who are the society; and possibly it might be well to look a little into the character of those who constituted it at Lisbon. If the officers who first went down to Lisbon from the army, they are people who ought not to be countenanced on any account, as they in fact deserted; and each of them, as he comes up, is in arrest, and he is obliged to give an account of himself. . . .'

Injudicious News.

To the Earl of Liverpool.

'Badajoz,
'November 21, 1809.

'I beg to draw Your Lordship's attention to the frequent paragraphs in the English newspapers, describing the position, the numbers, the objects, and the means of attaining them, possessed by the armies in Spain and Portugal.

'In some instances, the English newspapers have accurately stated, not only the regiments occupying a position, but the number of men fit for duty of which each regiment was composed; and this intelligence must have reached the enemy at the same time it did me, at a moment at which it was most important that he should not receive it.

'The newspapers have recently published an account of the defensive positions occupied by the different English and Portuguese corps, which certainly conveyed to the enemy the first knowledge he had of them; and I enclose a paragraph recently published, describing the line of operation which I should follow in case of the occurrence of a certain event, the preparations which I had made for that operation, and where I had formed my magazines.

'It is not necessary to inquire in what manner the newspapers acquire this description of information; but if the editors really feel an anxiety for the success of the military operations in the Peninsula, they will refrain from giving this information to the public, as they must know that their papers are read by the enemy, and that the information which they are desirous of conveying to their English readers is mischievous to the public, exactly in proportion as it is well founded and correct.

'Your Lordship will be the best judge whether any and what measures ought to be adopted to prevent the publication of this description of intelligence. I can only assure you that it will increase materially the difficulty of all operations in this country.'

Recommending a Brave Officer.

To Lieutenant-Colonel Torrens.

'Badajoz,
'November 30, 1809.

'I have to request that you will submit the enclosed memorial to the favourable consideration of the Commander-in-Chief; and I beg leave to recommend Major Coghlan, 61st Regiment, in the strongest manner, as an officer most deserving of the promotion he solicits.'

★★★★★★★★★★

Major Coghlan had been wounded and left at Talavera, and had escaped from prison on his march towards France. He was soon afterwards promoted to be Lieutenant-Colonel of the 61st, in the command of which regiment he was shot through the heart at the Battle ofToulouse, on April 10, 1814. He was buried, under fire, in a temporary grave, on the position captured from the enemy; but on the 12th was removed to the Protestant cemetery in Toulouse, where all the officers of the army then in Toulouse paid the last tribute of respect to his remains.

★★★★★★★★★★

'A Unanimous Army.'

To Colonel Malcolm.

'Badajoz,
'December 3,1809.

'I have in hand a most difficult task, from which I may not extricate myself; but I must not shrink from it. I command *a unanimous army*; I draw well with all the authorities in Spain and Portugal, and I believe I have the good wishes of the whole world. In such circumstances one may fail, but it would be dishonourable to shrink from the task. . . .'

Ignorant Spanish Officers.

To B. Frere, Esq.

'Badajoz,
'December 6, 1809.

'I shall not detain the messenger by any addition to my official letters of this day, excepting to lament that a cause which promised so well a few weeks ago should have been so completely lost by the ignorance, presumption, and mismanagement of those to whose direction it was intrusted.

'I declare that if they had preserved their two armies, or even one of them, the cause was safe. The French could have sent no reinforcements which could have been of any use; time would have been gained; the state of affairs would have improved daily; all the chances were in our favour; and in the first moment of weakness occasioned by any diversion on the Continent, or by the growing discontent of the French themselves with the war, the French Armies must have been driven out of Spain.

'But no! Nothing will answer excepting to fight great battles in plains, in which their defeat is as certain as is the commencement of the battle. They will not credit the accounts I have repeatedly given them of the superior number even of the French; they will seek them out, and they find them invariably in all parts in numbers superior to themselves.

'I am only afraid, now, that I shall be too late to save Ciudad Rodrigo; the loss of which will secure for the French Old Castille, and will cut off all communication with the northern provinces, and leave them to their fate.

'I wonder whether the Spanish officers ever read the history of the American war, or of their own war in the Dutch provinces, or of their own war in Portugal.'

A Too Zealous Reformer.

To the Right Hon. John Villiers.

'Badajoz,
'December 22, 1809.

'I am concerned to be obliged to make any complaint of a *protegé* of yours, but I must say that I think I have some cause to complain of Mr. ——.

'He was appointed by me to the Commissariat in June, and on July 11 he writes a letter to the Lords of the Treasury, in which he gives them to understand neither more nor less than that the Commissary-General and all his officers, as well as myself, are either knaves or fools; and that he can save thousands upon thousands to the public, by some new mode he has discovered of supplying the troops with bread. He disclaims, at the same time, any intention of making a charge against any of us!

'Now, I must say that, if Mr. —— has made any discovery upon this subject, it was his duty to apprise me of it; and at least to try whether our failure to save the public these thousands upon thousands was to be attributed to knavery or folly, before he wrote to the Treasury upon the subject.'

Assailed by Common Councilmen.

To the Right Hon. John Villiers.

'Pombal,
'January 2, 1810.

'. . . . You see the dash which the Common Council of the city of London have made at me! I act with a sword hanging over me, which will fall upon me whatever may be the result of affairs here; but they may do what they please, I shall not give up the game here as long as it can be played.'

EIGHT MONTHS' LOSS IN DEAD.

To the Earl of Liverpool.

'Pombal,

'January 2, 1810.

'. . . .I have lately had a return made out showing the total loss of the army in dead since I took the command in April last; which is only 4,500 men, including the Battle of Talavera, etc. Besides which, there are 1,500 prisoners. This is about one third of the loss which the French compute that they suffered in about the same period of time. . .'

FAITHFUL TO THE 33RD.

To Lieutenant-Colonel Torrens, Military Secretary to the Commander-in-Chief.

'Viseu,

'January 30, 1810.

'I shall esteem it a great favour if you will tell Sir David Dundas that I am very much obliged to him, but that I have no wish to be removed from the 33rd Regiment, of which I was Major, and Lieutenant-Colonel, and then Colonel.

(An offer had been made to remove Lord Wellington to a regiment with two battalions.)

'I must say, however, that my friend, the late Secretary at War, made it the least profitable of all the regiments of the army, and, I believe, a losing concern, having reduced the establishment at once from 1,200 to 800, when it consisted of above 750 men; and I had to pay the freight of the clothing to the East Indies, and its carriage to Hyderabad, about 500 miles from Madras. With all this, I have the reputation of having a good thing in a regiment in the East Indies!'

MILITARY STORES.

To the Earl of Liverpool.

'Viseu,

'January 30, 1810.

'I have the honour to enclose the returns of stores in His Majesty's magazines in Portugal up to January 1, 1810.'

'COMMISSARY-GENERAL'S OFFICE,
'VISEU, *January* 1, 1810.

Return of Provisions, Wine, Spirits, and Forage remaining in His Majesty's Magazines in Portugal on January 1, 1810.

Provisions, Wine, and Spirits.	Biscuit	1,792,160	Pounds.
	Flour	1,099,134	Pounds.
	Salt meat	1,797,190	Pounds.
	Wine	26	Pipes.
	Rum	113,990	Gallons.
Forage	Oats	1,444,640	Pounds.
	Barley	1,286,385	Pounds.
	Wheat	87,070	Pounds.
	Indian corn	212,551	Pounds.
	Beans	1,660	Pounds.
	Bran	5,100	Pounds.
	Hay	1,372,304	Pounds.

'J. MURRAY, *Commissary-General.*'

'COMMISSARY-GENERAL'S OFFICE,
'VISEU, *January* 1, 1810.

Return of Quartermaster-General's Stores remaining in His Majesty's Magazines in Portugal.

1,900	Flanders tents	Soldiers' tents.
1,900	Flanders poles	Soldiers' tents.
1,838	Iron collars	Soldiers' tents.
6,000	Mallets	Soldiers' tents.
124,600	Pins	Soldiers' tents.
724	Poles and cases	Camp colours.
431	Flags	Camp colours.
595	Powder bags.	
1,060	Drum cases.	
698	Hatchets.	
16	Tarpaulins.	
15½	Vals marq. tents	Hospital.
14½	Sets of poles	Hospital.
70	Bags of mallets and pins	Hospital.
3	Reels and lines.	
200	Langrels.	
626	Tin kettles.	
335	Kettle bags.	
604	Tin canteens.	
6,699	Wood canteens.	
5,286	Canteen straps.	
43	Felling axes.	
14,020	Haversacks.	
2,235	Blankets.	
542¾	Sets of forage cords, four to a set.	
785	Bill-hooks.	
3,493	Flanders kettles.	
264	Picket ropes.	
5	Pickaxes.	
453	Hair nose bags.	
461	Packsaddles with crooked haucums.	
264	Bridles and chain collars.	
167	Ammunition boxes.	
19	Medicine panniers.	
106	Bundles of blankets.	
735	Picket poles.	
1	Knapsack.	
618	Sets of bedding.	
5	Shovels.	
5	Spades.	
149	Casks of accoutrements.	
2	Cases of nails.	
75	Mule halters.	
34	French tent poles.	
20	Small water casks.	
13	Cases of buttons.	
9	Cases of officers' swords.	
99,062	Pairs of shoes.	
45	Bales of army clothing.	
10	Baskets.	
400	Palliasses.	

'J. MURRAY, *Commissary-General.*'

CONTINUED OUTRAGES.

(Written in connection with an allegation that a British soldier had murdered a man because the deceased had refused to mend his boots,—W.W.)

To Charles Stuart, Esq.

'Viseu,
'March 6, 1810.

'. . . . It is unfortunately but too true that outrages of all descriptions are committed.by the British soldiers in this country, notwithstanding the pains taken by me and the general and other superior officers of the army, to prevent them, and to punish those who commit them.

'It is useless to trouble you with a description of the causes of these evils, upon which I have written fully to the King's Ministers. One of them, undoubtedly, is the disinclination of the people of this country to substantiate upon oath, before a court-martial, their complaints of the conduct of the soldiers, without which it is well known that it is impossible for me to punish them: the consequence is that the criminals are tried and acquitted for want of evidence; for it is vain to expect evidence of an outrage from the comrades of the soldier who has committed it.

'The records of the embassy at Lisbon must be filled with complaints of the same general nature as that which I now return to you, and with demands from me of evidence on the facts stated; the result of which has invariably been, that no evidence has been adduced to substantiate the complaints made, and those who have committed the outrages complained of have remained unpunished.

'I am concerned to add that I know of no means which have not already been adopted to endeavour to keep the British soldiers in order.

'Detachments are never allowed to march, excepting under the command of an officer; and the most strict orders have been given for the regulation of the conduct of the soldiers when so employed; and an officer of the provost marshal establishment is employed whenever the numbers of any detachment will justify such an appointment.

'But all has hitherto been in vain; the outrages complained of are still perpetrated, and they will continue until the Government and people see the necessity of doing their utmost to convict, before a court-martial, those soldiers of the crimes of which, I am sorry to say, I am too well convinced they have reason to complain.'

Vagabonds from Hospital.

To Brigadier-General R. Craufurd.

'Viseu,
'March 20, 1810.

'. . . I shall speak to the Commissary-General about your wine, and I shall send you some shoes. We have, however, very few in this neighbourhood, as the vagabonds who come from the hospital sell everything upon the road, and it is generally necessary to supply them with all the requisites for a soldier as they pass through this place. I have, however, ordered forward a large supply, of which you shall have your share.'

The Third Year of the Contest.

To Major-General the Hon. W. Stewart.

'Viseu,
'March 27, 1810.

'. . . . The affairs of the Peninsula have invariably had the same appearance since I have known them; they have always appeared to be lost; means have always appeared inadequate to objects, and the sole dependence of the whole has apparently been upon us.

'The contest, however, still continues, and is in its third year, and we must continue it as long as we can with the means which the country affords, improving them as much as the people will allow us, as it is obvious that Great Britain cannot give us larger means than we have . . .'

The Affair at Barba de Puerco.

To the Earl of Liverpool.

'Viseu,
'March 28, 1810.

'. . . The French attacked the post at Barba de Puerco, which was occupied by four companies of the 95th Regiment under Lieutenant-Colonel Beckwith, on the night of the 19th instant.

'Immediately opposite to Barba de Puerco, on the other side of the river, is San Felices, and between these two villages the only bridge on the Agueda below Ciudad Rodrigo, and the recent fall of rain had filled the river, which was nowhere fordable.

'The enemy had collected a brigade of infantry at San Felices, and crossed the bridge with 600 men after dark, keeping the remainder on the other side.

'These followed the picket of the 95th up from the bridge, and immediately made their attack; but they were repulsed with the loss of two officers and seven men killed, six prisoners, and thirty firelocks.

'I am sorry to add that Lieutenant Mercer of the 95th and three men were killed, and ten were wounded, in this affair, which was highly creditable to Colonel Beckwith, and displayed the gallantry and discipline of the officers and troops under his command. The Adjutant, Lieutenant Stewart, distinguished himself.'

★★★★★★★★★★

This affair of posts is one of the most memorable incidents in the annals of the Rifle Brigade—the old 95th. Wellington issued a special complimentary Order in which he said that the action reflected great honour on the regiment.—W.W.

★★★★★★★★★★

Mutual Hatred.

To the Earl of Liverpool.

'Viseu,

'March 30, 1810.

'. . . I am fully aware of the mutual hatred of the Spanish and Portuguese people towards each other; and you may depend upon it that I adverted to that circumstance when I considered of the propriety of sending to Cadiz a Portuguese regiment.

'From experience of the manner in which the service of Portuguese troops was received in other Spanish garrisons, I did not consider it probable that this hatred was likely to affect the reception of the Portuguese regiment at Cadiz; and having that regiment at my disposal at the moment a garrison was wanted for Cadiz, I did not think it proper to allow the consideration of the hatred of these nations towards each other to deprive the cause of this timely assistance. . .'

Unfaltering Confidence.

To Lieutenant-Colonel Torrens.

'March 31, 1810.

'. . . . I am in a situation in which no mischief can be done to the army, or to any part of it; I am prepared for all events; and if I am in a scrape, as appears to be the general belief in England, although certainly not my own, I'll get out of it.'

To Encourage French Desertion

To Brigadier-General Cox, Governor of Almeida,

'Viseu,
'April 1, 1810.

'I request you to pay Señor Echevarria all the expenses which he has incurred for the encouragement of desertion from the French Army, and for the support of deserters, and to tell him that I request him to encourage desertion by the following measures. Let him send trusty persons to assure soldiers in the French Army, induced to desert, that they shall be received here and treated in every respect as British soldiers; that their arms and horses, if they should bring them, shall be bought from them and paid for; that they shall have their option of enlisting into the British service or not; that if they choose to enlist they shall receive a bounty and shall have the choice of enlisting into any of the foreign corps with this army, or in England; and that, if they do not choose to enlist, measures shall be taken to send them out of the Peninsula, and to facilitate their return to their own country.

'I request that all deserters may be sent to the headquarters of the army, and all expenses incurred on their account shall be paid.'

To Major-General Doyle.

'Celorico,
'May 3, 1810.

'. . . . I have received an answer to the reference which I had made to the Secretary of State on the subject of your raising a regiment from the deserters of the French Army; and His Lordship not only objects to your proposal, but objects to admitting deserters into the British service in any manner or upon any terms. However, any engagements into which you may have entered, under any former orders, shall be carried into execution, and the men shall be treated as British soldiers, shall be sent to England, and, if then discharged from the service, they shall have the means facilitated to them of returning to their own countries.'

Wellington and Sir John Moore.

To the Earl of Liverpool.

'Viseu,
'April 2, 1810.

'. . . . . The great disadvantage under which I labour is, that Sir John Moore, who was here before me, gave an opinion that this country could not be defended by the army under his command; and, although it is obvious that the country was in a very different situation at that time from what it is at present; that I am in a very different situation from that in which he found himself; and that, moreover, it can be proved, from the marches and operations of the army under Sir John Moore, and his despatches, that little was known of Portugal at that time; yet persons, who ought to be acquainted with these facts, entertain a prejudice against the adoption of any plans for opposing the enemy, of which Portugal is to be the theatre, or its means the instrument, and will not even consider them.

'I have as much respect as any man can have for the opinion and judgment of Sir John Moore; and I should mistrust my own, if opposed to his, in a case which he had had an opportunity of knowing and considering. But he positively knew nothing of Portugal, and could know nothing of its existing state. Besides this prejudice, founded on Sir John Moore's opinion, there is another very general prejudice against any military opinion in the Peninsula.

'My opinion is that, as long as we shall remain in a state of activity in Portugal, the contest must continue in Spain; that the French are most desirous that we should withdraw from the country, but know that they must employ a very large force indeed in the operations which will render it necessary for us to go away; and I doubt whether they can bring that force to bear upon Portugal without abandoning other objects, and exposing their whole fabric in Spain to great risk. If they should be able to invade it, and should not succeed in obliging us to evacuate the country, they will be in a very dangerous situation; and the longer we can oppose them, and delay their success, the more likely are they to suffer materially in Spain.

'All the preparations for embarking and carrying away the army, and everything belonging to it, are already made, and my intention is to embark it, as soon as I find that a military necessity exists for so doing. I shall delay the embarkation as long as it is in my power, and shall do everything in my power to avert the necessity of embarking at all.

'If the enemy should invade this country with a force less than that which I should think so superior to ours as to create the necessity for embarking, I shall fight a battle to save the country, for which I have made the preparations; and if the result should not be successful, of which I have no doubt, I shall still be able to retire and embark the army.

'In short, the whole of my conduct shall be guided by a fair and cool view of the circumstances of our situation at the moment, and a reference to Your Lordship's instructions of February 27.

ANXIOUS TO LEAVE BY THE HALL DOOR.

'When we do go, I feel a little anxiety to go, like gentlemen, out of the hall door, particularly after the preparations which I have made to enable us to do so, and not out of the back-door, or by the area.

'I am willing to be responsible for the evacuation of Portugal, under Your Lordship's instructions of February 27. Depend upon it, whatever people may tell you, I am not so desirous as they imagine of fighting desperate battles; if I was, I might fight one any day I please. But I have kept the army for six months in two positions, notwithstanding their own desire, and that of the allies, that I should take advantage of many opportunities which the enemy apparently offered of striking a blow against them; in some of which the single operation would certainly have been successful.

'But I have looked to the great result of our maintaining our position on the Peninsula, and have not allowed myself to be diverted from it by the wishes of the allies, and probably of some of our own army, that I should interfere more actively in some partial affairs; or by the opinion of others that we ought to quit the country prematurely; and I have not harassed my troops by marches and counter-marches in conformity to the enemy's movements. I believe that the world in the Peninsula begin to believe that I am right.

'I am convinced that, if the Spaniards had followed my advice, Spain would now have been out of danger, and that the conduct which I have pursued has given us at this moment an efficient army, which is the only hope of the Peninsula. I am perfectly aware of the risks which I incur personally, whatever may be the result of the operations in Portugal. All I beg is that, if I am to be responsible, I may be left to the exercise of my own judgment; and I ask for the fair confidence of Government upon the measures which I am to adopt.

'If Government take the opinions of others upon the situation of affairs here, and entertain doubts upon the measures which I propose to adopt, then let them give me their instructions in detail, and I will carry them strictly into execution. I may venture, however, to assure you that, with the exception of Marshal Beresford, who I believe concurs entirely in all my opinions respecting the state of the contest, and the measures to be adopted here, there is no man in the army who has taken half the pains upon subject that I have.'

The Hollowness of the Bonaparte System.

To Brigadier-General R. Craufurd.

'Viseu,
'April 4, 1810.

'The Austrian marriage is a terrible event, and must prevent any great movement on the Continent for the present. Still, I do not despair of seeing at some time or other a check to the Bonaparte system. Recent transactions in Holland show that it is all hollow within, and that it is so inconsistent with the wishes, the interests, and even the existence, of civilized society, that he cannot trust even his brothers to carry it into execution. . . .'

Desertion and Crime.

(In his evidence before the Royal Commission for inquiring into Military Punishments, Wellington emphatically said that drunkenness was invariably the great parent of all crime in the British Army.—W. W.)

To *the Adjutant-General of the Forces.*

'Viseu,
'April 6, 1810,

'I have had the honour of receiving your letters of March 2, relative to the desertion in the 2nd Battalion —th Regiment, appearing on the return of that regiment, to January 25; and I enclose the reports which I have received from Major-General Picton and Major Young upon that subject,

'The desertion from nearly all the regiments in this army must have appeared extraordinary to the commander-in-chief, and must have given him as much concern as it has to me. Till lately desertion from a British Army on service was a crime almost unknown; and I am concerned to add that I have reason to believe that many of those who have deserted have been guilty of the worst description of that offence, and have gone over to the enemy. I attribute the prevalence of this crime in a great measure to the bad description of men, of which many of the regiments are composed almost entirely, and who have been received principally from the Irish militia.

'A sufficient time has not elapsed, since these men have entered the regiments of the line, to form their habits to regularity and discipline; the non-commissioned officers, in the second battalions principally, are very bad; and I am sorry to add that the subaltern officers are not of the best description; and that I do not think so much attention has been given by them as might have been expected, to form either the non-commissioned officers or the soldiers to those habits of regularity which a soldier ought to have.

'I attribute the desertion from this army likewise, in some degree, to the irregular and predatory habits which those soldiers had acquired, who, having straggled from their regiments during the late service under the command of Sir John Moore, were some of them taken prisoners by the French, and have since escaped from them; and others, after having wandered in different parts of Portugal and Spain, have returned to the army. All these men have shifted for themselves in the country, by rapine and plunder, since they quitted their regiments in 1808; and they have informed others of their modes of proceeding, and have instilled a desire in others to follow their example, and live in the same mode and by the same means, free from the restraints of discipline and regularity.

'I can assure the commander-in-chief that I know of no cause for the desertion of the soldiers from this army, excepting those to which I have above referred. They have in general but little duty, and since the month of August no fatigue. Their quarters are, without exception, good; the inhabitants of the country are invariably kind to them; and not only has there been no distress for provisions since the month of August, but I really believe that there is not a soldier in the army who is not as well fed, and does not receive his food as regularly as he could in barracks in England. Their pay is also regularly given to them, and their accounts regularly settled, and the balances paid, although one month later than the period fixed by His Majesty's regulations, on account of the difficulty of procuring money in this country for the army.

'While writing upon this subject, it is proper that I should inform the commander-in-chief that desertion is not the only crime of which the soldiers of this army have been guilty to an extraordinary degree. A detachment seldom marches, particularly if under the command of a non-commissioned officer (which rarely happens), that a murder or a highway robbery, or some act of outrage, is not committed by the British soldiers composing it.

'They have killed eight people since the army returned to Portugal in December; and I am sorry to add that a convoy has seldom arrived with money that the chests have not been broken open, and some of the money stolen by the soldiers in whose charge it was placed, although invariably under the command of an officer; and they have never brought up either shoes or other necessaries which could be of use to them, or which they could sell, that they have not stolen some of the articles committed to their charge.

'The orders to the army, and the Provost's establishment, which is larger than was ever known with any British Army, will show the pains which the general officers, the commanding officers of regiments, and I, have taken to prevent the commission of these crimes, which, indeed, are not very frequent at the regiments, although they are committed sometimes even there: and the general courts martial which have been assembled, and sitting almost constantly while the army has been halted, and sometimes as many as three sitting at the same time in the different cantonments of the army, will show the pains which have been taken to convict and punish those who have been guilty of these crimes.

'But the inhabitants of the country have such a respect and affection for the British nation, and particularly for the military qualities of the soldier (who presumes upon his military reputation to commit many of the crimes of which he is guilty), that it is most difficult to prevail upon the inhabitants to give testimony of the injuries they have received, and they will rarely point out the person who has committed the offence; and the soldiers themselves will rarely tell the truth before a court-martial.

'The sentences of the courts-martial are also carried into execution; so that everything that precaution and discipline could do to prevent crimes, and that trial and execution of sentences could do to punish those who have been guilty of them, has been done, but hitherto without much success. I am concerned to be obliged to make to the commander-in-chief so unfavourable a report of an army which has shown that it possesses many excellent qualities; but it contains facts which ought not to be concealed from his knowledge.'

WRONGFUL ENLISTMENT.

To Brigadier-General Alex Campbell.

'Viseu,
'April 8, 1810.

'I sent you a warrant for £150, for bounty for your recruits, three or four days ago; but are you aware that your recruiting officer takes men (Frenchmen) from the prisons, who were made prisoners of war, some of them under a capitulation? No wonder that he has enlisted 150 men, and that Colonel Peacocke has approved of them. This positively must not be done. I write by this post to Colonel Peacocke upon the subject, and I beg you to lose no time in writing to the officer whom you employ.'

Irish Deserters from the French.

To Vice-Admiral the Hon. G. Berkeley.

'Viseu,
'April 9, 1810.

'Twenty seamen, who had belonged to an Irish regiment in the French service, and had deserted, have lately come in here, and I shall forward them to Lisbon, to be delivered over to your orders, as soon as the weather shall clear up a little. They all wish to enter the navy. . . .'

An Army spoiled by Plunder.

To the Earl of Liverpool.

'Viseu,
'April 11, 1810.

'. . . . I enclose the Inspector-General's returns of April 1, from which you will see the number actually sick, of those on the military returns "sick absent." The others are either convalescent, out of the hospitals, or on the road to join, and Your Lordship will be glad to observe how efficient and healthy the army is becoming. Indeed, it would now be an excellent army if the soldiers did not plunder.

'Several have lately been convicted before general courts-martial, and have been executed, an example which I hope will have effect, as well upon the officers as the men. Upon the former I hope it will operate to induce them to take more pains to keep their men in order, and support the authority of the non-commissioned officers, and to instil into them a proper sense of their situation and duty; and I hope it will convince the latter that I possess the power, and am determined to exert it, to punish those who are guilty of those disgraceful outrages. I am still apprehensive of the consequence of trying them in any nice operation before the enemy, for they really forget everything when plunder or wine is within their reach. . . .'

A Definition of Military Law.

To Charles Stuart, Esq.

'Viseu,
'April 19, 1810.

'I think it would be desirable to define with precision our ideas respecting the establishment of military law, before we determine to alter the established law of the country in any case.

'The following questions are worth consideration and decision on this topic. What is military law? Military law as applied to any persons, excepting the officers, soldiers, and followers of the army, for whose government there are particular provisions of law in all well-regulated countries, is neither more nor less than the will of the General of the army. He punishes, either with or without trial, for crimes either declared to be so, or not so declared by any existing law, or by his own orders. This is the plain and common meaning of the term military law. . . .

'Let us define our notions; and, depend upon it, we shall find that the establishment of military law will only increase our difficulties.'

Murder of Deserters.

To the Earl of Liverpool.

'Celorico,
'May 1, 1810.

'I enclose a copy of the letter which I wrote on April 1 to Brigadier-General Cox, containing the terms on which I was disposed to receive deserters from the French Army. I have been particularly cautious respecting the enlistment of persons of this description in the corps of this army; and none are taken who, or their families, are not known to some of the officers, non-commissioned officers, or privates already in the different corps. . . .

'The great impediment to desertion is the danger of being murdered, which all soldiers of the French Army incur in Spain, when they wander from their quarters, and are found singly, or in small bodies, by the inhabitants of the country. . . .

'But this is a service of serious danger to the person who undertakes it. I do not think the employment of officers in the manner proposed by Your Lordship would answer, as the enemy would immediately discover their stations, and would cut off all communication between their foreign corps and the stations in which these agents should have fixed themselves. It is best that the deserters should be received wherever they can reach a post of the Allied Armies, and be conveyed from thence to the sea-coast, which is the mode at present arranged for the conduct of this business. . . .'

Prejudice against German Troops.

To His Royal Highness the Duke of Cambridge.

'Celorico,
'May 7, 1810.

'. . . A very general prejudice against German officers and troops prevails throughout the Peninsula; and I think it very doubtful whether I shall be able to prevail upon any of the Spanish authorities to employ these officers; and if I should, I fear that the officers will have but too much reason to complain of the treatment which they will receive.

'I therefore considered it advisable to endeavour in the first instance to employ them in the Portuguese service, and I communicated with Marshal Beresford upon the subject, and I now enclose his answer.

'I must add to it that I am perfectly aware of the objections to which he refers, in giving employment to any foreign officers in the Portuguese service, and I have already been obliged to send some back to England.

'Your Royal Highness may depend upon my doing everything in my power to prevail upon the Spanish Government to employ these officers, and to make their situation as advantageous and agreeable to them as circumstances will admit.'

Deeds, not Words, required.

To Charles Stuart, Esq.

'Celorico,
'May 13, 1810.

'. . . . In my opinion the fault of all these proclamations in the Peninsula has been that the writers of them have followed the example of those published by the French during the Revolution; and they have invariably flattered and deceived the people. What we want is:

'First, an exposition of their danger;

'Secondly, a reference to the existing means of resistance;

'Thirdly, an exposition of their own duties;

'Fourthly, an exhortation to perform them, and,

'Lastly, a declaration by the Government that those who should not perform their duty would be punished without distinction of persons.

'This ought to be stated in plain language, without bombast, and ought, above all, to be short. But these. "*Corir sobre os nossos Inimigos*" will only tend to increase the existing evils.

'Every man in Portugal is sufficiently alive to the danger, and is very anxious to avert it; there is plenty of enthusiasm, there are cries of "*Viva!*" and illuminations and patriotic songs and feasts everywhere; but that which is wanting is the plain simple performance of his duty, each in his station, and obedience to order . . .'

British Troops in Time of War.

To Brigadier-General Cox, Governor of Almeida.

'Celorico,
'May 14, 1810.

'War is a terrible evil, particularly to those who reside in those parts of the country which are the seat of the operations of hostile armies; but I believe it will be found, upon inquiry, and will be acknowledged by the people of Portugal, that it is inflicted in a less degree by the British troops than by the others; and that eventually all they get from the country is paid for, and that they require only what is necessary. . .'

Soldiers' Funeral Expenses.

To the Right Hon. the Secretary at War.

'Celorico,
'June 10, 1810.

'I have the honour to transmit a statement of funeral expenses of men who have died in general hospital in this country, and which cannot be recovered from the circumstance of the regiments having left the country, or from the accounts of the men having been closed and sent to England previous to the charge having been received by the regiments.

'I have authorised the purveyor to enter these expenses in his accounts until he shall receive orders respecting them from England, and I request that Your Lordship will be pleased to give directions accordingly.'

Capitulation of Ciudad Rodrigo.

To Brigadier-General A. Campbell.

'Alverca,
'July 11, 1810, 6 p. m.

'The enemy got possession of Ciudad Rodrigo by capitulation yesterday evening, and this morning there was an affair with our pickets, of which I have not received the details, in which we lost Lieutenant-Colonel Talbot, 14th Light Dragoons, and 8 men killed and 23 men wounded; we have taken 31 men and 29 horses. General Craufurd has occupied Fuentes.'

Party Spirit the Bane of Armies.

To Brigadier-General R. Craufurd.

'Alverca,
'July 23, 1810.

'I have been much annoyed by the foolish conversations and reports and private letters about the 16th Light Dragoons. . . .

'I can only say that I have never seen an attack by our troops in which similar, if not greater, accidents and mistakes have not occurred, and in which orders have not been given, for which no authority had proceeded from the commander, and in which there were not corresponding accidents and failures. This is to be attributed to the inexperience of our officers, and, I must add, to some good qualities in them, as well as in the troops.

'All this would not much signify if our staff and other officers would mind their business, instead of writing news and keeping coffee-houses. But as soon as an accident happens, every man who can write, and who has a friend who can read, sits down to write his account of what he does not know, and his comments on what he does not understand; and these are diligently circulated and exaggerated by the idle and malicious, of whom there are plenty in all armies.

'The consequence is that officers and whole regiments lose their reputation; a spirit of party, which is the bane of all armies, is engendered and fomented; a want of confidence ensues, and there is no character, however meritorious, and no action, however glorious, which can have justice done to it. I have hitherto been so fortunate as to keep down this spirit in this army, and I am determined to persevere. . .

Affair at the Coa.

To the Right Hon. Henry Wellesley.

'Alverca,
'July 27, 1810.

'The enemy obliged us to evacuate Fort Concepcion on the 21st, which we destroyed; and on the morning of the 24th they attacked General R. Craufurd's advanced-guard close to Almeida, and obliged him to retire across the Coa with the loss of 4 officers killed, 25 wounded; and 28 men killed and 218 wounded. . . .

'The enemy's numbers were about four times his in cavalry, and at least three times in infantry. We hear that their loss has been great. They made three attempts afterwards to storm the bridge of the Coa, in all of which they failed. . . .'

Return of the Number of Killed, Wounded, and Missing, of a Division of the Army under the Command of His Excellency Lieutenant-General Viscount Wellington, K.B., in an Action with the French Army near Almeida, on July 24, 1810.

	Officers.	Sergeants.	Drummers.	Rank and File.	Troop Horses.	Total Loss of Officers, Non-commissioned Officers, and Rank and File.
Killed -	4	3	—	29	3	36
Wounded	23	10	2	164	12	199
Missing -	1	1	1	80	—	83

THE FRENCH FORCE IN SPAIN.

To Admiral Sir Richard Keats, K.B.

'Celorico,

'August 2, 1810.

'The enemy's force in Spain consists of 250,000 men, according to the best accounts I can make of it. Of this force above one third is engaged in the operations against this army. About 50,000 or 60,000 men, in three corps, are in Andalusia, of which 20,000 are engaged in the operations at Cadiz; 15,000 or 16,000 about Seville, etc., protecting their rear, and Sebastiani, with the remainder, towards Granada, etc. There are two strong corps in Catalonia and Aragon, but most of these troops are in the garrisons; and there are about 20,000 or 30,000 men about Madrid, in the Asturias, Biscay, Navarre, and keeping up the communication by the highroad from France....'

STERN WARNINGS.

To Lieutenant-General Sir Stapleton Cotton, Bart.

'Celorico,

'August 4, 1810. 2 p.m.

'Send round to the people that they must retire from the villages, and let the magistrates know that if any of them stay, or if any of the inhabitants have any communication with the enemy, they shall be hanged.'

To Major-General the Hon. L. Cole.

'Celorico,

'August 11, 1810, 3 p.m..

'Tell Captain Cocks to inform the inhabitants of Richosa that I will not pardon them till they give up those who committed the outrage on the troops, and that if they delay it much longer, I will destroy their village. Let them give up those who committed the outrage, and trust to my mercy. . . .'

Promotion in the Army.

To Lieutenant-Colonel Torrens.

'Celorico,
'August 4,1810.

'. . . I have never been able to understand the principle on which the claims of gentlemen of family, fortune, and influence in the country, to promotion in the army, founded on their military conduct, and character, and services, should be rejected, while the claims of others, not better founded on military pretensions, were invariably attended to. It would be desirable, certainly, that the only claim to promotion should be military merit; but this is a degree of perfection to which the disposal of military patronage has never been, and cannot be, I believe, brought in any military establishment. The commander-in-chief must have, friends, officers on the staff attached to him, etc., who will press him to promote their friends and relations, all doubtless very meritorious, and no man can at all times resist these applications; but if there is to be any influence in the disposal of military patronage, in aid of military merit, can there be any in our army so legitimate as that of family connection, fortune, and influence in the country?. . .

'While writing upon this subject, I am also tempted to communicate to you my opinion upon another branch of it, *viz*:, the disposal of the patronage of the troops serving on foreign service. In all services, excepting that of Great Britain, and in former times in the service of Great Britain, the commander-in-chief of an army employed against the enemy in the field had the power of promoting officers, at least to vacancies occasioned by the service, in the troops under his own command; and in foreign services the principle is carried so far, as that no person can venture to recommend an officer for promotion belonging to an army employed against the enemy in the field, excepting the commander of that army.

'It was pretty nearly the case formerly in our own service; and I believe the greater number of the general officers of the higher ranks of the present day were made lieutenant-colonels by Sir W. Howe, Sir Henry Clinton, Lord Cornwallis, General Burgoyne, Lord Dorchester, etc. But how is it now? The form remains still in some degree the same; that is to say, my secretary keeps the register of the applications, memorials, and regimental recommendations, a trouble which, by-the-by, might as well be saved; but the substance is entirely altered; and I, who command the largest British Army that has been employed against the enemy for many years, and who have upon my hands certainly the most extensive and difficult concern that was ever imposed upon any British officer, have not the power of making even a corporal!

'It is impossible that this system can last. It will do very well for trifling expeditions and short services, etc., but those who are to superintend the discipline, and to excite and regulate the exertions of the officers of the army, during a long-continued service, must have the power of rewarding them by the only mode in which they can be rewarded—-that is, by promotion.

'It is not known to the army and to strangers, and I am almost ashamed of acknowledging, the small degree (I ought to say nullity) of power of reward which belongs to my situation; and it is really extraordinary that I have got on so well hitherto without it; but the day must come when this system must be altered.

'I do not entertain these opinions, and communicate them to you, because there are any officers attached to me in the service for whom I desire promotion. All my *aides-de-camp*, respecting whom I do feel an interest, have been promoted in their turn in their regiments, or are to be promoted, for carrying home the accounts of victories. The only person respecting whose promotion I ever interested myself personally was that of Colin Campbell, which the Duke of York had promised him, in consequence of his having brought home the accounts of two victories at the same time; and the difficulty which I experienced in obtaining his promotion, notwithstanding that promise, is a strong practical proof of the effects of the system to which I have adverted.

'The consequence of the change of the system in respect to me would be only to give me the power of rewarding the services of those who have exerted, or should exert, themselves zealously in the service, and thus to stimulate others to similar exertions.

'Even admitting that the system of promotion by seniority, exploded in other armies, is the best for that of Great Britain, it would still be an advantage that those who become entitled to it should receive it immediately, and from the hand of the person who is obliged to expose them to danger, to enforce discipline, and to call for their exertions. I would also observe that this practice would be entirely consistent with the unvaried usage of the British navy.

'I admit that it may be urged with truth that a larger view may be taken of the interests of the public, in the mode of promoting officers of the army, than I am capable of taking; and this view may have suggested the expediency of adopting and adhering to the mode now in use; at the same time I must say that the public can have no greater interest than in the conduct and discipline of an army employed against the enemy in the field; and I am thoroughly convinced that, whatever may be the result in my hands, a British Army cannot be kept in the field for any length of time, unless the officers composing it have some hope that their exertions will certainly be rewarded by promotion; and that to be abroad on service, and to do their duty with zeal and intelligence, afford prospects of promotion not afforded by the mere presence of an officer with his regiment, and his bearing the King's commission for a certain number of years.

'I have been induced to communicate these opinions to you, from the consideration of the claims of those officers to which I have drawn your attention at the commencement of this letter, from a strong conviction of their truth, and not, I assure you, from any interest I feel in the result. I would not give one pin to have the disposal of every commission in the army.'

Mutual Good Treatment of the Wounded.

To the Right Hon. Henry Wellesley.

'Celorico,
'August 8, 1810.

'Since I have commanded the troops in this country, I have always treated the French officers and soldiers who have been made prisoners with the utmost humanity and attention; and in numerous instances I have saved their lives. The only motive which I have had for this conduct has been that they might treat our officers and soldiers well who might fall into their hands, and I must do the French the justice to say that they have been universally well treated, and in recent instances the wounded prisoners of the British Army have been taken care of before the wounded of the French Army. . . .'

Officers' Private Correspondence.

To Lieutenant-General Graham.

'Celorico,
'August 10, 1810.

'I beg to draw your attention to the orders which I have given this day respecting the private correspondence of the officers of the army. I was astonished some time ago to see in the English newspapers an accurate account of the batteries and works erecting at Cadiz and on the Isla, with the number of guns, and of what calibre each was to contain, and their distance from each other, and from the enemy's works. This information must have been extracted from the letter of an officer. If officers wish to give their friends this description of information, they should request them not to publish their letters in the newspapers.'

DESERTION OF A PORTUGUESE REGIMENT.

To Charles Stuart, Esq.

'Celorico,
'August 31, 1810.

'. . . I am sorry to add that the whole of the 24th Regiment, with the exception of the Major and of the English officers, have gone into the French service. It is said that their object is to have an opportunity of deserting from it, which is well enough for the private soldiers, but is highly disgraceful to the character of the officers.

'The major commanding the artillery was the person employed by Cox to settle the capitulation for him. He went out and informed the French of the exact state of the place after the explosion, and never returned!! Massena has made him a Colonel!! . . .'

To the Right Hon. Henry Wellesley.

'Gouvea,
'September 7, 1810.

'Seventeen officers and 500 men of the 24th Portuguese Regiment have already deserted from the French, and have come in at one place, and others have come into Braganza.'

To Charles Stuart, Esq.

'Gouvea,
'September 11, 1810.

'. . . I do not recollect a circumstance which made such an impression on the British Army, and upon the English officers serving with the Portuguese Army, as the account of the conduct of the officers of the 24th Regiment; and after full consideration, the measure which I recommended, and the distinct statement of the principle on which it was recommended, appeared the only means of reconciling the minds of the officers of the British Army to what had occurred, and to further service with the Portuguese—at the same time that it held out a standard of sentiment and principle for the officers of the Portuguese service on similar occasions.

'I wished to avail myself of this opportunity of showing them what the principles of men of honour, and the sentiments of officers and gentlemen, ought to induce them to do on similar occasions. I am sorry to say that this object is defeated by the publication of the notice of the Government; and it would have been accomplished if the Government would have waited for the official communication of the circumstances on which they have decided, as I am convinced that you would have seen at once my object in the measure which I recommended, and would have supported it with all your influence...'

To the Earl of Liverpool.

'Gouvea,
'September 13, 1810.

'I understand that, with the exception of about 200 men, the whole of the 24th Portuguese Regiment have quitted the enemy; and that they have relinquished their intention of making this regiment the foundation of their Portuguese levy, and have sent these men prisoners to France. I have every reason to believe that these men likewise would have returned to Portugal, if it had been in their power.'

Croaking in the Army.

To Marshal Beresford.

'Gouvea,
'September 8, 1810.

'Upon considering the subject which you mentioned to me last night, I do not think it so important as it appeared to me upon first hearing it. The remedy which we agreed upon will answer some purpose, and I have it in my power to make some arrangements immediately, and others hereafter, which will effectually prevent all mischief of the description supposed in that quarter. 'I beg you, however, not to mention the subject to anybody. The croaking which already prevails in the army, and particularly about headquarters, is disgraceful to us as a nation, and does infinite mischief to the cause; and it would become much worse if this story were known...'

The Battle of Busaco.

To Charles Stuart, Esq.

'Convent of Busaco,
'September 27,1810.

'We have been engaged with the enemy for the last three days,

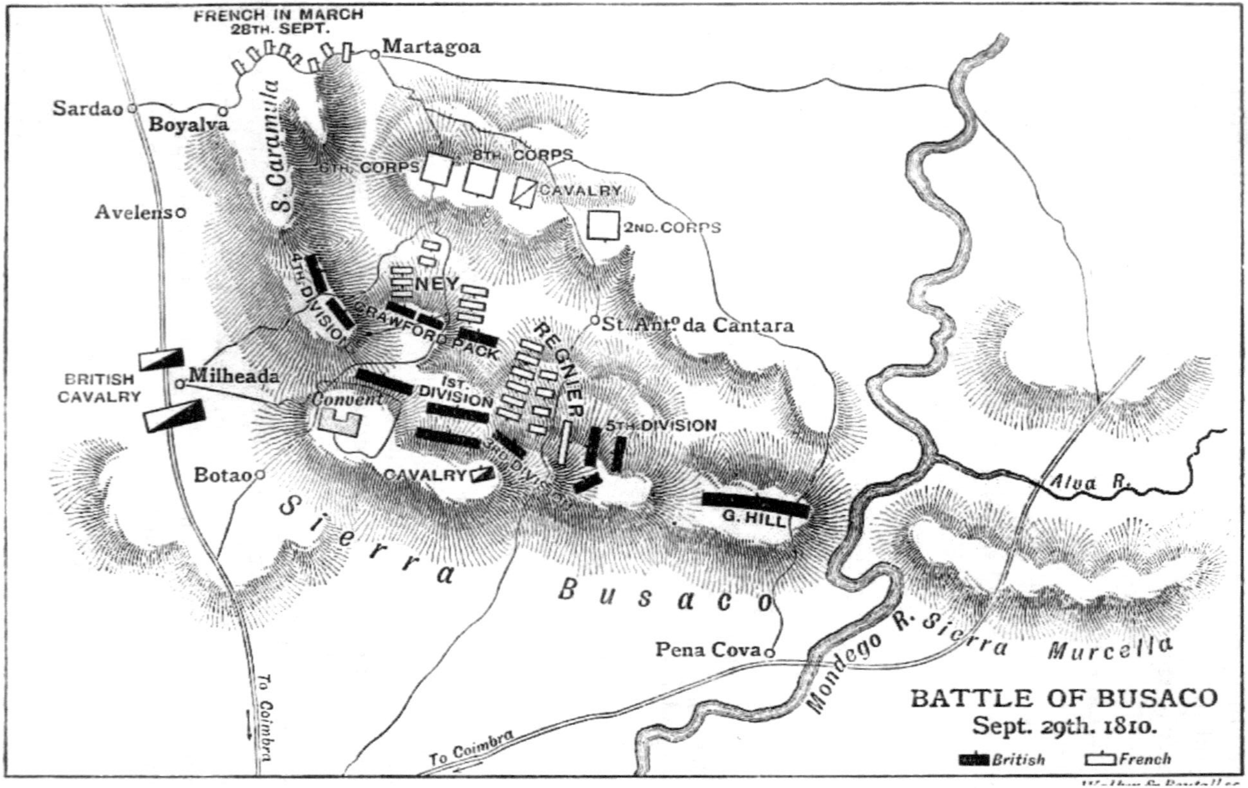

BATTLE OF BUSACO
Sept. 29th. 1810.

and I think we shall be attacked again tomorrow; as I understand they must carry our position, on which, however, they have as yet made no impression, or starve. Our loss has been trifling: that of the British troops about 300 men; that of the Portuguese, who have conducted themselves remarkably well in several brisk attacks, rather greater; the loss of the French must have been very large indeed, and we hear from deserters that they are much discouraged. Our position is an excellent one, and it is certainly no easy task to carry it; but I think they will make another trial. . . .'

To the Earl of Liverpool.

'Coimbra,
'September 30,1810.

'While the enemy was advancing from Celorico and Trancoso upon Viseu, the different divisions of militia and *ordenanza* were employed upon their flanks and rear; and Colonel Trant with his division attacked the escort of the military chest and reserve artillery near Tojal, on the 20th instant. He took two officers and eighty prisoners, but the enemy collected a force from the front and rear, which obliged him to retire again towards the Douro. I understand that the enemy's communication is completely cut off, and he possesses only the ground upon which his army stands.

'My despatch of the 20th instant will have informed you of the measures which I had adopted and which were in progress to collect the army in this neighbourhood, and, if possible, to prevent the enemy from obtaining possession of this town.

'On the 21st the enemy's advanced-guard pushed on to Sta. Combadaõ, at the junction of the Rivers Criz and Dao; and Brigadier-General Pack retired across the former and joined Brigadier-General Craufurd at Mortagoa, having destroyed the bridges over those two rivers.

'The enemy's advanced-guard crossed the Criz, having repaired the bridge, on the 23rd, and the whole of the 6th Corps was collected on the other side of the river. I therefore withdrew the cavalry through the Serra de Busaco, with the exception of three squadrons, as the ground was unfavourable for the operation of that arm.

'On the 25th, the whole of the 6th and of the 2nd Corps crossed the Criz in the neighbourhood of Sta. Combadaõ; and Brigadier-General Pack's brigade and Brigadier-General Craufurd's division retired to the position which I had fixed upon for the army on the top of the Serra de Busaco. These troops were followed in this movement by the whole of the corps of Ney and Regnier (the 6th and the 2nd); but it was conducted by Brigadier-General Craufurd with great regularity, and the troops took their position without sustaining any loss of importance.

'The 4th Portuguese Caçadores, which had retired on the right of the other troops, and the pickets of the 3rd Division of Infantry, which were posted at St. Antonio de Cantaro, under Major Smyth of the 45th Regiment, were engaged with the advance of Regnier's corps in the afternoon, and the former showed that steadiness and gallantry which others of the Portuguese troops have since manifested.

'The Serra de Busaco is a high ridge which extends from the Mondego in a northerly direction about eight miles. At the highest point of the ridge, about two miles from its termination, is the convent and garden of Busaco. The Serra de Busaco is connected by a mountainous tract of country with the Serra de Caramula, which extends in a north-easterly direction beyond Viseu, and separates the valley of the Mondego from the valley of the Douro. On the left of the Mondego, nearly in a line with the Serra de Busaco, is another ridge of the same description, called the Serra da Murcella, covered by the River Alva, and connected by other mountainous parts with the Serra d'Estrella.

'All the roads to Coimbra from the eastward lead over the one or the other of these Serras. They are very difficult for the passage of an army, the approach to the top of the ridge on both sides being mountainous.

'As the enemy's whole army was on the right of the Mondego, and it was evident that he intended to force our position, Lieutenant-General Hill crossed that river by a short movement to his left, on the morning of the 26th, leaving Colonel Le Cor with his brigade on the Serra da Murcella, to cover the right of the army, and Brigadier-General Fane, with his division of Portuguese cavalry and the 13th Light Dragoons, in front of the Alva, to observe and check the movements of the enemy's cavalry on the Mondego.

'With this exception, the whole army was collected upon the Serra de Busaco, with the British cavalry observing the plain in the rear of its left, and the road leading from Mortagoa to Oporto, through the mountainous tract which connects the Serra de Busaco with the Serra de Caramula.

'The 8th Corps joined the enemy in our front on the 26th, but he did not make any serious attack on that day. The light troops on both sides were engaged throughout the line.

'At six in the morning of the 27th the enemy made two desperate attacks upon our position, the one on the right, the other on the left of the highest part of the Serra. The attack upon the right was made by two divisions of the 2nd Corps, on that part of the Serra occupied by the 3rd Division of Infantry. One division of French infantry arrived at the top of the ridge, where it was attacked in the most gallant manner by the 88th Regiment, under the command of Lieutenant-Colonel Wallace; the 45th, under the command of Lieutenant-Colonel the Hon. R. Meade; and by the 8th Portuguese Regiment, under the command of Lieutenant-Colonel Douglas, directed by Major-General Picton.

'These three corps advanced with the bayonet, and drove the enemy's division from the advantageous ground which they had obtained. The other division of the 2nd Corps attacked farther on the right by the road leading by St. Antonia de Cantaro, also in front of Major-General Picton's division. These were repulsed before they could reach the top of the ridge, by the 74th, under the command of Lieutenant-Colonel the Hon. R. Trench, and the brigade of Portuguese infantry of the 9th and 21st Regiments, under the command of Colonel Champelmond, directed by Colonel Mackinnon. Major-General Leith also moved to his left to the support of Major-General Picton, and aided in the defeat of the enemy by the 3rd Battalion of Royals, the 1st Battalion of the 9th, and the 2nd Battalion of the 38th Regiments.

In these attacks Major-Generals Leith and Picton, Colonels Mackinnon and Champelmond, of the Portuguese service, who was wounded, Lieutenant-Colonel Wallace, Lieutenant-Colonel the Hon. R. Meade, Lieutenant-Colonel Sutton, of the 9th Portuguese, Major Smyth of the 45th, who was afterwards killed, Lieutenant-Colonel Douglas, and Major Birmingham, of the 8th Portuguese Regiment, distinguished themselves.

'Major-General Picton reports the good conduct of the 9th and 21st Portuguese Regiments, commanded by Lieutenant-Colonel Sutton and Lieutenant-Colonel A. Bacellar, and of the Portuguese artillery, under the command of Major Arentschildt. I have also to mention, in a particular manner, the conduct of Captain Dansey of the 88th.

'Major-General Leith reports the good conduct of the Royals, 1st Battalion, and 9th, and 2nd Battalion of the 38th Regiments; and I beg to assure Your Lordship that I have never witnessed a more gallant attack than that made by the 88th, 45th, and 8th Portuguese Regiments, on the enemy's division which had reached the ridge of the Serra.

'On the left the enemy attacked with three divisions of infantry of the 6th Corps, on the part of the Serra occupied by the light division of infantry commanded by Brigadier-General Craufurd, and by the brigade of Portuguese infantry commanded by Brigadier-General Pack.

'One division of infantry only made any progress to the top of the hill, and they were immediately charged with the bayonet by Brigadier-General Craufurd, with the 43rd, 52nd, and 95th, and the 3rd Portuguese Caçadores, and driven down with immense loss. (The 43rd, the 52nd, and the 95th formed the famous Light Division which Craufurd so often led to victory.—W. W.)

'Brigadier-General Coleman's brigade of Portuguese infantry, which was in reserve, was moved up to the right of Brigadier-General Craufurd's division, and a battalion of the 19th Portuguese Regiment, under the command of Lieutenant-Colonel MacBean, made a gallant and successful charge upon a body of another division of the enemy, which was endeavouring to penetrate in that quarter.

'In this attack, Brigadier-General Craufurd, Lieutenant-Colonels Beckwith, of the 95th, and Barclay, of the 52nd, and the Commanding Officers of the regiments, distinguished themselves.

'Besides these attacks, the light troops of the two armies were engaged throughout the 27th; and the 4th Portuguese Caçadores, and the 1st and 16th Regiments, directed by Brigadier-General Pack, and commanded by Lieutenant-Colonel Hill, Lieutenant-Colonel Luis de Regoa, and Major Armstrong, showed great steadiness and gallantry.

'The loss sustained by the enemy in his attack of the 27th has been enormous. I understand that the Generals of Division, Merle, Loison, and Maucune, are wounded, and General Simon was taken prisoner by the 52nd Regiment; and 3 colonels,—officers, and 250 men.

'The enemy left 2,000 killed upon the field of battle, and I understand from the prisoners and deserters that the loss in wounded is immense.

'The enemy did not renew his attack, excepting by the fire of his light troops on the 28th; but he moved a large body of infantry and cavalry from the left of his centre to the rear, from whence I saw his cavalry in march on the road from Mortagoa over the mountains towards Oporto.

'Having thought it probable that he would endeavour to turn our left by that road, I had directed Colonel Trant, with his division of militia, to march to Sardaõ, with the intention that he should occupy the mountains, but, unfortunately, he was sent round by Oporto, by the General Officer commanding in the north, in consequence of a small detachment of the enemy being in possession of S. Pedro do Sul; and, notwithstanding the efforts which he made to arrive in time, he did not reach Sardaõ till the 28th at night, after the enemy were in possession of the ground.

As it was probable that, in the course of the night of the 28th, the enemy would throw the whole of his army upon the road, by which he could avoid the Serra de Busaco and reach Coimbra by the high road of Oporto, and thus the army would have been exposed to be cut off from that town or to a general action in less favourable ground, and as I had reinforcements in my rear, I was induced to withdraw from the Serra de Busaco,

'The enemy did break up in the mountains at eleven at night of the 28th, and he made the march I expected. His advanced-guard was at Avelans, on the road from Oporto to Coimbra, yesterday, and the whole army was seen in march through the mountains. That under my command, however, was already in the low country, between the Serra de Busaco and the sea; and the whole of it, with the exception of the advanced-guard, is this day on the left of the Mondego.

'Although, from the unfortunate circumstance of the delay of Colonel Trant's arrival at Sardaõ, I am apprehensive that I shall not succeed in effecting the object which I had in view in passing the Mondego and in occupying the Serra.de Busaco, I do not repent my having done so. This movement has afforded me a favourable opportunity of showing the enemy the description of troops of which this army is composed; it has brought the Portuguese levies into action with the enemy for the first time in an advantageous situation; and they have proved that the trouble which has been taken with them has not been thrown away, and that they are worthy of contending in the same ranks with British troops in this interesting cause, which they afford the best hopes of saving.

'Throughout the contest on the Serra, and in all the previous marches, and those which we have since made, the whole army have conducted themselves in the most regular manner. Accordingly, all the operations have been carried on with ease; the soldiers have suffered no privations, have undergone no unnecessary fatigue, there has been no loss of stores, and the army is in the highest spirits. . . .

'I should not do justice to the service, or to my own feelings, if I did not take this opportunity of drawing Your Lordship's attention to the merits of Marshal Beresford. To him exclusively, under the Portuguese Government, is due the merit of having raised, formed, disciplined, and equipped the Portuguese Army, which has now shown itself capable of engaging and defeating the enemy. . . .'

Return of the Killed, Wounded, and Missing of the Army under the Command of Lieutenant-General Viscount Wellington, K.B., on September 25 and 26, and in the Action with the French Army, commanded by Marshal Massena, at Busaco, on September 27, 1810.

	Officers.	Sergeants.	Rank and File.	Horses.	Total Loss of Officers, Non-commissioned Officers, and Rank and File.
Killed	11	6	180	5	197
Wounded	62	32	920	12	1,014
Missing	1	3	54	10	58

The Portuguese loss is included in the above numbers.

AN ABSURD AND ODIOUS TRANSACTION.

To Charles Stuart, Esq.

'Pero Negro,
'October 21, 1810.

'I enclose you a newspaper, which contains a paragraph which I have marked, to which I request you to draw the attention of the Government. I have sins enough of my own to answer for; and it is rather hard upon me to incur the odium of having recommended acts to this Government, which they committed without my knowledge, and of which I could not approve.

'I must request that they will publish my letter to them upon the absurd and odious transaction to which this paragraph refers.'

A SATISFACTORY SITUATION.

To the Earl of Liverpool.

'Pero Negro,
'October 27, 1810.

'My despatches of this date will give you an idea of our situation, which I hope will be satisfactory to you. In my opinion the enemy ought to retire, for he has no chance of annoying our position; and delay will only aggravate his distress, and make his retreat more difficult.

'I calculate that a reinforcement of 15,000 men would not give him so good an army as he had at Busaco. He had 2,000 men killed there: Trant took 5,000 prisoners at Coimbra: above 1,000 prisoners have gone through this army: many men have been killed by the peasantry, and in the skirmishes with our different detachments; and they had 200 or 300 men wounded in the affair with our outposts about Sobral. They cannot have less than 4,000 sick, after the march they have made, the distress they have suffered, and the weather to which they were exposed. Indeed, the deserters and prisoners tell us that almost everybody is sick. . . .

'We have an excellent position, which we are improving every day; and the army is in good order and spirits, and not sickly. By the last returns, we had 4,200 in hospital, and no serious disorder. We had 8,500 sick in the military returns, but these include convalescents at Belem, of whom, I hope, under better regulations, not to have quite so many . . .'

The Evils of Wine.

To Lieutenant-Colonel Torrens.

'Pero Negro,
'November 2, 1810.

'No soldier can withstand the temptation of wine. This is constantly before their eyes in this country, and they are constantly intoxicated when absent from their regiments, and there is no crime which they do not commit to obtain money to purchase it; or if they cannot get money, to obtain it by force. . .'

A Hearty Wish.

To Major-General Fane.

'Pero Negro,
'November 3, 1810.

'. . . I wish I had it in my power to give you well-clothed troops, or to hang those who ought to have given them their clothing. . . .'

Strength of the Opposing Forces.

To the Earl of Liverpool.

'Pero Negro,
'November 3, 1810.

'I enclose Your Lordship an account of the number of battalions, squadrons, etc., which entered Portugal with Massena, and I cannot believe that they composed an army of less than 70,000 men at the

Battle of Busaco. I calculate their loss, including sick, since that time, at 15,000 men, which would leave them with 55,000 men, of which 6,000 or 7,000 are cavalry, at the present moment.

'The effective strength of the British Army, according to the last returns, was 29,000 infantry, cavalry, and artillery, and one regiment at Lisbon, and one at Torres Vedras, which, in the view of the contest, ought not to be taken into the account; and I enclose a statement of the Portuguese force, according to the last returns.

'Besides this force, the Marques de la Romana's corps consists of about 5,000 men; making a total of 58,615, of which I could command the services, in case I should act offensively against the enemy, of which about —— would be cavalry. . . .'

THE WEARING OF RIBANDS.

To Lieutenant-Colonel Torrens.

'Cartaxo,
'December 11, 1810.

'. . . Some of the General Officers have applied to me to know whether, upon ordinary occasions, they might not wear the riband of the medal at the buttonhole, instead of round the neck. This would be a more convenient way of wearing it, and they would wear it consequently more frequently, which would be desirable; and I shall be obliged to you if you will let me know whether there is any objection to what is proposed. . .'

****

Honours and medals for the Peninsular War were long withheld. Honours were granted for eighteen of the battles, sieges, and stormings; but it was not until 1848 that Queen Victoria distributed medals for the Pyrenees. There were then 690 survivors who were entitled to the medal. There are in existence Peninsular medals with fourteen clasps. At a London sale in 1901 a group of Peninsular decorations, awarded to Colonel Galiffe, 60th Foot, realised £500—WW.

****

ONE OF THE CAUSES OF SICKNESS.

To the Earl of Liverpool.

'Cartaxo,
'December 15, 1810.

'I enclose the weekly state of the 8th, and the weekly return of the sick to the 9th instant.

'I am concerned to add that, since this report has been made, an increased degree of sickness has appeared in the 3rd Battalion of the Royals, the 4th and 9th Regiments, all of which had been in Walcheron. But I attribute the sickness of these regiments not to that cause alone, but to the irregularity of the soldiers; who, contrary to repeated orders, have burnt as firewood the doors and windows, and in some instances the roofs, of the houses in which they have been cantoned; and they have been, consequently, exposed to the weather.

'The troops of the 5th Division, to which these regiments belong, have been less exposed by their duty than any others in the army; and yet they are now the only division in which there is any appearance of sickness.'

Wellington and Newspapers.

To Dr. Frank.

'Cartaxo,
'January 7, 1811.

'. . . I hope that the opinions of the people in Great Britain are not influenced by paragraphs in newspapers, and that those paragraphs do not convey the public opinion or sentiment upon any subject. Therefore I (who have more reason that any other public man of the present day to complain of libels of this description) never take the smallest notice of them; and have never authorised any contradiction to be given, or any statement to be made in answer to the innumerable falsehoods, and the heaps of false reasoning, which have been published respecting me and the operations which I have directed. . .'

The History of the War.

To Dr. Holliday.

'Cartaxo,
'January 15, 1811.

'I have received your letter of the 13th instant, and I am highly flattered by your desire to write the history of the war in Portugal.

'The events in this country of the three last years are fit subjects for the historian, and, if well and truly related, may be deemed deserving the consideration of politicians and military men. But I am apprehensive that the time is not yet arrived in which either the facts themselves can be stated with accuracy or truth, or the motives for the different occurrences be stated.

'I feel that I could not give an answer to many of the questions which it is probable you would be desirous of asking, without disclosing facts, opinions, and reasonings, which are not yet before the public, and which could not be disclosed by me without a breach of confidence. I would therefore recommend to you to postpone the execution of your design to some future period.'

Admiration of the French Army.

To the Marquis Wellesley.

'Cartaxo,
'January 26, 1811.

'. . . . The French Army is certainly a wonderful machine; but if we are to form such a one, we must form such a Government as exists in France, which can with impunity lose one half of the troops employed in the field every year, only by the privations and hardships imposed upon them. Next, we must compose our army of soldiers drawn from all classes of the population of the country; from the good and middling, as well as in rank as in education, as from the bad, and not as all other nations, and we in particular, do, from the bad only.

'Thirdly, we must establish such a system of discipline as the French have—a system founded upon the strength of the tyranny of the Government, which operates upon an army composed of soldiers, the majority of whom are sober, well disposed, amenable to order, and in some degree educated.

'When we shall have done all this, and shall have made these armies of the strength of those employed by the French, we may require of them to live as the French do, *viz.*, by authorised and regulated plunder of the country and its inhabitants, if any should remain; and we may expose them to the labour, hardships, and privations which the French soldier suffers every day; and we must expect the same proportion of loss every campaign, *viz.*, one half of those who take the field.

'This plan is not proposed for the British Army, nor has it yet been practised in any great degree by the Portuguese; but I shall state the effect which, in my opinion, the attempt has had upon the Spaniards.

'There is neither subordination nor discipline in the army, among either officers or soldiers; and it is not even attempted (as, indeed, it would be in vain to attempt) to establish either. It has, in my opinion, been the cause of the dastardly conduct which we have so frequently witnessed in the Spanish troops; and they have become odious to their country; and the peaceable inhabitants, much as they detest and suffer from the French, almost wish for the establishment of Joseph's

Government, to be protected from the outrages of their own troops. These armies, therefore, must be paid and supported, if any service is expected from them; and at present, at least, I see no chance of their being paid, except by British assistance. . . .'

Misery in Badajoz.

To the Right Hon. Henry Wellesley.

'Cartaxo,
'February 3, 1811.

'. . . I have a miserable account of affairs from Badajoz. There is not a grain of provision in the public magazines: the town is full of women and children, and refugees of all descriptions, and nothing can be in a worse state than the public mind in that place. There is no chance, I fear, of ever opening a communication, excepting by British troops, and those I cannot send. Unfortunate cause! how has it been frittered away!. . .'

Chaplains for the Army.

To Lieutenant-General Calvert, Adjutant-General of the Forces.

'Cartaxo,
'February 6, 1811.

'I believe that you have attended a good deal to the establishment of the chaplains to the army, upon which I am now about to trouble you. Notwithstanding all that has been done upon the subject, with a view to making their situation such as to induce respectable persons to accept of them, I fear that they are not yet sufficiently advantageous to insure the object. I believe the income, while they are employed abroad, to be sufficiently good, but that of retired chaplains, after service, is not; and the period of service required of them is too long. You will observe that a man can scarcely be eligible to be an army chaplain till he is six or eight and twenty, after an expensive education; and it can scarcely be said that the pay of a retired chaplain, at thirty-six years of age, is what a respectable person would have acquired if he had followed any other line of the clerical profession besides the army,

'In my opinion, the period of service ought to be reduced from ten to six years; but they ought to be years of service, without leave of absence, excepting on account of health, and the pay of the retired chaplain ought to be augmented. My reason for making these suggestions is that really, we do not get respectable men for the service. I have one excellent young man in this army, Mr. Briscall, who is attached to headquarters, who has never been one moment absent from his duty; but I have not yet seen another who has not applied and made a pitiable case for leave of absence immediately after his arrival; and, excepting Mr. Dennis at Lisbon, who was absent all last year, I believe Mr. Briscall is the only chaplain doing duty.

'I am very anxious upon this subject, not only from the desire which every man must have that so many persons as there are in this army should have the advantage of religious instruction, but from a knowledge that it is the greatest support and aid to military discipline and order.'

****

Mr. Briscall remained with the army till the end of the war. He was also with the army in the Low Countries and France from 1815 to 1818, and was afterwards curate at Strathfieldsaye.

****

The Duke and Methodism.

'It has, besides, come to my knowledge that Methodism is spreading very fast in the army. There are two, if not three, Methodist meetings in this town, of which one is in the Guards. The men meet in the evening, and sing psalms; and I believe a sergeant (Stephens) now and then gives them a sermon. Mr. Briscall has his eye upon these transactions, and would give me notice were they growing into anything which ought to be put a stop to; and the respectability of his character and conduct has given him an influence over these people which will prevent them from going wrong.

'These meetings likewise prevail in other parts of the army. In the 9th Regiment there is one, at which two officers attend, Lieutenant —— and Dr. ——; and the commanding officer of the regiment has not yet been able to prevail upon them to discontinue this practice. Here, and in similar circumstances, we want the assistance of a respectable clergyman. By his personal influence and advice, and by that of true religion, he would moderate the zeal and enthusiasm of these gentlemen, and would prevent their meetings from being mischievous, if he did not prevail upon them to discontinue them entirely.

'This is the only mode in which, in my opinion, we can touch these meetings. The meeting of soldiers in their cantonments to sing psalms or hear a sermon read by one of their comrades is, in the abstract, perfectly innocent, and it is a better way of spending their time than many others to which they are addicted; but it may become otherwise, and yet, till the abuse has made some progress, the commanding officer would have no knowledge of it, nor could he interfere. Even at last his interference must be guided by discretion, otherwise he will do more harm than good; and it can in no case be so effectual as that of a respectable clergyman. I wish, therefore, you would turn your mind a little more to this subject, and arrange some plan by which the number of respectable and efficient clergymen with the army may be increased.'

'I Have Done with the Portuguese Army.'

To Charles Stuart, Esq.

'Cartaxo,
'February 16, 1811.

'. . .I am exceedingly hurt at the contents of Dom Miguel Forjaz's note, marked B in your letter. It contains statements which are absolutely false; and attributes to me and the British commissariat the distresses of the Portuguese Army, which Dom Miguel Forjaz knows ought to be attributed to the want of arrangement by the *Junta de Viveres*, and to the want of money by the Government; and he also knows that if I had not relieved those distresses the army would have disbanded.

'In the present situation of affairs, I shall give no answer to this note, as I could not answer it without detailing facts which, under existing circumstances, I do not think proper to detail officially. But I have done with the Portuguese Army. They shall starve before they receive any further assistance from me.'

Desertion of a Mad Officer.

To Marshal Beresford.

'Cartaxo,
'March 1, 1811, 13 at noon.

'. . . I am sorry to tell you that an officer, Lieutenant Burke, 45th, has deserted to the enemy, and has arrived at Santarem. . . .' (This officer was mad, and was left behind by Marshal Massena when he retreated.)

Barbarity of French Troops.

To the Earl of Liverpool.

'Villa Seca,
'March 14, 1811

'The enemy retired from the position which they had occupied at Santarem and the neighbourhood on the night of the 5th instant.

I put the British Army in motion to follow them on the morning of the 6th. . . .

'The whole country affords many advantageous positions to a retreating army, of which the enemy have shown that they know how to avail themselves. They are retreating from the country, as they entered it, in one solid mass, covering their rear on every march by the operations of either one or two *corps d'armée* in the strong positions which the country affords, which *corps d'armée* are closely supported by the main body.

'Before they quitted their position, they destroyed a part of their cannon and ammunition, and they have since blown up whatever the horses were unable to draw away. They have no provisions, excepting what they plunder on the spot, or, having plundered, what the soldiers carry on their backs, and live cattle.

'I am concerned to be obliged to add to this account that their conduct throughout this retreat has been marked by a barbarity seldom equalled, and never surpassed. Even in the towns of Torres Novas, Thomar, and Pernes, in which the headquarters of some of the corps had been for four months, and in which the inhabitants had been invited, by promises of good treatment, to remain, they were plundered, and many of their houses destroyed, on the night the enemy withdrew from their position, and they have since burnt every town and village through which they have passed. The convent of Alcobaca was burnt by order from the French headquarters.

'The bishop's palace and the whole town of Leyria, in which General Drouet had had his headquarters, shared the same fate; and there is not an inhabitant of the country of any class or description who has had any dealing or communication with the French Army who has not had reason to repent of it and to complain of them. This is the mode in which the promises have been performed and the assurances have been fulfilled which were held out in the proclamation of the French Commander-in-Chief, in which he told the inhabitants of Portugal that he was not come to make war upon them, but with a powerful army of 110,000 men to drive the English into the sea.

'It is to be hoped that the example of what has occurred in this country will teach the people of this and of other nations what value they ought to place on such promises and assurances; and that there is no security for life, or for anything which makes life valuable, excepting in decided resistance to the enemy. . .'

Heavy Spanish Losses.

'The Spanish nation have lost Tortosa, Oliveira, and Badajoz, in the course of two months, without sufficient cause; and in the same period Marshal Soult, with a corps never supposed to be more than 20,000 men, has taken, besides the last two places, or destroyed above 22,000 Spanish troops.'

A Plea for the British Soldier.

To Charles Stuart, Esq.

'Louzão,
'March 16, 1811.

'I have had the honour of receiving your letter of the 9th instant, on a complaint said by Dom Miguel Forjaz to be made of the conduct of the British troops at Salvaterra, which complaint you will observe refers not to the conduct of the British troops, but to that of the Portuguese regiments Nos. 4 and 10.

'In respect to the charge of cutting barren wood in the royal parks for firewood, I have to reply that I suppose His Royal Highness does not propose that His Majesty's troops shall want firewood in Portugal. It is reasonable that His Royal Highness, as well as other proprietors, should be paid for the wood cut upon his demesnes; but either the troops must be allowed to cut firewood, paying for the same, wherever the defence of His Royal Highness's dominions renders it necessary that they should be stationed, or they must be removed to the places where they can cut firewood, by which His Royal Highness's interests must suffer.

'I cannot avoid adverting to the disposition recently manifested by the Government to complain of the conduct of the British troops, certainly, in this instance, without foundation.

'Acts of misconduct, and even outrage, I admit, have been committed, but never with impunity in any instance in which the complaint could be substantiated; and I have not yet been able to obtain the punishment of any individual of this country, be his crimes what they may.

'If the British soldiers have committed, as all soldiers do commit, acts of misconduct, they have at least fought bravely for the country. They have, besides, recently shown that commiseration for the misfortunes of the people of this country which I am convinced will be equally felt by their countrymen at home, and actually fed the poor inhabitants of all the towns in which they were cantoned on the Rio Mayor River. Yet I have not heard that the Portuguese Government have expressed their approbation of this conduct, very unusual in people of this class and description; nor do I find that either their bravery in the field, or their humanity, or their generosity, can induce those whom they are serving to look with indulgence at their failings, or to draw a veil over the faults of the few, in consideration of the military and other virtues of the many.'

BUNGLING THE COMMISSARIAT.

To Charles Stuart, Esq.

'Oliveira do Hospital,
'March 22, 1811.

'I have just heard that the vessels arrived for the Portuguese troops at Figueira contained, one *sardinias*, one *bacalao*, the third rice!!!'

'Gouvea,
'March 27, 1811.

'. . . Since writing the other side, I have heard that Colonel Ashworth's brigade of Portuguese infantry are as badly off as General Pack's; they have nothing to eat and have sent here for it, having before sent to Coimbra and Figueira, where they found nothing!! So much for rice, *bacalao*, and *sardinias*!'

THE HORRORS OF WAR.

To the Earl of Liverpool

'Sta. Marinha,
'March 23,1811.

'. . . I shall be sorry if Government should think themselves under the necessity of withdrawing from this country on account of the expense of the contest. From what I have seen of the objects of the French Government, and the sacrifices they make to accomplish them, I have no doubt that if the British Army were for any reason to withdraw from the Peninsula, and the French Government were relieved from the pressure of military operations on the Continent, they would incur all risks to land an army in His Majesty's dominions. Then, indeed, would commence an expensive contest; then would His Majesty's subjects discover what are the miseries of war, of which, by the blessing of God, they have hitherto had no knowledge; and the cultivation, the beauty, and prosperity of the country, and the virtue and happiness of its inhabitants, would be destroyed, whatever might be the result of the military operations.

'God forbid that I should be a witness, much less an actor in the scene; and I only hope that the King's Government will consider well what I have above stated to Your Lordship; will ascertain as nearly as is in their power the actual expense of employing a certain number of men in this country beyond that of employing them at home or elsewhere; and will keep up their force here on such a footing as will at all events secure their possession without keeping the transports, if it does not enable their commander to take advantage of events and assume the offensive.'

The Battle of Barrosa.

To Lieutenant-General Sir Brent Spencer, K.B.

'Sta. Marinha,
'March 25,1811.

'The French retired from Celorico yesterday, and they appear to intend to take up a line on the Coa. Their left has gone by Guarda, apparently for Sabugal.

'I enclose Graham's despatches on his action.'

'Lieutenant-General Graham to the Earl of Liverpool, Secretary of State.

'Isla de Leon,
'March 6, 1811.

'Captain Hope, my first *Aide-de-Camp*, will have the honour of delivering this despatch, to inform Your Lordship of the glorious issue of an action fought yesterday by the division under my command against the army commanded by Marshal Victor, composed of the two divisions, Rufin's and Laval's.'

"The circumstances were such as compelled me to attack this very superior force. . . . The Allied Army, after a night march of sixteen hours from the camp near Veger, arrived in the morning of the 5th on the low ridge of Barrosa, about four miles to the southward of the mouth of the Santi Petri River. This height extends inland about a mile and a half, continuing on the north the extensive heathy plain of Chiclana. A great pine forest skirts the plain, and circles round the height at some distance, terminating down to Santi Petri, the intermediate space between the north side of the height and the forest being uneven and broken. . . .

'Trusting to the known heroism of British troops, regardless of the numbers and position of their enemy, an immediate attack was determined on. . . .

BATTLE OF BARROSA, March 5, 1811.

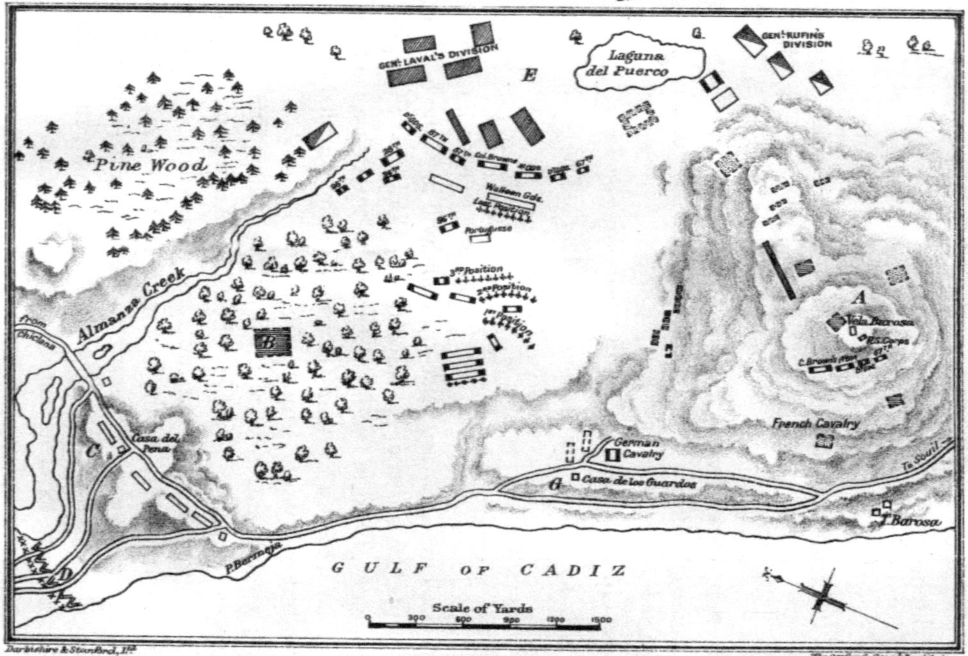

Darbishire & Stanford, Ltd.

The Oxford Geogl. Institute.

A Hill of Barosa.
B Graham's Division on its march to join La Peña, when the news of the enemy's approach was received.
C Position of La Peña.
D French post taken by Ladrizabal.
E Plain on which the enemy made its appearance.

'In less than an hour and a half from the commencement of the action the enemy was in full retreat. . . .

'The exhausted state of the troops made pursuit impossible. . . .

'An eagle, (this was the first eagle captured by the British in action in the Peninsula, it belonged to the 8th Regiment of Light Infantry, and was captured by the Royal Irish Fusiliers, whose badge is inscribed '8.'—W. W.), six pieces of cannon, the General of Division Rufin, and the General of Brigade Rousseau, wounded and taken; the Chief of the Staff, General Bellegarde, an *Aide-de-Camp* of Marshal Victor, and the Colonel of the 8th Regiment, with many other officers, killed, and several wounded and taken prisoners; the field covered with the dead bodies and arms of the enemy attests that my confidence in this division was nobly repaid.

'Where all have so distinguished themselves, it is scarcely possible to discriminate any as the most deserving of praise. Your Lordship will, however, observe how gloriously the brigade of Guards maintained the high character of His Majesty's household troops. . . .

'The animated charges of the 87th Regiment were most conspicuous. (Now the 1st Battalion Princess Victoria's—Royal Irish Fusiliers). . .'

'Lieutenant-General Graham to the Earl of Liverpool, Secretary of State.

'Isla de Leon,
'March 10, 1811.

'I have the honour to transmit to Your Lordship the return of the killed and wounded in the action of the 5th instant, and I have the satisfaction to add that the wounded in general are doing well.

'By the best account that can be collected from the wounded French officers, the enemy had about 8,000 men engaged. Their loss, by reports from Chiclana, in killed, wounded, and prisoners, is supposed to amount to 3,000; I have no doubt of its being very great.

'I transmit, too, a return of the ordnance in our possession, and also the most accurate note that can be obtained of prisoners, most of whom are wounded. They are so dispersed in different hospitals that an exact return has not yet been obtained.

'*P.S.* Detachments of cavalry and infantry have been daily employed in carrying off the wounded and burying the dead, till the evening of the 8th instant, by which time all the enemy's wounded that could be found among the brushwood and heath were brought in.

'*Return of the Nature and Number of Pieces of Ordnance taken in the Action of Barrosa, on March 5, 1811.*

'Two 7-inch howitzers, three heavy 8-pounders, one 4-pounder, with their ammunition waggons, and a proportion of horses.

'*Return of Prisoners of War taken in the Action of Barrosa, on March 5, 1811.*

'Two general officers, 1 field officer, 9 captains, 8 subalterns, 420 rank and file.

'*N.B.* The General of Brigade Rousseau and 2 captains since dead of their wounds.

Return of the Killed, Wounded, and Missing of the Troops under the Command of Lieutenant-General Graham, in the Action of Barrosa, with the French Corps d'Armée commanded by Marshal Victor, on March 5, 1811.

	Officers.	Non-commissioned Officers and Drummers.	Rank and File.	Horses.	Total Loss of Officers, Non-commissioned Officers, and Rank and File.
Killed -	7	6	189	24	202
Wounded -	55	45	940	42	1,040
Missing -	—	—	—	—	—

To Lieutenant-General Graham.

'Sta. Marinha,
'March 25, 1811.

'I beg to congratulate you and the brave troops under your command on the signal victory which you gained on the 5th instant. I have no doubt whatever that their success would have had the effect of raising the siege of Cadiz if the Spanish corps had made any effort to assist them; and I am equally certain, from your account of the ground, that if you had not decided with the utmost promptitude to attack the enemy, and if your attack had not been a most vigorous one, the whole allied army would have been lost. . . .

'The conduct of the Spaniards throughout this expedition is precisely the same as I have ever observed it to be. They march the troops night and day, without provisions or rest, and abusing everybody who proposes a moment's delay to afford either to the famished and fatigued soldiers.

They reach the enemy in such a state as to be unable to make any exertion, or to execute any plan, even if any plan had been formed; and then, when the moment of action arrives, they are totally incapable of movement, and they stand by to see their allies destroyed, and afterwards abuse them because they do not continue, unsupported, exertions to which human nature is not equal. . . .'

To Marshal Beresford.

'Sta. Marinha,
'March 25, 1811.

'General Graham has returned to the Isla, after having fought the hardest action that has been fought yet. The Spaniards left him very much to his own exertions. The Spanish General is to be brought to a court-martial. Graham took two general officers, six pieces of cannon, an eagle, and 500 prisoners. He lost 1,100, principally wounded. The two Portuguese companies of the 20th behaved remarkably well; Bushe is wounded. I will send you the despatches as soon as Sir Brent shall return them.

'I am sorry to tell you that the Portuguese troops here are diminishing in numbers terribly. Pack's brigade has only 1,700; the 21st Regiment but little more than 500; Pakenham tells me either the 3rd or 15th only 300, but I have not seen this return. They are fed, and, indeed, have been ever since they marched, by our commissaries, except Pack's, Ashworth's, and Barbacena's cavalry.'

A Handsome Dressing for the French.

To Captain Chapman, Royal Engineers.

'Villar Mayor,
'April 8, 1811.

'. . . We have given the French a handsome dressing, and I think they will not say again that we are not a manoeuvring army. We may not manoeuvre so beautifully as they do; but I do not desire better sport than to meet one of their columns *en masse* with our lines. The poor 2nd Corps received a terrible beating from the 43rd and 52nd on the 3rd.'

Violating Hospitality.

To Charles Stuart, Esq.

'Villar Mayor,
'Aprils, 1811.

'I have had the honour of receiving your letter of March 16, regarding a complaint of Captain —— of the ——, forwarded by the Governors of the Kingdom.

'I enclose a letter of March 5, which Captain —— had written to his commanding officer, under the expectation that his conduct might be complained of; and another letter of March 31, written in answer to one which I desired might be sent to him, to inquire whether he wrote the letters enclosed in yours of the 16th instant.

'Excepting in cases in which it appears that there has been some gross and flagrant departure from the laws of hospitality, or violence has been used, or gross fraud practised, it does not answer to bring cases of seduction under the cognisance of the military tribunals. It is probable that Captain —— would be acquitted, and the young lady and family would be disgraced by the sentence.

'I acknowledge that, from what I have heard upon this subject, I would recommend to the family to drop it entirely. If, however, they should determine to bring it forward in the Portuguese civil courts, it will be necessary that the Government should apply to me to have Captain —— made over to them to answer for his conduct.'

Immense French Losses.

To the Earl of Liverpool.

'Villa Fermosa,
'April 9, 1811.

'The enemy's loss in this expedition to Portugal is immense; I should think not less than 45,000 men including the sick and wounded; and I think that, including the 9th Corps, they may have 40,000 on this frontier. I enclose a letter which I have received this day from one of my correspondents at Salamanca, which shows the state in which they are. The whole army is dispirited and dissatisfied. Ney left them about a fortnight ago, it is said, in arrest; and I understand that the other generals are equally dissatisfied with Massena's operations . . .'

The French Defeats,

To the Right Hon. Henry Wellesley.

Villa Fermosa, April 10, 1811.

'. . . . We have given the French some terrible beatings, and they are completely dispirited and disorganised. . . .'

FUENTES DE OÑORO.

To the Earl of Liverpool.

'Villa Fermosa,
'May 8, 1811.

'. . . The Allied Army had been cantoned along the River Dos Casas, and on the sources of the Azava, the Light Division at Gallegos and Espeja. This last fell back upon Fuentes de Oñoro, on the Dos Casas, with the British cavalry, in proportion as the enemy advanced, and the 1st, 3rd, and 7th Divisions were collected at that place; the 6th Division, under Major-General Campbell, observed the bridge at Alameda; and Major-General Sir William Erskine, with the 5th Division, the passages of the Dos Casas at Fort Concepcion and Aldea del Obispo. Brigadier-General Pack's brigade, with the Queen's Regiment from the 6th Division, kept the blockade of Almeida; and I had prevailed upon Don Julian Sanchez to occupy Nave d'Aver with his corps of Spanish cavalry and infantry.

'The Light Division were moved in the evening to join Major-General Campbell, upon finding that the enemy were in strength in that quarter; and they were brought back again to Fuentes de Oñoro on the morning of the 5th, when it was found that the 8th Corps had joined the 6th on the enemy's left.

'Shortly after the enemy had formed on the ground on the right of the Dos Casas, on the afternoon of the 3rd, they attacked with a large force the village of Fuentes de Oñoro, which was defended in a most gallant manner by Lieutenant-Colonel Williams, of the 5th Battalion 60th Regiment, in command of the light infantry battalion belonging to Major-General Picton's division, supported by the light infantry battalion in Major-General Nightingall's brigade, commanded by Major Dick of the 42nd Regiment, and the light infantry battalion in Major-General Howard's brigade, commanded by Major M'Donnell of the 92nd, and the light infantry battalion of the King's German Legion, commanded by Major Aly, of the 5th Battalion of the Line, and by the 2nd Battalion 83rd Regiment, under Major Carr.

'The troops maintained their position; but having observed the repeated efforts which the enemy were making to obtain possession of the village, and being aware of the advantage which they would derive from the possession in their subsequent operations, I reinforced the village successively with the 71st Regiment under Lieutenant-Col-

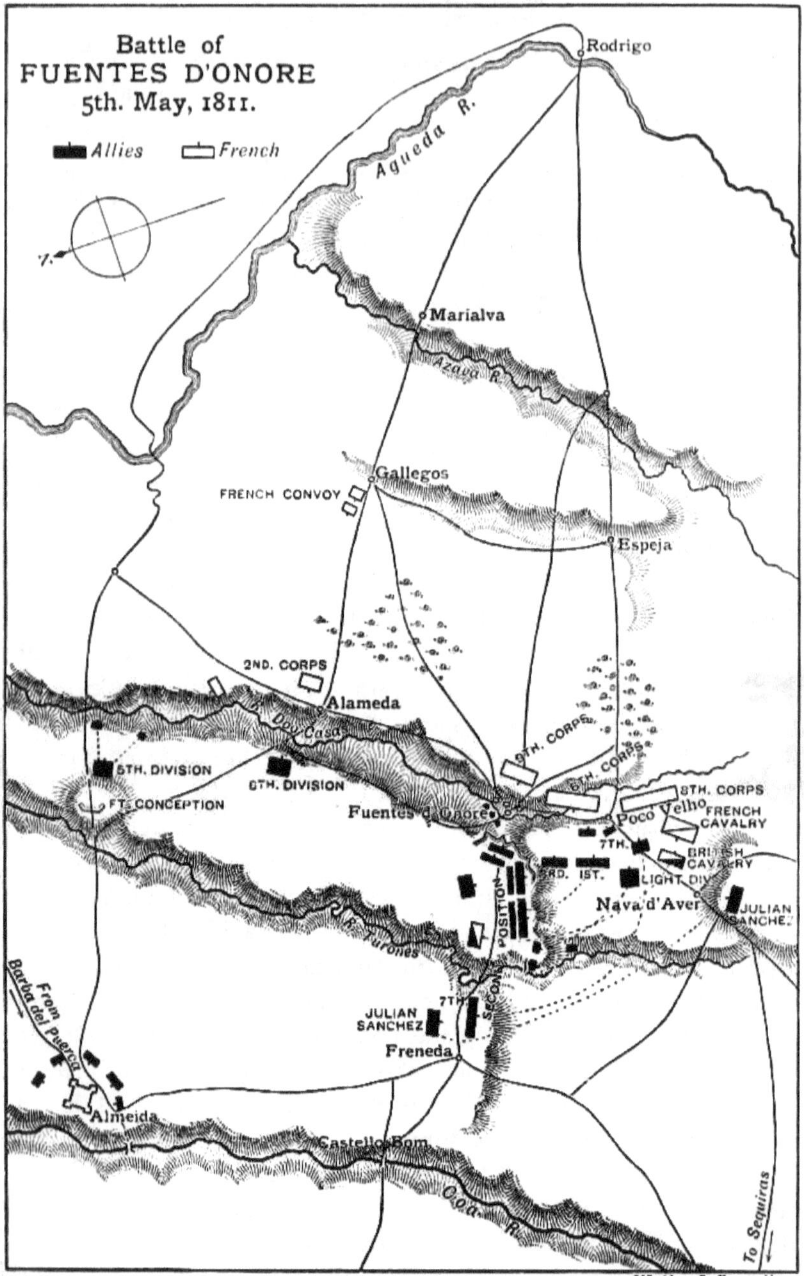
Battle of
FUENTES D'ONORE
5th. May, 1811.
Allies
French
Rodrigo
Agueda R.
Marialva
Azava R.
Gallegos
FRENCH CONVOY
Espeja
2ND. CORPS
Alameda
R. Dos Casas
9TH. CORPS
6TH. CORPS
8TH. CORPS
5TH. DIVISION
6TH. DIVISION
FT. CONCEPTION
Fuentes d'Onore
Poco Velho
FRENCH CAVALRY
7TH.
BRITISH CAVALRY
3RD.
1ST.
LIGHT DIV.
Nava d'Aver
JULIAN SANCHEZ
POSITION
R. Turones
SECOND
7TH.
JULIAN SANCHEZ
Freneda
From Barba del Puerca
Almeida
Castello Bom
Coa R.
To Sequiras
Walker & Boutall sc.

onel the Hon. H. Cadogan, and the 79th under Lieutenant-Colonel Cameron, and the 24th under Major Chamberlain. The former, at the head of the 71st Regiment, charged the enemy, and drove them from a part of the village of which they had obtained a momentary possession.

'Nearly at this time Lieutenant-Colonel Williams was unfortunately wounded, but I hope not dangerously, and the command devolved upon Lieutenant-Colonel Cameron of the 79th.

'The contest continued till night, when our troops remained in possession of the whole.

'I then withdrew the light infantry battalions and the 83rd Regiment, leaving the 71st and 79th Regiments only in the village, and the 2nd Battalion 24th Regiment to support them.

'On the 4th the enemy reconnoitred the position which we had occupied on the Dos Casas River; and during that night they moved the Duc d'Abrantes' corps from Alameda to the left of the position occupied by the 6th Corps, opposite to Fuentes de Oñoro.

'From the course of the reconnaissance on the 4th I had imagined that the enemy would endeavour to obtain possession of Fuentes de Oñoro, and of the ground occupied by the troops behind that village, by crossing the Dos Casas at Pozo Velho; and in the evening I moved the 7th Division, under Major-General Houstoun, to the right, in order, if possible, to protect that passage.

'On the morning of the 5th the 8th Corps appeared in two columns, with all the cavalry, on the opposite side of the valley of the Dos Casas and Pozo Velho; and as the 6th and 9th Corps also made a movement to their left, the Light Division, which had been brought back from the neighbourhood of Alameda, were sent with the cavalry, under Sir Stapleton Cotton, to support Major-General Houstoun; while the 1st and 3rd Divisions made a movement to their right, along the ridge between the Turon and Dos Casas Rivers, corresponding to that of the 6th and 9th Corps, on the right of the Dos Casas.

'The 8th Corps attacked Major-General Houstoun's advanced guard, consisting of the 85th Regiment, under Major Macintosh, and the 2nd Portuguese Caçadores, under Lieutenant-Colonel Nixon, and obliged them to retire; and they retired in good order, although with some loss. The 8th Corps being thus established in Pozo Velho, the enemy's cavalry turned the right of the 7th Division, between Pozo Velho and Nave d'Aver, from which last place Don Julian Sanchez had been obliged to retire, and the cavalry charged.

'The charge of the advanced guard of the enemy's cavalry was met by two or three squadrons of the different regiments of British Dragoons, and the enemy were driven back; and Colonel La Motte, of the 13th Chasseurs, and some prisoners taken.

'The main body were checked and obliged to retire by the fire of Major-General Houstoun's division, and I particularly observed the *Chasseurs Britanniques*, under Lieutenant-Colonel Eustace, as behaving in the most steady manner; and Major-General Houstoun mentions in high terms the conduct of a detachment of the Duke of Brunswick's Light Infantry.

'Notwithstanding that this charge was repulsed, I determined to concentrate our force towards the left, and to move the 7th and Light Divisions and the cavalry from Pozo Velho towards Fuentes de Oñoro and the other two divisions.

'I had occupied Pozo Velho and that neighbourhood in hopes that I should be able to maintain the communication across the Coa by Sabugal, as well as provide for the blockade, which objects it was now obvious were incompatible with each other; and I therefore abandoned that which was the least important, and placed the Light Division in reserve in the rear of the left of the 1st Division, and the 7th Division on some commanding ground beyond the Turon, which protected the right flank and rear of the 1st Division, and covered the communication with the Goa, and prevented that of the enemy with Almeida by the roads between the Turon and that river....

'Our position thus extended on the high ground from the Turon to the Dos Casas. The 7th Division, on the left of the Turon, covered the rear of the right; the 1st Division, in two lines, were on the right; Colonel Ashworth's brigade, in two lines, in the centre; and the 3rd Division, in two lines, on the left; the Light Division and British Artillery in reserve; and the village of Fuentes in front of the left. Don Julian's infantry joined the 7th Division in Freneda, and I sent him with his cavalry to endeavour to intercept the enemy's communication with Ciudad Rodrigo.

'The enemy's efforts on the right part of our position, after it was occupied as I have above described, were confined to a cannonade, and to some charges with his cavalry upon the advanced posts. The regiments of the 1st Division, under Lieutenant-Colonel Hill of the 3rd Regiment of Guards, repulsed one of these; but as they were falling back, they did not see the direction of another in sufficient time to form to oppose it, and Lieutenant-Colonel Hill was taken prisoner, and many men were wounded and some taken, before a detachment of the British cavalry could move up to their support.

'The 2nd Battalion 42nd Regiment, under Lord Blantyre, also repulsed a charge of the cavalry directed against them.

'The enemy's principal effort was throughout this day again directed against Fuentes de Oñoro; and, notwithstanding that the whole of the 6th Corps were at different periods of the day employed to attack this village, they could never gain more than a temporary possession of it. It was defended by the 24th, 71st, and 79th Regiments, under the command of Lieutenant-Colonel Cameron; and these troops were supported by the light infantry battalions of the 3rd Division, commanded by Major Woodgate; the light infantry battalions of the 1st Division, commanded by Major Dick, Major M'Donald, and Major Aly; the 6th Portuguese Caçadores, commanded by Major Pinto; by the light companies in Colonel Champelmond's Portuguese brigade, under Colonel Sutton; and those in Colonel Ashworth's Portuguese brigade, under Lieutenant-Colonel Pynn, and by the piquets of the 3rd Division, under the command of Colonel the Hon. R. Trench. Lieutenant-Colonel Cameron was severely, (mortally), wounded in the afternoon, and the command in the village devolved upon Lieutenant-Colonel the Hon. H. Cadogan.

'The troops in Fuentes were besides supported, when pressed by the enemy, by the 74th Regiment, under Major Russell Manners, and the 1st Battalion 88th Regiment, under Lieutenant-Colonel Wallace, belonging to Colonel Mackinnon's brigade; and on one of these occasions, the 88th, with the 71st and 79th, under the command of Colonel Mackinnon, charged the enemy, and drove them through the village; and Colonel Mackinnon has reported particularly the conduct of Lieutenant-Colonel Wallace, Brigade-Major Wilde, and Lieutenant and Adjutant Stewart.

'The contest again lasted in this quarter till night, when our troops still held their post, and from that time the enemy have made no fresh attempt on any part of our position.

'The enemy manifested an intention to attack Major-General Sir William Erskine's post at Alde del Obispo on the same morning, with a part of the 2nd Corps, but the Major-General sent the 2nd Battalion Lusitanian Legion across the ford of the Dos Casas, which obliged them to retire.

'In the course of last night, the enemy commenced retiring from their position on the Dos Casas, and this morning, at daylight, the whole was in motion. I cannot yet decide whether this movement is preparatory to some fresh attempt to raise the blockade of Almeida, or is one of decided retreat; but I have every reason to hope that they will not succeed in the first, and that they will be obliged to have recourse to the last. Their superiority in cavalry is very great, owing to the weak state of our horses from recent fatigue and scarcity of forage, and the reduction of numbers in the Portuguese brigade of cavalry with this part of the army, in exchange for a British brigade sent into Estremadura with Marshal Sir William Beresford, owing to the failure of the measures reported to have been adopted to supply horses and men with food on the service.

'The result of a general action, brought on by an attack upon the enemy by us, might, under those circumstances, have been doubtful; and if the enemy had chosen to avoid it, or if they had met it, they would have taken advantage of the collection of our troops to fight this action, and throw relief into Almeida.

'From the great superiority of force to which we have been opposed upon this occasion Your Lordship will judge of the conduct of the officers and troops. The actions were partial, but very severe, and our loss has been great. The enemy's loss has also been very great, and they left 400 killed in the village of Fuentes, and we have many prisoners . . .'

Return of the Killed, Wounded, and Missing of the Army under the Command of Lieutenant-General Viscount Wellington, K.B., in the Affairs at Fuentes da Oñoro, on May 3 and 5, 1811.

	Officers.	Non-commissioned Officers and Drummers.	Rank and File.	Horses.	Total Loss of Officers, Non-commissioned Officers, and Rank and File.
Killed -	11	16	208	49	235
Wounded -	81	72	1,081	101	1,234
Missing -	7	10	300	5	317

The Portuguese killed, wounded, and missing are included in the above numbers.

To the Right Hon. Henry Wellesley.

'Villa Fermosa,
'May 8,1811

'. . . We have had warm work in this quarter, but I hope we shall succeed in the end. The French, it is said, lost 5,000 men, we 1,200, in the affair of the 5th; on the 3rd we lost about 250; the French left 400 dead in the village of Fuentes de Oñoro. We lost the prisoners by the usual dash and imprudence of the soldiers.'

Over-zealous Leaders.

To Major-General Alexander Campbell.

'Villa Fermosa,
'May 15, 1811.

'. . . The frequent instances which have occurred lately of severe loss, and, in some instances, of important failure, by officers leading the troops beyond the point to which they are ordered and beyond all bounds, such as the loss of the prisoners taken in front of the village of Fuentes, on the 3rd and 5th instant; the loss incurred by the 13th Light Dragoons, near and at Badajoz, on March 25; the severe loss incurred by the troops in the siege of Badajoz on the right of the Guadiana on the 10th instant; and the loss incurred by Lieutenant-Colonel —— on the 11th instant, have induced me to determine to bring before a general court-martial, for disobedience of orders, any officer who shall, in future, be guilty of this conduct.

'I entertain no doubt of the readiness of the officers and soldiers of the army to advance upon the enemy; but it is my duty, and that of every general and other officer in command, to regulate this spirit, and not to expose the soldiers to contend with unequal numbers in situations disadvantageous to them, and, above all, not to allow them to follow up trifling advantages to situations in which they cannot be supported, from which their retreat is not secure, and in which they incur the risk of being prisoners to the enemy they had before beaten.

'The desire to be forward in engaging the enemy is not uncommon in the British Army; but that quality which I wish to see the officers possess, who are at the head of the troops, is a cool, discriminating judgment in action, which will enable them to decide with promptitude how far they can and ought to go with propriety, and to convey their orders, and act with such vigour and decision that the soldiers will look up to them with confidence in the moment of action, and obey them with alacrity.

'The officers of the army may depend upon it that the enemy to whom they are opposed are not less prudent than they are powerful. Notwithstanding what has been printed in gazettes and newspapers, we have never seen small bodies, unsupported, opposed to large; nor has the experience of any officer realised the stories, which all have read, of whole armies being driven by a handful of light infantry or dragoons.

'I trust that this letter, copies of which I propose to circulate to the general officers commanding divisions, with directions to circulate it among the officers of the army, will have the effect of inducing them to reflect seriously upon the duties which they have to perform before the enemy, and to avoid the error which is the subject of it, which is really become one of serious detriment to the army and to the public interests.'

The Battle of Albuera.

To Charles Stuart, Esq.

'Elvas,
'May 20, 1811.

'. . . I think it very desirable that, if possible, no flying details of the Battle of Albuera should go home till Sir William Beresford's report shall be sent. I conclude that the account that there had been a battle went by the mail yesterday, which is of no importance; but where there are many killed and wounded the first reports are not favourable, and it is not doing justice to the Marshal to allow them to circulate without his.'

To Lieutenant-General Sir Brent Spencer.

'Elvas,
'May 22, 1811.

'I went yesterday to Albuera, and saw the field of battle. We had a very good position, and I think should have gained a complete victory in it, without any material loss, if the Spaniards could have manoeuvred; but unfortunately, they cannot.

'The French are retiring, but I do not think it clear that they are going beyond the Sierra Morena. As I know you have plenty of correspondents, I do not give you any details of the action here, or of our loss. I think the action, upon the whole, to be the most honourable to the troops that they have been engaged in during the war.

'*P.S*—I received your letter of the 20th this morning; I think it appears that the enemy's loss cannot be less than between 8,000 and 9,000 men. . . .'

To the Right Hon. Henry Wellesley.

'Elvas,
'May 22, 1811.

'We have had warm work here; however, I hope that the French have suffered more than we have. I mean, if Soult goes far enough from me, to renew the operations of the siege of Badajoz; but he will

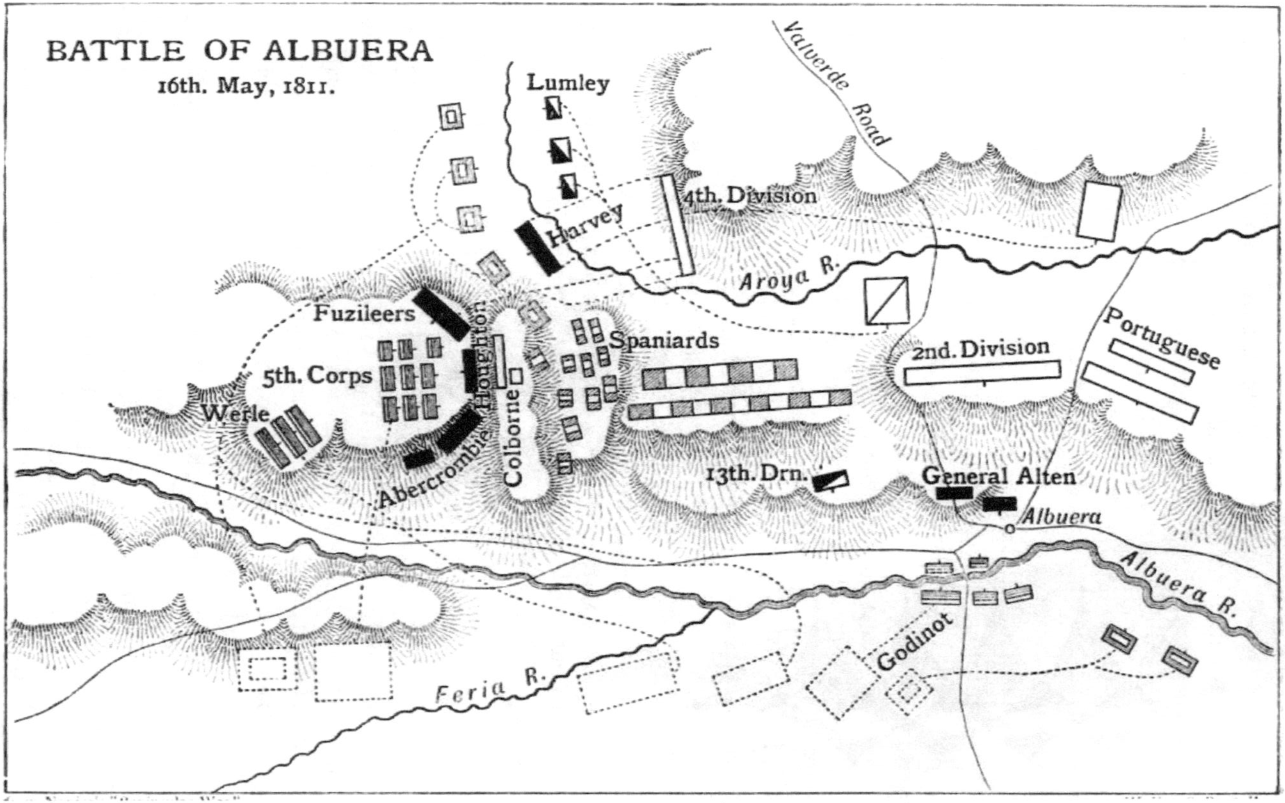
BATTLE OF ALBUERA
16th. May, 1811.
Lumley
Valverde Road
4th. Division
Harvey
Aroya R.
Fuzileers
Houghton
Spaniards
2nd. Division
Portuguese
5th. Corps
Werle
Colborne
Abercrombie
13th. Drn.
General Alten
Albuera
Albuera R.
Godinot
Feria R.

soon have a large reinforcement from Castille, and another such battle would ruin us.

'The Spanish troops, I understand, behaved admirably; they stood like stocks, both parties at times firing on them, but they were quite immovable; and this is the great cause of all our losses. After they had lost their position, the natural thing to do would have been to attack it with the nearest Spanish troops, but they could not be moved; the British troops were the next, and they were brought up, and must always in these cases be brought up, and they suffered accordingly.

'The Battle of Talavera was an example of the same defect in the Spanish troops; they could not be moved, however advantageous this movement might have been; and I suspect that the Battle of Barrosa was something of the same kind.

'It is scarcely to be believed that any officer, who could depend upon the discipline of his troops in their movements, would have remained the quiet spectator of such an action at such a moment.

'From these circumstances you will believe that I am not very easy about the result of another action, if we should be obliged to fight one. What a pity it is that the Spaniards will not set to work seriously to discipline their troops! We do what we please now with the Portuguese troops; we manoeuvre them under fire equally with our own, and have some dependence on them; but these Spaniards can do nothing, but stand still, and we consider ourselves fortunate if they do not run away. . . .'

To the Earl of Liverpool.

'Elvas,
'May 22, 1811.

'On the night of the 15th instant I received from Marshal Sir William Beresford letters of the 12th and 13th instant, which reported that Marshal Soult had broken up from Seville and had advanced towards Estremadura about the 10th, notwithstanding the reports which had been previously raised that he was busily occupied in strengthening Seville, and the approaches to that city, by works, and that all his measures indicated an intention to remain on the defensive in Andalusia.

'I therefore set out on the following morning from Villa Fermosa, and having received further information of the 14th from Sir William Beresford of the enemy's movements, I hastened my progress, and arrived here on the 19th, and found that Sir William Beresford had raised the siege of Badajoz without the loss of ordnance or stores of any description, had collected the troops under his command, and had formed a junction with Generals Castaños and Blake at Albuera in the course of the 15th instant. He was attacked there on the 16th by the French Army under the command of Marshal Soult, and, after a most severe engagement, in which all the troops conducted themselves in the most gallant manner, Sir William Beresford gained the victory. The enemy retired in the night of the 17th instant, leaving between 900 and 1,000 wounded on the ground. Sir William Beresford sent the Allied cavalry after them, and on the 19th in the morning reinvested Badajoz.

'I enclose the reports of Sir William Beresford of the 16th and the 18th instant, on the operations of the siege to the moment of raising it, and on the battle at Albuera, and I beg to draw Your Lordship's attention to the ability, the firmness, and the gallantry manifested by Marshal Sir William Beresford throughout the transaction on which he has written. I shall add nothing to what he has said of the conduct of all the officers and troops, excepting to express my admiration of it and my cordial concurrence in the favourable reports made by Sir William Beresford of the good conduct of all.'

Marshal Sir W. C. Beresford, K.B.,
to Lieutenant-General Viscount Wellington, K.B.

'Albuera,
'May 18, 1811.

'I have infinite satisfaction in communicating to Your Lordship that the allied army, united here under my orders, obtained, on the 16th instant, after a most sanguinary conquest, a complete victory over that of the enemy, commanded by Marshal Soult.

'In a former report I have informed Your Lordship of the advance of Marshal Soult from Seville, and I had in consequence judged it wise entirely to raise the siege of Badajoz, and prepare to meet him with our united forces, rather than, by looking to two objects at once, to risk the loss of both.

'Marshal Soult, it appears, had been long straining every nerve to collect a force which he thought fully sufficient to his object for the relief of Badajoz, and for this purpose he had drawn considerable numbers from the corps of Marshal Victor and General Sebastiani, and also, I believed, from the French Army of the centre. Having thus completed his preparations, he marched from Seville on the 10th instant with a corps then estimated at 15,000 or 16,000 men, and was joined, on descending into Estremadura, by the corps under General Latour Maubourg, stated to be 5,000 men. . . .

'As remaining at Valverde, though a stronger position, left Badajoz entirely open, I determined to take up a position (such as could be got in this widely open country) at this place, thus standing directly between the enemy and Badajoz.

'The army was assembled here on the 15th instant. The corps of General Blake, though making a forced march to effect it, only joined in the night, and could not be placed in its position till the morning of the 16th instant, when General Cole's division, with the Spanish Brigade under Don Carlos de España, also joined, and a little before the commencement of the action. Our cavalry had been forced on the morning of the 15th instant to retire from Santa Marta, and joined here.

'In the afternoon of that day the enemy appeared in front of us. The next morning our disposition for receiving the enemy was made, being formed in two lines, nearly parallel to the River Albuera, on the ridge of the gradual ascent rising from that river, and covering the roads to Badajoz and Valverde, though Your Lordship is aware that the whole face of this country is everywhere passable for all arms. General Blake's corps was on the right in two lines; its left, on the Valverde road, joined the right of Major-General the Hon. William Stewart's division, the left of which reached the Badajoz road, where commenced the right of Major-General Hamilton's division, which closed the left of the line. General Cole's division, with one brigade of General Hamilton's, formed the second line of the British and Portuguese Army.

'The enemy, on the morning of the 16th, did not long delay his attack. At eight o'clock he was observed to be in movement, and his cavalry was seen passing the rivulet of Albuera, considerably above our right; and shortly after he marched out of the wood opposite to us a strong force of cavalry, and two heavy columns of infantry, pointing them to our front, as if to attack the bridge and village of Albuera. During this time, under cover of his vastly superior cavalry, he was filing the principal body of his infantry over the river beyond our right, and it was not long before his intention appeared to be to turn us by that flank, and to cut us off from Valverde. . . .

'The enemy commenced his attack at nine o'clock, not ceasing at the same time to menace our left, and after a strong and gallant resistance of the Spanish troops, he gained the heights upon which they had been formed. . . .

'As the heights the enemy had gained raked and entirely commanded our whole position, it became necessary to make every effort to retake and maintain them, and a noble one was made by the division of General Stewart, headed by that gallant officer.

'Nearly at the beginning of the enemy's attack a heavy storm of rain came on, which, with the smoke from the firing, rendered it impossible to discern anything distinctly. This, with the nature of the ground, had been extremely favourable to the enemy in forming his columns, and in his subsequent attack.

'The right brigade of General Stewart's division, under Lieutenant-Colonel Colborne, first came into action, and behaved in the most gallant manner, and finding that the enemy's column could not be shaken by fire, proceeded to attack it with the bayonet; and, while in the act of charging, a body of Polish lancers (cavalry), which the thickness of the atmosphere and the nature of the ground had concealed (and which was, besides, mistaken by those of the brigade, when discovered, for Spanish cavalry, and therefore not fired upon), turned it, and, being thus attacked unexpectedly in the rear, was unfortunately broken, and suffered immensely, The 31st Regiment, being the left one of the brigade, alone escaped this charge, and, under the command of Major L'Estrange, kept its ground until the arrival of the 3rd Brigade, under Major-General Houghton. The conduct of this brigade was most conspicuously gallant, and that of the 2nd Brigade, under the command of Lieutenant-Colonel the Hon. A. Abercrombie, was not less so. Major-General Houghton, cheering on his brigade to the charge, fell pierced by wounds.

'Though the enemy's principal attack was on this point of the right, he also made a continual attempt upon that part of our original front at the village and bridge, which were defended in the most gallant manner by Major-General Baron Alten, and the light infantry brigade of the German Legion, whose conduct was, in every point of view, conspicuously good. This point now formed our left, and Major-General Hamilton's division had been brought up there; and he was left to direct the defence of that point, whilst the enemy's attack continued on our right, a considerable proportion of the Spanish troops supporting the defence of this place.

'The enemy's cavalry, on his infantry attempting to force our right, had endeavoured to turn it, but, by the able manoeuvres of Major-General the Hon. William Lumley, commanding the allied cavalry, though vastly inferior to that of the enemy in number, his endeavours were foiled. Major-General Cole, seeing the attack of the enemy, very judiciously bringing up his left a little, marched in line to attack the enemy's left, and arrived most opportunely to contribute, with the charges of the brigades of General Stewart's division, to force the enemy to abandon his situation, and retire precipitately, and to take refuge under his reserve. Here the fusilier brigade particularly distinguished itself.

'He was pursued by the allies to a considerable distance, and as far as I thought it prudent, with his immense superiority of cavalry, and I contented myself to see him driven across the Albuera. . . . .

'It is impossible to enumerate every instance of discipline and valour shown on this severely contested day, but there never were troops that more valiantly or more gloriously maintained the honour of their respective countries. I have not been able to particularise the Spanish divisions, brigades, or regiments, that were particularly engaged, because I am not acquainted with their denominations or names, but I have great pleasure in saying that their behaviour was most gallant and honourable, and though, from the superior number and weight of the enemy's force, that part of them that were in the position attacked were obliged to cede the ground, it was after a gallant resistance, and they continued in good order to support their allies; and I doubt not His Excellency General Blake will do ample justice on this head by making honourable mention of the deserving.

'The battle commenced at nine o'clock, and continued without interruption till two in the afternoon, when, the enemy having been driven over the Albuera, for the remainder of the day there was but cannonading and skirmishing.

'It is impossible by any description to do justice to the distinguished gallantry of the troops, but every individual most nobly did his duty, which will be well proved by the great loss we have suffered, though repulsing the enemy; and it was observed that our dead, particularly the 57th Regiment, were lying as they had fought in ranks, and every wound was in front...

****

Albuera gave to the 57th, now the 1st Battalion the Duke of Cambridge's Own (Middlesex Regiment), its famous nickname of 'the Die Hards.' The regiment have a badge in the shape of a laurel leaf, inscribed 'Albuhera.' The 57th went into action 570 strong, and of that number 22 officers and more than 400 men were killed or wounded. The King's colour was shot through by thirty bullets, but in spite of its heavy losses the regiment never flinched. Colonel Inglis repeatedly inspired his men by shouting, 'Die hard, my men, die hard!'—W. W.

****

'I annex the return of our loss in this hard contested day—it is very severe; and in addition to it is the loss of the troops under His Excellency General Blake, who are killed, missing, and wounded, but of which I have not the return. The loss of the enemy, though I cannot know what it is, must be still more severe. He has left on the field of battle about 2,000 dead, and we have taken from 900 to 1,000 prisoners. He has had five generals killed and wounded; of the former, Generals of Divisions Werle and Pesim; and Gazan and two others amongst the latter. His force was much more considerable than we had been informed of, as I do not think he displayed less than from 20,000 to 22,000 infantry, and he certainly had 4,000 cavalry, with a numerous and heavy artillery. His overbearing cavalry cramped and confined all our operations, and, with his artillery, saved his infantry after its rout.

'He retired after the battle to the ground he had been previously on, but occupying it in position; and on this morning, or rather during the night, commenced his retreat on the road he came, towards Seville, and has abandoned Badajoz to its fate. He left a number of his wounded on the ground he had retired to, and to whom we are administering what assistance we can. I have sent our cavalry to follow the enemy, but in that arm, he is too powerful for us to attempt anything against him in the plains he is traversing.

'Thus, we have reaped the advantage we proposed from our opposition to the attempts of the enemy, and, whilst he has been forced to abandon the object for which he has almost stripped Andalusia of troops, instead of having accomplished the haughty boasts with which Marshal Soult harangued his troops on leaving Seville, he returns there with a curtailed army, and, what perhaps may be still more hurtful to him, with a diminished reputation. . . .'

Return of Killed, Wounded, and Missing of the Corps of the Army tinder the Command of Lieutenant-General Viscount Wellington, K.B., under the Immediate Orders of Marshal Sir William Carr Beresford, K.B., in the Battle with the French Army, commanded by Marshal Soult, at Albuera, on May 16, 1811.

	Officers.	Non-commissioned Officers and Drummers.	Rank and File.	Horses.	Total Loss of Officers, Non-commissioned Officers, and Rank and File.
Killed -	34	33	917	63	984
Wounded -	181	146	2,666	35	2,993
Missing -	14	28	528	17	570

The Portuguese loss, but not the Spanish, is included in this return.

To the Earl of Liverpool.

'Elvas,
'May 22, 1811,

'I enclose a letter of the 21st instant, which I have received from Marshal Sir William Beresford, containing a letter from General Gazan to Marshal Soult, which had been intercepted by some of our parties.

'General Gazan, wounded himself, was marching with the wounded, and from his account of those with him, from the account of those at Almendralejo, and those left on the ground at Albuera, from the number found dead on the field, and the prisoners, the Marshal computes the enemy's loss not to fall short of 9,000 men.'

Raising of the Siege of Badajoz.

To the Earl of Liverpool.

'Quinta de Granicha,
'June 13, 1811.

'In consequence of a report from the Chief Engineer, Lieutenant-Colonel Fletcher, that the fire from San Christoval might occasion the loss of many lives in the operations on the left of the Guadiana, and the breach in that outwork having been apparently much improved by the fire throughout the 6th, I directed that an attempt might be made to carry San Christoval by storm that night. Major-General Houstoun, who conducted the operations of the siege on the right of the Guadiana, accordingly ordered a detachment under Major Macintosh, of the 85th Regiment, to make the attempt. The men advanced under a very heavy fire of musketry and hand grenades from the outworks, and of shot and shells from the town, with the utmost intrepidity, and in the best order, to the bottom of the breach, the advanced-guard being led by Ensign Dyas, of the 51st Regiment, who volunteered to perform this duty; but they found that the enemy had cleared the rubbish from the bottom of the escarp, and, notwithstanding that they were provided with ladders, it was impossible to mount it. They retired with some loss.

'The fire upon San Christoval, as well as upon the place, continued on the 7th, 8th, and 9th, on which day the breach in the wall of San Christoval appeared practicable, and I directed that a second attempt should be made on that night to obtain possession of that outwork. Major-General Houstoun ordered another detachment for this service, under the command of Major M'Geechy, of the 17th Portuguese Regiment, who, with the officers destined to command the different parties composing the detachment, had been employed throughout the 8th and 9th in reconnoitring the breach and the different approaches to it.

'They advanced at about nine at night, in the best order, though opposed by the same means, and with the same determination as had been opposed to the detachment which had made the attempt on the 6th.

'Ensign Dyas again led the service, and the storming party arrived at the foot of the breach; but they found it impossible to mount it, the enemy having again cleared the rubbish from the bottom of the escarp. The detachment suffered considerably, and Major M'Geechy, the Commanding Officer, was unfortunately killed, and others of the officers fell; but the troops continued to maintain their station till Major-General Houstoun ordered them to retire.

'When the reinforcements had arrived from the frontiers of Castille, after the battle of Albuera, I undertook the siege of Badajoz, entertaining a belief that the means of which I had the command would reduce the place before the end of the second week in June, at which time I expected that the reinforcement for the enemy's southern army, detached from Castille, would join Marshal Soult. I was, unfortunately, mistaken in my estimate of the quality of these means.

'The ordnance belonging to the garrison of Elvas is very ancient and incomplete, unprovided with the improvements adopted by modern science to facilitate and render more certain the use of cannon; and although classed generally as 24-pounders, the guns were found to be of a calibre larger than the shot in the garrison of that weight. The fire from this ordnance was therefore very uncertain, and the carriages proved to be worse even than we supposed they were; and both guns and carriages were rendered useless so frequently by the effect of our own fire as to create delay, in consequence of the necessity which existed for exchanging both in the advanced batteries.

'Those who are accustomed to observe the effect of the fire of artillery will be astonished to learn that fire was kept up from the 2nd to the 10th instant from fourteen 24-pounders, upon the wall of the castle of Badajoz, constructed of rammed earth and loose stones, of which the foot was seen at the distance of from 400 to 600 yards, and that it had not at last effected a practicable breach. It was impossible to estimate the length of time which would elapse before a practicable breach could have been effected in this wall; and, even if one had been effected, it was the opinion of the engineers and others, as well as my own, that although the breach could have been stormed, we could not have formed our troops to attack the enemy's intrenchment within unless we had possession of Fort San Christoval.

'We had failed in two attempts to obtain possession of Fort San Christoval, and it was obvious to me that we could not obtain possession of that outwork without performing a work which would have required the labour of several days to accomplish it.

'On the morning of the 10th instant I received the enclosed intercepted despatch, from the Duke of Dalmatia to the Duke of Rogusa, which pointed out clearly the enemy's design to collect in Estremadura their whole force, and I had reason to believe that Bonet's corps, which had marched from Toledo on the 28th and 29th of May, and was expected at Cordova on the 5th and 6th instant, would have joined the Southern Army by the 10th; and it was generally expected in the country that the southern army would have moved by that time.

'The movement of this army alone would have created a necessity for raising the siege; but on the same morning I received accounts from the frontiers of Castille, which left no doubt of the destination of the Army of Portugal to the southward, and gave ground for belief that they would arrive at Merida on the 15th instant.

'I therefore ordered that the siege should be raised.

'I am concerned to add that this measure was rendered expedient, not only by the military considerations to which I have above referred, but by others relative to the security of Elvas. . . .

'I enclose a return of the killed and wounded throughout the siege, from which Your Lordship will observe that, excepting in the attempts to obtain possession of San Christoval, our loss has not been severe. We still maintain the blockade of Badajoz; and I know from an intercepted letter that the enemy had in the place, on the 28th of May, only three weeks' provisions.'

Return of Killed, Wounded, and Missing of the Army under the Command of Lieutenant-General Lord Viscount Wellington, K.B., in the Several Affairs with the French Army, from May 30 to June 11, 1811, inclusive.

Headquarters, Quinta de St. João,
'June 13, 1811.

	Officers.	Non-commissioned Officers and Drummers.	Rank and File.	Horses.	Total Loss of Officers Non-commissioned Officers, and Rank and File.
Killed -	9	3	106	—	118
Wounded -	22	17	315	—	354
Missing -	3	—	6	—	9

The Grant of Medals.

To the Earl of Liverpool.

'Quinta de St. João,
'July 11, 1811.

'I have had the honour of receiving Your Lordship's letter of June 22, in which Your Lordship desires to have my opinion as to the restrictions which it may be expedient to put upon the grant of medals to British officers, for distinguished merit displayed upon Such occasions as the Battles of Vimeiro, Coruna, Talavera, and Barrosa.

'My opinion has always been that the grant of a medal to an individual officer ought to have been founded originally, partly on the importance of the occasion or action which it was intended to commemorate, and partly on the share which the individual officer had had in the action to be commemorated; and that medals should have been granted for important actions only, and to those engaged in them in a conspicuous manner, whatever might be their rank in the service.

'It was decided, however, that medals should be granted on the same principle only, but following strictly the example of the grant of medals to the navy, notwithstanding that an action on shore is very different from an action at sea; and the merits of the different classes of individuals are likewise entirely different. At the same time, this principle was departed from in some of the grants made.

'If the principle adopted in the grant of medals to the navy is adhered to in the grant of medals to officers of the army, and that medals are to be granted to general officers, and lieutenant-colonels commanding regiments, on an occasion to be commemorated, because, on a similar occasion, they would be granted to admirals and captains of ships of the line, it is difficult to restrict the grant, or to make a selection of officers to whom they should be granted, to commemorate the battles at Busaco and Fuentes de Oñoro, if Government determine that these actions should be commemorated in that manner. If, however, that principle is departed from, it is not difficult to make out a list of the names of officers already reported to Your Lordship, who were at the head of corps or detachments upon these occasions, and who had a conspicuous share in the event which it is the intention of the Government to commemorate in this manner.

'It is not probable, however, that the adoption of this principle will decrease the number of those to whom the honour would be granted; but, as I have already represented to Your Lordship, I do not think this important: that which is important in the establishment of the principle on which the grant of this honour should be made, is, that every officer should feel that he shall receive the mark of distinction, if he should be in the place to distinguish himself, and should act in the manner to deserve to be distinguished, whatever may be his military rank. It may be contended by me that the officers of the British Army do not require an honour of this description to stimulate their exertions, and that the grant of the medal is therefore useless; but, however, those who contend for this principle must admit that a selection of those who have had an opportunity of distinguishing themselves in an action is a less objectionable mode of granting it than the grant of it by classes, whether the individuals composing those classes have distinguished themselves or not.

'I have now the honour to enclose lists of the names of the officers who, on the principle of selection, ought, in my opinion, to receive medals for the Battles of Busaco and Fuentes de Oñoro, if Government think proper to distinguish these battles by medals. In respect to the Battle of Albuera, I was not there, and I am not able to give an opinion upon it. (Wellington was too late for Albuera because he waited to see if Almeida would be repaired after it was blown up.—W. W.)

'One brigade of the 4th Division of Infantry, however, was not in the action, nor Brigadier-General Madden's brigade of cavalry. The brunt of the action was on the right; but some of the corps of infantry, I believe, and certainly General Otway's brigade of cavalry, on the left, were not engaged.

'At all events, these troops were not engaged, as far as I understand, in a greater degree than the whole army were at Busaco, and every corps on the field at Fuentes de Oñoro. I mention these circumstances only to point out to Your Lordship that in every action on shore, however severe, there must be some to whose lot it does not fall to have an opportunity to distinguish themselves; and that the principle of selection, without reference to ranks, ought to be adopted in every instance of the grant of medals to the army.'

Astonishing Numbers of the French.

To Marshal Beresford.

'Quinta de St. João,
'July 12, 1811.

'The devil is in the French for numbers! A deserter came in yesterday, and told me he heard Broissard say to another officer that the two armies had 60,000 infantry and nearly 10,000 cavalry! I made them from 48,000 to 50,000 infantry, without the garrison of Badajoz, and 7,000 cavalry. . . .'

This Extraordinary War.

To Major-General the Hon. G. L. Cole.

'Portalegre,
'July 26, 1811.

'The scene shifts in this extraordinary war so frequently, and so many unexpected circumstances occur affecting our situation, that it is difficult to say at what period it is possible to allow an officer to quit the army. . . .'

An Incorrigible Boy.

To Vice-Admiral the Hon. George Berkeley.

'Portalegre,
'July 29, 1811.

'Lord Blantyre has written to me to propose to transfer to the navy a boy by the name of John Fraser, who is so prone to desertion that they cannot keep him with the 42nd Regiment. I have sent him to the Provost at Lisbon, and, if you have no objection to taking him, I request you to desire General Peacocke to send him on board any ship you please, and I will discharge him from the 42nd. He will not be at Lisbon for some days.'

Friendly British and Portuguese.

To the Earl of Liverpool.

'Pedrogão,
'August 4, 1811.

'...The people of Portugal agree remarkably well with the British soldiers. I have never known an instance of the most trifling disagreement among the soldiers or officers of the two nations. The Portuguese soldiers eat the same food, and, as military men, adopt the same habits as our soldiers, including, in some instances, their disposition to intoxication.

'And therefore, I should think it a preferable mode of introducing them into the British service, to place them indiscriminately in the same companies with recruits raised in His Majesty's dominions. Each individual would then be more likely to conduct himself on every occasion, and in all circumstances, as a British soldier....'

'Hell to Pay.'

To Marshal Beresford.

'Fuente Guinaldo,
'August 28, 1811.

'....You will see the despatches to Government, but I have no doubt that, unless the design has been altered since the end of June and beginning of July, we shall have the Emperor in Spain and *hell* to *pay* before much time elapses....'

Absurd Enough for an Encyclopaedia.

To the Right Hon. Henry Wellesley.

'Fuente Guinaldo,
'September 4, 1811.

'...I have not often seen so absurd a paper as —— ——'s.

'It would do very well for the *Encyclopaedia*; but there is not one word in the whole paper applicable to the present situation of Valencia.'

Buonaparte and his Fleet.

To His Excellency Charles Stuart.

'Quadraseis,
'September 29, 1811.

'. . . . I recommended the measure of arming the forts, not on any suspicion of the enemy's intentions founded on intelligence, but from the suggestions of my own mind, reflecting upon what it was probable the enemy might attempt. I am certain, that if Buonaparte does not remove us from the Peninsula, he must lower his tone with the world; and I am equally certain that he will make every effort to avoid this necessity. He has a fleet, and does not want for armies; and he is just the man to sacrifice his fleet, and to make a great effort with his armies to effect this object, I fear the results of neither the one nor the other if we are prepared. But as we are not prepared with a fleet at Lisbon, which, in my opinion, we ought always to be, I thought it proper to desire that the sea forts might be armed, as the only measure in my power at the time it was supposed probable that he was coming himself to take command of his armies.

'The mail was robbed by some of my vagabond soldiers.'

The Affair at El Bodon

(This celebrated affair, with which the 5th Regiment, now the Northumberland Fusiliers, are particularly associated, was stated by the Marquis of Londonderry to be the first instance on record of a charge by the bayonet being made upon cavalry by infantry in line.—W.W.)

To the Earl of Liverpool.

'Quadraseis,
'September 29, 1811.

'The enemy commenced their movements towards Ciudad Rodrigo with the convoys of provisions from the Sierra de Bejar, and from Salamanca on the 21st instant, and on the following day I collected the British Army in positions, from which I could either advance or retire without difficulty, and which would enable me to see all that was going on, and the strength of the enemy's army . . . .

'On the morning of the 25th the enemy sent a reconnaissance of cavalry towards the Lower Azava, consisting of about fourteen squadrons of the cavalry of the Imperial Guard. . . .

'But the enemy's attention was principally directed during this day to the position of the 3rd Division, in the hills between Fuente Guinaldo and Pastores. About eight in the morning they moved a column, consisting of between thirty and forty squadrons of cavalry, and fourteen battalions of infantry, and twelve pieces of cannon, from Ciudad Rodrigo, in such a direction that it was doubtful whether they would attempt to ascend the hills by La Encina, or by the direct road of El Bodon, towards Fuente Guinaldo: and I was not certain by which road they would make their attack till they actually commenced it upon the last.

'As soon as I saw the direction of their march, I had reinforced the 2nd Battalion 5th Regiment, which occupied the post on the hill over which the road passes to Guinaldo, by the 77th Regiment and the 21st Portuguese Regiment, under the command of Major-General the Hon. C. Colville, and Major-General Alton's brigade, of which only three squadrons remained which had not been detached, drawn from El Bodon; and I ordered there a brigade of the 4th Division from Fuente Guinaldo, and afterwards, from El Bodon, the remainder of the troops of the 3rd Division, with the exception of those at Pastores, which were too distant.

'In the meantime, however, the small body of troops in this post sustained the attack of the enemy's cavalry and artillery. One regiment of French dragoons succeeded in taking two pieces of cannon which had been posted on a rising ground on the right of our troops; but they were charged by the 2nd Battalion 5th Regiment, under the command of Major Ridge, and the guns were immediately retaken.

'While this operation was going on on the flank, an attack was made on the front by another regiment, which was repulsed in a similar manner by the 77th Regiment; and the three squadrons of Major-General Alten's brigade charged repeatedly different bodies of the enemy which ascended the hill on the left of the two regiments of British infantry, the Portuguese regiment being posted in the rear of their right.

'At length, the division of the enemy's infantry, which had marched with the cavalry from Ciudad Rodrigo, were brought up to the attack on the road of Fuente Guinaldo, and seeing that they would arrive and be engaged before the troops could arrive either from Guinaldo or El Bodon, I determined to withdraw our post, and to retire with the whole on Fuente Guinaldo. The 2nd Battalion 5th Regiment and the 77th Regiment were formed into one square, and the 21st Portuguese Regiment into another, supported by Major-General Alten's small body of cavalry and the Portuguese artillery.

'The enemy's cavalry immediately rushed forward, and obliged our cavalry to retire to the support of the Portuguese regiment, and the 5th and 77th Regiments were charged on three faces of the square by the French cavalry; but they halted, and repulsed the attack with the utmost steadiness and gallantry. We then continued the retreat, and joined the remainder of the 3rd Division, also formed in squares, on their march to Fuente Guinaldo; and the whole retired together in the utmost order, and the enemy never made another attempt to charge any of them, but were satisfied with firing upon them with their artillery, and with following them. . . . .

'The enemy brought up a second division of infantry from Ciudad Rodrigo in the afternoon of the 25th; and in the course of that night, and of the 26th, they collected their whole army in front of our position at Guinaldo, and, not deeming it expedient to stand their attack in that position, I retired about three leagues. . . .

'On the 28th, I formed the army on the heights behind Soito, having the Serra de Meras on their right, and the left at Rendo, on the Coa, about a league in rear of the position which they had occupied on the 27th. The enemy also retired from Aldea da Ponte, and had their advanced posts at Albergueria; and as it appears that they are about to retire from this part of the country, and as we have already had some bad weather, and may expect more at the period of the equinoctial gales, I propose to canton the troops in the nearest villages to the position which they occupied yesterday.

'I cannot conclude this report of the occurrences of the last week without expressing to Your Lordship my admiration of the conduct of the troops engaged in the affairs of the 25th instant. The conduct of the 2nd Battalion 5th Regiment, commanded by Major Ridge, in particular, affords a memorable example of what the steadiness and discipline of the troops, and their confidence in their officers, can effect in the most difficult and trying situations. The conduct of the 77th Regiment, under the command of Lieutenant-Colonel Bromhead, was equally good, and I have never seen a more determined attack than was made by the whole of the enemy's cavalry, with every advantage of the assistance of a superior artillery, and repulsed by these two weak battalions. I must not omit also to report the good conduct on the same occasion of the 21st Portuguese Regiment.

'Your Lordship will have observed, by the details of the action which I have given you, how much reason I had to be satisfied with the conduct of the 1st Hussars and the 11th Light Dragoons of Major-General Alten's brigade. There were not more than three squadrons of the two regiments on the ground, this brigade having for some time furnished the cavalry for the outposts of the army, and they charged the enemy's cavalry repeatedly; and notwithstanding the superiority of the latter, the post would have been maintained if I had not preferred to abandon it to risking the loss of these brave men by continuing the unequal contest under additional disadvantages, in consequence of the immediate entry of fourteen battalions of infantry into the action before the support which I had ordered up could arrive.'

Return of the Killed, Wounded, and Missing of the Army under the Command of General Viscount Wellington, K.B., in an affair with the Enemy on the Heights of El Bodon, on the 25th, and near Aldea da Ponte, on September 27, 1811.

	Officers.	Non-commissioned Officers and Drummers.	Rank and File.	Horses.	Total Loss of Officers, Non-commissioned Officers, and Rank and File.
Killed -	1	1	40	40	42
Wounded -	16	13	156	63	185
Missing -	—	1	33	9	34

THE WALCHEREN FEVER.

(This disease, to which Wellington often referred, was contracted in the disastrous expedition against Antwerp in 1809. In fourteen days more than 12,000 soldiers were in hospital on board ship or sent to England, and the malady eventually destroyed thousands of the men who had been sent to the Peninsula and elsewhere.—W.W.)

To the Earl of Liverpool.

'Freneda,
'October 2, 1811.

'I enclose the last morning state.

'Your Lordship will be concerned to observe the number of sick it contains; but I am happy to say that there is no serious disorder, and that that which prevails is principally a return of the Walcheren fever, or a disorder of the same description produced among the newly-arrived troops by previous derangement of their bowels, in consequence of their eating unripe fruit and drinking to excess on their arrival in this country.

'I yesterday saw the 4th Dragoon Guards. Of 470 men, they could produce only 230 mounted, and these looked more like men come out of the hospitals than troops just arrived from England.

'These men have to take care of the horses of the whole regiment, and allowing that one man can take care of three horses, they could not produce in the field for any service at this moment above no men.

'All the newly-arrived regiments of cavalry are in nearly the same state.'

Changes in General Officers.

To Lieutenant-Colonel Torrens.

'Freneda,
'October 30, 1811.

'I am sorry to tell you that Dr. Frank, the Inspector of Hospitals, is so unwell as to be obliged to go home; and the department under him is so important, that if, as I fear, he should not be able to come out again, it will be necessary that we should have the most active and intelligent person that can be found to fill his station.

'I am very unlucky in this respect. Excepting in the Quartermaster-General's department, I have had two, and in some instances three, different persons at the head of every department in the army. Here have been three officers second in command, and General Officers commanding divisions and brigades, and officers, have been changed repeatedly; and there is not one General Officer now with the army who came out with it, excepting Hill, and he was at home for six months last year; and Campbell, and he was at home for the same period the year before last, and is now going again; and General Henry Campbell, who was at home for two years.'

Changes in Uniform.

To Lieutenant-Colonel Torrens.

'Freneda,
'November 6, 1811.

'I hear that measures are in contemplation to alter the clothing, caps, etc., of the army.

'There is no subject of which I understand so little, and, abstractedly speaking, I think it indifferent how a soldier is clothed, provided it is in a uniform manner, and that he is forced to keep himself clean and smart, as a soldier ought to be. But there is one thing I deprecate, and that is any imitation of the French in any manner.

'It is impossible to form an idea of the inconveniences and injury which result from having anything like them either on horseback or on foot. ——— and his piquet were taken in June because the 3rd

Hussars had the same caps as the French *Chasseurs à Cheval* and some of their hussars, and I was near being taken on September 25 from the same cause.

'At a distance or in an action colours are nothing: the profile and shape of the man's cap, and his general appearance, are what guide us; and why should we make our people look like the French? A *cocked-tailed* horse is a good mark for a dragoon, if you can get a side view of him; but there is no such mark as the English helmet, and, as far as I can judge, it is the best cover a dragoon can have for his head.

'I mention this because in all probability you may have something to say to these alterations, and I only beg that we may be as different as possible from the French in everything.

'The narrow top caps of our infantry, as opposed to their broad top caps, are a great advantage to those who are to look at long lines of posts opposed to each other.'

Arroyo Dos Molinos.

To the Earl of Liverpool.

'Freneda,

'November 6, 1811.

'I informed Your Lordship, in my despatches of October 23 and 30, of the orders which I had given to Lieutenant-General Hill to move into Estremadura with the troops under his command, and with his progress to October 26.

'He marched on the 27th by Aldea del Cano to Alcuescar, and, on the 28th, in the morning, surprised the enemy's troops under General Girard at Arroyo Molinos, and dispersed the division of infantry and the cavalry which had been employed under the command of that General, taking General Brun, the Prince d'Aremberg, and above 1,300 prisoners, three pieces of cannon, etc., and having killed many in the action with the enemy and in the subsequent pursuit. General Girard escaped wounded, and, by all the accounts which I have received, General Dombrowski was killed.

'I beg to refer Your Lordship, for the details of Lieutenant-General Hill's operations to October 30, to his despatch to me of that date from Merida, a copy of which I enclose. . . .'

'*Lieutenant-General R. Hill to General Viscount Wellington, K.B.*

'Merida,

'October 30, 1811.

'In pursuance of the instructions which I received from

Your Excellency to drive the enemy out of that part of Estremadura which lies between the Tagus and the Guadiana, and to replace the corps under the command of Brigadier-General the Conde de Penne Villemur in Carceres (from which town it had been obliged to retire by the superior force of the enemy), I put a portion of the troops under my orders in motion on the 22nd instant from their cantonments in the neighbourhood of Portalegre, and advanced with them towards the Spanish frontier . . . .

'Having received certain information that the enemy had marched on Torremocha, I put the troops at Malpartida in motion on the morning of the 27th, and advanced by the road leading to Merida, through Aldea del Cano and Casas de don Antonio, being a shorter route than that followed by the enemy, and which afforded a hope of being able to intercept and bring him to action, and I was here joined by the Spaniards from Caceres. On the march I received information that the enemy had only left Torremocha that morning, and that he had again halted his main body at Arroyo Molinos, leaving a rear guard at Albala, which was a satisfactory proof that he was ignorant of the movements of the troops under my command. I therefore made a forced march to Alcuescar that evening, where the troops were so placed as to be out of sight of the enemy, and no fires were allowed to be made.

'On my arrival at Alcuescar, which is within a league of Arroyo Molinos, everything tended to confirm me in the opinion that the enemy was not only in total ignorance of my near approach, but extremely off his guard, and I determined upon attempting to surprise, or at least to bring him to action.

'The town of Arroyo Molinos is situated at the foot of one extremity of the Sierra de Montanches, the mountain running from it to the rear in the form of a crescent, almost everywhere inaccessible, the two points being about two miles asunder. The Truxillo road runs round that to the eastward.

'The road leading from the town to Merida runs at right angles with that from Alcuescar, and the road to Medellin passes between those to Truxillo and Merida, the grounds over which the troops had to manoeuvre being a plain thinly scattered with oak and cork trees. My object, of course, was to place a body of troops so as to cut off the retreat of the enemy by these roads.

'The troops moved from their bivouac near Alcuescar about two o'clock in the morning of the 28th, in one column, right in front, direct on Arroyo Molinos. . . .

'As the day dawned a violent storm of rain and thick mist came on, under cover of which the columns advanced in the direction and in the order which had been pointed out to them. The left column, under Lieutenant-Colonel Stewart, marched direct upon the town, the 71st, one company of the 60th, and 92nd Regiments, at quarter distance, and the 50th in close column, somewhat in the rear with the guns as a reserve. . . .

'The advance of our column was unperceived by the enemy until they approached very near, at which moment he was filing out of the town upon the Merida road, the rear of his column, some of his cavalry, and part of his baggage being still in it. One brigade of his infantry had marched for Medellin an hour before daylight.

'The 71st and 92nd Regiments charged into the town with cheers, and drove the enemy everywhere at the point of the bayonet, having a few men cut down by the enemy's cavalry.

'The enemy's infantry, which had got out of the town, had, by the time these regiments arrived at the extremity of it, formed into two squares, with the cavalry on their left; the whole were posted between the Merida and Medellin roads, fronting Alcuescar, the right square being formed within half musket-shot of the town, the garden walls of which were promptly lined by the 71st Light Infantry, while the 92nd Regiment filed out and formed line on their right, perpendicular to the enemy's right flank, which was much annoyed by the well-directed fire of the 71st. In the meantime, one wing of the 50th Regiment occupied the town and secured the prisoners, and the other wing, along with the three 6-pounders, skirted the outside of it, the artillery as soon as within range firing with great effect upon the squares.

'Whilst the enemy was thus occupied on his right, Major-General Howard's column continued moving round his left, and our cavalry, advancing and crossing the head of the column, cut off the enemy's cavalry from his infantry, charging it repeatedly and putting it to the rout. The 13th Light Dragoons at the same time took possession of the enemy's artillery; one of the charges made by two squadrons of the 2nd Hussars and one of the 9th Light Dragoons was particularly gallant, the latter commanded by Captain Gore and the whole under Major Busche, of the Hussars.

'I ought previously to have mentioned that the British cavalry having, through the darkness of the night and the badness of the roads, been somewhat delayed, the Spanish cavalry under the Conde de Penne Villemur was on this occasion the first to form upon the plain and engage the enemy until the British was enabled to come up.

'The enemy was now in full retreat, but Major-General Howard's column, having gained the point to which it was directed, and the left column gaining fast upon him, he had no resource but to surrender, or to disperse and ascend the mountain. He preferred the latter, and ascending near the eastern extremity of the crescent, and which might have been deemed inaccessible, was followed closely by the 28th and 34th Regiments, whilst the 39th Regiment and Colonel Ashworth's brigade of Portuguese infantry followed round the foot of the mountain by the Truxillo road to take him again in flank.

★★★★★★★★★★

The 34th, now the 1st Battalion the Border Regiment, is the only regiment in the British Army bearing the honour of 'Arroyo dos Molinos.' The 34th cut off and captured the French 34th Regiment of the Line, and made prisoners of a large number of officers. For a long time the 34th used the brass drum, and drum-major's staff which they took in the action. When 'Arroyo dos Molinos 'was granted, it was a unique honour, only general actions having been previously inscribed on colours and appointments.—W. W.

★★★★★★★★★★

'At the same time Brigadier-General Morillo's infantry ascended at some distance to the left with the same view.

'As may be imagined, the enemy's troops were by this time in the utmost panic; his cavalry was flying in every direction, the infantry threw away their arms, and the only effort of either was to escape. The troops under Major-General Howard's immediate command, as well as those he had sent round the point of the mountain, pursued them over the rocks, making prisoners at every step, until his own men became so exhausted and few in number that it was necessary for him to halt and secure the prisoners, and leave the further pursuit to the Spanish infantry.

'The ultimate consequences of these operations I need not point out to Your Lordship; their immediate result is the capture of one General of Cavalry (Brun), one Colonel of Cavalry (the Prince d'Aremberg), one Lieutenant-Colonel (*Chef d'État Major*), one *aide-de-camp* of General Girard, two lieutenant-colonels, one *Commissaire de Guerre,* thirty captains and inferior officers, and upwards of 1,000 men, already sent off under an escort to Portalegre; the whole of the enemy's artillery, baggage, and commissariat, some magazines of corn which he had collected at Caceres and Merida, and the contribution of money which he had collected on the former town, besides the total dispersion of General Girard's corps. The loss of the enemy in killed must also have been severe, while that on our side was comparatively trifling. . . . .

'Thus, has ended an expedition which, although not bringing into play to the full extent the gallantry and spirit of those engaged, will, I trust, give them a claim to Your Lordship's approbation. No praise of mine can do justice to their admirable conduct, the patience and goodwill shown by all ranks during forced marches in the worst weather, their strict attention to the orders they received, the precision with which they moved to the attack, and their obedience to command during the action. . . .'

Shameful Treatment of British Prisoners.

To Lieutenant-General Hill.

'Freneda,

'November 8, 1811, 10 p.m.

'I beg you to inform the Comte d'Erlon that I have received with the greatest concern the accounts which have reached me of the ill-treatment of the prisoners of the Allied British and Portuguese Army taken by the French Army of the South. He who has served in the French Army of Portugal knows how I have treated the French officers and soldiers who have fallen into my hands, and how many of them I have saved; indeed, nobody ought to know this better than Marshal Soult, yet I am sorry to say that the officers and soldiers who have been taken by the Army of the South have been treated most shamefully.'

A Garbled Version.

To Major-General Alexander Campbell.

'Freneda,
'November 13, 1811.

'I see that Colonel —— has published his letter in answer to mine on the affair of the Barba de Puerco, I imagine garbled in the usual Jacobin style, and preceded by a statement the meaning of which is (as far as I can understand it) to insinuate that I, or my friends, have published my letter. I write in hopes that this will catch you at Lisbon, to intreat you on no account to be drawn into a war in the newspapers with this fellow.'

The Enmity of Marshals.

To the Earl of Liverpool.

'Freneda,
'November 13, 1811.

'I enclose a very curious intercepted letter, which was in cipher, from Marmont to Foy, which shows how these gentry are going on; in fact, each marshal is the natural enemy of the king and of his neighbouring marshal. Pray take care that this letter is not made public, as it would disclose that we have the key of the cipher. . . .'

Return of Killed, Wounded, and Missing of the Corps of the Army under the Command of General Viscount Wellington, K.B., under the Immediate Orders of Lieutenant-General R. Hill, in the action with the French Army near Arroyo Molinos, on October 28, 1811.

	Officers.	Non-commissioned Officers and Drummers.	Rank and File.	Horses.	Total Loss of Officers, Non-commissioned Officers, and Rank and File.
Killed - -	—	—	7	6	7
Wounded -	7	4	53	11	64
Missing -	1	—	—	4	1

The Portuguese loss, but not the Spanish, is included in this return.

An Affectionate Letter.

To Major-General Alexander Campbell.

'Freneda,
'November 22, 1811.

'I was very much obliged to you for the kindness of the letter which you wrote to me on your departure from this part of the world, and I assure you that I lament the chance which certainly exists that I may never meet you again. I acknowledge that, with this chance before your eyes, I am astonished that you should think, at your time of life, of returning to the East Indies. With the income of your regiment, and on the staff in England or Ireland, or at Gibraltar, or Malta, or Sicily, or in America, you might live with your family. I do not think that any man's family have a right to expect that he should die a few years sooner to put a little more money in their pockets after his death; and I should think that your wife, who, in a pecuniary way, would be the person most interested in your return to the East Indies, would prefer your prolonged life to increase of pounds.

'God bless you, my dear Campbell.'

Dubious Officers.

To Lieutenant-Colonel Torrens.

'Freneda,
'Decembers, 1811.

'I am obliged to you for attending to our wants of general officers. —— did not succeed very well when he was here before, but I dare say he will do so now. I have a high opinion of General Kempt from all that I have heard of him. We have now more than we can well dispose of, particularly if Beckwith comes out again, and there are two with whom we could dispense with advantage, —— and ——. They are both respectable officers as commanders of regiments, but they are neither of them very fit to take charge of a large body. I understand that —— wishes to return home to unite himself with a lady of *easy virtue,* and —— has been very ill lately, and I think might be induced to go. I shall try if I can get them away in this manner, as I would not on any account hurt the feelings of either.'

Retaliation.

To Lieutenant-Colonel Sir Howard Douglas, Bart.

'Freneda,
'December 7, 1811.

'. . . Before the allies are called upon to protect the guerrillas by retaliating upon the enemy the injuries, they do to those who are prisoners, it is proper that the Spanish Government and the regular Spanish Armies should protect them and that the several guerrilla parties should protect each other.

'We have frequently heard of declarations that injuries should be retaliated, and but few instances of those declarations being carried into execution, notwithstanding that the French murder the Spanish prisoners every day. When the Spanish Government and armies shall take up this subject as they ought, it will rest with the British Government (not me) to determine whether they will enter into this system of retaliation in favour of the Spaniards. . . .'

The Tyranny of Buonaparte.

To Lieutenant-General Lord William Bentinck.

'Freneda,
'December 24, 1811.

'. . . I have long considered it probable that even we should witness a general resistance throughout Europe to the fraudulent and disgusting tyranny of Buonaparte, created by the example of what has passed in Spain and Portugal; and that we should be actors and advisers in these scenes, and I have reflected frequently upon the measures which should be pursued to give a chance of success.

'Those who embark in projects of this description should be made to understand, or to act as if they understood, that having once drawn the sword they must not return it till they shall have completely accomplished their object. They must be prepared and must be forced to make all sacrifices to the cause. Submission to military discipline and order is a matter of course; but when a nation determines to resist the authority, and to shake off the Government of Buonaparte, they must be prepared and forced to sacrifice the luxuries and comforts of life, and to risk all in a contest which, it should be clearly understood before it is undertaken, has for its object to save all or nothing. . . .'

A Year's Casualties.

To Dr. Frank.

'Gallegos,
'January 7, 1812.

'I am very much obliged to you for your account of my little boy, and for your kindness in going to see him. I trust that your own health is re-established.

'You will be glad to hear that the health of the troops is much improved, though not yet what I could wish it to be. We lost a great many men upon the change from warm to cold weather; but the whole of our casualties in this year, including some bloody affairs, amounts only to 6,000 men.'

Storm of Ciudad Rodrigo.

To the Earl of Liverpool.

'Gallegos,
'January 9, 1812.

'According to the intention which I informed Your Lordship that I entertained, I invested Ciudad Rodrigo yesterday.

'Since the enemy have had possession of the place, they have constructed a palisaded redoubt on the hill of San Francisco, and have fortified three convents in the suburbs, the defences of which are connected with the work on the hill of San Francisco, and with the old line by which the suburb was surrounded. By these means the enemy have increased the difficulty of approaching the place; and it was necessary to obtain possession of the work on the hill of San Francisco before we could make any progress in the attack. Accordingly, Major-General Craufurd directed a detachment of the Light Division, under the command of Lieutenant-Colonel Colborne of the 52nd, to attack the work, shortly after it was dark. The attack was very ably conducted by Lieutenant-Colonel Colborne, and the work was taken by storm in a short time. Two captains and forty-seven men were made prisoners, the remainder of the garrison being put to the sword in the storm. We took three pieces of cannon.

'I cannot sufficiently applaud the conduct of Lieutenant-Colonel Colborne, and of the detachment under his command, upon this occasion. I am happy to add that our loss in this affair has not been severe. . . .'

To the Earl of Liverpool.

'Gallegos,
'January 20, 1812.

'I informed Your Lordship in my despatch of the 9th that I had attacked Ciudad Rodrigo, and in that of the 15th of the progress of the operations to that period, and I have now the pleasure to acquaint Your Lordship that we took the place by storm yesterday evening after dark.

'We continued, from the 15th to the 19th, to complete the second parallel, and the communications with that work, and we had made some progress by sap towards the crest of the glacis. On the night of the 15th, we likewise advanced, from the left of the first parallel down the slope of the hill towards the Convent of San Francisco, to a situation from which the walls of the *fausse braie* and of the town were

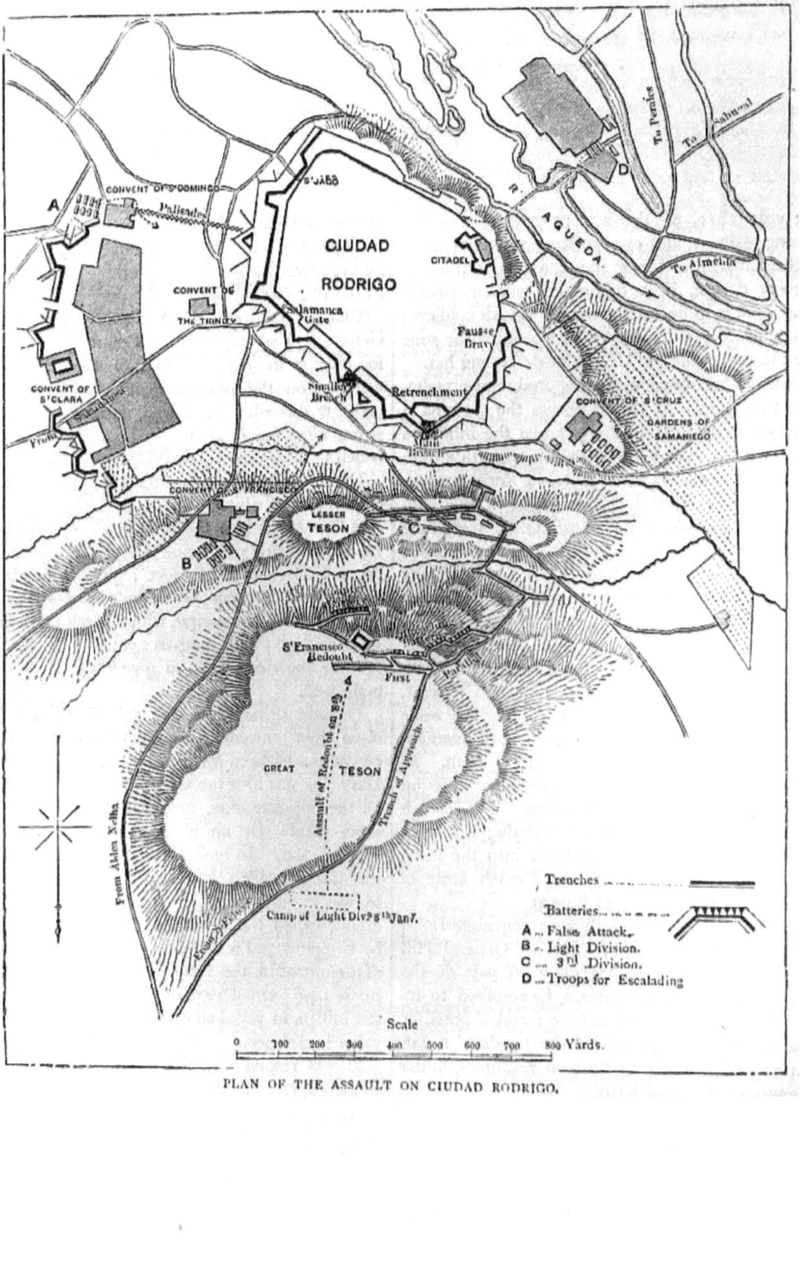

PLAN OF THE ASSAULT ON CIUDAD RODRIGO.

seen, on which a battery for seven guns was constructed, and these commenced their fire on the morning of the 18th.

'In the meantime the batteries in the first parallel continued their fire; and yesterday evening their fire had not only considerably injured the defences of the place, but had made breaches in the *fausse braie* wall, and in the body of the place, which were considered practicable; while the battery on the slope of the hill, which had been commenced on the night of the 15th, and had opened on the 18th, had been equally efficient still farther to the left, and opposite to the suburb of San Francisco.

'I therefore determined to storm the place, notwithstanding that the approaches had not been brought to the crest of the glacis, and the counterscarp of the ditch was still entire. The attack was accordingly made yesterday evening, in five separate columns, consisting of the troops of the 3rd and Light Divisions, and of Brigadier-General Pack's brigade. The two right columns, conducted by Lieutenant-Colonel O'Toole of the 2nd Caçadores, and Major Ridge of the 5th Regiment, were destined to protect the advance of Major-General Mackinnon's brigade, forming the 3rd, to the top of the breach in the *fausse braie* wall; and all these, being composed of troops of the 3rd Division, were under the direction of Lieutenant-General Picton.

'The fourth column, consisting of the 43rd and 52nd Regiments, and part of the 95th Regiment, being of the Light Division, under the direction of Major-General Craufurd, attacked the breaches on the left in front of the suburb of San Francisco, and covered the left of the attack of the principal breach by the troops of the 3rd Division; and Brigadier-General Pack was destined, with his brigade, forming the fifth column, to make a false attack upon the southern face of the fort.

'Besides these five columns, the 94th Regiment, belonging to the 3rd Division, descended into the ditch in two columns, on the right of Major-General Mackinnon's brigade, with a view to protect the descent of that body into the ditch and its attack of the breach in the *fausse braie*, against the obstacles which it was supposed the enemy would construct to oppose their progress.

'All these attacks succeeded, and Brigadier-General Pack even surpassed my expectations, having converted his false attack into a real one; and his advanced-guard, under the command of Major Lynch, having followed the enemy's troops from the advanced works into the *fausse braie,* where they made prisoners, all opposed to them.

'Major Ridge, of the 2nd Battalion 5th Regiment, having escaladed the *fausse braie* wall, stormed the principal breach in the body of the place, together with the 94th Regiment, commanded by Lieutenant-Colonel Campbell, which had moved along the ditch at the same time, and had stormed the breach in the *fausse braie*, both in front of Major-General Mackinnon's brigade. Thus, these regiments not only effectually covered the advance from the trenches of Major-General Mackinnon's brigade by their first movements and operations, but they preceded them in the attack.

'Major-General Craufurd, and Major-General Vandeleur, and the troops of the Light Division, on the left, were likewise very forward on that side; and in less than half an hour from the time the attack commenced our troops were in possession, and formed on the ramparts of the place, each body contiguous to the other. The enemy then submitted, having sustained a considerable loss in the contest.

'Our loss was also, I am concerned to add, severe, particularly in officers of high rank and estimation in this army. Major-General Mackinnon was unfortunately blown up by the accidental explosion of one of the enemy's expense magazines close to the breach, after he had gallantly and successfully led the troops under his command to the attack. Major-General Craufurd likewise received a severe wound while he was leading on the Light Division to the storm, and I am apprehensive that I shall be deprived for some time of his assistance. . . .

'I have already reported, in my letter of the 9th instant, my sense of the conduct of Major-General Craufurd, and of Lieutenant-Colonel Colborne, and of the troops of the Light Division, in the storm of the redoubt of San Francisco, on the evening of the 8th instant. The conduct of these troops was equally distinguished, throughout the siege; and, in the storm, nothing could exceed the gallantry with which these brave officers and troops advanced and accomplished the difficult operation allotted to them, notwithstanding that all their leaders had fallen. . . .

'The conduct of Captain Duffy, of the 43rd, and that of Lieutenant Gurwood, of the 52nd Regiment, who was wounded, have likewise been particularly reported to me.

'I shall hereafter transmit to Your Lordship a detailed account of what we have found in the place; but I believe that there are 153 pieces of ordnance, including the heavy train belonging to the French Army, and great quantities of ammunition and stores. We have the Governor, General Barrié, about 78 officers, and 1,700 men prisoners. . . .'

****

Lieutenant-Colonel Gurwood, the compiler of this work. Lieutenant Gurwood, 52nd Regiment, led the 'forlorn hope' of the Light Division in the assault of the lesser breach. He afterwards took the French Governor, General Barrié, in the citadel, and, from the hands of Lord Wellington, on the breach by which he had entered, he received the sword of his prisoner. The permission accorded by the Duke of Wellington to compile this work has doubtless been one of the distinguished consequences resulting from this service, and Lieutenant-Colonel Gurwood feels pride, as a soldier of fortune, in here offering himself as an encouraging example to the subaltern in future wars

****

Return of Killed, Wounded, and Missing of the Army under the Command of General Viscount Wellington, K.B., during the Siege and in the Assault of Ciudad Rodrigo, from January 8 to 19, 1812.

	Officers.	Non-commissioned Officers and Drummers.	Rank and File.	Horses.	Total Loss of Officers, Non-commissioned Officers, and Rank and File.
Killed - -	9	11	158	—	178
Wounded -	70	35	713	—	818
Missing -	—	—	7	—	7

To the Earl of Liverpool.

'Gallegos,

'January 20, 1812.

'You will receive with this the account of the successful termination of our operation, in half the time that I told you it would take, and less than half that which the French spent in taking the same place from the Spaniards, as you will see by referring to the despatches of that period. . . .'

Death of General Craufurd.

To the Earl of Liverpool.

'Gallegos,

'January 29, 1812.

'Major-General Craufurd died on the 24th instant, of the wounds which he received on the 19th, while leading the Light Division of this army to the assault of Ciudad Rodrigo. . . .'

(He was buried at the foot of the little breach. The Commander of the Forces and all the officers of the besieging army attended the funeral, which, from place and circumstances, was more than usually impressive.)

A New Principle in Sieges.

To the Duke of Richmond.

'Gallegos,
'January 29, 1812.

'. . . We proceeded at Ciudad Rodrigo on quite a new principle in sieges. The whole object of our fire was to lay open the walls. We had not one mortar, nor a howitzer, excepting to prevent the enemy from clearing the breaches, and for that purpose we had only two; and we fired upon the flanks and defences only when we wished to get the better of them, with a view to protect those who were to storm. This shows the kind of place we had to attack, and how important it is to cover the works of a place well by a glacis. The French, however, who are supposed to know everything, could not take this place in less than forty days after it was completely invested, or than twenty-five days after breaking ground . . .'

Superiority of French Tools.

To the Earl of Liverpool.

'Freneda,
'February 11, 1812.

'. . . The cutting tools which we have found in Ciudad Rodrigo belonging to the French Army are infinitely better than ours. Is it not shameful that they should have better cutlery than we have?'

Poor Artillery Practice.

To Lieutenant-General Graham.

'Freneda,
'February 18, 1812, 9 a.m.

'. . . Some of our concerns to the south are going on well. I am not quite so certain of others. Those to whom I was obliged to have recourse to get the ordnance I wanted seem to be of opinion that there is no more occasion for precision in the fire of artillery in a siege than there is in an action at sea! . . .'

Spanish Selfishness.

To the Right Hon. Henry Wellesley.

'Freneda,
'February 19, 1812.

'Extravagant as we are, there is no officer with us who draws more than one ration, the same as a soldier. He besides draws a ration for every servant not a soldier. Just observe that, for 123 artillerymen and 22 pioneers, making 145 troops, and some of the staff of the garrison, the Spaniards draw 269 rations, each officer drawing three, five, six, seven, and as far as sixteen rations.'

SHRAPNEL'S SHELLS.

To the Earl of Liverpool.

'Elvas,
'March 12, 1812.

'. . . I have spoken to Sir William Beresford, and shall speak to General Graham, respecting Shrapnel's shells. I have seen our artillery produce great effect on the enemy, and I have been induced to attribute this effect to the use of Shrapnel's shells. But my opinion in favour of these shells has been much shaken lately. First, I have reason to believe that their effect is confined to wounds of a very trifling description, and they kill nobody.

'I saw General Simon, who was wounded by the balls from shrapnel's shells, of which he had several in his face and head; but they were picked out of his face as duck-shot would be out of the face of a person who had been hit by accident while out shooting, and he was not much more materially injured.

'Secondly, from the difficulty of judging of direct distances and in knowing whether the shell has burst in the air in the proper place, I suspect that an original error in throwing the shells is seldom corrected; and that if the shell is not effectual the first shot, the continuance of the fire of these shells seldom becomes more effectual.

'I can entertain no doubt, however, that if the shell should be accurately thrown, and burst as it is intended, it must wound a great number of men, but probably none very materially.'

STORM OF BADAJOZ.

Memorandum for the Attack of Badajoz.

'Camp,
'April 6, 1812.

'1. The Fort of Badajoz is to be attacked at ten o'clock this night.

'2. The attack must be made on three points: the castle, the face of the bastion of La Trinidad, and the flank of the bastion of Sta. Maria.

'3. The attack of the castle to be by escalade; that of the two bastions by the storm of the breaches. . .'

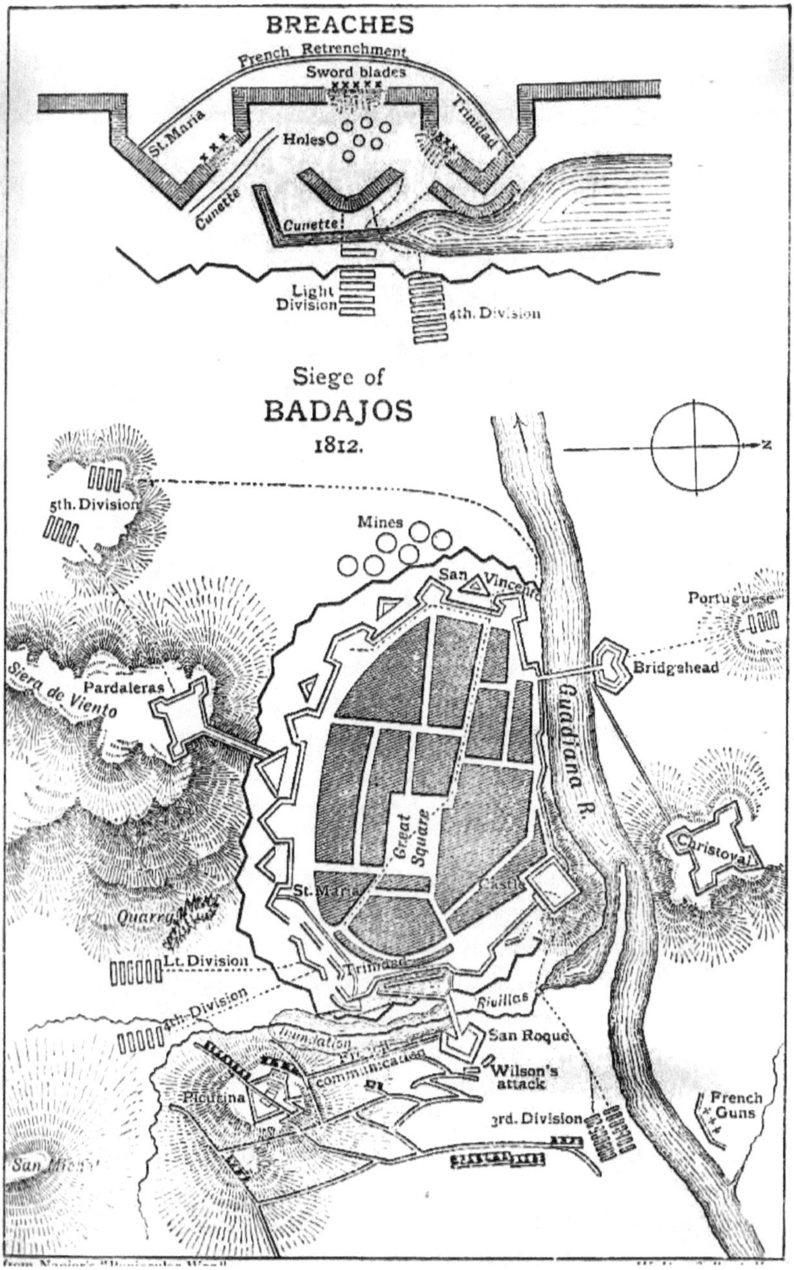
BREACHES
French Retrenchment
Sword blades
St. Maria
Trinidad
Holes
Cunette
Cunette
Light Division
4th. Division
Siege of
BADAJOS
1812.
N
5th. Division
Mines
San Vincente
Portuguese
Bridgehead
Pardaleras
Siera de Viento
Guadiana R.
Great Square
Christoval
St. Maria
Castle
Quarry
Lt. Division
Trinidad
4th. Division
Rivillas
San Roque
Inundation
communication
Wilson's attack
Picurina
3rd. Division
French Guns

To the Earl of Liverpool.

'Camp before Badajoz,
'April 7, 1812.

'My despatch of the 3rd instant will have apprised Your Lordship of the state of the operations against Badajoz to that date, which were brought to a close on the night of the 6th by the capture of the place by storm.

'The fire continued during the 4th and 5th against the face of the bastion of La Trinidad, and the flank of the bastion of Sta. Maria, and on the 4th, in the morning, we opened another battery of six guns in the second parallel against the shoulder of the ravelin of San Roque, and the wall in its gorge.

'Practicable breaches were effected in the bastions above mentioned on the evening of the 5th, but as I had observed that the enemy had entrenched the bastion of La Trinidad, and the most formidable preparations were making for the defence as well of the breach in that bastion, as of that in the bastion of Sta. Maria, I determined to delay the attack for another day, and to turn all the guns in the batteries in the second parallel on the curtain of La Trinidad, in hopes that by effecting a third breach the troops would be enabled to turn the enemy's works for the defence of the other two, the attack of which would besides be connected by the troops destined to attack the breach in the curtain.

'This breach was effected in the evening of the 6th, and the fire of the face of the bastion of Sta. Maria, and of the flank of the bastion of La Trinidad, being overcome, I determined to attack the place that night.

'I had kept in reserve in the neighbourhood of this camp the 5th Division, under Lieutenant-General Leith, which had left Castille only in the middle of March, and had but lately arrived in this part of the country, and I brought them up on that evening. The plan for the attack was that Lieutenant-General Picton should attack the Castle of Badajoz by escalade with the 3rd Division, and a detachment from the guard in the trenches, furnished that evening by the 4th Division, under Major Wilson, of the 48th Regiment, should attack the ravelin of San Roque upon his left; while the 4th Division, under Major-General the Hon. C, Colville, and the Light Division, under Lieutenant-Colonel Barnard, should attack the breaches in the bastions of La Trinidad and Sta. Maria, and in the curtain by which they are connected.

'The 5th Division were to occupy the ground which the 4th and Light Divisions had occupied during the siege, and Lieutenant-General Leith was to make a false attack upon the outwork called the Pardaleras, and another on the works of the fort towards the Guadiana, with the left brigade of the division, under Major-General Walker, which he was to turn into a real attack if circumstances should prove favourable; and Brigadier General Power, who invested the place with his Portuguese brigade on the right of the Guadiana, was directed to make false attacks on the *tête-de-pont*, the Fort San Christoval, and the new redoubt called Mon Coeur.

'The attack was accordingly made at ten at night, Lieutenant-General Picton preceding by a few minutes the attacks by the remainder of the troops. Major-General Kempt led this attack, which went out from the right of the first parallel. He was unfortunately wounded in crossing the River Rivillas below the inundation, but notwithstanding this circumstance, and the obstinate resistance of the enemy, the castle was carried by escalade, and the 3rd Division established in it at about half-past eleven.

'While this was going on, Major Wilson, of the 48th, carried the ravelin of San Roque by the gorge, with a detachment of 200 men of the guard in the trenches, and with the assistance of Major Squire, of the Engineers, established himself within that work.

'The 4th and Light Divisions moved to the attack from the camp along the left of the River Rivillas, and of the inundation. They were not perceived by the enemy till they reached the covered-way; and the advanced guards of the two divisions descended without difficulty into the ditch, protected by the fire of the parties stationed on the glacis for that purpose; and they advanced to the assault of the breaches, led by their gallant officers, with the utmost intrepidity. But such was the nature of the obstacles prepared by the enemy at the top and behind the breaches, and so determined their resistance, that our troops could not establish themselves within the place.

'Many brave officers and soldiers were killed or wounded by explosions at the top of the breaches; others who succeeded to them were obliged to give way, having found it impossible to penetrate the obstacles which the enemy had prepared to impede their progress. These attempts were repeated till after twelve at night, when, finding that success was not to be attained, and that Lieutenant-General Picton was established in the castle, I ordered that the 4th and Light Divisions might retire to the ground on which they had been first assembled for the attack.

'In the meantime, Lieutenant-General Leith had pushed forward Major-General Walker's brigade on the left, supported by the 38th Regiment, under Lieutenant-Colonel Nugent, and the 15th Portuguese Regiment, under Colonel 'Do Rego, and he had made a false attack upon the Pardaleras with the 8th Caçadores, under Major Hill. Major-General Walker forced the barrier on the road of Olivença, and entered the covered-way on the left of the bastion of San Vicente, close to the Guadiana. He there descended into the ditch, and escaladed the face of the bastion of San Vicente. Lieutenant-General Leith supported this attack by the 38th Regiment and 15th Portuguese Regiment; and our troops being thus established in the castle, which commands all the works of the town, and in the town, and the 4th and Light Divisions being formed again for the attack of the breaches, all resistance ceased; and at daylight in the morning the Governor, General Philippon, who had retired to Fort San Christoval, surrendered, together with General Vielande, and all the staff, and the whole garrison.

'I have not got accurate returns of the strength of the garrison, or of the number of prisoners; but General Philippon has informed me that it consisted of 5,000 men at the commencement of the siege, of which 1,200 were killed or wounded during the operations, besides those lost in the assault of the place. There were five French battalions, besides two of the regiment of Hesse Darmstadt, and the artillery, engineers, etc., and I understand there are 4,000 prisoners.

'It is impossible that any expressions of mine can convey to Your Lordship the sense which I entertain of the gallantry of the officers and troops upon this occasion. The list of killed and wounded will show that the General Officers, the staff attached to them, the commanding and other officers of the regiments, put themselves at the head of the attacks which they severally directed, and set the example of gallantry which was so well followed by their men . . . .

'The officers and men of the corps of engineers and artillery were equally distinguished during the operations of the siege and in its close. . . . .

'It would be very desirable that I should have it in my power to strike a blow against Marshal Soult before he could be reinforced; but the Spanish authorities having omitted to take the necessary steps to provision Ciudad Rodrigo, it is absolutely necessary that I should return to the frontiers of Castille within a short period of time. It is not very probable that Marshal Soult will risk an action in the province of Estremadura, which it would not be difficult for him to avoid, and it is very necessary that he should return to Andalusia, as General Ballesteros was in movement upon Seville on the 29th of last month, and the Conde de Penne Villemur moving on the same place from the Lower Guadiana.

'It will be quite impossible for me to go into Andalusia till I shall have secured Ciudad Rodrigo. I therefore propose to remain in the positions now occupied by the troops for some days; indeed, a little time is required to take care of our wounded; and if Marshal Soult should remain in Estremadura, I shall attack him; if he should retire into Andalusia, I must return to Castille.

'I have the honour to enclose returns of the killed and wounded from March 31, and in the assault of Badajoz, and a return of the ordnance, small arms, and ammunition found in the place. I shall send the returns of provisions in the place by the next despatch. This despatch will be delivered to Your Lordship by my *aide-de-camp*, Captain Canning, whom I beg leave to recommend to your protection.

'He has likewise the colours of the garrison, and the colours of the Hesse Darmstadt's regiment, to be laid at the feet of His Royal Highness the Prince Regent. The French battalions in the garrison had no eagles.'

Return of the Killed, Wounded, and Missing of the Army under the Command of General the Earl of Wellington, K.B., at the Siege and Capture of Badajoz, from March 18 to April 7, 1812, inclusive.

	Officers.	Sergeants.	Rank and File.	Horses.	Total Loss of Officers, Non-commissioned Officers, and Rank and File.
Killed -	72	51	912	—	1,035
Wounded -	306	216	3,265	—	3,787
Missing -	—	1	62	—	63

The Portuguese loss is included in the above numbers.

Ill Equipped for Sieges.

To Colonel Torrens.

'Camp at Badajoz,
'April y, 1812.

'. . . Our loss has been very great; but I send you a letter to Lord Liverpool which accounts for it. The truth is that, equipped as we are, the British Army are not capable of carrying on a regular siege.

To Major-General George Murray.

'Fuente Guinaldo,
'May 28, 1812.

'. . . . You will have appreciated the difficulty and importance of our late operations. The siege of Badajoz was a most serious undertaking, and the weather did not favour us. The troops were up to their middles in mud in the trenches, and in the midst of our difficulties the Guadiana swelled and carried away our bridge, and rendered useless for a time our flying bridge. However, we never stopped, and a fair day or two set all to rights. The assault was a terrible business, of which I foresaw the loss when I was ordering it. But we had brought matters to that state that we could do no more, and it was necessary to storm or raise the siege. I trust, however, that future armies will be equipped for sieges, with the people necessary to carry them on as they ought to be; and that our engineers will learn how to put their batteries on the crest of the glacis, and to blow in the counterscarp, instead of placing them wherever the wall can be seen, leaving the poor officers and troops to get into and cross the ditch as they can. . .'

A Brilliant Exploit.

To the Earl of Liverpool.

'Fuente Guinaldo,
'May 28, 1812,

'When I found that the enemy had retired from this frontier on April 24, and that I was enabled to make a disposition of the army, to give me the command of the means of transport attached to the troops, and to enable me to throw provisions into the fortresses of Ciudad Rodrigo and Almeida, and to move up the magazines of the army, with a view to the further operations of the campaign, I directed Lieutenant-General Sir Rowland Hill to carry into execution the operations against the posts and establishments of the enemy at the passage of the Tagus, at Almaraz, which I had in contemplation before the siege of Badajoz, and which I had then delayed for reasons into which it is not now necessary to enter.

'Owing to the necessary preparations for this expedition, and to the unexpected delays of the repairs of the bridge over the Guadiana at Merida, which I had destroyed during the siege of Badajoz, Lieutenant-General Sir R. Hill could not begin his operation with part of the 2nd Division till the 12th instant; and he attained the object of his expedition on the 19th instant, by taking by storm Forts Napoleon and Ragusa, and the *têtes-de-pont*, and other works by which the enemy's bridge was guarded, by destroying those forts and works, and the enemy's bridge and establishments, and by taking their magazines, and about 259 prisoners, and 18 pieces of cannon.

'I have the honour to enclose Sir R. Hill's report of this brilliant exploit; and I beg to draw Your Lordship's attention to the difficulties with which he had to contend, as well from the nature of the country as from the works which the enemy had constructed, and to the ability and characteristic qualities displayed by Lieutenant-General Sir R. Hill, in persevering in the line, and confining himself to the objects chalked out by his instructions, notwithstanding the various obstacles opposed to his progress. . . . .'

Return of the Killed, Wounded, and Missing of the Army under the Command of His Excellency General the Earl of Wellington, K.B., under the Immediate Orders of Lieutenant-General Sir R. Hill, K.B., at the Storm and Capture of Fort Napoleon, and the Enemy's, other Works in the Neighbourhood of Almaraz, on the morning of May 19, 1812.

	Officers.	Sergeants.	Rank and File.	Horses.	Total Loss of Officers, Non-commissioned Officers, and Rank and File.
Killed - -	2	1	30	—	33
Wounded - -	13	10	121	—	144
Missing - -	—	—	—	—	—

Spanish Volunteers for British Regiments.

To the General Officers commanding Divisions.

'Fuente Guinaldo,
'May 18, 1812.

'The Spanish Government having been pleased to allow a limited number of the natives of Spain to serve His Majesty in the British regiments composing this army, I have to request that you will authorise the regiments named in the margin to enlist and bear on their strength 100 Spanish volunteers. . . . .'

Form of the Attestation.

'I, A. B., do make oath that I will serve His Majesty the King of Great Britain and Ireland in the — Battalion of the — Regiment of Foot, during the existing war in the Peninsula, if His

Majesty should so long require my services, and provided that the — Battalion of the — Regiment of Foot shall continue in the Peninsula during that period. . . .'

'In communicating this arrangement to the several regiments, I request you to point out to the commanding officers of regiments how desirable it is that these volunteers should be treated with the utmost kindness and indulgence, and brought by degrees to the system of discipline of the army.'

Unfit for Service.

To Major-General Peacock.

'Fuente Guinaldo,
'May 19, 1812.

'I enclose a letter which has been put into my hands by the Inspector-General of Hospitals, and I beg that, according to the recommendation which it contains, the —th Regiment may be removed to the seaside as soon as possible.

'I beg that you will inform the commanding and other officers of the —th Regiment that they have been sent, and are detained at Lisbon, because their regiment is *unfit for service*—a circumstance not very creditable to any regiment, and that I trust that by their attention to the discipline as well as the health and necessary comfort of the soldiers, by their obedience to orders, and by their endeavours to establish in the regiment a system of order and subordination, they will render their regiment fit to belong to this army.'

No Second in Command desired.

To the Earl of Liverpool.

'Fuente Guinaldo,
'June 3, 1812.

'. . . There are few officers who understand the situation of the officer second in command of these armies. Unless he should be posted to command a division of cavalry or infantry, and perform that duty, he has really, on ordinary occasions, nothing to do, and at the same time that his opinion relieves me but little from responsibility, and that after all I must act according to my own judgment in case of a difference of opinion; there are but few officers who should be sent from England as second in command who would not come here with opinions formed, probably on very bad grounds, and with very extravagant pretensions. To this add that, when necessary to detach a body of troops in any situation, but few would be satisfied to remain with the detachment, unless indeed it should consist of nearly the whole army. . . .'

To Earl Bathurst.

'Freneda,
'January 26, 1813.

'In my opinion the office of second in command of an army in these days, in which the use of councils of war has been discontinued, and the chief in command is held severely responsible for everything that passes, is not only useless, but injurious to the service. A person; without defined duties, excepting to give flying opinions from which he may depart at pleasure, must be a nuisance in moments of decision; and whether I have a second in command or not,

I am determined always to act according to the dictates of my own judgment, being quite certain that I shall be responsible for the act, be the person who he may, according to whose opinion it has been adopted.'

CONTINUED OUTRAGES.

To the Earl of Liverpool.

'Fuente Guinaldo,
'June 10, 1812.

'The outrages committed by the British soldiers belonging to this army have become so enormous, and they have produced an effect upon the minds of the people of the country so injurious to the cause, and likely to be so dangerous to the army itself, that I request Your Lordship's early attention to the subject.

'I am sensible that the best measures to be adopted on this subject are those of prevention, and I believe there are few officers who have paid more attention to the subject in this view of it than I have done; and I have been so far successful, that few outrages are committed by the soldiers who are with their regiments, after the regiments have been a short time in this country.

'But in the extended system on which we are acting, small detachments of soldiers must be marched long distances through the country, either as escorts or returning from being escorts to prisoners, or coming from hospitals, etc.; and notwithstanding that none of these detachments are ever allowed to march excepting under the command of an officer, or more, in proportion to its size, and that every precaution is taken to provide for the regularity of their subsistence, there is no instance of the march of one of these detachments that outrages of every description are not committed, and, I am sorry to say, with impunity.

'The foundation of every system of discipline which has for its object the prevention of crimes must be the non-commissioned officers of the army. But I am sorry to say that, notwithstanding the encouragement which I have given to this class, they are still as little to be depended upon as the private soldiers themselves; and they are just as ready to commit irregularities and outrages. I attribute this circumstance very much to the lowness of their pay in comparison with that of the soldiers.

'Within my recollection, the pay of the soldiers of the army has been increased from sixpence to one shilling *per diem*, with other advantages, while that of the corporals, which was eightpence, has in the same period been raised only to one shilling and twopence, and that of the sergeants, which was one shilling, has been raised only to one shilling and sixpence, both with the same advantages as the private soldiers.

'Your Lordship will observe that the old proportions have not been preserved, and the non-commissioned officers of the army not only feel no inclination to preserve a distinction between them and the private soldiers, but they feel no desire to incur the responsibility, and take the trouble, and submit to the privations of their situation for so trifling a difference in their pay as that of twopence in fourteen pence to corporals, and that of sixpence in eighteen pence to sergeants, and they are indifferent whether they continue non-commissioned officers or not.

'The remedy for this evil is to increase the pay of the corporals and sergeants, so as at least to restore the old proportions between non-commissioned officers and soldiers before the first increase of pay to the army at the commencement of the last war. This measure becomes particularly necessary in consequence of the opinions generally prevalent in respect to the punishment of soldiers, which are certainly so far well founded that it must be admitted by all that the best mode of insuring regularity among soldiers is to prevent the commission of crimes.

'Then, not only is it difficult, if not impossible, to preserve order in one of these detachments upon a march, owing to the badness of the non-commissioned officers of the army, but the crimes which the soldiers commit remain unpunished.

'It is impossible to try these offences while the soldiers are on the march, from the want of a sufficient number of officers to constitute a court, and I refer Your Lordship to my letter to the Judge Advocate-General of November 13, 1811, for a detail of the difficulties attending the procuring evidence against them when they join the army. I proposed remedies for this evil which have not been entirely adopted. . . .

'The guard-rooms are therefore crowded with prisoners, and the offences of which they have been guilty remain unpunished, to the destruction of the discipline of the army, and to the injury of the reputation of the country for justice.

'I have thought it proper to lay these circumstances before Your Lordship. I am about to move the army further forward into Spain, and I assure Your Lordship that I have not a friend in that country who has not written to me in dread of the consequences which must result to the army, and to the cause, from a continuance of these disgraceful irregularities, which I declare I have it not in my power to prevent.'

A Regrettable Affair.

To Lieutenant-General Sir R. Hill, K.B.

'Salamanca,
'June 18, 1812.

'I have received your letters of the 13th and 14th. I have never been more annoyed than by —— ——'s affair, and I entirely concur with you in the necessity of inquiring into it. It is occasioned entirely by the trick our officers of cavalry have acquired of galloping at everything, and their galloping back as fast as they gallop on the enemy. They never consider their situation, never think of manoeuvring before an enemy—so little that one would think they cannot manoeuvre, excepting on Wimbledon Common—and when they use their arm as it ought to be used—*viz.*, offensively—they never keep or provide for reserve.

'All cavalry should charge in two lines, of which one should be in reserve; if obliged to charge in one line, part of the line, at least one-third, should be ordered beforehand to pull-up and form in second line as soon as the charge should be given, and the enemy has been broken and has retired.

'The Royals and the 3rd Dragoon Guards were the best regiments in the cavalry in this country, and it annoys me particularly that the misfortune has happened to them. I do not wonder at the French boasting of it; it is the greatest blow they have struck.'

To the Earl of Liverpool.

'Salamanca,
'June 18, 1812.

'. . . I enclose a letter from Lieutenant-General Sir Rowland Hill, and its enclosures, being two from Major-General Slade, giving an account of an affair which he had with the enemy on the 11th instant, in which, owing to the eagerness and impetuosity of the soldiers, considerable loss was sustained . . .'

Return of the Killed, Wounded, and Missing, in the Affair near Maguilla, on June 11, 1812.

	Officers.	Sergeants.	Rank and File.	Horses.	Total Loss of Officers, Non-commissioned Officers, and Rank and File.
Killed - -	—	2	20	6	22
Wounded -	—	—	26	14	26
Missing - -	2	10	106	127	118

BATTLE OF SALAMANCA.

To the Earl of Liverpool.

'Fuente la Peña,
'June 30, 1812.

'The ammunition to enable us to carry on the attack of the forts having arrived at Salamanca in the afternoon of the 26th, the fire was immediately recommenced upon the gorge of the redoubt of Los Cayetanos, in which a practicable breach was effected at about ten o'clock in the morning of the 27th; and we had succeeded nearly about the same time in setting fire to the buildings in the large fort of San Vicente, by the fire from which the approach to Los Cayetanos by its gorge was defended.

'Being in Salamanca at this moment, I gave directions that the forts of Los Cayetanos and La Merced should be stormed, but some little delay occurred in consequence of the commanding officer of these forts in the first instance, and afterwards the commanding officer of San Vicente, having expressed a desire to capitulate after the lapse of a certain number of hours.

'As it was obvious that these propositions were made in order to gain time till the fire in San Vicente should be extinguished, I refused to listen to any terms unless the forts should be instantly surrendered; and having found that the commanding officer of Los Cayetanos, who

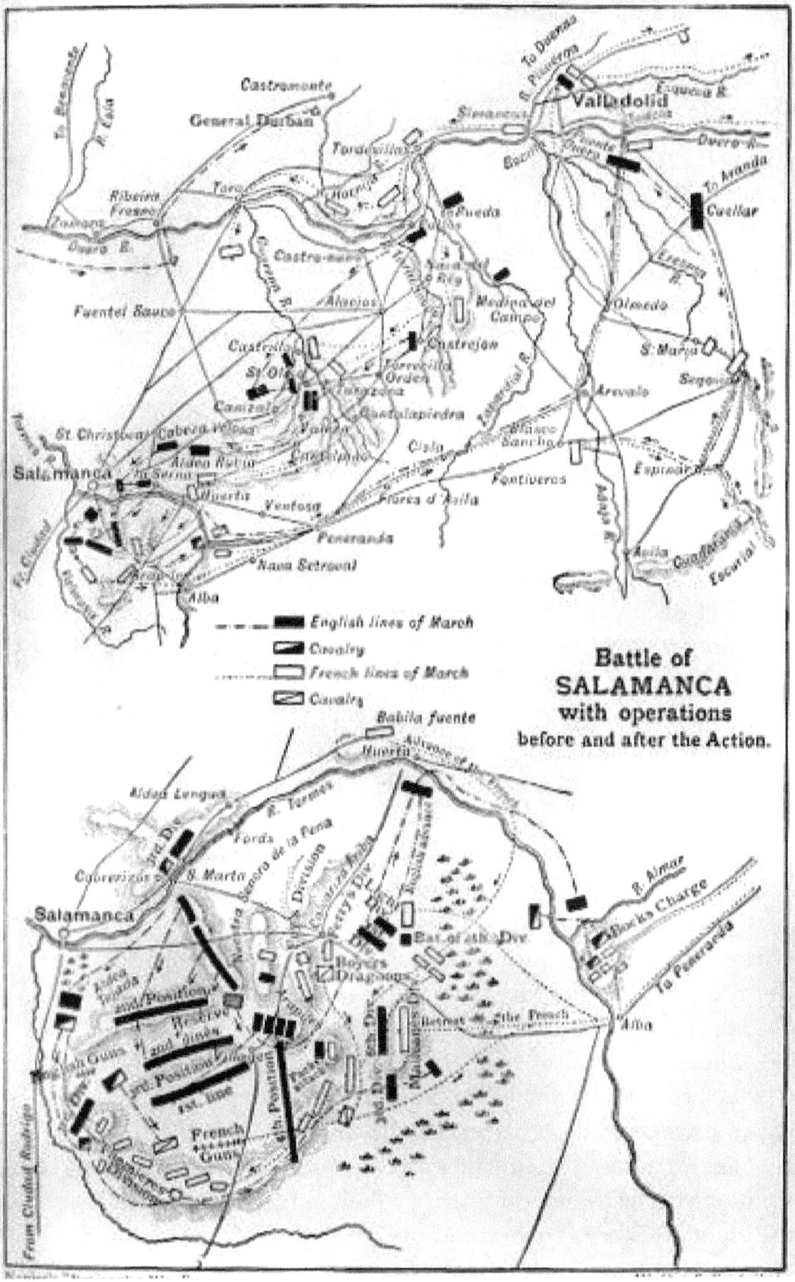

Battle of SALAMANCA with operations before and after the Action.

was the first to offer to surrender, was entirely dependent upon the Governor of San Vicente, and could not venture to carry into execution the capitulation which he had offered to make, I gave directions that his fort and that of La Merced might be stormed forthwith.

'These operations were effected in the most gallant manner by a detachment of the 6th Division, under the command of Lieutenant-Colonel Davis, of the 36th Regiment, under the direction of Major-General Clinton.

'The troops entered the fort of Los Cayetanos by the gorge, and escaladed that of La Merced, and I am happy to add that our loss was but trifling.

'The Governor of San Vicente then sent out a flag of truce to ratify the surrender of that fort on the terms I had offered him—*viz*,, the garrison to march out with the honours of war, to be prisoners of war, and the officers to retain their personal military baggage, and the soldiers their knapsacks—and notwithstanding that the 9th Regiment of Caçadores had actually stormed one of the outworks of San Vicente, and were in possession of it, I deemed it expedient to accept the fort by capitulation on those terms, and to stop the attack.

'The enemy had been employed for nearly three years in constructing these works, but with increased activity for the last eight or nine months. A large expense had been incurred, and these works, sufficiently garrisoned by about 800 men, and armed with 30 pieces of artillery, were of a nature to render it quite impossible to take them, excepting by a regular attack; and it is obvious that the enemy relied upon their strength, and upon their being sufficiently garrisoned and armed, as they had left in San Vicente large depots of clothing, and military stores of every description.

'I was mistaken in my estimate of the extent of the means which would be necessary to subdue these forts, and I was obliged to send to the rear for a fresh supply of ammunition.

This necessity occasioned a delay of six days.

'The enemy withdrew their garrison from Alba de Tormes as soon as they heard of the fall of the Forts of Salamanca, and I have ordered that the works at both places may be destroyed.

'The operations against the forts of Salamanca were carried on in sight of Marshal Marmont's army, which remained in its position, with the right at Cabeza Vellosa, and the left at Huerta, till the night of the 27th instant, when they broke up and retired in three columns towards the River Duero, one of them directing its march upon Toro, and the others upon Tordesillas.

'The Allied Army broke up the following day, and are this day encamped upon the Guareña. . . .'

Return of the Killed, Wounded, and Missing of the Army under the Command, of General the Earl of Wellington, K.B., in the Siege of the Forts of San Vicente, Los Cayetanos, and La Merced, and in the Position on the Heights of Villares, from June 16 to June 27, 1812, inclusive.

	Officers.	Sergeants.	Rank and File.	Horses.	Total Loss of Officers, Non-commissioned Officers, and Rank and File.
Killed - -	6	5	104	28	115
Wounded -	28	44	340	—	412
Missing - -	2	—	11	5	13

To the Earl of Liverpool.

'Fuente la Peña,
'June 30, 1812.

'I omitted to report to Your Lordship in my last despatch the particulars of a very gallant affair of the cavalry in Estremadura, under the command of Lieutenant Strenuwitz, the *aide-de-camp* of Lieutenant-General Sir William Erskine. Lieutenant-General Sir Rowland Hill having learnt that the enemy had left at Maguilla a great proportion of the soldiers who had been taken prisoners in Major-General Slade's affair of the 11th instant, sent Lieutenant Strenuwitz on the 13th with a detachment consisting of 50 men of the 3rd Dragoon Guards and Royal Dragoons, under the command of Lieutenant Bridges, of the Royal Dragoons, to bring them in. On his arrival there he found a detachment of French Dragoons, consisting of 80 men, whom he attacked with such conduct and effect as to kill many, and to take prisoners 1 officer, 20 men, and 25 horses, with the loss of 1 man of his detachment killed. . .'

To Earl Bathurst.

'Cabrerizos, near Salamanca,
'July 21,1812.

'In the course of the 15th and 16th the enemy moved all their troops to the right of their position on the Duero, and their army was concentrated between Toro and San Roman. A considerable body passed the Duero at Toro on the evening of the 16th, and I moved the allied army to their left on that night, with an intention to concentrate on the Guareña.

'It was totally out of my power to prevent the enemy from passing the Duero at any point at which he might think it expedient, as he had in his possession all the bridges over that river and many of the fords; but he recrossed that river at Toro in the night of the 16th, moved his whole army to Tordesillas, where he again crossed the Duero on the morning of the 17th, and assembled his army on that day at La Nava del Rey, having marched not less than ten leagues in the course of the 17th.

'The 4th and Light Divisions of infantry, and Major-General Anson's brigades of cavalry, had marched to Castrejon on the night of the 16th, with a view to the assembly of the army on the Guareña, and were at Castrejon under the orders of Lieutenant-General Sir Stapleton Cotton on the 17th, not having been ordered to proceed further, in consequence of my knowledge that the enemy had not passed the Duero at Toro, and there was not time to call them in between the hour at which I received the intelligence of the whole of the enemy's army being at La Nava and daylight on the morning of the 18th. I therefore took measures to provide for their retreat and junction by moving the 5th Division to Torrecillade la Orden, and Major-General Le Marchant's, Major-General Alten's, and Major-General Bock's brigades of cavalry to Alaejos.

'The enemy attacked the troops at Castrejon at the dawn of day of the 18th, and Sir Stapleton Cotton maintained the post without suffering any loss till the cavalry had joined him. Nearly about the same time the enemy turned, by Alaejos, the left flank of our position at Castrejon.

'The troops retired in admirable order to Torrecilla de la Orden, having the enemy's whole army on their flank, or in their rear, and thence to the Guareña, which river they passed under the same circumstances, and effected their junction with the army.

'The Guareña, which runs into the Duero, is formed by four streams, which unite about a league below Cañizal, and the enemy took a strong position on the heights on the right of that river; and I placed the 5th, 4th, and Light Divisions on the opposite heights, and had directed the remainder of the army to cross the Upper Guareña at Vallesa, in consequence of the appearance of the enemy's intention to turn our right.

'Shortly after his arrival, however, the enemy crossed the Guareña at Castrillo, below the junction of the streams, and manifested an intention to press upon our left, and to enter the valley of Cañizal. Major-General Alten's brigade of cavalry, supported by the 3rd Dragoons, were already engaged with the enemy's cavalry, and had taken, among other prisoners, the French General de Carrie; and I desired Lieutenant-General the Hon. L. Cole to attack with Major-General William Anson's and Brigadier-General Harvey's brigades of infantry, the latter under the command of Colonel Stubbs, the enemy's infantry, which were supporting their cavalry. He immediately attacked and defeated them with the 27th and 40th Regiments, which advanced to the charge with bayonets, Colonel Stubbs' Portuguese brigade supporting, and the enemy gave way. Many were killed and wounded, and Major-General Alten's brigade of cavalry having pursued the fugitives, 240 prisoners were taken. . . .

'The enemy did not make any further attempt on our left, but, having reinforced their troops on that side, and withdrawn those which had moved to their left, I brought back ours from Vallesa.

'On the 19th, in the afternoon, the enemy withdrew all the troops from their right, and marched to their left by Tarazona, apparently with an intention of turning our right: I crossed the Upper Guareña at Vallesa and El Olmo, with the whole of the Allied Army, in the course of that evening and night, and every preparation was made for the action which was expected on the plain of Vallesa on the morning of the 20th.

'But shortly after daylight the enemy made another movement, in several columns, to his left, along the heights of the Guareña, which river he crossed below Cantalapiedra, and encamped last night at Babila-fuente and Villoruela; and the Allied Army made a corresponding movement to its right to Cantalpino, and encamped last night at Cabeza Vellosa, the 6th Division and Major-General Alten's brigade of cavalry being upon the Tormes at Aldea Lengua.

'During these movements there have been occasional cannonades, but without loss on our side.

'I have this morning moved the left of the army to the Tormes, where the whole are now concentrated, and I observe that the enemy have also moved towards the same river near Huerta.

'The enemy's object hitherto has been to cut off my communication with Salamanca and Ciudad Rodrigo, the want of which, he knows well, would distress us very materially. The wheat harvest has not yet been reaped in Castille, and, even if we had money, we could not now procure anything from the country, unless we should follow the example of the enemy, and lay waste whole districts, in order to procure a scanty subsistence of unripe wheat for the troops.

'It would answer no purpose to attempt to retaliate upon the enemy, even if it were practicable. The French Armies in Spain have never had any secure communication beyond the ground which they occupy, and provided the enemy opposed to them is not too strong for them, they are indifferent in respect to the quarter from which their operations are directed, or on which side they carry them on.

'The Army of Portugal has been surrounded for the last six weeks, and scarcely even a letter reaches its commander; but the system of organised rapine and plunder, and the extraordinary discipline so long established in the French Armies, enable it to subsist at the expense of the total ruin of the country in which it had been placed, and I am not certain that Marshal Marmont has not now at his command a greater quantity of provisions and supplies of every description than we have. Any movement upon his flank, therefore, would only tend to augment the embarrassments of our own situation, while it would have no effect whatever upon that of the enemy, even if such a movement could have been made with advantage as an operation purely military. This, however, was not the case, and when the French attempted to turn our right, I had the choice only of marching towards Salamanca, or of attacking the enemy in a position highly advantageous to him, which, for several reasons, I did not think expedient.

'I have invariably been of opinion that, unless forced to fight a battle, it is better that one should not be fought by the Allied Army, unless under such favourable circumstances as that there would be reason to hope that the Allied Army would be able to maintain the field, while those of the enemy should not.

'Your Lordship will have seen by the returns of the two armies that we have no superiority of numbers, even over that single army immediately opposed to us; indeed, I believe that the French Army is of the two the strongest, and it is certainly equipped with a profusion of artillery double ours in numbers, and of larger calibres. It cannot be attacked, therefore, in a chosen position without considerable loss on our side.

'To this circumstance add that I am quite certain that Marshal Marmont's army is to be joined by the King's, which will be 10,000 or 12,000 men, with a large proportion of cavalry, and that troops are still expected from the army of the north, and some are ordered from that of the south; and it will be seen that I ought to consider it almost impossible to remain in Castille after an action, the circumstances of which should not have been so advantageous as to have left the Allied Army in a situation of comparative strength, while that of the enemy should have been much weakened.'

'I have, therefore, determined to cross the Tormes, if the enemy should, to cover Salamanca as long as I can; and above all, not to give up our communication with Ciudad Rodrigo, and not to fight an action unless under very advantageous circumstances, or it should become absolutely necessary. . . .'

Return of the Killed, Wounded, and Missing of the Army under the Command of General the Earl of Wellington, K.B., near Castrejon, on July 18, 1812.

	Killed.	Wounded.	Missing.
British	61	297	27
Portuguese	34	96	27
Total	95	393	54

To Lieutenant-General Hill.

'On the Heights near Alba de Tormes,
'July 23, 1812.

'I write to let you know that we beat Marshal Marmont's army yesterday evening, near Salamanca, and they are now in full retreat, and we are following them. . . .

'We have taken a good many prisoners and cannon—above 3,000 of the former, and I should think 20 of the latter, and, I understand, two eagles. All the troops behaved admirably.'

To Earl Bathurst.

'Flores de Avila,
'July 24, 1812.

'My *aide-de-camp,* Captain Lord Clinton, will present to Your Lordship this account of a victory which the allied troops under my command gained in a general action fought near Salamanca on the evening of the 22nd instant, which I have been under the necessity of delaying to send till now, having been engaged ever since the action in the pursuit of the enemy's flying troops.

In my letter of the 21st I informed Your Lordship that both armies were near the Tormes, and the enemy crossed that river with the greatest part of his troops in the afternoon, by the fords between Alba de Tormes and Huerta, and moved by their left towards the roads leading to Ciudad Rodrigo.

'The Allied Army, with the exception of the 3rd Division and General D'Urban's cavalry, likewise crossed the Tormes in the evening by the bridge of Salamanca and the fords in the neighbourhood, and I placed the troops in a position, of which the right was upon one of the two heights called Dos Arapiles, and the left on the Tormes, below the ford of Sta. Marta.

'The 3rd Division and Brigadier General D'Urban's cavalry were left at Cabrerizos, on the right of the Tormes, as the enemy had still a large corps on the heights above Babila-Fuente, on the same side of the river, and I considered it not improbable that, finding onr army prepared for them in the morning on the left of the Tormes, they would alter their plan and manoeuvre by the other bank.

'In the course of the night of the 21st I received intelligence, of the truth of which I could not doubt, that General Clausel had arrived at Polios on the 20th with the cavalry and horse artillery of the Army of the North, to join Marshal Marmont; and I was quite certain that these troops would join him on the 22nd or 23rd at latest.

'There was no time to be lost therefore, and I determined that, if circumstances should not permit me to attack him on the 22nd, I would move towards Ciudad Rodrigo without further loss of time, as the difference of the numbers of cavalry might have made a march of manoeuvre, such as we have had for the last four or five days, very difficult, and its result doubtful.

'During the night of the 21st the enemy had taken possession of the village of Calvarassa de Arriba, and of the heights near it called Nuestra Señora de la Peña, our cavalry being in possession of Calvarassa de Abaxo; and shortly after daylight detachments from both armies attempted to obtain possession of the more distant from our right of the two hills called Dos Arapiles.

'The enemy, however, succeeded, their detachments being the strongest, and having been concealed in the woods nearer the hill than we were, by which success they strengthened materially their own position, and had in their power increased means of annoying ours.

'In the morning the light troops of the 7th Division and the 4th Caçadores belonging to General Pack's Brigade were engaged with the enemy on the height called Nuestra Senora de la Pena, on which height they maintained themselves with the enemy throughout the day. The possession by the enemy, however, of the more distant of the Arapiles rendered it necessary for me to extend the right of the army *en potence* to the height behind the village of Arapiles, and to occupy that village with light infantry; and here I placed the 4th Division, under the command of Lieutenant-General the Hon. L. Cole, and although, from the variety of the enemy's movements, it was difficult to form a satisfactory judgment of his intentions, I considered that upon the whole his objects were upon the left of the Tormes.

'I therefore ordered Major-General the Hon. E. Pakenham, who commanded the 3rd Division in the absence of Lieutenant-General Picton, on account of ill-health, to move across the Tormes with the troops under his command, including Brigadier-General D'Urban's cavalry, and to place himself behind Aldea Tejada—Brigadier-General Bradford's brigade of Portuguese infantry and Don Carlos de Espana's infantry having been moved up likewise to the neighbourhood of Las Torres, between the 3rd and 4th Divisions.

'After a variety of evolutions and movements the enemy appears to have determined upon his plan about two in the afternoon, and, under cover of a very heavy cannonade, which, however, did us but very little damage, he extended his left, and moved forward his troops apparently with an intention to embrace, by the position of his troops, and by his fire, our post on that of the two Arapiles which we possessed, and from thence to attack and break our line, or, at all events, to render difficult any movement of ours to our right.

'The extension of his line to his left, however, and its advance upon our right, notwithstanding that his troops still occupied very strong ground, and his position was well defended by cannon, gave me an opportunity of attacking him, for which I had long been anxious.

'I reinforced our right with the 5th Division, under Lieutenant-General Leith, which I placed behind the village of Arapiles, on the right of the 4th Division, and with the 6th and 7th Divisions in reserve; and as soon as these troops had taken their station, I ordered Major-General the Hon. E. Pakenham to move forward with the 3rd Division and General D'Urban's cavalry, and two squadrons of the 14th Light Dragoons, under Lieutenant-Colonel Hervey, in four columns, to turn the enemy's left on the heights; while Brigadier-General Bradford's Brigade, the 5th Division, under Lieutenant-General Leith, the 4th Division, under Lieutenant-General the Hon. L. Cole, and the cavalry under Lieutenant-General Sir Stapleton Cotton, should attack them in front, supported in reserve by the 6th Division, under Major-General Clinton, the 7th under Major-General Hope, and Don Carlos de Espana's Spanish Division; and Brigadier-General Pack should support the left of the 4th Division by attacking that of the Dos Arapiles which the enemy held. The 1st and Light Divisions occupied the ground on the left, and were in reserve.

'The attack upon the enemy's left was made in the manner above described, and completely succeeded. Major-General the Hon. E. Pakenham formed the 3rd Division across the enemy's flank, and overthrew everything opposed to him. These troops were supported in the most gallant style by the Portuguese cavalry, under Brigadier-General D'Urban, and Lieutenant-Colonel Hervey's squadron of the 14th, who successfully defeated every attempt made by the enemy on the flank of the 3rd Division.

'Brigadier-General Bradford's Brigade, the 5th and 4th Divisions, and the cavalry under Lieutenant-General Sir Stapleton Cotton, attacked the enemy in front, and drove his troops before them from one height to another, bringing forward their right, so as to acquire strength upon the enemy's flank in proportion to the advance. 'Brigadier General Pack made a very gallant attack upon the Arapiles, in which, however, he did not succeed, excepting in diverting the attention of the enemy's corps placed upon it from the troops under the command of Lieutenant-General Cole in his advance.

'The cavalry under Lieutenant-General Sir Stapleton Cotton made a most gallant and successful charge against a body of the enemy's infantry, which they overthrew and cut to pieces. In this charge Major-General Le Marchant was killed at the head of his brigade, and I have to regret the loss of a most able officer.

'After the crest of the height was carried, one division of the enemy's infantry made a stand against the 4th Division, which, after a severe contest, was obliged to give way in consequence of the enemy having thrown some troops on the left of the 4th Division, after the failure of Brigadier-General Pack's attack upon the Arapiles and Lieutenant-General the Hon. L. Cole having been wounded.

'Marshal Sir William Beresford, who happened to be on the spot, directed Brigadier-General Spry's brigade of the 5th Division, which was in the second line, to change its front, and to bring its fire on the flank of the enemy's division; and I am sorry to add that, while engaged in this service, he received a wound which I am apprehensive will deprive me of the benefit of his counsel and assistance for some time. Nearly about the same time Lieutenant-General Leith received a wound which unfortunately obliged him to quit the field. I ordered up the 6th Division under Major-General Clinton, to relieve the 4th, and the battle was soon restored to its former success.

'The enemy's right, however, reinforced by the troops which had fled from his left, and by those which had now retired from the Arapiles, still continued to resist, and I ordered the 1st and Light Divisions, and Colonel Stubbs's Portuguese brigade of the 4th Division, which was re-formed, and Major-General William Anson's brigade, likewise of the 4th Division, to turn the right, while the 6th Division, supported by the 3rd and 5th, attacked the front. It was dark before this point was carried by the 6th Division, and the enemy fled through the woods towards the Tormes. I pursued them with the 1st and Light Divisions, and Major-General William Anson's brigade of the 4th Division, and some squadrons of cavalry under Lieutenant-General Sir Stapleton Cotton, as long as we could find any of them together, directing our march upon Huerta and the fords of the Tormes, by which the enemy had passed on their advance; but the darkness of the night was highly advantageous to the enemy, many of whom escaped under its cover who must otherwise have been in our hands.

'I am sorry to report that, owing to this same cause, Lieutenant-General Sir Stapleton Cotton was unfortunately wounded by one of our own sentries after we had halted.

'We renewed the pursuit at break of day in the morning with the same troops, and Major-General Bock's and Major-General Anson's brigades of cavalry, which joined during the night, and, having crossed the Tormes, we came up with the enemy's rear of cavalry and infantry near La Serna. They were immediately attacked by the two brigades of dragoons, and the cavalry fled, leaving the infantry to their, fate. I have never witnessed a more gallant charge than was made on the enemy's infantry by the heavy brigade of the King's German Legion, under Major-General Bock, which was completely successful, and the whole body of infantry, consisting of three battalions of the enemy's 1st Division, were made prisoners.

'The pursuit was afterwards continued as far as Penaranda last night, and our troops were still following the flying enemy.

'Their headquarters were in this town, not less than ten leagues from the field of battle, for a few hours last night; and they are now considerably advanced on the road towards Valladolid, by Arevalo. They were joined yesterday on their retreat by the cavalry and artillery of the Army of the North, which have arrived at too late a period, it is to be hoped, to be of much use to them.

'It is impossible to form a conjecture of the amount of the enemy's loss in this action, but, from all reports, it is very considerable. We have taken from them 11 pieces of cannon, (the official returns only account for 11 pieces, but it is believed that 20 have fallen into our hands), several ammunition waggons, 2 eagles, and 6 colours; and 1 general, 3 colonels, 3 lieutenant-colonels, 130 officers of inferior rank, and between 6,000 and 7,000 soldiers, are prisoners and our detachments are sending in more at every moment. (The prisoners are supposed to amount to 7,000; but it has not been possible to ascertain their number exactly, from the advance of the army immediately after the action was over). The number of dead on the field is very large.

'I am informed that Marshal Marmont is badly wounded, and has lost one of his arms, and that four general officers have been killed, and several wounded.

'Such an advantage could not have been acquired without material loss on our side; but it certainly has not been of a magnitude to distress the army, or to cripple its operations. (The Devonshire Regiment—the old 11th Foot—is known as the. 'Bloody Eleventh,' a sobriquet arising out of the state of the corps after the Battle of Salamanca.—W. W.)

'I have great pleasure in reporting to Your Lordship that throughout this trying day, of which I have related the events, I had every reason to be satisfied with the conduct of the general officers and troops.

'The relation which I have written of its events will give a general idea of the share which each individual had in them, and I cannot say too much in praise of the conduct of every individual in his station. . . .

'In a case in which the conduct of all has been conspicuously good, I regret that the necessary limits of a despatch prevent me from drawing Your Lordship's notice to the conduct of a larger number of individuals, but I can assure Your Lordship that there was no officer or corps engaged in this action who did not perform his duty by his sovereign and his country. 'Captain Lord Clinton will have the honour of laying at the feet of His Royal Highness the Prince Regent the eagles and colours taken from the enemy in this action. . . .'

Return of Killed, Wounded and Missing of the Allied Army, under the Command of General the Earl of Wellington, K.B., in the Battle near Salamanca, on July 22, 1812.

	Officers.	Sergeants.	Rank and File.	Horses.	Total.	British.	Portuguese.	Spanish.
Killed -	41	28	625	114	694	388	304	2
Wounded	252	178	3,840	133	4,270	2,714	1,552	4
Missing -	1	1	254	44	256	74	182	—

To Earl Bathurst.

'Flores de Avila,
'July 24, 1812.

'I hope that you will be pleased with our battle, of which the despatch contains as accurate an account as I can give you.

'There was no mistake; everything went on as it ought; and there never was an army so beaten in so short a time.

'If we had had another hour or two of daylight, not a man would have passed the Tormes. . . .'

To Lieutenant-General Sir T. Graham, K.B.

'Flores de Avila,
'July 25, 1812.

'. . . I am in great hopes that our loss has not been great.

'In two divisions, the 3rd and 5th, it is about 1,200 men, including Portuguese. There are more in the 4th and 6th, but there are many men who left the ranks with wounded officers and soldiers, who are eating and drinking, and engaged in *regocijos* with the inhabitants of Salamanca; I have sent, however, to have them all turned out of the town. . . .'

Continued Distress.

To Earl Bathurst.

'Olmedo,
'July 28, 1812.

'. . . We are absolutely bankrupt. The troops are now five months in arrears, instead of being one month in advance. The staff have not been paid since February; the muleteers not since June, 1811; and we are in debt in all parts of the country. . .'

To Earl Bathurst.

'Cuellar,
'August 4, 1812.

'I have the pleasure to send you a letter from Dr. M'Grigor, which I have received since I wrote my despatch on our sickness this day. However, it is very bad, and it is melancholy to see the finest and bravest soldiers in the world falling down, owing to their own irregularities, and the ignorant presumption of those who think they know better what is good for them than those do who have been serving so long in this country. . .'

Arrival in Madrid.

To Earl Bathurst.

'Madrid,
'August 13, 1812.

'. . . It is impossible to describe the joy manifested by the inhabitants of Madrid upon our arrival; and I hope that the prevalence of the same sentiments of detestation of the French yoke, and of a strong desire to secure the independence of their country, which first induced them to set the example of resistance to the usurper, will induce them again to make exertions in the cause of their country, which being more wisely directed, will be more efficacious than those formerly made. . . .'

Proclamation.

'Madrid,
'August 29, 1812.

'Spaniards,

'It is unnecessary to take up your time by recalling to your recollection the events of the last two months, or by drawing your attention to the situation in which your enemies now find themselves.

'Listen to the accounts of the numerous prisoners daily brought in and deserters from their army; hear the details of the miseries endured by those who, trusting to the promises of the French, have followed the vagabond fortunes of the Usurper, driven from the capital of your monarchy; hear these details from their servants and followers who have had the sense to quit this scene of desolation, and if the sufferings of your oppressors can soften the feeling of those inflicted upon yourselves, you will, find ample cause for consolation.

'But much remains still to be done to consolidate and secure the advantages acquired. It should be clearly understood that the pretended king is a usurper, whose authority it is the duty of every Spaniard to resist; that every Frenchman is an enemy, against whom it is the duty of every Spaniard to raise his arm. 'Spaniards! resist this odious tyranny, and be independent and happy. Wellington.'

Misunderstanding in England.

To Colonel Torrens.

'Torquemada,
'September 13, 1812.

'. . . In truth, my dear Torrens, the difficulties under which we labour are but little known in England. First, there is no soldier in the army who has at present been paid to a later date than April 24 for want of money. His accounts are settled every month.

'But, secondly, if a soldier has been in hospital since the month of March last, at which time the soldiers had not been paid later than January, and the pay for March not received till June or July, I should like to know how it is possible for any officer to come to a settlement by a correspondence with one officer, who has to settle the accounts of probably 500 men going to England at the same moment? It is quite impossible; and the consequence is, that the poor men are detained three, four, or five months, to the loss of many, till the correspondence respecting their accounts is finished, during which time many settle all accounts with this world. It is a great error to suppose that the lower orders are always right in their complaints, and the higher orders always in the wrong.

'My experience has taught me that, nine times in ten, the soldiers loudest in their complaints and claims have no ground for either the one or the other, and are generally in debt to their captains. Those who are wounded invariably either throw away or sell their necessaries; and whether the ground is held or not by the army, they claim compensation from the public.

'Their claim can be settled only by a Board. No officer of a regiment has the power either to admit or to refuse it. Yet if a soldier makes such a claim at Lisbon, the officer who is to settle the soldier's claims before they go to England must detain at least as many as one transport will contain, till the claims of one for losses of this description shall be inquired into by post; every letter now requiring three weeks to get an answer. While this is going on, many die who might be saved; and, after all, a soldier's account can never be settled satisfactorily excepting with his regiment. . . . .'

Capture of San Miguel.

To Earl Bathurst.

'Villa Toko,
'September 21, 1812.

'I continued to follow the enemy with the troops under my command till the 16th, when I was joined at Pampliega by three divisions of infantry and a small body of cavalry of the army of Galicia, His Excellency the Captain-General Castanos having arrived at headquarters on the 14th. The enemy had on the 16th taken a strong position on the heights behind Celada del Camino, and arrangements were made to attack them on the morning of the 17th; but the enemy retired in the night; and they were driven on the 17th to the heights close to Burgos. They retired through the town in the night, leaving behind them some clothing and other stores, and a large quantity of wheat and barley; and have since continued their retreat to Briviesca, where it is reported that they have been joined by 7,000 conscripts. It is likewise reported that the Prince of Essling has been ordered by the local government in France to come and take the command of the army.

'The Castle of Burgos commands the passages of the River Arlanzon in the neighbourhood and the roads communicating with them so completely that we could not pass the river till the 19th; when we effected that operation in two columns, the 5th Division and General Bradford's brigade above, and the 1st Division and General Pack's brigade and General Anson's cavalry below the town.

'Burgos is situated in that division of Spain allotted to the army of the North; and General Caffarelli, who had been here on the 17th, had placed in the castle a garrison of the troops of that army, consisting, as is reported, of 2,500 men.

'The enemy had taken considerable pains to fortify the Castle of Burgos; and had occupied with a horn work the hill of San Miguel, which has a considerable command over some of the works of the castle at the distance of 300 yards. They had likewise occupied other parts of the hill with *flèches* and other works for the protection of their piquets and outposts.

'As soon as the 1st Division crossed the Arlanzon on the 19th, the enemy's outposts were driven in by the light infantry battalion of Colonel Stirling's brigade, under the command of Major the Hon. C. Cocks, supported by Brigadier-General Pack's brigade; and the enemy's outworks on the hill of San Miguel, with the exception of the horn work, were occupied by our troops, which were posted close to the horn work.

'As soon as it was dark, the same troops, with the addition of the 42nd Regiment, attacked and carried by assault the horn work which the enemy had occupied in strength. . . .

'We took three pieces of cannon and one captain and 62 prisoners; but I am sorry to add that our loss was severe, as appears by the enclosed return. . . .'

Return of the Killed, Wounded, and Missing of the Army under the Command of General the Marquis of Wellington, K.B., in the Assault and Capture of the Fort of San Miguel, on September 19, 1812.

	Officers.	Sergeants.	Rank and File.	Horses.	Total Loss of Officers, Non-commissioned Officers, and Rank and File.
Killed - -	6	5	60	—	71
Wounded -	15	21	297	—	333
Missing -	—	—	16	—	16

The Siege of Burgos.

To Earl Bathurst.

'Villa Toro,
'September 27, 1812.

'The operations against the Castle of Burgos have been continued since I addressed you on the 20th; and on the night of the 22nd I directed that an attempt might be made to take by storm the exterior line of the enemy's works, one of the batteries destined to support our position within them having been in such a state of preparation as to afford hopes that it would be ready to open on the morning of the 23rd. The attack was to have been made by detachments of Portuguese troops belonging to the 6th Division, which occupied the town of Burgos and invested the castle on the S.W. side on the enemy's left, while a detachment of the 1st Division under Major Lawrie of the 79th should scale the wall in front. Unfortunately, the Portuguese troops were so strongly opposed that they could not make any progress on the enemy's flank; and the escalade could not take place. I am sorry to say that our loss was severe. . . .

'We have since established ourselves close to the exterior wall, and have carried a gallery towards it, and I hope that a mine under it will be completed in the course of tomorrow. In the meantime, our batteries are completed, and ready to open upon the enemy's interior lines, as soon as we shall have established our troops within the exterior lines.'

Return of the Killed, Wounded, and Missing of the Army under the Command of General the Marquis of Wellington, K.B., in the Siege of the Castle of Burgos, from September 20 to 26, 1812, inclusive.

	Officers.	Sergeants.	Rank and File.	Horses.	Total Loss of Officers, Non-commissioned Officers, and Rank and File.
Killed - -	7	2	50	—	59
Wounded -	12	13	264	—	289
Missing -	—	—	—	—	—

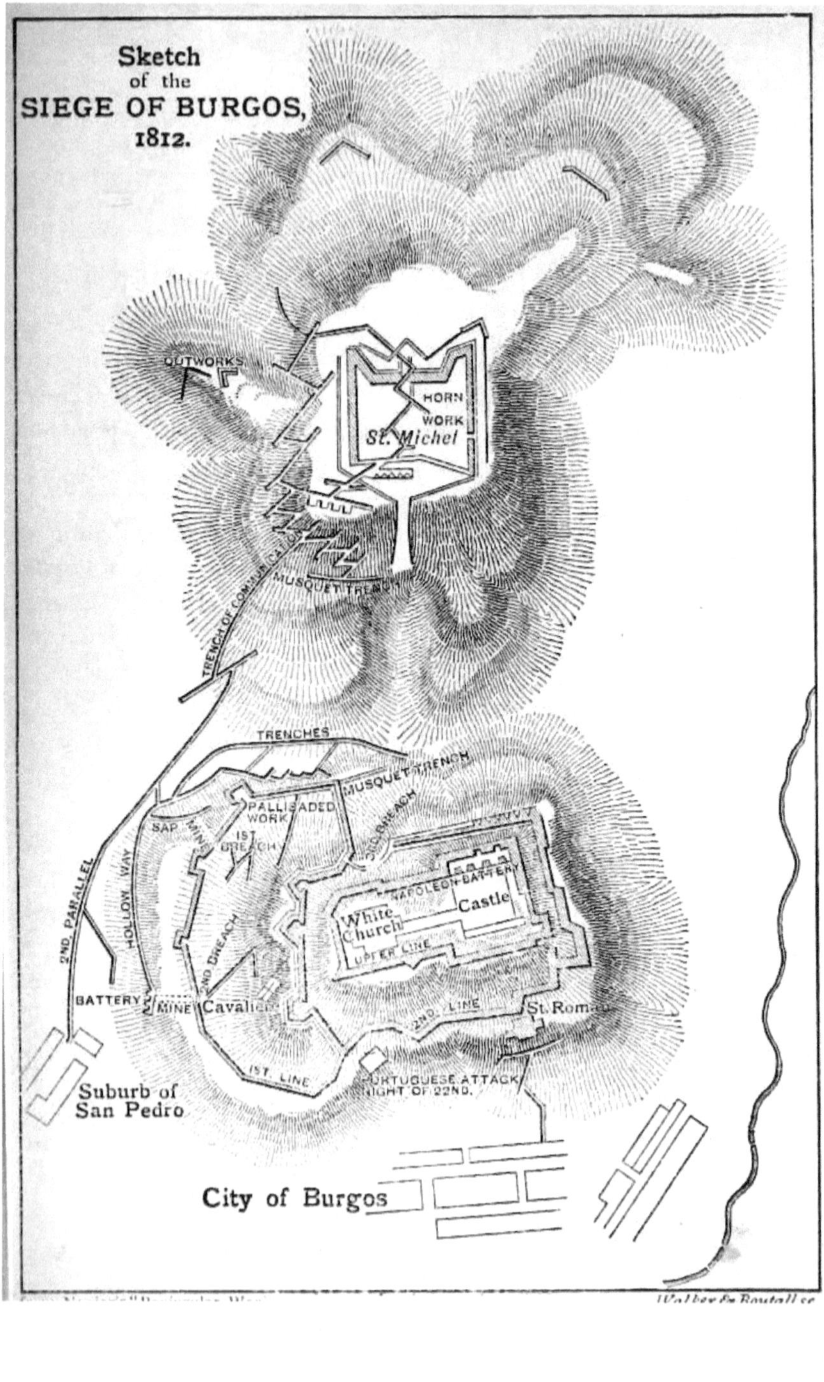

Sketch
of the
SIEGE OF BURGOS,
1812.

Walker & Boutall sc.

To Marshal Beresford.

'Villa Toro,
'October 5, 1812.

'Something or other has made a terrible alteration in the troops for the worse. They have lately, in several instances, behaved very ill, and whether it be owing to the nature of the service or their want of pay I cannot tell; but they are not at all in the style they were. I am rather inclined to attribute their misbehaviour to the misery and consequent indifference of both officers and soldiers, on account of their want of pay. . . .

'I do not know what to say of this d——d place. Our success of yesterday evening has opened a new scene to us, but our final success is still doubtful. Luckily, the French give me more time than I had a right to expect.'

To Earl Bathurst.

'Villa Toro,
'October 5, 1812.

'One of the mines which had been prepared under the exterior line of the Castle of Burgos was exploded at midnight of the 29th, and effected a breach in the wall, which some of the party, destined to attack it, were enabled to storm; but owing to the darkness of the night the detachment who were to support the advanced party missed their way, and the advance were driven off the breach again before they could be effectually supported. The breach effected by the mine was not of a description to be stormed except at the moment of the explosion, and it was necessary to improve it by fire, before the attempt could be repeated.

'But all our endeavours to construct batteries in the best situation to fire upon the wall failed, in consequence of the great superiority of the enemy's fire. One of the only three battering guns we had and two carriages were destroyed, and another gun was much injured. In the meantime, another mine had been placed under the wall, which was ready yesterday, and a fire was opened yesterday morning from a battery constructed under cover of the horn work.

'The fire from this battery improved the breach first made, and the explosion of the mine, at five o'clock yesterday evening, effected a second breach. Both were immediately stormed by the 2nd Battalion of the 24th Regiment, under the command of Captain Hedderwick, which I had ordered into the trenches for that purpose, and our troops were established within the exterior line of the works of the Castle of Burgos. The conduct of the 24th Regiment was highly praiseworthy, and Captain Hedderwick and Lieutenants Holmes and Fraser, who led the two storming parties, particularly distinguished themselves. (Now the South Wales Borderers. In later years—at Chillianwallah and Isandhlwana—the 24th was almost annihilated.—W. W.) I am happy to add, the operation was effected without suffering a very severe loss. . . .'

Return of the Killed, Wounded, and Missing of the Army under the Command of General the Marquis of Wellington, K.B., in the Siege of the Castle of Burgos, from September 27 to October 5, inclusive.

	Officers.	Sergeants.	Rank and File.	Horses.	Total Loss of Officers, Non-commissioned Officers, and Rank and File.
Killed - -	—	5	71	—	76
Wounded -	11	10	302	—	323
Missing -	—	—	4	—	4

Return of the Killed, Wounded, and Missing of the Army under the Command of General the Marquis of Wellington, K.B., in the Siege of the Castle of Burgos, from October 6 to 10, 1812, inclusive.

	Officers.	Sergeants.	Rank and File.	Horses.	Total Loss of Officers, Non-commissioned Officers, and Rank and File.
Killed - -	7	4	116	—	127
Wounded -	16	8	268	—	292
Missing -	—	—	18	—	18

To Major-General the Hon. C. Stewart.

'Villa Toro,
'October 14, 1812.

'I have in hand the toughest job I have ever undertaken, but notwithstanding deficiencies of means of all kinds, I hope I shall succeed yet. If I do, I shall be better satisfied than I have ever been with any success.'

Return of the Killed, Wounded, and Missing of the Army under the Command of General the Marquis of Wellington, K.B., in the Siege of the Castle of Burgos, from October 11 to 17, inclusive.

	Officers.	Sergeants.	Rank and File.	Horses.	Total Loss of Officers, Non-commissioned Officers, and Rank and File.
Killed	—	1	27	—	28
Wounded	4	3	66	—	73
Missing	—	—	—	—	—

Return of the Killed, Wounded, and Missing of the Army under the Command of General the Marquis of Wellington, K.B., in the Siege of the Castle of Burgos, from October 18 to 21, inclusive.

	Officers.	Sergeants.	Rank and File.	Horses.	Total Loss of Officers, Non-commisioned Officers, and Rank and File.
Killed	4	3	89	—	96
Wounded	10	4	160	—	174
Missing	—	—	4	—	4

To Earl Bathurst.

'Cabezon,
'October 26, 1812.

'I have been so much occupied by the movements and operations of the army since the 18th instant that I have not been able to write to Your Lordship. The operations of the siege of the Castle of Burgos continued nearly in the state in which they were when I addressed Your Lordship on the 11th instant, until the 18th. . . .

'I had long had reports of the enemy's intention to advance for the relief of the Castle of Burgos with the Army of Portugal, reinforced by troops recently arrived from France and with that part of the Army of the North which was disposable; and they did advance in considerable force against the post of Monasterio, on the evening of the 18th. . . .

'I assembled the troops, excepting those necessary for carrying on the operations of the siege, as soon as it appeared, by the enemy's movement of the 18th, that they entertained serious intentions of endeavouring to raise it, and placed the Allied Army on the heights, having their right at Ibeas, on the Arlanzon, the centre at Riobena and Mijaradas, and the left at Soto Palacios. The enemy's army likewise assembled in the neighbourhood of Monasterio.

'They moved forward on the evening of the 20th with about 10,000 men, to drive in our outposts from Quintanapalla and Olmos.

'On the morning of the 21st I received a letter from Sir Rowland Hill of the 17th, in which he acquainted me with the enemy's intention to move towards the Tagus, which was already fordable by individuals in many places, and was likely to become so by an army.

'The Castle of Chinchilla had surrendered on the 9th instant, and General Ballesteros, although he had entered Granada on September 17, had not assumed the position in La Mancha which he had been ordered to assume by the Spanish Government, at my suggestion.

'The enemy's force in Valencia was supposed to amount to not less than 70,000 men, a very large proportion of which, it was expected, would be disposable for service out of that kingdom.

'I had desired Lieutenant-General Sir Rowland Hill to retire from his position on the Tagus, if he should find that he could not maintain himself in it with advantage, and it was necessary that I should be near him, in order that the corps under my command might not be insulated in consequence of the movements which he should find himself under the necessity of making. I therefore raised the siege of Burgos on the night of the 21st, and moved the whole army back towards the Duero.

'I felt severely the sacrifice I was obliged to make. Your Lordship is well aware that I never was very sanguine in my expectations of success in the siege of Burgos, notwithstanding that I considered that success was attainable, even with the means in my power, within a reasonably limited period. If the attack on the first line, made on the 22nd or the 29th, had succeeded, I believe we should have taken the place, notwithstanding the ability with which the governor conducted the defence, and the gallantry with which it was executed by the garrison. Our means were very limited, but it appeared to me that if we should succeed, the advantage to the cause would be great, and the final success of the campaign would have been certain.

'I had every reason to be satisfied with the conduct of the officers and troops during the siege of Burgos, particularly with the brigade of Guards. During the latter part of the siege the weather was very unfavourable, and the troops suffered much from the rain...'

Return of the Killed, Wounded, and Missing in the Movements of the Army under the Command of General the Marquis of Wellington, K.B., from October 22 to 29, inclusive.

	Officers.	Sergeants.	Rank and File.	Horses.	Total Loss of Officers, Non-commissioned Officers, and Rank and File.
Killed -	4	14	109	74	127
Wounded -	45	35	442	65	522
Missing -	8	12	223	59	243

The Revolution in Spain.

To the Right Hon. Sir Henry Wellesley.

'Rueda,
'November 1, 1812.

'.... It is extraordinary that the revolution in Spain should not have produced one man with any knowledge of the real situation of the country. It really appears as if they were all drunk, and thinking and talking of any other subject but Spain. How it is to end God knows! ..'

Alba de Tormes.

To Earl Bathurst.

'Ciudad Rodrigo,
'November 19, 1812.

'.... I enclose Lieutenant-General Hamilton's report to Sir Rowland Hill of the transactions at Alba, which were highly creditable to the troops employed....'

Return of the Killed and Wounded of the Army under the Command of General the Marquis of Wellington, K.B., in the Defence of Alba de Tormes, on November 10 and 11, 1812.

	Officers.	Sergeants.	Rank and File.	Horses.	Total Loss of Officers, Non-commissioned Officers, and Rank and File.
Killed - -	—	—	21	—	21
Wounded -	3	4	85	—	92
Missing -	—	—	—	—	—

Return of the Killed, Wounded, and Missing in the Operations of the Army under the Command of General the Marquis of Wellington, K.B., from November 15 to 19, inclusive.

	Officers.	Sergeants.	Rank and File.	Horses.	Total Loss of Officers, Non-commissioned Officers, and Rank and File.
Killed - -	5	2	43	15	50
Wounded -	6	7	126	9	139
Missing -	1	3	174	58	178

A Successful Campaign.

To the Earl of Liverpool.

'Ciudad Rodrigo,
'November 23, 1812.

' . . . From what I see in the newspapers, I am much afraid that the public will be disappointed at the result of the last campaign, notwithstanding that it is, in fact, the most successful campaign in all its circumstances, and has produced for the cause more important results than any campaign in which a British Army has been engaged for the last century. We have taken by siege Ciudad Rodrigo, Badajoz, and Salamanca; and the Retiro surrendered. In the meantime, the allies have taken Astorga, Guadalaxara and Consuegra, besides other places taken by Duran and Sir H. Popham. In the months elapsed since January this army has sent to England little short of 20,000 prisoners, and they have taken and destroyed or have themselves the use of the enemy's arsenals in Ciudad Rodrigo, Badajoz, Salamanca, Valladolid, Madrid, Astorga, Seville, the lines before Cadiz, etc.; and upon the whole we have taken and destroyed, or we now possess, little short of 3,000 pieces of cannon. The siege of Cadiz has been raised, and all the countries south of the Tagus have been cleared of the enemy . . . .

'I see that a disposition already exists to blame the Government for the failure of the siege of Burgos. The Government had nothing to say to the siege; it was entirely my own act. In regard to means, there were ample means both at Madrid and at Santander for the siege of the strongest fortress. That which was wanting at both places was means of transporting ordnance and military stores to the place where it was desirable to use them.

'The people in England, so happy as they are in every respect, so rich in resources of every description, having the use of such excellent roads, *etc.*, will not readily believe that important results here frequently depend upon fifty or sixty mules, more or less, or a few bundles of straw to feed them; but the fact is so, notwithstanding their incredulity. . .'

Irregularities and Outrages.

To Officers commanding Divisions and Brigades.

'Freneda,
'November 28, 1812.

'I have ordered the army into cantonments, in which I hope that circumstances will enable me to keep them for some time, during which the troops will receive their clothing, necessaries, etc., which are already in progress by different lines of communication to the several divisions of brigades.

'But besides these objects, I must draw your attention in a very particular manner to the state of discipline of the troops. The discipline of every army, after a long and active campaign, becomes in some degree relaxed, and requires the utmost attention on the part of the general and other officers to bring it back to the state in which it ought to be for service; but I am concerned to have to observe that the army under my command has fallen off in this respect in the late campaign to a greater degree than any army with which I have ever served, or of which I have ever read.

****

At the inquiry into military punishments, Wellington, asked if he conceived that the army, when it left France from the Pyrenees, was in as efficient a state for service as an army can well be brought to, made his famous answer: 'I always thought that I could have gone anywhere and done anything with that army.' He also stated that he considered the discipline of his Peninsular Army to be infinitely superior to that of the French troops opposed to him.—W. W.

****

'Yet this army has met with no disaster; it has suffered no privations which but trifling attention on the part of the officers could not have prevented, and for which there existed no reason whatever in the nature of the service; nor has it suffered any hardships, excepting those resulting from the necessity of being exposed to the inclemencies of the weather at a moment when they were most severe.

'It must be obvious, however, to every officer that from the moment the troops commenced their retreat from the neighbourhood of Burgos on the one hand, and from Madrid on the other, the officers lost all command over their men. Irregularities and outrages of all descriptions were committed with impunity, and losses have been sustained which ought never to have occurred.

'Yet, the necessity for retreat existing, none was ever made on which the troops had such short marches, none on which they made such long and repeated halts, and none on which the retreating armies were so little pressed on their rear by the enemy.

'We must look, therefore, for the existing evils, and for the situation in which we now find the army, to some cause besides those resulting from the operations in which we have been engaged.

'I have no hesitation in attributing these evils to the habitual inattention of the officers of the regiments to their duty, as prescribed by the standing regulations of the service, and by the orders of this army.

'I am far from questioning the zeal, still less the gallantry and spirit, of the officers of the army; and I am quite certain that if their minds can be convinced of the necessity of minute and constant attention to understand, recollect, and carry into execution the orders which have been issued for the performance of their duty, and that the strict performance of this duty is necessary to enable the army to serve the country as it ought to be served, they will in future give their attention to these points.

'Unfortunately, the inexperience of the officers of the army has induced many to consider that the period during which an army is on service is one of relaxation from all rule, instead of being, as it is, the period during which of all others every rule for the regulation and control of the conduct of the soldier, for the inspection and care of his arms, ammunition, accoutrements, necessaries, and field equipments, and his horse and horse appointments, for the receipt and issue and care of his provisions, and the regulation of all that belongs to his food and the forage for his horse, must be most strictly attended to by the officers of his company or troop, if it is intended that an army, a British Army in particular, shall be brought into the field of battle in a state of efficiency to meet the enemy on the day of trial. These are the points, then, to which I most earnestly intreat you to turn your attention, and the attention of the officers of the regiments under your command, Portuguese as well as English, during the period in which it may be in my power to leave the troops in their cantonments.

'The commanding officers of regiments must enforce the orders of the army regarding the constant inspection and superintendence of the officers over the conduct of the men of their companies in their cantonments; and they must endeavour to inspire the non-commissioned officers with a sense of their situation and authority; and the non-commissioned officers must be forced to do their duty by being constantly under the view and superintendence of the officers.

'By these means the frequent and discreditable recourse to the authority of the provost, and to punishments by the sentence of courts-martial, will be prevented, and the soldiers will not dare to commit the offences and outrages of which there are too many complaints, when they well know that their officers and their non-commissioned officers have their eyes and attention turned towards them. The commanding officers of regiments must likewise enforce the orders of the army regarding the constant, real inspection of the soldiers' arms, ammunition, accoutrements, and necessaries, in order to prevent at all times, the shameful waste of ammunition, and the sale of that article and of the soldiers' necessaries. With this view, both should be inspected daily.

'In regard to the food of the soldier, I have frequently observed and lamented in the late campaign the facility and celerity with which the French soldiers cooked in comparison with those of our army.

'The cause of this disadvantage is the same with that of every other description—the want of attention of the officers to the orders of the army, and the conduct of their men, md the consequent want of authority over their conduct.

'Certain men of each company should be appointed to cut and bring in wood, others to fetch water, and others to get the meat, etc., to be cooked; and it would soon be found that if this practice were daily enforced, and a particular hour for seeing the dinners, and for the men dining, named, as it ought to be, equally as for parade, that cooking would no longer require the inconvenient length of time which it has lately been found to take, and that the soldiers would not be exposed to the privation of their food at the moment at which the army may be engaged in operations with the enemy.

'You will, of course, give your attention to the field exercise and discipline of the troops. It is very desirable that the soldiers should not lose the habits of marching, and the division should march ten or twelve miles twice in each week, if the weather should permit, and the roads in the neighbourhood of the cantonments of the division should be dry. But I repeat that the great object of the attention of the general and field officers must be to get the captains and subalterns of the regiments to understand and perform the duties required from them, as the only mode by which the discipline and efficiency of the army can be restored and maintained during the next campaign.'

Ladies in Billets.

To Marshal Beresford.

'Cadiz,

'December 29, 1812.

'. . . In regard to the ladies, they have certainly no right to be lodged in billets, but it would be cruel to deprive them of that accommodation. I do not believe I can authorise their having this advantage by an order, and the point can be settled only in communication with the Government. If the matter could be allowed to go on, as it is now,

I would write a letter to Peacocke to be circulated among the ladies, which would give them a little advice on this subject, and make them better behaved . . .'

The Publication of Despatches.

To Don J. de Carvajal.

'Xerez,
'January 10, 1813.

'Before I left Cadiz I omitted to communicate personally with Your Excellency regarding those parts of the despatches and reports to Your Excellency which should be published, and those which should be kept for the information of the Regency alone.

'It is obvious that it may be necessary to keep parts of every despatch from the knowledge of the public for some time, and therefore I shall take the liberty of marking in the margin of every despatch, for the information of the public, those parts of it, and of its enclosures, which it shall appear to me ought not to be made public.'

Quitting the 33rd.

To Colonel Arthur Gore, commanding 33rd Regiment.

'Freneda,
'February 3, 1813.

'Before you receive this letter you will have heard that His Royal Highness the Prince Regent has been pleased to appoint me to be Colonel of the Royal Horse Guards, an honour entirely unexpected by me. I do not know who is to be my successor in the 33rd Regiment.

'Although highly gratified by the honour which has been thus conferred upon me, as well as by the manner in which it has been conferred, I cannot avoid feeling a regret at one of its circumstances, *viz.*, that I should be separated from the 33rd Regiment, to which I have belonged, with so much satisfaction to myself, for more than twenty years . . .'

Punishment for Desertion.

To Major-General the Hon. C. Colville.

'Headquarters, Freneda,
'February 9, 1813.

'It appearing that the sentence of the enclosed court-martial is, at present, in part illegal, by exceeding the powers given by the Mutiny Act to the court, I return the proceedings for the purpose of revision.

'By the twentieth section of the Act, upon which this sentence must be founded, the court is enabled to sentence a deserter to any *one* of the following three *distinct* punishments:

'First: "to service in such country, or place, or places abroad, or otherwise, and in such regiment, or regiments, or corps, as His Majesty shall please to direct." That is, to general service.

'Secondly: "to service for life as a soldier."

'Thirdly: "to service for any term of years beyond the period for which such non-commissioned officer or soldier shall have enlisted, and to a forfeiture of all, or any part, of the benefit, or advantage as to increase of pay, or as to pension, or discharge, which might otherwise have accrued to such non-commissioned officer or soldier from the length or nature of the service."

'But the court is not authorised to pass the cumulative sentence of any *two* or more of these three distinct punishments, which in this case it has done, namely, *general service, and for life.*

'By the sixth section, the marking with the letter D, as described there, may be added to any *one* of the former three punishments.' (To mark a soldier with the letter "D" signified deserter.—W. W.)

A Money-Chest robbed.

To the Adjutant-General.

'Freneda,
'March 9, 1813.

'I have received your letter of January 18, in regard to four soldiers of the —th Regiment.

'These soldiers were part of a guard who, when escorting treasure from Lisbon and Badajoz in the year 1809, robbed the money-chest of £2,500 sterling. Shortly after the robbery was committed, 2,500 dollars were found in the possession of the prisoners, but no proof could ever be obtained that they had robbed the military chest, although I, and those who considered the subject with me, never entertained the slightest doubt upon the subject.

'For this reason, I did not think it proper to bring these persons to trial before a court-martial. They must have been acquitted, and they would have had a claim to the money which had been found in their possession. As the robbery by the soldiers of the guard of the money and other articles under their charge was but too common a practice, I did not deem it expedient to hold forth to the army this example of the success with which such an outrage to such a serious extent might be committed with impunity. . . .

'I now request to have orders what I am to do with these men, and particularly whether I am to restore to them the money taken from them and locked in the military chest in the year 1809. . . .'

Medals.

To Earl Bathirst.

'Freneda,
'March 16, 1813.

'I have received your letter of February 24 in regard to the medals, and I concur entirely with you regarding all the improvements you propose on the subject. You have provided a remedy for a difficulty which I could never get over in a way at all satisfactory to myself.

'I likewise agree with you in the propriety of having a cross with eight bars, or a star with eight points, for those who are entitled to more than seven distinctions.

'I am not certain that it would not be best that all general officers, as well as others, should wear the medal or cross at the buttonhole till they should receive the last distinction. It is very awkward to ride in round the neck. . . .'

To Earl Bathurst.

'Freneda,
'April 20, 1813.

'. . . . We must have the orders of the Secretary of State for any alteration in the mode of wearing the medal by the general officers. It may do very well for an admiral to wear his medal round his neck on his quarter-deck, but we on horseback ought to wear it always at our buttonhole . . .'

Abduction by an Officer.

To Lieutenant-General Cole.

'Freneda.
'March 19, 1813.

'The mother of the lady carried off by —— of the —th Regiment, having complained to me of his conduct, and having desired my assistance to remove her daughter from the disgraceful situation in which she is now placed, I consented to grant it, on the condition of a promise on her part that the daughter should not be ill-treated, and, above all, should not be confined in a convent.

'I enclose the letter from the lady, in which she makes the engagement as above pointed out; and I beg that you will call upon —— —— to restore the young lady to her family. If he should decline to do so upon your order, I beg you to put him in close arrest, and then to take measures to remove the young lady from his power into that of her family at ——; as I cannot allow any officer of this army to be guilty of such a breach of the laws of Portugal as to carry away a young lady, and retain her in the cantonments of the army, contrary to the wishes of her parents and relations. . . .'

'Freneda,
'March 25, 1813.

'I have received your letter of the 22nd instant; and being satisfied myself of the validity of the promise made by the mother of the young lady who has been carried off by —— —— of the —th Regiment, I do not conceive that doubts entertained by any other person on that subject ought to prevent or delay the execution of the directions which I gave on that subject.

'In regard to—— ——'s inclination to marry the young lady, I cannot but observe that he has it in his power, whenever he pleases, to compensate in that manner the injury which he has done to the family; and it is no excuse that the influence of the family has prevented the clergy in the neighbourhood from performing the ceremony. That influence could not extend to the clergy in Spain, from which country —— —— is distant but a few miles.

'—— —— has been guilty of a gross breach, not only of the laws of Portugal, but of the laws of his own and of all civilized countries, and if I should be called upon by the Government, as I most probably shall, to deliver over —— —— to the Portuguese tribunals, to be dealt with according to the Portuguese law, I shall most undoubtedly comply with their desire.

'I cannot but observe upon —— ——'s complaint "that he is to be placed at the disposal of a foreign tribunal," that the notion is too common among the officers and soldiers of the army that they are not obliged to obey the laws of the country in which they are acting; or, in other words, that they may act as they please, and may commit such outrages as they think proper, provided they do not offend against the Mutiny Act and Articles of War. I cannot, however, admit of such a doctrine; and —— —— will be an instance that the laws of the country must be obeyed, if the Portuguese Government shall desire that he may be delivered over to the tribunals of that country . . . .'

Gallantry of the 10th Hussars.

To Earl Bathurst.

'Ampudia,
'June 6, 1813.

'. . . . The English hussars, being in the advanced-guard, fell in, between Toro and Morales, with a considerable body of the enemy's cavalry, which were immediately attacked by the 10th, supported by the 18th and 15th. The enemy were overthrown, and pursued for many miles; and 210 prisoners, with many horses, and two officers, fell into our hands.

'I enclose Colonel Grant's report of this gallant affair, which reflects great credit upon Major Robarts and the 10th Hussars, and upon Colonel Grant, under whose directions they acted. . .'

Battle of Vitoria.

To Earl Bathurst.

'Salvatierra,
'June 22, 1813.

'The enemy, commanded by King Joseph, having Marshal Jourdan as the Major-General of the army, took up a position, on the night of the 19th instant, in front of Vitoria; the left of which rested upon the heights which end at La Puebla de Arganzon, and extended from thence across the valley of the Zadorra, in front of the village of Ariñez. They occupied with the right of the centre a height which commanded the valley to the Zadorra. The right of their army was stationed near Vitoria, and was destined to defend the passages of the River Zadorra, in the neighbourhood of that city. They had a reserve in rear of their left, at the village of Gomecha.

'The nature of the country through which the army had passed since it had reached the Ebro had necessarily extended our columns; and we halted on the 20th, in order to close them up, and moved the left to Murguia, where it was most likely it would be required. I reconnoitred the enemy's position on that day, with a view to the attack to be made on the following morning, if they should still remain in it.

'We accordingly attacked the enemy yesterday, and I am happy to inform Your Lordship that the Allied Army under my command gained a complete victory, having driven them from all their positions; having taken from them 151 pieces of cannon, waggons of ammunition, all their baggage, provisions, cattle, treasure, etc., and a considerable number of prisoners.

'The operations of the day commenced by Lieutenant-General Sir Rowland Hill obtaining possession of the heights of La Puebla, on which the enemy's left rested, which heights they had not occupied in great strength. He detached for this service one brigade of the Spanish division under General Morillo; the other brigade being employed in keeping the communication between his main body on the highroad from Miranda to Vitoria, and the troops detached to the heights. The enemy, however, soon discovered the importance of these heights, and reinforced their troops there to such an extent that Lieutenant-General Sir Rowland Hill was obliged to detach, first, the 71st Regiment, (now the 1st Battalion the Highland Light Infantry), and the light infantry battalion of General Walker's brigade, under the command of Lieutenant-Colonel the Hon. H. Cadogan, and successively other troops to the same point; and the allies not only gained, but maintained possession of these important heights throughout their operations, notwithstanding all the efforts of the enemy to retake them. (A piper of the 71st at Vitoria valiantly encouraged his comrades in the battle by playing '*Up an'waur them a', Willie.*'—W.W.)

'The contest here was, however, very severe, and the loss sustained considerable. General Morillo was wounded, but remained in the field, but I am concerned to have to report that Lieutenant-Colonel the Hon. H. Cadogan has died of a wound which he received. In him His Majesty has lost an officer of great merit and tried gallantry, who had already acquired the respect and regard of the whole profession, and of whom it might have been expected that, if he had lived, he would have rendered the most important services to his country.

'Under cover of the possession of these heights, Sir Rowland Hill successively passed the Zadorra, at La Puebla, and the defile formed by the heights and the River Zadorra, and attacked and gained possession of the village of Subijana de Alava in front of the enemy's line, which the enemy made repeated attempts to regain.

'The difficult nature of the country prevented the communication between our different columns moving to the attack from their stations on the River Bayas at as early an hour as I had expected; and it was late before I knew that the column, composed of the 3rd and 7th Divisions, under the command of the Earl of Dalhousie, had arrived at the station appointed for them. The 4th and Light Divisions, however, passed the Zadorra immediately after Sir Rowland Hill had possession of Subijana de Alava, the former at the bridge of Nanclares, and the latter at the bridge of Trespuentes; and almost as soon as these had crossed, the column under the Earl of Dalhousie arrived at Mendoza, and the 3rd Division, under Lieutenant-General Sir Thomas Picton, crossed at the bridge higher up, followed by the 7th Division, under the Earl of Dalhousie.

'These four divisions, forming the centre of the army, were destined to attack the height on which the right of the enemy's centre was placed, while Lieutenant-General Sir Rowland Hill should move forward from Subijana de Alava to attack the left. The enemy, however, having weakened his line to strengthen his detachment on the hills, abandoned his position in the valley as soon as he saw our disposition to attack it, and commenced his retreat in good order towards Vitoria.

'Our troops continued to advance in admirable order, notwithstanding the difficulty of the ground. In the meantime, Lieutenant-General Sir Thomas Graham, who commanded the left of the army, consisting of the 1st and 5th Divisions, and the General Pack's and Bradford's brigades of infantry, and General Bock's and Anson's of cavalry, and who had been moved on the 20th to Murguia, moved forward from thence on Vitoria, by the highroad from that town to Bilbao. He had, besides, with him the Spanish division under Colonel Longa, and General Giron, who had been detached to the left, under a different view of the state of affairs, and had afterwards been recalled, and had arrived on the 20th at Orduna, marched that morning from thence, so as to be in the field in readiness to support Lieutenant-General Sir Thomas Graham, if his support had been required.

'The enemy had a division of infantry with some cavalry advanced on the great road from Vitoria to Bilbao, resting their right on some strong heights covering the village of Gamarra Mayor. Both Gamarra and Abechuco were strongly occupied as *têtes de pont* and the bridges over the Zadorra at these places. Brigadier-General Pack with his Portuguese brigade, and Colonel Longa with his Spanish division, were directed to turn and gain the heights, supported by Major-General Anson's brigade of light dragoons, and the 5th Division of Infantry under the command of Major-General Oswald, who was desired to take the command of all these troops.

'Lieutenant-General Sir Thomas Graham reports that in the execution of this service the Portuguese and Spanish troops behaved admirably. The 4th Battalion of Caçadores and the 8th Caçadores particularly distinguished themselves. Colonel Longa, being on the left, took possession of Gamarra Menor.

'As soon as the heights were in our possession, the village of

Gamarra Mayor was most gallantly stormed and carried by Major-General Robertson's brigade of the 5th Division, which advanced in columns of battalions, under a very heavy fire of artillery and musketry, without firing a shot, assisted by two guns of Major Lawson's brigade of artillery. The enemy suffered severely, and lost three pieces of cannon.

'The Lieutenant-General then proceeded to attack the village of Abechuco with the 1st Division, by forming a strong battery against it, consisting of Captain Dubourdieu's brigade and Captain Ramsay's troop of Horse Artillery; and under cover of this fire Colonel Halkett's brigade advanced to the attack of the village, which was carried; the light battalions having charged and taken three guns and a howitzer on the bridge. This attack was supported by General Bradford's brigade of Portuguese infantry.

'During the operation at Abechuco the enemy made the greatest efforts to repossess themselves of the village of Gamarra Mayor, which were gallantly repulsed by the 5th Division, under the command of Major-General Oswald. The enemy had, however, on the heights on the left of the Zadorra, two divisions of infantry in reserve, and it was impossible to cross by the bridges till the troops which had moved upon the enemy's centre and left had driven them through Vitoria.

'The whole then co-operated in the pursuit, which was continued by all till after it was dark.

'The movement of the troops under Lieutenant-General Sir Thomas Graham, and their possession of Gamarra and Abechuco, intercepted the enemy's retreat by the highroad to France. They were then obliged to turn to the road towards Pamplona, but they were unable to hold any position for a sufficient length of time to allow their baggage and artillery to be drawn off. The whole, therefore, of the latter which had not already been taken by the troops in their attack of the successive positions taken up by the enemy in their retreat from their first position at Ariñez and on the Zadorra, and all their ammunition and baggage, and everything they had, were taken close to Vitoria. I have reason to believe that the enemy carried off with them one gun and one howitzer only.

'The army under King Joseph consisted of the whole of the armies of the South, and of the Centre, and of four divisions and all the cavalry of the Army of Portugal, and some troops of the Army of the North. General Foy's division of the Army of Portugal was in the neighbourhood of Bilbao; and General Clausel, who commanded the Army of the North, was near Logroño with one division of the army of Portugal commanded by General Taupin, and General Vander-Maesen's division of the Army of the North.

****

The 14th (King's) Hussars took King Joseph's carriage, and with it a remarkable silver trophy—which the regiment still possesses—known throughout the service as 'The Emperor.'—W. W.

****

'The 6th Division of the Allied Army, under Major-General the Hon. E. Pakenham, was likewise absent, having been detained at Medina de Pomar for three days, to cover the march of our magazines and stores.

'I cannot extol too highly the good conduct of all the General Officers, officers, and soldiers of the army in this action. . . .

'It was impossible for the movements of any troops to be conducted with more spirit and regularity than those of their respective divisions by Lieutenant-Generals the Earl of Dalhousie, Sir Thomas Picton, Sir Lowry Cole, and Major-General Baron Charles Alton. The troops advanced in *échelons* of regiments in two, and occasionally three, lines; and the Portuguese troops in the 3rd and 4th Divisions, under the command of Brigadier-General Power and Colonel Stubbs, led the march with steadiness and gallantry never surpassed on any occasion.

'Major-General the Hon. C. Colville's brigade of the 3rd Division was seriously attacked in its advance by a very superior force well formed, which it drove in, supported by General Inglis's brigade of the 7th Division, commanded by Colonel Grant of the 82nd. These officers and the troops under their command distinguished themselves. . . .

'Mariscal de Campo Don Luis Wimpffen, and the Inspector-General Don Thomas O'Donoju, and the officers of the staff of the Spanish Army, have invariably rendered me every assistance in their power in the course of these operations, and I avail myself of this opportunity of expressing my satisfaction with their conduct, as likewise with that of Mariscal de Campo Don Miguel Alava, and of the Brigadier-General Don Josef O'Lalor, who have been so long and usefully employed with me.

'The artillery was most judiciously placed by Lieutenant-Colonel Dickson, and was well served, and the army is particularly indebted to that corps.

'The nature of the ground did not allow of the cavalry being generally engaged, but the General Officers commanding the several brigades kept the troops under their command respectively close to the infantry to support them, and they were most active in the pursuit of the enemy after they had been driven through Vitoria.

'I send this despatch by my *aide-de-camp*, Captain Fremantle, whom I beg leave to recommend to Your Lordship's protection. He will have the honour of laying at the feet of His Royal Highness the colours of the 4th Battalion 100th Regiment, and Marshal Jourdan's baton of a Marshal of France taken by the 87th Regiment.

'I enclose a return of the killed and wounded in the late operations, and a return of the ordnance, carriages, and ammunition taken from the enemy in the action of the 21st instant.'

Return of the Killed, Wounded, and Missing of the Allied Army, under the Command of General the Marquis of Wellington, K.G., in the Action with the French Army, under the Command of King Joseph Buonaparte, at Vitoria, on June 21, 1813.

	Officers.	Serjeants.	Rank and File.	Total Loss of Officers, Non-commissioned Officers, and Rank and File.	British.	Spanish.	Portuguese.	Horses.
Killed -	33	19	688	740	501	89	150	92
Wounded -	230	158	3,782	4,174	2,807	464	899	68
Missing -	—	1	265	266	—	—	—	26

1 sergeant, 2 drummers, and 263 rank and file have been returned missing by the several corps of the army, British and Portuguese. It is supposed that the greater number of them lost their regiments in the course of the night, and that very few of them have fallen into the hands of the enemy.

Aylmer, Deputy Adjutant-General.

Return of Ordnance, Carnages, and Ammunition, captured from the Enemy in the Action at Vitoria, on June 21, 1813.

151 brass ordnance, on travelling carriages.
415 caissons.
14,249 rounds of ammunition.
1,973,400 musket-ball cartridges.
40,668 pounds of gunpowder.
56 forage waggons.
44 forge waggons.

A. Dickson, Lieutenant-Colonel
commanding the Artillery.

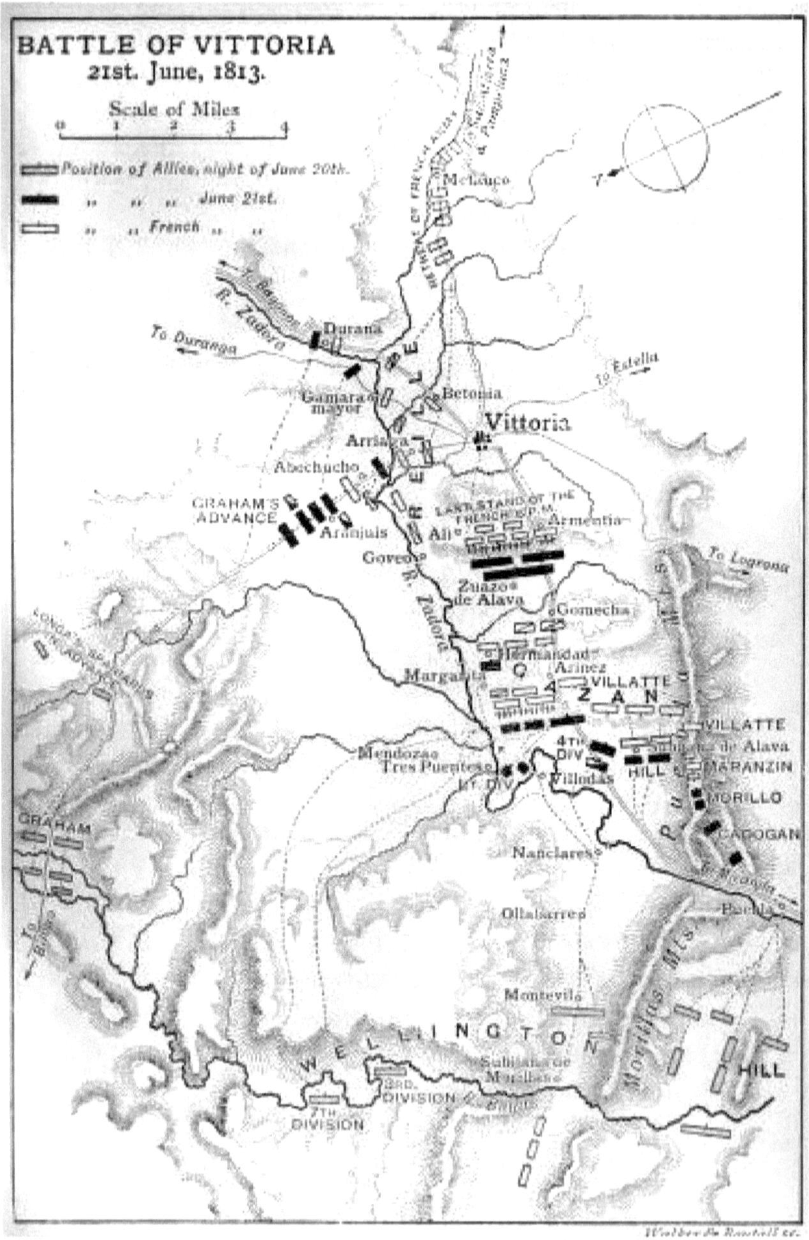

Walker & Boutall sc.

To Don Juan O'Donoju.

'Salvatierra,
'June 22, 1813.

'I have the honour to inform you that I yesterday attacked the enemy's army, commanded by King Joseph, in the neighbourhood of Vittoria, and gained a complete victory, having taken from the enemy more than 120 pieces of cannon, all their ammunition, baggage, cattle, provisions, treasure, etc.

'The enemy, prevented from retiring by the direct road to France, are on their retreat to Pamplona. I followed them this day with the advanced-guard to within six leagues of that place, to which the whole army are in march.

'Our loss has not been severe...'

'Our Vagabond Soldiers.'

To Earl Bathurst.

'Caseda, on the River Aragon,
'June 29, 1813.

'It is desirable that any reinforcements of infantry which you may send to this army may come to Santander, notwithstanding that I am very apprehensive of the consequence of marching our vagabond soldiers through the province of Biscay in that state of discipline in which they and their officers generally come out to us. It may be depended upon, that the people of this province will shoot them as they would the French, if they should misbehave.

'We started with the army in the highest order, and up to the day of the battle nothing could get on better; but that event has, as usual, totally annihilated all order and discipline. The soldiers of the army have got among them about a million sterling in money, with the exception of about 100,000 dollars, which were got for the military chest. The night of the battle, instead of being passed in getting rest and food to prepare them for the pursuit of the following day, was passed by the soldiers in looking for plunder. The consequence was that they were incapable of marching in pursuit of the enemy, and were totally knocked up. The rain came on and increased their fatigue, and I am quite convinced that we have now out of the ranks double the amount of our loss in the battle; and that we have lost more men in the pursuit than the enemy have, and have never in any one day made more than an ordinary march.

'This is the consequence of the state of discipline of the British

Army. We may gain the greatest victories, but we shall do no good until we shall so far alter our system as to force all ranks to perform their duty. The new regiments are, as usual, the worst of all. The —th —— —— are a disgrace to the name of a soldier, in action as well as elsewhere, and I propose to draft their horses from them, and to send the men to England, if I cannot get the better of them in any other manner.'

Unrivalled Fighters.

To Colonel Torrens.

'Lesaca,
'July 18, 1813.

'I have received your letter of the 5th, and I am sorry that I cannot recommend —— —— for promotion, because I have, had him in arrest since the battle for disobeying an order given to him by me verbally. The fact is, that if discipline means habits of obedience to orders, as well as military instruction, we but have little of it in the army. Nobody ever thinks of obeying an order, and all the regulations of the Horse Guards, as well as of the War Office, and all the orders of the army applicable to this peculiar service, are so much waste paper.

'It is, however, an unrivalled army for fighting, if the soldiers can only be kept in their ranks during the battle; but it wants some of those qualities which are indispensable to enable a General to bring them into the field in the order in which an army ought to be to meet an enemy, or to take all the advantage to be derived from a victory; and the cause of these defects is the want of habits of obedience and attention to orders by the inferior officers, and, indeed, I might add, by all. They never attend to an order with an intention to obey it, or sufficiently to understand it, be it ever so clear, and therefore never obey it when obedience becomes troublesome, or difficult, or important. . . .'

'The Fighting Cocks of the Army.'

To the Earl of Liverpool.

'Lesaca,
'July 25, 1813.

'As far as I have any knowledge, there are no troops paid in Spain at present excepting those to whom I have been enabled to spare money out of our military chest in payment of the Spanish subsidy. Your Lordship must have seen enough of the Spanish character, during the contest and our connection with them, to be aware that it will not answer to press any measure upon them which they do not like. I have not seen amongst them the slightest inclination to employ English officers to discipline their troops to such an extent as would answer any useful purpose; and I believe that one of the reasons for which they like me so well is that, contrary to their expectations, I have not pressed them to take English officers. Besides, as I have above stated to Your Lordship, the Spanish troops do not want discipline—if by discipline is meant instruction—so much as they do a system of order, which can be founded only on regular pay and food, and good care and clothing. These British officers could not give them; and, notwithstanding that the Portuguese are now the *fighting cocks* of the army, I believe we owe their merits more to the care we have taken of their pockets and bellies than to the instruction we have given; them. . . .'

THE PYRENEES.

To Earl Bathurst.

'San Estevan,
'August 1, 1813.

'Two practicable breaches having been effected at San Sebastian on July 24, orders were given that they should be attacked on the morning of the 25th.

'I am concerned to have to report that this attempt to obtain possession of the place failed, and that our loss was very considerable.

'I went to the siege on the 25th, and, having conferred with Lieutenant-General Sir Thomas Graham and the officers of the engineers and artillery, it appeared to me that it would be necessary to increase the facilities of the attack before it should be repeated. But, upon adverting to the state of our ammunition, I found that we had not a sufficiency to do anything effectual till that should arrive for which I had written on June 26, which I had reason to believe was embarked at Portsmouth, and to expect every hour. I therefore desired that the siege should for the moment be converted into a blockade, a measure which I found to be the more desirable when I returned to Lesaca in the evening.

'The Allied Army was posted in the passes of the mountains, with a view to cover the blockade of Pamplona and the siege of San Sebastian. . . .

'The defect of this position was that the communication between the several divisions was very tedious and difficult, while the communication of the enemy in front of the passes was easy and short; and in case of attack those in the front line could not support each other, and could look for support only from their rear.

'On the 24th Marshal Soult collected the right and left wings of his army, with one division of the centre and two divisions of cavalry at St. Jean Pied de Port, and on the 25th attacked, with between 30,000 and 40,000 men, General Byng's post at Roncesvalles. Lieutenant-General Sir Lowry Cole moved up to his support with the 4th Division, and these officers were enabled to maintain their post throughout the day, but the enemy turned it in the afternoon, and Lieutenant-General Sir Lowry Cole considered it to be necessary to withdraw in the night, and he marched to the neighbourhood of Zubiri.

'In the actions which took place on this day the 20th Regiment distinguished themselves.

'Two divisions of the centre of the enemy's army attacked Sir R. Hill's position in the Puerto de Maya at the head of the valley of Baztan, in the afternoon of the same day. The brunt of the action fell upon Major-General Pringle's and Major-General Walker's brigades, in the 2nd Division, under the command of Lieutenant-General the Hon. W. Stewart. These troops were at first obliged to give way, but having been supported by Major-General Barnes's brigade of the 7th Division, they regained that part of their post which was the key of the whole, and which would have enabled them to reassume it if circumstances had permitted it. But Sir R. Hill, having been apprised of the necessity that Sir Lowry Cole should retire, deemed it expedient to withdraw his troops likewise to Irurita, and the enemy did not advance on the following day beyond the Puerto de Maya.

'Notwithstanding the enemy's superiority of numbers, they acquired but little advantage over these brave troops during the seven hours they were engaged. All the regiments charged with the bayonet. The conduct of the 82nd Regiment, which moved up with Major-General Barnes's brigade, is particularly reported.

'I was not apprised of these events till late in the nights of the 25th and 26th, and I adopted immediate measures to concentrate the army to the right, still providing for the siege of San Sebastian, and for the blockade of Pamplona. . . .

'The British cavalry under Lieutenant-General Sir Stapleton Cotton were placed near Huarte on the right, being the only ground on which it was possible to use the cavalry. . . .

'I joined the 3rd and 4th Divisions just as they were taking up their ground on the 27th, and shortly afterwards the enemy formed their army on a mountain the front of which extends from the highroad to Ostiz to the highroad to Zubiri; and they placed one division on the left of that road on a height, and in some villages in front of the 3rd Division; they had here also a large body of cavalry.

'In a short time after they had taken up their ground, the enemy attacked the hill on the right of the 4th Division, which was then occupied by one battalion of the 4th Portuguese Regiment, and by the Spanish regiment of Pravia. These troops defended their ground, and drove the enemy from it with the bayonet. Seeing the importance of this hill to our position, I reinforced it with the 40th Regiment, and this regiment, with the Spanish regiments El Principe and Pravia, held it from this time, notwithstanding the repeated efforts of the enemy during the 27th and 28th to obtain possession of it.

'Nearly at the same time that the enemy attacked this height on the 27th, they took possession of the village of Sorauren on the road to Ostiz, by which they acquired the communication by that road, and they kept up a fire of musketry along the line till it was dark.

'We were joined on the morning of the 28th by the 6th Division of Infantry, and I directed that the heights should be occupied on the left of the valley of the Lanz, and that the 6th Division should form across the valley in rear of the left of the 4th Division, resting their right on Orcain, and their left on the heights above mentioned.

'The 6th Division had scarcely taken their position when they were attacked by a very large force of the enemy which had been assembled in the village of Sorauren.

'Their front was, however, so well defended by the fire of their own light troops from the heights on their left, and by the fire from the heights occupied by the 4th Division and Brigadier-General Campbell's Portuguese brigade, that the enemy were soon driven back with immense loss from a fire on their front, both flanks, and rear.

'In order to extricate their troops from the difficulty in which they found themselves in their situation in the valley of the Lanz, the enemy now attacked the height on which the left of the 4th Division stood, which was occupied by the 7th Caçadores, of which they obtained a momentary possession. They were attacked, however, again by the 7th Caçadores, supported by Major-General Ross with his brigade of the 4th Division, and were driven down with great loss.

'The battle now became general along the whole front of the heights occupied by the 4th Division, and in every part in our favour, excepting where one battalion of the 10th Portuguese Regiment of

Major-General Campbell's brigade was posted. This battalion having been overpowered, and having been obliged to give way immediately on the right of Major-General Ross's brigade, the enemy established themselves on our line, and Major-General Ross was obliged to withdraw from his post.

'I, however, ordered the 27th and 48th Regiments to charge, first, that body of the enemy which had first established themselves on the height, and next, those on the left. Both attacks succeeded, and the enemy were driven down with immense loss, and the 6th Division, having moved forward at the same time to a situation in the valley nearer to the left of the 4th, the attack upon this front ceased entirely, and was continued but faintly on other points of our line.

'In the course of this contest, the gallant 4th Division, which had so frequently been distinguished in this army, surpassed their former good conduct. Every regiment charged with the bayonet, and the 40th, 7th, 20th, and 23rd, four different times. Their officers set them the example, and Major-General Ross had two horses shot under him.

'The Portuguese troops likewise behaved admirably, and I had every reason to be satisfied with the conduct of the Spanish regiments El Principe and Pravia. . . .

'The enemy's force which had been in front of Sir Rowland Hill followed his march, and arrived at Ostiz on the 29th. The enemy, thus reinforced, and occupying a position on the mountains which appeared little liable to attack, and finding that they could make no impression on our front, determined to endeavour to turn our left by an attack on Sir Rowland Hill's corps. They reinforced with one division the troops which had been already opposed to him, still occupying the same points in the mountain on which was formed their principal force, but they drew in to their left the troops which occupied the heights opposite the 3rd Division, and they had, during the night of the 29th and 30th, occupied in strength the crest of the mountain on our left of the Lanz opposite to the 6th and 7th Divisions, thus connecting their right in their position with the divisions detached to attack Lieutenant-General Sir Rowland Hill.

'I, however, determined to attack their position, and ordered Lieutenant-General the Earl of Dalhousie to possess himself of the top of the mountain in his front, by which the enemy's right would be turned, and Lieutenant-General Sir Thomas Picton to cross the heights on which the enemy's left had stood, and to turn their left by the road to Roncesvalles. All the arrangements were made to attack the front of the enemy's position, as soon as the effect of these movements on their flanks should begin to appear. Major-General the Hon. Edward Pakenham, whom I had sent to take the command of the 6th Division, Major-General Pack having been wounded, turned the village of Sorauren as soon as the Earl of Dalhousie had driven the enemy from the mountain by which that flank was defended, and the 6th Division, and Major-General Byng's brigade, which had relieved the 4th Division on the left of our position on the road to Ostiz, instantly attacked and carried that village.

'Lieutenant-General Sir Lowry Cole likewise attacked the front of the enemy's main position with the 7th Caçadores, supported by the 11th Portuguese Regiment, the 40th, and the battalion under Colonel Bingham, consisting of the 53rd and Queen's Regiment. All these operations obliged the enemy to abandon a position which is one of the strongest and most difficult of access that I have yet seen occupied by troops.

'In their retreat from this position, the enemy lost a great number of prisoners. I cannot sufficiently applaud the conduct of all the general officers, officers, and troops throughout these operations. The attack made by Lieutenant-General the Earl of Dalhousie was admirably conducted by His Lordship, and executed by Major-General Inglis and the troops composing his brigade; and that by Major-General the Hon. E. Pakenham, and Major-General Byng, and that by Lieutenant-General Sir Lowry Cole; and the movement made by Sir Thomas Picton merited my highest commendation. The latter officer co-operated in the attack of the mountain, by detaching troops to his left, in which Lieutenant-Colonel the Hon. R. Trench was wounded, but I hope not seriously.

'While these operations were going on, and in proportion as I observed their success, I detached troops to the support of Lieutenant-General Sir Rowland Hill.

'The enemy appeared in his front late in the morning, and immediately commenced an extended manoeuvre upon his left flank, which obliged him to withdraw from the height which he occupied behind Lizasso to the next range. He there, however, maintained himself, and I enclose his report of the conduct of the troops.

'I continued the pursuit of the enemy after their retreat from the mountain to Olague, where I was at sunset immediately in the rear of their attack upon Lieutenant-General Sir Rowland Hill. They withdrew from his front in the night, and yesterday took up a strong position with two divisions to cover their rear on the pass of Dona Maria.

'Lieutenant-General Sir Rowland Hill and the Earl of Dalhousie attacked and carried the pass, notwithstanding the vigorous resistance of the enemy, and the strength of their position. . . . .'

'In the meantime, I moved with Major-General Byng's brigade, and the 4th Division, under Lieutenant-General the Hon. Sir Lowry Cole, by the Pass of Velate, upon Irurita, in order to turn the enemy's position on Dona Maria. Major-General Byng took in Elizondo a large convoy going to the enemy, and made many prisoners.

'We have this day continued the pursuit of the enemy in the valley of the Bidasoa, and many prisoners and much baggage have been taken. Major General Byng has possessed himself of the valley of Baztan, and of the position on the Puerto de Maya, and the army will be this night nearly in the same positions which they occupied on July 25. . . .

'The enemy, having been considerably reinforced and reequipped after their late defeat, made a most formidable attempt to relieve the blockade of Pamplona, with the whole of their forces, excepting the reserve, under General Villatte, which remained in front of our troops on the great road from Irun. This attempt has been entirely frustrated by the operations of a part only of the allied army, and the enemy has sustained a defeat, and suffered a severe loss in officers and men. . . .'

Return of the Killed, Wounded, and Missing of the Army under the Command of Field-Marshal the Marquis of Wellington, K.G., at the Siege of San Sebastian, from July 7 to 27, 1813.

	Officers.	Sergeants.	Rank and File.	Horses.	Total Loss of Officers, Non-commissioned Officers, and Rank and File.
Killed -	11	9	184	—	204
Wounded -	44	34	696	—	774
Missing -	6	6	288	—	300

Portuguese loss included.

To Earl Bathurst,

'Lesaca,

'August 3, 1813.

'. . . . We have had some desperate fighting in these mountains, and I have never known the troops behave so well. In the battle of the 28th we had hard fighting, and in my life, I never saw such an attack as was made by General Barnes's brigade in the 7th Division upon the enemy above Echalar yesterday; the loss of the French is immense.

'I understand they say themselves that they have lost 15,000 men. That is what I estimated their loss; but if they acknowledge that number, I ought to estimate it at 20,000 men, which is the number more generally believed.'

To Lieutenant-General Sir T. Graham, K.B.

'Lesaca,
'August 4, 1813, 9 a.m.

'I have received your letters to the 3rd instant, which I have been obliged to delay acknowledging till this moment. The troops are, of course, a good deal fatigued, and we have suffered very considerably, particularly the English troops in the 2nd Division, in the affair in the Puerto de Maya, which, with the existing want of shoes and of musket ammunition, induces me to delay for a day or two any forward movement, and to doubt the expediency of making one at all. I keep everything in readiness, however.

'I am perfectly aware of the objections to our positions in the Pyrenees; but if we should not be able to advance from them without incurring more loss than we ought, or than we can well afford, I am afraid that we cannot well retire from them.

'Many events turned out unfortunately for us on the 1st instant, each of which ought to have been in our favour; and we should have done the enemy a great deal more mischief than we did in his passage down this valley.

'But as it is, I hope that Soult will not feel an inclination to renew his expedition on this side at least. The French Army must have suffered, terribly.

'Between the 25th of last month and 2nd of this they were engaged seriously not less than ten times; on many occasions in attacking very strong positions, in others beat from them or pursued. .'

To the Earl of Liverpool.

'August 4, 1813.

'The enemy had no success on any other ground, and were terribly beat after I joined the troops at Sorauren. Their loss cannot be less than 15,000 men, and I am not certain that it is not 20,000 men. We have about 4,000 prisoners. I never saw such fighting as on July 27 and 28, the anniversary of the Battle of Talavera, nor such determination as the troops showed.

'I wish some measures could be adopted to punish the recruiters for the foreign corps.

'Above 150 men deserted from the *Chasseurs Britanniques* from Lizasso in one night, and the Brunswick *Oels* lost by desertion 90 men in the course of a very few days on the outposts. The fact is, the men were enlisted from the prisons.

'There are now not less than 800 deserters in confinement at Lisbon, whom the Admiralty have forbidden should be sent home; and they are excessively discontented with their treatment, which has now effectually stopped desertion in the French Army in aid of the enlistment of deserters by the York Light Infantry.

'The desertion of the foreign troops has had the bad effect of teaching desertion to our own troops.'

To Earl Bathurst.

'Lesaca,
'August 4, 1813.

'The enemy still continued posted on the morning of the 2nd, with a force of two divisions, in the Puerto de Echalar, and nearly the whole army behind the Puerto, when the 4th, 7th and Light Divisions advanced by the valley of the Bidasoa to the frontier; and I had determined to dislodge them by a combined attack and movement of the three divisions.

'The 7th Division, however, having crossed the mountains from Sumbilla, and having necessarily preceded the arrival of the 4th, Major-General Barnes's brigade was formed for the attack, and advanced before the 4th and Light Divisions could co-operate, with a regularity and gallantry which I have seldom seen equalled, and actually drove two divisions of the enemy from the formidable heights, notwithstanding the resistance opposed to them.

'It is impossible that I can extol too highly the conduct of Major-General Barnes, and of these brave troops, which was the admiration of all who were witnesses of it.

'Major-General Kempt's brigade of the Light Division likewise drove a very considerable force from the rock which forms the left of the Puerto.

'There is now no enemy in the field within this part of the Spanish frontier.'

General Return of the Killed, Wounded, and Missing in the Operations of the Allied Army, under the Command of Field-Marshal the Marquis of Wellington, K.G., from July 25 to August 2, 1813, inclusive.

	Officers.	Sergeants.	Rank and File.	Total Loss of Officers, Non-commissioned Officers, and Rank and File.	British.	Portuguese.
Killed -	43	59	779	881	559	322
Wounded	331	261	4,918	5,510	3,693	1,817
Missing -	17	16	672	705	504	201

This return includes the whole of the casualties during the operations between July 25 and August 2, enclosed in the despatch of August 1 as well as that of August 4.

To Earl Bathurst.

'Lesaca,

'August 9, 1813.

'I have not had a great deal of reason to complain of the conduct of the troops since the last battles, but we pulled up on the frontiers of France, and they are getting into good order again. As we are getting many men out of hospital, I hope that we shall soon have in the ranks within 2,000 or 3,000 men of the number we had before the late battles.

'But our soldiers are terrible fellows for everything but fighting with their regiments. What do you think of seventy or eighty of them, having wandered from their regiments during the late operations, and having surrendered themselves to some of the French peasantry who accompanied the French Army, and whom they ought, and would at other times, have eaten up? The foreign troops desert terribly; 150 men deserted from the *Chasseurs Britanniques* in one night at Lizasso.

'Our having so much money has enabled me to adopt a plan for paying every non-commissioned officer and soldier a day's pay every day, which will, I think, produce a great reform in their conduct. Many of their outrages are certainly to be attributed to want of money.

'Nothing has yet been done, my dear lord, about a naval force for us, which is really necessary.'

Naval Help needed.

To Viscount Melville.

'Lesaca,

'August 21, 1813.

'I have received your letter of July 28. I do not know what Sir Charles Stuart has written to Government regarding want of naval means on the Lisbon station. What I have written has been founded upon my own sense of the want of naval assistance on this coast, as well as on the coast of Portugal; and I assure you that I neither know nor care what has passed, or may pass, in Parliament or in the newspapers on the subject.

'I complain of an actual want of necessary naval assistance and co-operation with the army, of which I believe no man will entertain a doubt who reads the facts stated in my reports to Government. I know nothing about the cause of the evil; it may be owing to a general deficiency of naval force for all the objects to which it is necessary to attend in an extended system of war.

'It may be owing to a proper preference of other services over this, or it may be owing to the inapplication of the force intrusted to their command by the admirals and captains. I state the fact, which nobody will deny; and leave it to Government to apply a remedy or not as they may think proper, hoping only that they will let me know whether they propose to apply a remedy or not. . . .'

A Rare Loss.

To Earl Bathurst

'Lesaca,
'August 23, 1813.

'I have received your letter of the 14th, with —— ——'s scheme. It is like all those which I have received from French officers, and might answer well enough if I could afford, or the British Government or nation would allow of my being as prodigal of men as every French General is. They forget, however, that we have but one army, and that the same men who fought at Vimeiro and Talavera fought the other day at Sorauren; and that, if I am to preserve that army, I must proceed with caution.

'Indeed, this becomes doubly necessary, as I see that, notwithstanding the fondness of the British nation for the sport, and their exultation upon our success, they began to cry out the other day upon the loss of 300 or 500 men in the unsuccessful storm of San Sebastian, and of the men in the affair at the —— ——. The troops, however, will sometimes behave ill, and posts will sometimes be surprised, and the troops engaged be roughly handled.

'The affair at the —— —— is certainly the worst that has ever occurred to the troops under my command, and the only one in which any guns have been lost, excepting at the Battle of ———; and it was entirely owing to ——'s settling in his own mind that the enemy would not attack him. If the troops had not regained their post, and behaved remarkably well, I should not have passed this affair without notice.

'Your Lordship may depend upon it that I am by no means tired of success; and that I shall do everything in my power to draw the attention of the enemy to this quarter, as soon as I shall know that hostilities are really renewed in Germany.'

To Lieutenant-General Sir William Stewart.

'Lesaca,
'September 13, 1813.

'I feel very unwilling to draw the attention of the Secretary of State again to the loss of the guns in the Puerto de Maya, in order to show that they were lost going to a position to which you had ordered them by the very same road, and under the very circumstances, under which I had stated they were lost, retiring to Elizondo. I was very sorry to have lost those guns, as they are the only guns that have ever been lost by troops acting under my command; but I attributed their loss then, as I do now, to unfortunate accident to which the best arrangements must be liable, and, above all, to that most unfortunate accident of your being absent when the attack was made, and —— ——, who commanded, having been with the division only two days. . .'

The Capture of San Sebastian.

To Earl Bathurst.

'Lesaca,
'September 2, 1813.

'The fire against the Fort of San Sebastian was opened on August 26, and directed against the towers which flanked the bastion on the eastern face; against the demi-bastion on the south-east angle, and the termination of the curtain of the south face.

'Lieutenant-General Sir Thomas Graham had directed that an establishment should be formed on the island of Sta. Clara, which was effected on the night of the 26th, and the enemy's detachment on the island were made prisoners. Captain Cameron of the 9th had the command of the detachment which effected this operation, and Lieutenant-General Sir Thomas Graham particularly applauds his conduct and that of Lieutenant Chadwick, of the Royal Engineers. The conduct of Lieutenant the Hon. James Arbuthnot, of the Royal Navy, who commanded the boats, was highly meritorious, as likewise that of Lieutenant Bell of the Royal Marines.

'All that was deemed practicable to carry into execution in order

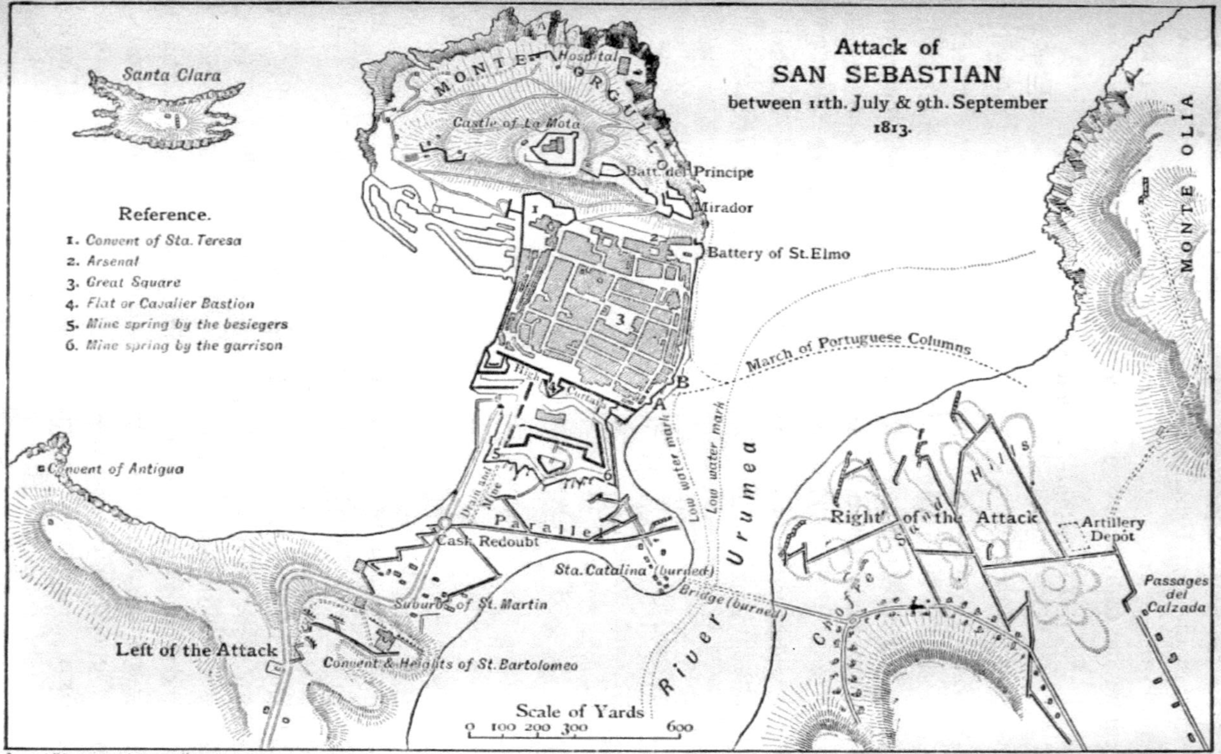

Jones' "Journal of Sieges."

Walker & Boutall sc.

to facilitate the approach to the breaches before made in the wall of San Sebastian, having been effected on August 30, and the breach having been made at the termination of the bastion, the place was stormed at eleven o'clock in the day on the 31st, and carried.

'The loss on our side has been severe. Lieutenant-General Sir James Leith, who had joined the army only two days before, and Major-Generals Oswald and Robinson, were unfortunately wounded in the breach; and Colonel Sir Richard Fletcher was killed by a musket-ball at the mouth of the trenches.

'I have the honour to enclose Lieutenant-General Sir Thomas Graham's report of this operation below, in which Your Lordship will observe with pleasure another distinguished instance of the gallantry and perseverance of His Majesty's officers and troops under the most trying difficulties. . . .

To Field-Marshal the Marquis of Wellington, K.G.

'Oyarzun,
'September 1, 1813.

'In obedience to Your Lordship's orders of the preceding day to attack and form a lodgement on the breach of San Sebastian, which now extended to the left, so as to embrace the outermost tower, the end and front of the curtain immediately over the left bastion, as well as the faces of the bastion itself, the assault took place at eleven o'clock a.m. yesterday; and I have the honour to report to Your Lordship that the heroic perseverance of all the troops concerned was at last crowned with success.

'The column of attack was formed of the 2nd Brigade of the 5th Division, commanded by Major-General Robinson, with an immediate support of detachments as per margin, and having in reserve the remainder of the 5th Division, consisting of Major-General Spry's Portuguese brigade and the 1st Brigade under Major-General Hay, as also the 5th Battalion of Caçadores of General Bradford's brigade, under Major Hill, the whole under the direction of Lieutenant-General Sir James Leith, commanding the 5th Division.

'Having arranged everything with Sir J. Leith, I crossed the Urumea to the batteries of the right attack, where everything could be most distinctly seen, and from whence the orders for the fire of the batteries, according to circumstances, could be immediately given.

'The column, in filing out of the right of the trenches, was as before exposed to a heavy fire of shells and grape-shot, and a mine was exploded in the left angle of the counterscarp of the hornwork, which did great damage, but did not check the ardour of the troops in advancing to the attack. There never was anything so fallacious as the external appearance of the breach; without some description, the almost insuperable difficulties of the breach cannot be estimated. Notwithstanding its great extent, there was but one point where it was possible to enter, and there by single files.

'All the inside of the wall to the right of the curtain formed a perpendicular scarp of at least 20 feet to the level of the streets, so that the narrow ridge of the curtain itself, formed by the breaching of its end and front, was the only accessible point. During the suspension of the operations of the siege, from want of ammunition, the enemy had prepared every means of defence which art could devise, so that great numbers of men were covered by entrenchments and traverses, in the hornwork, on the ramparts of the curtain, and inside of the town opposite to the breach, and ready to pour a most destructive fire of musketry on both flanks of the approach to the top of the narrow ridge of the curtain.

'Everything that the most determined bravery could attempt was repeatedly tried in vain by the troops, who were brought forward from the trenches in succession. No man outlived the attempt to gain the ridge, and though the slope of the breach afforded shelter from the enemy's musketry, yet still the nature of the stone rubbish prevented the great exertions of the engineers and working parties from being able to form a lodgement for the troops, exposed to the shells and grape from the batteries of the castle, as was particularly directed, in obedience to Your Lordship's instructions; and, at all events, a secure lodgement could never have been obtained without occupying a part of the curtain.

'In this almost desperate state of the attack, after consulting with Colonel Dickson, commanding the Royal Artillery, I ventured to order the guns to be turned against the curtain. A heavy fire of artillery was directed against it, passing a few feet only over the heads of our troops on the breach, and was kept up with a precision of practice beyond all example.

'Meanwhile, I accepted the offer of a part of Major-General Bradford's Portuguese brigade to ford the river near its mouth. The advance of the 1st Battalion 13th Regiment, under Major Snodgrass, over the open beach and across the river, and of a detachment of the 24th Regiment, under Lieutenant-Colonel M'Bean, in support, was made in the handsomest style, under a very severe fire of grape.

'Major Snodgrass attacked, and finally carried the small breach on the right of the great one, and Lieutenant-Colonel M'Bean's detachment occupied the right of the great breach. I ought not to omit to mention that a similar offer was made by the 1st Portuguese Regiment of Brigadier-General Wilson's brigade, under Lieutenant-Colonel Fearon, and that both Major-General Bradford and Brigadier-General Wilson had from the beginning urged most anxiously the employment of their respective brigades in the attack, as they had had so large a share in the labour and fatigues of the right attack.

'Observing now the effect of the admirable fire of the batteries against the curtain, though the enemy was so much covered, a great effort was ordered to be made to gain the high ridge at all hazards, at the same time that an attempt should be made to storm the horn work.

'It fell to the lot of the 2nd Brigade of the 5th Division, under the command of Colonel the Hon. Charles Greville, to move out of the trenches for this purpose, and the 3rd Battalion of the Royal Scots, under Lieutenant-Colonel Barns, supported by the 38th, under Lieutenant-Colonel Miles, fortunately arrived to assault the breach of the curtain about the time when an explosion on the rampart of the curtain (occasioned by the fire of the artillery) created some confusion among the enemy.

'The narrow pass was gained, and was maintained, after a severe conflict, and the troops on the right of the breach, having about this time succeeded in forcing the barricades on the top of the narrow line wall, found their way into the houses that joined it. Thus, after an assault which lasted above two hours, under the most trying circumstances, a firm footing was obtained.

'It was impossible to restrain the impetuosity of the troops, and in an hour more the enemy were driven from all the complication of defences prepared in the streets, suffering a severe loss on their retreat to the castle, and leaving the whole town in our possession. . . .'

'The garrison retired to the castle, leaving about 270 prisoners in our hands, and I hope that I shall soon have the pleasure to inform Your Lordship that we have possession of that post.

'Since the fire against San Sebastian had been recommenced, the enemy had drawn the greatest part of their force to the camp of Urogne, and there was every reason to believe that they would make an attempt to relieve the place. . . . .

'The enemy crossed the Bidasoa by the fords between Andara and the destroyed bridge on the highroad, before daylight on the morning of the 30th, with a very large force, with which they made a most desperate attack along the whole front of the position of the Spanish troops on the heights of San Marcial. They were beat back, some of them even across the river, in the most gallant style by the Spanish troops, whose conduct was equal to that of any troops that I have ever seen engaged; and the attack, having been frequently repeated, was upon every occasion defeated with the same gallantry and determination.

'The course of the river being immediately under the heights on the French side, on which the enemy had placed a considerable quantity of cannon, they were enabled to throw a bridge across the river three-quarters of a mile above the highroad, over which, in the afternoon, they marched again a considerable body, who, with those who had crossed the fords, again made a desperate attack upon the Spanish positions. This was equally beat back, and at length, finding all their efforts on that side fruitless, the enemy took advantage of the darkness of a violent storm to retire their troops from this front entirely.

Return of the Killed, Wounded, and Missing of the Army under the Command of Field-Marshal the Marquis of Wellington, K.G., at the Siege, Assault, and Capture of San Sebastian, from July 28 to August 31, 1813.

	Officers.	Sergeants.	Rank and File.	Total Loss of Officers, Non-commissioned Officers, and Rank and File.	British.	Portuguese.	Horses.
Killed	45	40	676	761	572	189	—
Wounded	105	93	1,499	1,697	1,103	594	—
Missing	1	—	44	45	41	4	—

'Notwithstanding that I had a British division on each flank of the 4th Spanish Army, I am happy to be able to report that the conduct of the latter was so conspicuously good, and they were so capable of defending their post without assistance, in spite of the desperate efforts of the enemy to carry it, that, finding that the ground did not allow of my making use of the 1st or 4th Divisions on the flanks of the enemy's attacking corps, neither of them were in the least engaged during the action.

'Nearly at the same time that the enemy crossed the Bidasoa in front of the heights of San Marcial, they likewise crossed that river with about three divisions of infantry in two columns, by the fords below Salin, in front of the position occupied by the 9th Portuguese Brigade. I ordered General Inglis to support this brigade with that of the 7th Division under his command; and as soon as I was informed of the course of the enemy's attack, I sent to Lieutenant-General the Earl of Dalhousie to request that he would likewise move towards the Bidasoa with the 7th Division, and to the Light Division to support Major-General Inglis by every means in their power. Major-General Inglis found it impossible to maintain the heights between Lesaca and the Bidasoa, and he withdrew to those in front of the Convent of San Antonio, which he maintained.

'In the meantime, Major-General Kempt moved one brigade of the Light Division to Lesaca, by which he kept the enemy in cheek, and covered the march of the Earl of Dalhousie to join General Inglis.

'The enemy, however, having completely failed in their attempt upon the position of the Spanish Army on the heights of San Marcial, and finding that Major-General Inglis had taken a position from which they could not drive him, at the same time that it covered and protected the right of the Spanish Army, and the approaches to San Sebastian by Oyarzun, and that their situation on the left of the Bidasoa was becoming at every moment more critical, retired during the night.

'The fall of rain during the evening and night had so swollen the Bidasoa that the rear of their column was obliged to cross the bridge ofVera. In order to effect this object, they attacked the post of Major-General Skerrett's brigade of the Light Division, at about three in the morning, both from the Puerto de Vera, and from the left of the Bidasoa.

'Although the nature of the ground rendered it impossible to prevent entirely the passage of the bridge after daylight, it was made under the fire of a great part of Major-General Skerrett's brigade, and the enemy's loss in the operation must have been very considerable.

'While this was going on upon the left of the army, Mariscal de Campo Don P.A. Giron attacked the enemy's posts in front of the Pass of Echalar on the 30th and 31st.

'Lieutenant-General the Earl of Dalhousie made General Lecor attack those in front of Zugarramurdi with the 6th Portuguese Brigade on the 31st, and the Hon. Major-General Colville made Colonel Douglas attack the enemy's posts in front of the Pass of Maya on the same day with the 7th Portuguese Brigade. All these troops conducted themselves well.

'The attack made by the Earl of Dalhousie delayed his march till late in the afternoon of the 31st, but he was in the evening in a favourable situation for his further progress, and in the morning of the 1st in that allotted for him.

'In these operations, in which a second attempt by the enemy to prevent the establishment of the Allies upon the frontier has been defeated by the operations of a part only of the Allied Army, at the very moment at which the Fort of San Sebastian was taken by storm, I have had great satisfaction in observing the zeal and ability of the officers, and the gallantry and discipline of the troops ....

'I fully concur in the lieutenant-general's report of the cordial assistance which he has received from Captain Sir George Collier, and the officers, seamen, and marines under his command, who have done everything in their power to facilitate and ensure our success. The seamen have served with the artillery in the batteries, and have upon every occasion manifested that spirit which is characteristic of the British navy....'

Return of the Killed, Wounded, and Missing of the Allied Army, under the Command of Field-Marshal the Marquis of Wellington, K.G., in Action with the Enemy on August 31 and September 1, 1813.

	Officers.	Sergeants.	Rank and File.	Total Loss of Officers, Non-commissioned Officers, and Rank and File.	British.	Spanish.	Portuguese.	Horses.
Killed	29	20	351	400	51	261	88	2
Wounded	159	115	1,823	2,067	334	1,347	386	4
Missing	5	3	148	156	32	71	53	—

King Joseph's Papers.

To Earl Bathurst.

'Lesaca,
'September 3, 1813.

'. . . . I will send you a selection of Joseph's papers; but as the Secretary of State's Office is a sink of papers, and these are really curious, and will hereafter tend to illustrate many things that have occurred here, particularly in the last year, I shall be glad to have them again, and that they should remain among my papers.'

Heavy Losses in Officers.

To Earl Bathurst.

'Lesaca,
'September 3, 1813.

'. . . It would be very desirable to adopt some measure respecting the 51st and 68th Regiments—that is to say, either to order them home, or to allow me to form them into a provisional battalion. They are fully officered with very few men, and it is quite shocking to see the list of killed and wounded officers when they go into action. The other day the 51st lost 12 officers killed and wounded, and, I believe, not quite 100 men. As to sending them home, I must tell you that, in this country in particular, one old soldier is worth at least five new ones. This place is about eighteen miles from Pasages, where the drafts recently arrived have been landed, and they came that distance in two marches. But they had two mountains to pass, and they are so knocked up by marching over them, that I have not seen one detachment go through entire.

'Lord Aylmer's brigade cannot, I am convinced, march five miles in corps.'

Capitulation of San Sebastian.

To Earl Bathurst.

'Lesaca,
'September 10, 1813.

'A battery was constructed in the hornwork with great difficulty against the works of the Castle of San Sebastian, which opened on the morning of the 8th instant; and I have the pleasure to inform you that the garrison surrendered before evening. I enclose Lieutenant-General Sir Thomas Graham's report, and the terms of capitulation agreed upon with the garrison, returns of ordnance, ammunition, etc., in the place.

'The loss of the garrison during the siege is stated to have amounted to two-thirds of their number at its commencement. . . . .'

Return of Killed, Wounded, and Missing of the Army under the Command of Field-Marshal the Marquis of Wellington, K.G., in the Siege of the Castle of San Sebastian, from September 1 to 8, 1813.

	Officers.	Sergeants.	Rank and File.	Horses.	Total Loss of Officers, Non-commissioned Officers, and Rank and File.
Killed -	1	—	1	—	2
Wounded -	1	—	9	—	10
Missing -	—	—	—	—	—

Portuguese loss not included.

Renewed Plundering.

To Lieutenant-General Sir John Hope, K.B.

'Lesaca,
'October 8, 1813.

'. . . I have sad accounts of the plunder of the soldiers yesterday, and I propose again to call the attention of the officers to the subject. I saw yesterday many men coming in from Olague drunk and loaded with plunder; and it cannot be prevented unless the general and other officers exert themselves.'

****

'G. O. 'Lesaca,
'October 8, 1813.

'*1.* The Commander of the Forces is concerned to be under the necessity of publishing over again his orders of July 9 last, as they have been unattended to by the officers and troops which entered France yesterday.

'*2.* According to all the information which the Commander of the Forces has received, outrages of all descriptions were committed by the troops in presence even of their officers, who took no pains whatever to prevent them.

'*3.* The Commander of the Forces has already determined that some officers, so grossly negligent of their duty, shall be sent to England, that their names may be brought under the attention of the Prince Regent, and that His Royal Highness may give such directions respecting them as he may think proper, as the Commander of the Forces is determined not to command officers who will not obey his orders.'

****

Entrance into France.

To Earl Bathurst.

'Lesaca,

'October 9, 1813.

'Having deemed it expedient to cross the Bidasoa with the left of the army, I have the pleasure to inform Your Lordship that that object was effected on the 7th instant. . . .

'Lieutenant-General Sir Thomas Graham, having thus established within the French territory the troops of the Allied British and Portuguese Army, which had been so frequently distinguished under his command, resigned the command to Lieutenant-General Sir John Hope, who had arrived from Ireland on the preceding day. . . .

'The 52nd Regiment, under the command of Major Mayne, charged, in a most gallant style, and carried the entrenchment with the bayonet. The 1st and 3rd Caçadores, and the 2nd Battalion 95th Regiment, as well as the 52nd Regiment, distinguished themselves in this attack. . . .

'The Light Division took 22 officers, and 400 prisoners, and three pieces of cannon; and I am particularly indebted to Major-General Charles Baron Alten for the manner in which he executed this service.

'On the right, the troops of the army of reserve of Andalusia, under the command of Don P. A. Giron, attacked the enemy's post and entrenchments on the mountain of La Rhune in two columns, under the command of Spaniards only.

'These troops carried everything before them in the most gallant style, till they arrived at the foot of the rock on which the hermitage stands, and they made repeated attempts to take even that post by storm; but it was impossible to get up, and the enemy remained during the night in possession of the hermitage, and on a rock on the same range of the mountain with the right of the Spanish troops. Some time elapsed yesterday morning before the fog cleared away sufficiently to enable me to reconnoitre the mountain, which I found to be least inaccessible by its right, and that the attack of it might be connected with advantage with the attack of the enemy's works in front of the camp of Sarre.

'I accordingly ordered the army of reserve to concentrate to their right, and as soon as the concentration commenced Mariscal de Campo Don P. A. Giron ordered the battalion *de Las Ordenes* to attack the enemy's post on the rock, on the right of the position occupied by his troops, which was instantly carried in the most gallant style. These troops followed up their success, and carried an entrenchment on a hill, which protected the right of the camp of Sarre; and the enemy immediately evacuated all their works to defend the approaches to the camp, which were taken possession of by detachments from the 7th Division, sent by Lieutenant-General the Earl of Dalhousie through the Puerto de Echalar for this purpose.

'Don P. A. Giron then established the battalion of *Las Ordenes* on the enemy's left, on the rock of the hermitage. It was too late to proceed farther last night; and the enemy withdrew from their post at the hermitage, and from the camp of Sarre during the night.

'It gives me singular satisfaction to report the good conduct of the officers and troops of the Army of Reserve of Andalusia, as well in the operations of the 7th instant as in those of yesterday. The attack made by the battalion of *Las Ordenes*, under the command of Colonel Hore, yesterday, was made in as good order and with as much spirit as any that I have seen made by any troops, and I was much satisfied with the spirit and discipline of the whole of this corps. . . . . .

'When on my way to Roncesvalles, on the 1st instant, I directed Brigadier-General Campbell to endeavour to carry off the enemy's pickets in his front, which he attacked on that night; and completely succeeded, with the Portuguese troops under his command, in carrying the whole of one picket, consisting of seventy men. A fortified post on the mountain of Airola was likewise stormed, and the whole garrison put to the sword. . . .'

Return of Killed, Wounded, and Missing of the Army under the Command of Field-Marshal the Marquis of Wellington, K.G., in Action with the Enemy on October 7 and 8, 1813.

	Officers.	Sergeants.	Rank and File.	Total Loss of Officers, Non-commissioned Officers, Rank and File.	British.	Portuguese.	Horses.
Killed -	4	5	70	127	79	48	—
Wounded	40	33	422	674	495	179	—
Missing -	—	—	5	13	5	8	—

BADLY PAID GENERALS.

To Earl Bathurst.

'Vera,
'October 10, 1813.

'I wish to draw your attention to the situation of Sir Rowland Hill and Sir John Hope.

'They each of them command very large corps, and great expenses must be incurred by them; and I know that the former, and I believe the latter, has not the means of defraying those expenses.

'The general officers of the British Army are altogether very badly paid, and, adverting to the deductions from their pay, they receive less than they did fifty years ago, while their expenses are more than doubled; and their allowances of all kinds are smaller than those of corresponding ranks in other services, while, from the custom of the British Army, they are all obliged to keep tables for their staff, and their expenses are greater.

'It would not probably be possible to increase the pay of general officers generally; but I earnestly recommend that Sir John Hope and Sir Rowland Hill should have an allowance each equal to that of the second in command in Sicily, or to the commanding officer at Cadiz.

'I would beg Your Lordship to observe likewise that the expenses of an officer, who must spend more than he receives here, are vastly increased by the disadvantageous rate at which he is obliged to draw his money; and I believe that, in this way, even Sir Thomas Graham, who has a large private fortune, has been frequently in distress here.'

'Infamous Libels.'

To the Magistrates of San Sebastian.

'Vera,

'November 2, 1813.

'I received only this day your letter of October 15, and I am very sorry that it is not in my power to be of any use to the town of San Sebastian.

'The course of the operations of the war rendered necessary the attack of that town, in order to expel the enemy from the Spanish territory; and it was a subject of the utmost concern to me to see that the enemy wantonly destroyed it.

'The infamous libels which have been circulated upon this subject, in which the destruction of the town has been attributed to the troops under my command, *by order of their officers* (notwithstanding that it was in great part burned, and was on fire in six places before they entered it by storm), render it a matter of delicacy for me to interfere in any manner in this affair; and I am very desirous not to be applied to again, and not again to have occasion to write upon it.'

Wholesale Desertion.

To Earl Bathurst.

'Vera,

'November 9, 1813.

'Although I am very well pleased with the German troops, (and in one respect, their health, they are very superior to any you could send us), they desert so terribly, and in this respect set our men so bad an example, that I should not be sorry to get rid of them. It is really quite disgraceful. I do not believe a man remains of the last recruits sent out to the German Legion. They were raised from the prisoners sent home after the Battle of Vitoria; and I would observe, that if this is to be allowed it would be much better to enlist them here, as Government would at least save the expense of their passage to England and back. They generally belong to the Nassau regiment, which we are endeavouring to bring over in a body, and in the meantime are recruiting it in detail.

'Between the Spaniards, Germans, and, I am sorry to add, English, I believe we have not lost less than 1,200 men in the last four months. The Portuguese (to their honour be it recollected) do not desert to the enemy. When they go, it is to return to their own country.'

The Passage of the Nivelle.

To Earl Bathurst.

'St. Pé,

'November 13, 1813.

'The enemy had since the beginning of August occupied a position with their right upon the sea in front of St. Jean de Luz, and on the left of the Nivelle, their centre on La Petite Rhune, and on the heights behind that village; and their left consisting of two divisions of infantry under the Comte d'Erlon on the right of that river, on a strong height in rear of Ainhoüé, and on the mountain of Mondarrain, which protected the approach to that village.

'They had had one division under General Foy at St. Jean Pied de Port, which was joined by one of the Army of Aragon under General Paris, at the time the left of the Allied Army crossed the Bidasoa. General Foy's division joined those on the heights behind Ainhoüé, when Sir R. Hill moved into the valley of Baztan. The enemy, not satisfied with the natural strength of this position, had the whole of it fortified; and their right in particular had been made so strong that I did not deem it expedient to attack it in front.

'Pamplona having surrendered on October 31, and the right of the army having been disengaged from covering the blockade of that place, I moved Lieutenant-General Sir Rowland Hill on the 6th and 7th into the valley of Baztan, as soon as the state of the roads, after the recent rains, would permit, intending to attack the enemy on the 8th; but the rain which fell on the 7th having again rendered the roads impracticable, I was obliged to defer the attack till the 10th, when we completely succeeded in carrying all the positions on the enemy's left and centre, in separating the former from the latter, and by these means turning the enemy's strong positions occupied by their right on the Lower Nivelle, which they were obliged to evacuate during the night, having taken 51 pieces of cannon and 1,400 prisoners.

'The object of the attack being to force the enemy's centre, and to establish our army in rear of their right, the attack was made in columns of divisions, each led by the general officer commanding it, and each forming its own reserve. Lieutenant-General Sir Rowland Hill directed the movements of the right, consisting of the 2nd Division under Lieutenant-General the Hon. Sir William Stewart; the 6th Division under Lieutenant-General Sir Henry Clinton; a Portuguese division under Lieutenant-General Sir John Hamilton, and a Spanish division under General Morillo, and Colonel Grant's brigade of cavalry and a brigade of Portuguese artillery, under Lieutenant-Colonel Tulloh, and three mountain guns under Lieutenant Robe, which attacked the positions of the enemy behind Ainhoüé.

'Marshal Sir William Beresford directed the movements of the right of the centre, consisting of the 3rd Division under Major-General the Hon. C. Colville, the 7th Division under Mariscal de Campo Le Cor, and the 4th Division under Lieutenant-General the Hon. Sir Lowry Cole.

'The latter attacked the redoubts in front of Sarre, that village, and the heights behind it, supported on their left by the Army of Reserve of Andalusia, under the command of Mariscal de Campo Don P. A. Giron, which attacked the enemy's positions on the right of Sarre, on the slopes of La Petite Rhune, and the heights behind the village on the left of the 4th Division.

'Major-General Charles Baron Alten attacked, with the Light Division, and General Longa's Spanish division, the enemy's positions on La Petite Rhune; and, having carried them, co-operated with the right of the centre in the attack of the heights behind Sarre.

'General V. Alten's brigade of cavalry, under the direction of Lieutenant-General Sir Stapleton Cotton, followed the movements of the centre; and there were three brigades of British artillery with this part of the army, and three mountain guns with General Giron, and three with Major-General C. Alten.

'Lieutenant-General Don Manuel Freyre moved in two columns from the heights of Mandate towards Ascain, in order to take advantage of any movement the enemy might make from the right of their position towards their centre; and Lieutenant-General Sir John Hope with the left of the army drove in the enemy's outposts in front of their entrenchments on the Lower Nivelle, carried the redoubt above Urogne, and established himself on the heights immediately opposite Siboure, in readiness to take advantage of any movement made by the enemy's right.

'The attack began at daylight; and Lieutenant-General Sir Lowry Cole having obliged the enemy to evacuate the redoubt on their right in front of Sarre by a cannonade, and that in front of the left of the village having been likewise evacuated on the approach of the 7th Division under General Le Cor to attack it, Lieutenant-General Sir Lowry Cole attacked and possessed himself of the village, which was turned on its left by the 3rd Division, under Major-General the Hon. C. Colville; and on its right, by the reserve of Andalusia under Don P. A. Giron; and Major-General C. Baron Alten carried the positions on La Petite Rhune.

'The whole then co-operated in the attack of the enemy's main position behind the village. The 3rd and 7th Divisions immediately carried the redoubts on the left of the enemy's centre, and the Light Division those on the right, while the 4th Division with the reserve of Andalusia on their left, attacked their positions in their centre. By these attacks the enemy were obliged to abandon their strong positions which they had fortified with much care and labour; and they left in the principal redoubt on the height the 1st Battalion 88th Regiment, which immediately surrendered.

'While these operations were going on in the centre, I had the pleasure of seeing the 6th Division, under Lieutenant-General Sir H. Clinton, after having crossed the Nivelle, and having driven in the enemy's pickets on both banks, and having covered the passage of the Portuguese division under Lieutenant-General Sir John Hamilton on its right, make a most handsome attack upon the right of the enemy's position behind Ainhoüé and on the right of the Nivelle, and carry all the entrenchments, and the redoubt on that flank. Lieutenant-General

Sir John Hamilton supported, with the Portuguese division, the 6th Division on its right; and both co-operated in the attack of the second redoubt, which was immediately carried.

'Major-General Pringle's brigade of the 2nd Division, under the command of Lieutenant-General Sir W. Stewart, drove in the enemy's pickets on the Nivelle and in front of Ainhoüé, and Major-General Byng's brigade of the 2nd Division carried the entrenchments and a redoubt further on the enemy's left: in which attack the Major-General and these troops distinguished themselves. Major-General Morillo covered the advance of the whole to the heights behind Ainhoüé, by attacking the enemy's posts on the slopes of Mondarrain, and following them towards Itsassu.

'The troops on the heights behind Ainhoüé were, by these operations, under the direction of Lieutenant-General Sir Rowland Hill, forced to retire towards the bridge of Cambo, on the Nive, with the exception of the division on Mondarrain, which, by the march of a part of the 2nd Division, under Lieutenant-General Sir William Stewart, was pushed into the mountain towards Baygorry.

'As soon as the heights were carried on both banks of the Nivelle, I directed the 3rd and 7th Divisions, being the right of our centre, to move by the left of that river upon St. Pé, and the 6th Division by the right of the river on the same place, while the 4th and Light Divisions, and General Giron's reserve, held the heights above Ascain, and covered this movement on that side, and Lieutenant-General Sir Rowland Hill covered it on the other.

'A part of the enemy's troops had retired from their centre and had crossed the Nivelle at St. Pé; and as soon as the 6th Division approached, the 3rd Division, under Major-General the Hon. C. Colville, and the 7th Division, under General Le Cor, crossed that river, and attacked, and immediately gained possession of, the heights beyond it. We were thus established in the rear of the enemy's right; but so much of the day was now spent that it was impossible to make any further movement; and I was obliged to defer our further operations till the following morning.

'The enemy evacuated Ascain in the afternoon, of which village Lieutenant-General Don Manuel Freyre took possession, and quitted all their works and positions in front of St. Jean de Luz during the night, and retired upon Bidart, destroying all the bridges on the Lower Nivelle. Lieutenant-General Sir John Hope followed them with the left of the army as soon as he could cross the river, and Marshal Sir W.

Beresford moved the centre of the army as far as the state of the roads, after a violent fall of rain, would allow; and the enemy retired again on the night of the 11th into an entrenched camp in front of Bayonne.

'In the course of the operations, of which I have given Your Lordship an outline, in which we have driven the enemy from positions which they had been fortifying with great labour and care for three months, in which we have taken 51 pieces of cannon and 6 tumbrils of ammunition, and 1,400 prisoners, I have great satisfaction in reporting the good conduct of all the officers and troops. . . .

'I likewise particularly observed the gallant conduct of the 51st and 68th Regiments, under the command of Major Rice and Lieutenant-Colonel Hawkins, in Major-General Inglis's brigade, in the attack of the heights above St. Pé, in the afternoon of the 30th. . . .

'Out loss, although severe, has not been so great as might have been expected, considering the strength of the positions attacked and the length of time, from daylight in the morning till night, during which the troops were engaged . . . .

'The artillery which was in the field was of great use to us, and I cannot sufficiently acknowledge the intelligence and activity with which it was brought to the point of attack under the directions of Colonel Dickson, over the bad roads through the mountains in this season of the year. . .'

Return of the Killed, Wounded, and Missing in the Operations of the Army under the Command of General the Marquis of Wellington, K.G., in the Passage of the Nivelle on November 10, 1813.

	Officers.	Sergeants.	Rank and File.	Horses.	Total Loss of Officers, Non-commissioned Officers, and Rank and File.
Killed .	26	28	289	16	343
Wounded .	155	132	1,991	25	2,278
Missing .	3	1	69	—	73

Terrible Punishments.

'St. Jean de Luz,
'December 3, 1813.

'I have received your letter of November 17, with eight proceedings of a general court-martial on certain soldiers of Dillon's regiment at Carthagena, all of which I have confirmed.

'I desire that —— —— and —— —— may be pardoned, that—

— ——, and Lance-Corporal, —— ——, may be executed by being shot, and that the remainder of the prisoners should first draw lots for one more to be executed by being shot, according to the sentence of the general court-martial.

'The other eleven prisoners are then to have the choice of suffering corporal punishment, or to be executed according to sentence; and those who shall prefer to be executed are to be shot; those who prefer to receive corporal punishment are to receive a punishment not exceeding three hundred lashes.

'The punishments are to be carried into execution in the most solemn manner at Carthagena, in presence of the British troops to be paraded there for that purpose; and care is to be taken to impress upon the troops that their entrance into the British service is voluntary, that they are well treated, well fed, and taken care of, and that they must expect that any attempt to desert and break their engagement will be followed by certain punishment.'

The Passage of the Nive

To Earl Bathurst.

'St. Jean de Luz,
'December 14, 1813.

'Since the enemy's retreat from the Nivelle they had occupied a position in front of Bayonne, which had been entrenched with great labour since the battle fought at Vitoria in June last. . . .

'I had determined to pass the Nive immediately after the passage of the Nivelle, but was prevented by the bad state of the roads, and the swelling of all the rivulets occasioned by the fall of rain in the beginning of that month; but the state of the weather and roads having at length enabled me to collect the materials, and make the preparations for forming bridges for the passage of that river, I moved the troops out of their cantonments on the 8th, and ordered that the right of the army, under Lieutenant-General Sir Rowland Hill, should pass on the 9th at and in the neighbourhood of Cambo, while Marshal Sir William Beresford should favour and support his operation by passing the 6th Division, under Lieutenant-General Sir H. Clinton, at Ustaritz. Both operations succeeded completely.

'The enemy were immediately driven from the right bank of the river, and retired towards Bayonne by the great road of St. Jean Pied de Port. Those posted opposite Cambo were nearly intercepted by the 6th Division, and one regiment was driven from the road and obliged

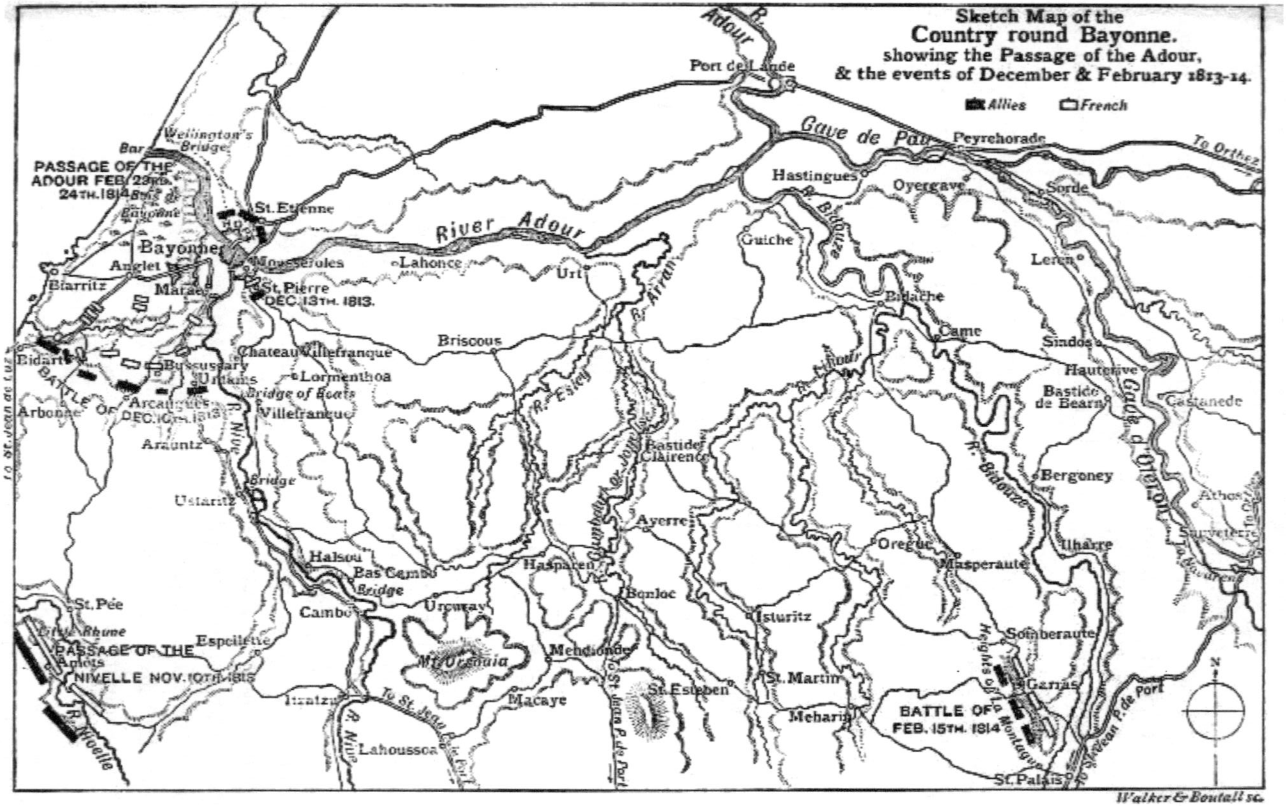
Sketch Map of the
Country round Bayonne.
showing the Passage of the Adour,
& the events of December & February 1813-14.
Allies
French
R. Adour
Port de Lande
Gave de Pau
Peyrehorade
To Orthez
Bar
Wellington's Bridge
PASSAGE OF THE ADOUR FEB. 23RD. & 24TH. 1814
St. Etienne
Bayonne
River Adour
Hastingues
Oyergave
Sorde
Guiche
R. Bidouze
Leren
Anglet
Mousseroles
Lahonce
Urt
R. Arran
Biarritz
Marac
St. Pierre
DEC. 13TH. 1813.
Bidache
Came
Briscous
Sindos
Bidart
Chateau Villefranque
Lormenthoa
Bussussary
Urdains
Bridge of Boats
R. Estey
R. Lihour
Hauterive
BATTLE OF DEC. 10TH. 1813
Arcangues
Arbonne
Villefranque
R. Nive
Bastide de Bearn
Gave d'Oleron
Castanede
Arauntz
Bastide Clairence
Bergoney
R. Bidouze
Bridge
Ustaritz
Ayerre
Athos
Halsou
Bas Cambo
Bridge
Hasparen
Oregue
Masperaute
Ilharre
St. Pée
Cambo
Urcuray
Bonloc
Isturitz
Little Rhune
PASSAGE OF THE
Ainhoa
NIVELLE NOV. 10TH. 1813
Espelette
Mt. Ursuia
Mendionde
To St. Jean P. de Port
St. Esteben
St. Martin
Someraute
Heights of La Montagne
Garris
N
Itxatzu
R. Nive
To St. Jean P. de Port
Macaye
Meharin
BATTLE OF FEB. 15TH. 1814
To St. Jean P. de Port
Lahoussoa
R. Nivelle
St. Palais
To St. Jean de Luz
Walker & Boutall sc.

to march across the country.

'The enemy assembled in considerable force on a range of heights running parallel with the Adour, and still keeping Ville Franque by their right. The 8th Portuguese Regiment, under Colonel Douglas, and the 9th Caçadores, under Colonel Brown, and the British Light Infantry battalion of the 6th Division, carried this village and the heights in the neighbourhood. The rain which had fallen the preceding night, and on the morning of the 8th, had so destroyed the road that the day had nearly elapsed before the whole of Sir Rowland Hill's corps had come up, and I was therefore satisfied with the possession of the ground which we occupied. . . .

'On the morning of the 10th Lieutenant-General Sir Rowland Hill found that the enemy had retired from the position which they had occupied the day before on the heights, into the entrenched camp on that side of the Nive, and he therefore occupied the position intended for him, with his right towards the Adour, and his left at Ville Franque, and communicating with the centre of the army under Marshal Sir William Beresford by a bridge laid over the Nive; and the troops under the Marshal were again drawn to the left of the Nive . . . .

'On the 10th in the morning the enemy moved out of the entrenched camp with their whole army, with the exception only of what occupied the works opposite to Sir Rowland Hill's position, and drove in the pickets of the Light Division and of Sir John Hope's corps, and made a most desperate attack upon the post of the former at the *château* and church of Arcangues, and upon the advanced posts of the latter on the highroad from Bayonne to St. Jean de Luz, near the Mayor's house of Biaritz. Both attacks were repulsed in the most gallant style by the troops, and Sir John Hope's corps took about 500 prisoners. The brunt of the action with Sir John Hope's advanced post fell upon the 1st Portuguese Brigade, under Major-General A. Campbell, which were on duty, and upon Major-General Robinson's brigade of the 5th Division, which moved up to their supports. . .

'When the night closed the enemy were still in large force in front of our posts, on the ground from which they had driven the pickets. They retired, however, during the night, from Lieutenant-General Sir John Hope's front, leaving small posts, which were immediately driven in. They still occupied in force the bridge on which the pickets of the Light Division had stood, and it was obvious that the whole army was still in front of our left, and about three in the afternoon they again drove in Lieutenant-General Sir John Hope's pickets, and attacked his post. They were again repulsed with considerable loss. The attack was recommenced on the morning of the 12th, with the same want of success. The 1st Division, under Major-General Howard, having relieved the 5th Division, the enemy discontinued it in the afternoon, and retired entirely within the entrenched camp on that night. They never renewed the attack on the posts of the Light Division after the 10th. . . .

'The enemy, having thus failed in all their attacks with their whole force upon our left, withdrew into their entrenchments on the night of the 12th, and passed a large force through Bayonne, with which, on the morning of the 13th, they made a most desperate attack upon Lieutenant-General Sir Rowland Hill.

'In expectation of this attack, I had requested Marshal Sir William Beresford to reinforce the Lieutenant-General with the 6th Division, which crossed the Nive at daylight in the morning, and I further reinforced him by the 4th Division and two brigades of the 3rd.

'The expected arrival of the 6th Division gave the Lieutenant-General great facility in making his movements, but the troops under his own immediate command had defeated and repulsed the enemy with immense loss before their arrival. The principal attack having been made along the highroad from Bayonne to St. Jean Pied de Port, Major-General Barnes's brigade of British infantry, and the 5th Brigade of Portuguese infantry under Brigadier-General Ashworth, were particularly engaged in the contest with the enemy on that point, and these troops conducted themselves admirably.

'The Portuguese division of infantry, under the command of Mariscal de Campo F. Le Cor, moved to their support on their left in a very gallant style, and regained an important position between those troops and Major-General Pringle's brigade engaged with the enemy in front of Ville Franque. I had great satisfaction also in observing the conduct of Major-General Byng's brigade of British infantry, supported by the Portuguese brigade under the command of Major-General Buchan, in carrying an important height from the enemy on the right of our position, and maintaining it against all their efforts to regain it.

'Two guns and some prisoners were taken from the enemy, who, being beat in all points, and having suffered considerable loss, were obliged to retire upon their entrenchments. . . .

'The enemy marched a large body of cavalry across the bridge of the Adour yesterday evening, and retired their force opposite to Sir Rowland Hill this morning towards Bayonne. . . .'

Return of the Killed, Wounded, and Missing of the Army under the Command of Field-Marshal the Marquis of Wellington, K.G., in the Operations connected with the Passage of the Nive, from December 9 to 13, 1813.

	Officers.	Sergeants.	Rank and File.	Horses.	Total Loss of Officers, Non-commissioned Officers, and Rank and File.
Killed	32	15	603	13	650
Wounded	233	215	3,459	21	3,907
Missing	17	14	473	1	504

UNFOUNDED CHARGES.

To General Don Manuel Freyre.

'St. Jean de Luz,
'January 8, 1814.

'. . . . I had repeatedly sent to General Morillo, through Sir Rowland Hill and by other channels, to request he would keep his troops in order; in answer to which the General stated to Sir Rowland Hill that it was impossible, *as the officers and soldiers received by every post letters from their friends congratulating them upon their good fortune in being in France, and urging them to take advantage of their situation to make their fortunes.* This Sir Rowland Hill told me, and I therefore saw there was no remedy but a strong one.

'I can assure you that, in my opinion, it was essentially necessary to put an effectual stop to the evils complained of; and I can equally assure you that neither in the measure adopted, nor in the orders given to carry that measure into execution, had I the most distant intention to insult or injure the officers. I considered what General Morillo told General Hill as an acknowledgment that neither he nor his officers could stop the evil, and I acted accordingly.

'I might satisfy myself with this answer to General Morillo's complaints, and justify myself as the Commander-in-Chief of the British Army to those who have a right to call upon me for such justification.

'General Morillo is, however, entirely mistaken in his assertions respecting the measures adopted to preserve discipline among the British troops; and, instead of asserting, as he has, that they may commit what crimes they please with impunity, he ought, if informed, to say that no crime ever goes unpunished when the criminal can be discovered. Hundreds of times in Spain and Portugal whole corps and divisions have been placed and kept under arms, not only to prevent disorder, but to obtain the discovery of criminals; and in no instance has a criminal been discovered that he has not been tried, and the sentence of the court-martial put into execution.

'I defy General Morillo—I defy any man—to show an instance in which injury has been done to any individual, of which proof could be adduced that the officer or soldier doing it has not been punished. Let him inquire how many soldiers have been hanged in Spain for plundering, and how many more have been otherwise punished and made to pay for the damage done, and he will find that there is no reason to complain on this ground. . . .

'The British officers and soldiers, like others, require to be kept in order, and till I read General Morillo's letter I imagined that the last accusation that could be made against me was that I neglected this duty. But however I may endeavour to perform it, I must admit that, in a large and widely extended army, evils and injuries may be committed without my knowing it; but with this admission I must say that it is quite groundless to assert or suppose that British officers and soldiers are allowed to do what they please with impunity.

'I beg Your Excellency to ask the question whether the British officers and soldiers have no ground of complaint. During the summer and autumn there were frequent instances of officers and soldiers shot at and robbed by the Spanish troops on the roads, and one soldier was murdered between Oyarzun and Lesaca. Our stores and convoys are frequently robbed, and only yesterday the accounts were received of an officer put to death at Vitoria; and a few days ago, I had accounts of others ill-treated at Santander; and other events of the same kind occur frequently.

'I must produce some much stronger proof of a design to ill-treat the officers and soldiers of the British Army than the death and ill-treatment of these individuals would give, supposing I were inclined to assert that such design existed; and yet this proof would be stronger than any General Morillo could adduce to support his assertion; as I again defy him to produce a single instance of a complaint made and proof adduced, and a denial or even a delay of redress.

'General Morillo has made two complaints, one of injustice and breach of the *Ordenanza* of the Spanish Army by me, the other of unjust and improper conduct in allowing officers and soldiers of the British Army to misconduct themselves with impunity.

'I hope this letter will show the general that there is no foundation for either complaint, and that he will withdraw them, as made in a moment of irritation, to which every man is liable. If he does not do so, I hope that he is prepared to prove them.

'I feel the same respect and regard for General Morillo and his troops that I do for all the other troops under my command, and I do everything in my power for them. This very regard must prevent me from allowing these charges of injustice to remain unrefuted, and they must be proved or formally withdrawn.'

Accommodation for Women.

To the Junta of Bilbao.

'St. Jean de Luz,
'January 12, 1814.

'I have had the honour of receiving your letter of December 24, to which I should have replied at an earlier period if I had not been engaged with the operations of the army, and I assure you that I feel the utmost concern that you should conceive that you have any reason to complain of any of the persons attached to the British Army.

'There can be no doubt that no person can have a right to claim quarters in any town to which he is not obliged to go upon duty, or by wounds or sickness acquired in the service; and the grant of quarters to ladies, the wives of officers of the army, can be considered in no other light than as an indulgence.

'I should not do justice to the town of Bilbao if I could believe it possible that they would withhold this indulgence from the wives of the officers of the British Army, more particularly as I have reason to believe that in that, any more than in other towns in Spain, it is not easy to get lodgings fit for the reception of respectable females; and that I have every reason to hope that those ladies, feeling that they owe the accommodation they possess in the town to the desire of the town to gratify the officers of the British Army, will, on their parts, refrain from giving any cause whatever for future complaint.

'I cannot expect that the *Ayuntamiento* will grant this indulgence to women not married; indeed, I am astonished that any officer should have ventured to ask for billets for such persons; and I beg that, in future, a quarter may not be granted to any woman with an officer, or to any lady singly, unless, the military *commandant* of the hospital should certify that she is the wife of an officer.

'There is no reason whatever, also, why the wives of non-commissioned officers and soldiers of the army should be quartered in the houses with the officers of the army, unless their husbands should be in the house as the servant or orderly of the officer in question; and, in case there should be any of that description, I beg you to apply for the interference of the military *commandant* of the hospital, to have them removed to their husbands.'

Battle of Orthez.

To Earl Bathurst.

'St. Sever,

'March 1, 1814.

'The sense which I had of the difficulties attending the movement of the army by its right, across so many rivers as must have been and as have lately been passed in its progress, induced me to determine to pass the Adour below the town of Bayonne, notwithstanding the difficulties which opposed this operation; and I was the more induced to adopt this plan as, whatever might be the mode in which I should eventually move upon the enemy, it was obvious that I could depend upon no communication with Spain and the seaports of that kingdom and with St. Jean de Luz, excepting that alone which is practicable in the winter, *viz.*, by the highroads leading to and from Bayonne.

'I likewise hoped that the establishment of a bridge below Bayonne would give me the use of the Adour as a harbour.

'The movements of the right of the army were intended to divert the enemy's attention from the preparations at St. Jean de Luz and Pasages for the passage of the Adour below Bayonne, and to induce the enemy to move his force to his left, in which objects they succeeded completely; but upon my return to St. Jean de Luz on the 19th, I found the weather so unfavourable at sea, and so uncertain, that I determined to push forward my operations on the right, notwithstanding that I had still the Gave d'Oleron, the Gave de Fau, and the Adour to pass.

'Accordingly, I returned to Garris on the 21st, and ordered the 6th and Light Divisions to break up from the blockade of Bayonne, and General Don Manuel Freyre to close up the cantonments of his corps towards Irun, and to be prepared to move when the left of the army should cross the Adour.

'I found the pontoons collected at Garris, and they were moved forward on the following days to and across the Gave de Mauleon, and the troops of the centre of the army arrived.

'On the 24th, Lieutenant-General Sir Rowland Hill passed the Gave d'Oleron at Villenave, with the Light, 2nd, and Portuguese Divisions, under the command of Major-General Baron Charles Alten,

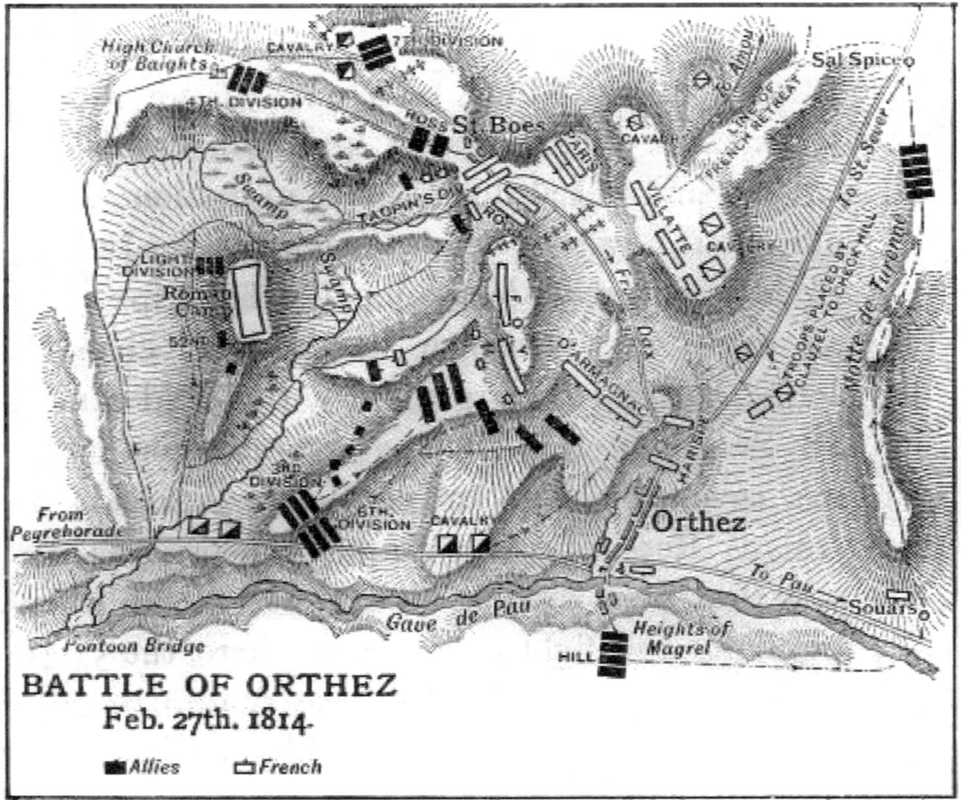

BATTLE OF ORTHEZ
Feb. 27th. 1814.

Lieutenant-General Sir William Stewart, and Mariscal de Campo Le Cor; while Lieutenant-General Sir Henry Clinton passed with the 6th Division between Monfort and Laas, and Lieutenant-General Sir Thomas Picton made demonstrations, with the 3rd Division, of an intention to attack the enemy's position at the bridge of Sauveterre, which induced the enemy to blow up the bridge.

'Mariscal de Campo Don Pablo Morillo drove in the enemy's posts near Navarreins, and blockaded that place.

'Field-Marshal Sir William Beresford likewise, who, since the movement of Sir Rowland Hill on the 14th and 15th, had remained with the 4th and 7th Divisions, and Colonel Vivian's brigade, in observation on the Lower Bidouze, attacked the enemy on the 23rd in their fortified posts at Hastingues and Oeyregave, on the left of the Gave de Pau, and obliged them to retire within the *tête de pont* at Peyrehorade.

'Immediately after the passage of the Gave d'Oleron was effected, Sir Rowland Hill and Sir Henry Clinton moved towards Orthez and the great road leading from Sauveterre to that town; and the enemy retired in the night from Sauveterre across the Gave de Pau, and assembled their army near Orthez on the 25th, having destroyed all the bridges on the river.

'The right and right of the centre of the army assembled opposite Orthez, Lieutenant-General Sir Stapleton Cotton, with Lord Edward Somerset's brigade of cavalry, and the 3rd Division, under Lieutenant-General Sir Thomas Picton, were near the destroyed bridge of Berenx; and Field-Marshal Sir William Beresford, with the 4th and 7th Divisions, under Lieutenant-General Sir Lowry Cole and Major-General Walker and Colonel Vivian's brigade, towards the junction of the Gave de Pau with the Gave d'Oleron.

'The troops opposed to the Marshal having moved on the 25th, he crossed the Gave de Pau below the junction of the Gave d'Oleron on the morning of the 26th, and moved along the highroad from Peyrehorade towards Orthez, on the enemy's right. As he approached, Lieutenant-General Sir Stapleton Cotton crossed with the cavalry, and Lieutenant-General Sir Thomas Picton with the 3rd Division, below the bridge of Berenx; and I moved the 6th and Light Divisions to the same point, and Lieutenant-General Sir Rowland Hill occupied the heights opposite Orthez and the highroad leading to Sauveterre.

'The 6th and Light Divisions crossed in the morning of the 27th at daylight, and we found the enemy in a strong position near Orthez, with his right on a height on the highroad to Dax, and occupying the village of St. Boés, and his left on the heights above Orthez and that town, and opposing the passage of the river by Sir Rowland Hill.

'The course of the heights on which the enemy had placed his army necessarily retired his centre, while the strength of the position gave extraordinary advantages to the flanks.

'I ordered Marshal Sir William Beresford to turn and attack the enemy's right with the 4th Division under Lieutenant-General Sir Lowry Cole, and the 7th Division under Major-General Walker and Colonel Vivian's brigade of cavalry; while Lieutenant-General Sir Thomas Picton should move along the great road leading from Peyrehorade to Orthez, and attack the heights on which the enemy's centre and left stood, with the 3rd and 6th Divisions under Lieutenant-General Sir Henry Clinton, supported by Sir Stapleton Cotton, with Lord Edward Somerset's brigade of cavalry. Major-General Baron Charles Alten, with the Light Division, kept the communication, and was in reserve between these two attacks. I likewise desired Lieutenant-General Sir Rowland Hill to cross the Gave, and to turn, and attack the enemy's left.

'Marshal Sir William Beresford carried the village of St. Boés with the 4th Division, under the command of Lieutenant-General Sir Lowry Cole, after an obstinate resistance by the enemy; but the ground was so narrow that the troops could not deploy to attack the heights, notwithstanding the repeated attempts of Major-General Ross and Brigadier-General Vasconcellos' Portuguese brigade; and it was impossible to turn them by the enemy's right without an excessive extension of our line.

'I therefore so far altered the plan of the action as to order the immediate advance of the 3rd and 6th Divisions, and I moved forward Colonel Barnard's brigade of the Light Division to attack the left of the height on which the enemy's right stood.

'This attack, led by the 52nd Regiment under Lieutenant-Colonel Colborne, and supported on their right by Major-General Brisbane's and Colonel Keane's brigades of the 3rd Division, and by simultaneous attacks on the left by Major-General Anson's brigade of the 4th Division, and on the right by Lieutenant-General Sir Thomas Picton, with the remainder of the 3rd Division and the 6th Division, under Lieutenant-General Sir Henry Clinton, dislodged the enemy from the heights and gave us the victory.

'In the meantime, Lieutenant-General Sir Rowland Hill had forced the passage of the Gave above Orthez, and seeing the state of the action he moved immediately, with the 2nd Division of infantry under Lieutenant-General Sir William Stewart and Major-General Fane's brigade of cavalry, direct for the great road from Orthez to St. Sever, thus keeping upon the enemy's left.

'The enemy retired at first in admirable order, taking every advantage of the numerous good positions which the country afforded him. The losses, however, which he sustained in the continued attacks of our troops, and the danger with which he was threatened by Lieutenant-General Sir Rowland Hill's movement, soon accelerated his movements, and the retreat at last became a flight, and the troops were in the utmost confusion.

'Lieutenant-General Sir Stapleton Cotton took advantage of the only opportunity which offered to charge with Major-General Lord Edward Somerset's brigade, in the neighbourhood of Sault de Navailles, where the enemy had been driven from the highroad by Lieutenant-General Sir Rowland Hill. The 7th Hussars distinguished themselves upon this occasion, and made many prisoners.

'We continued the pursuit till it was dusk, and I halted the army in the neighbourhood of Sault de Navailles. I cannot estimate the extent of the enemy's loss; we have taken six pieces of cannon and a great many prisoners, the numbers I cannot at present report. The whole country is covered by their dead. The army was in the utmost confusion when I last saw it passing the heights near Sault de Navailles, and many soldiers had thrown away their arms. The desertion has since been immense.

'We followed the enemy on the following day to this place, and we this day passed the Adour. Marshal Sir William Beresford marched with the Light Division and General Vivian's brigade upon Mont de Marsan, where he has taken a very large magazine of provisions. Lieutenant-General Sir Rowland Hill has moved upon Aire, and the advanced posts of the centre are at Cazères.

'The enemy are apparently retiring upon Agen, and have left open the direct road towards Bordeaux.

'While the operations of which I have above given the report were carrying on on the right of the army, Lieutenant-General Sir John Hope, in concert with Rear-Admiral Penrose, availed himself of an opportunity which offered on February 23 to cross the Adour below Bayonne, and to take possession of both banks of the river at its mouth. The vessels destined to form the bridge could not get in till the 24th, when the difficult, and at this season of the year dangerous, operation of bringing them in was effected with a degree of gallantry and skill seldom equalled.

'Lieutenant-General Sir John Hope particularly mentions Captain O'Reilly, Lieutenant Cheshire, Lieutenant Douglas, and Lieutenant Collins of the navy, and also Lieutenant Debenham, Agent of Transports; and I am infinitely indebted to Rear-Admiral Penrose for the cordial assistance I received from him in preparing for this plan, and for that which he gave Lieutenant-General Sir John Hope in carrying it into execution.

'The enemy, conceiving that the means of crossing the river which Lieutenant-General Sir John Hope had at his command, *viz.*, rafts made of pontoons, had not enabled him to cross a large force in the course of the 23rd, attacked the corps which he had sent over on that evening. This corps consisted of 600 men of the 2nd Brigade of Guards under the command of Major-General the Hon. E. Stopford, who repulsed the enemy immediately. The Rocket brigade was of great use upon this occasion.

'Three of the enemy's gunboats were destroyed this day; and a frigate lying in the Adour received considerable damage from the fire of a battery of eighteen-pounders, and was obliged to go higher up the river to the neighbourhood of the bridge.

'Lieutenant-General Sir John Hope invested the citadel of Bayonne on the 25th; and Lieutenant-General Don Manuel Freyre moved forward with the 4th Spanish Army in consequence of directions which I had left for him.

'On the 27th, the bridge having been completed, Lieutenant-General Sir John Hope deemed it expedient to invest the citadel of Bayonne more closely than he had done before; and he attacked the village of St. Etienne, which he carried, having taken a gun and some prisoners from the enemy; and his posts are now within 900 yards of the outworks of the place.

'The result of the operations which I have detailed to Your Lordship is that Bayonne, St. Jean Pied de Port, and Navarreins, are invested; and the army, having passed the Adour, are in possession of all the great communications across that river, after having beaten the enemy and taken their magazines. . . .

'The charge made by the 7th Hussars under Lord Edward Somerset was highly meritorious.

'The conduct of the artillery throughout the day deserved my highest approbation. . .'

Return of the Killed, Wounded, and Missing of the Allied Army under the Command of Marshal the Marquis of Wellington, K.G., in Action with the French Army under the Command of Marshal Soult, on February 27, at Orthez.

	Officers.	Sergeants.	Rank and File.	Horses.	Total Loss of Officers, Non-commissioned Officers, and Rank and File.
Killed -	18	25	234	7	277
Wounded -	134	89	1,700	33	1,923
Missing -	1	5	64	51	70

To Earl Bathurst.

'St. Sever,

'March 4, 1814.

'The rain which fell in the afternoon of the 1st swelled the Adour and all the rivulets falling into that river so considerably as materially to impede our further progress, and to induce me on the next day to halt the army till I could repair the bridges, all of which the enemy had destroyed.

'The rain continued till last night, and the river is so rapid that the pontoon cannot be laid upon it.

'The enemy had collected a corps at Aire, probably to protect the evacuation of a magazine which they had at that place. Sir Rowland Hill attacked this corps on the 2nd, and drove them from their post with considerable loss, and took possession of the town and magazine.'

Return of the Killed, Wounded, and Missing of the Army under the Command of Field-Marshal the Marquis of Wellington, K.G., in the Various Operations from February 28 to March 2, inclusive.

	Officers.	Sergeants.	Rank and File.	Horses.	Total Loss of Officers Non-commissioned Officers, and Rank and File.
Killed -	3	1	16	5	20
Wounded -	13	9	114	11	136
Missing -	—	—	2	—	2

Affair at Tarbes.

The Rifle Brigade is particularly associated with Tarbes. The 95th were the only British troops who fired on the hill where the fight took place, although other regiments were in reserve; and consequently Tarbes is regarded as the regimental fight of the Rifle Brigade.—W.W.

To Earl Bathurst.

'Samatan,
'March 25, 1814.

'The enemy continued his retreat after the affair near Tarbes on the 20th, during the night and following days and arrived yesterday at Toulouse. Then troops have marched with such celerity that, excepting the advanced-guard of the cavalry attached to Lieutenant-General Sir Rowland Hill's corps under Major-General Fane, who attacked the enemy's rear-guard at St Gaudens, our troops have never been able to come up with them.

'I enclose Major-General Fane's report to Lieutenant-General Sir Rowland Hill of this affair, which is highly creditable to the 13th Light Dragoons. . . .'

Return of Killed, Wounded, and Missing of the Army under the Command of Field-Marshal the Marques of Wellington, K.G., in the Operations from March 7 to 20, 1814.

	Officers.	Sergeants.	Rank and File.	Horses.	Total Loss of Officers, Non-commissioned Officers, and Rank and File.
Killed	4	3	41	21	51
Wounded	36	29	360	40	425
Missing	4	1	33	34	38

THE BATTLE OF TOULOUSE.

To Earl Bathurst.

'Toulouse,
'April 12, 1814.

'I have the pleasure to inform Your Lordship that I entered this town this morning, which the enemy evacuated during the night, retiring by the road of Carcassone.

'The continued fall of rain and the state of the river prevented me from laying the bridge till the morning of the 8th, when the Spanish corps and the Portuguese artillery, under the immediate orders of Lieutenant-General Don Manuel Freyre, and the headquarters, crossed the Garonne.

'We immediately moved forward to the neighbourhood of the town, and the 18th Hussars, under the immediate command of Colonel Vivian, had an opportunity of making a most gallant attack upon a superior body of the enemy's cavalry, which they drove through the

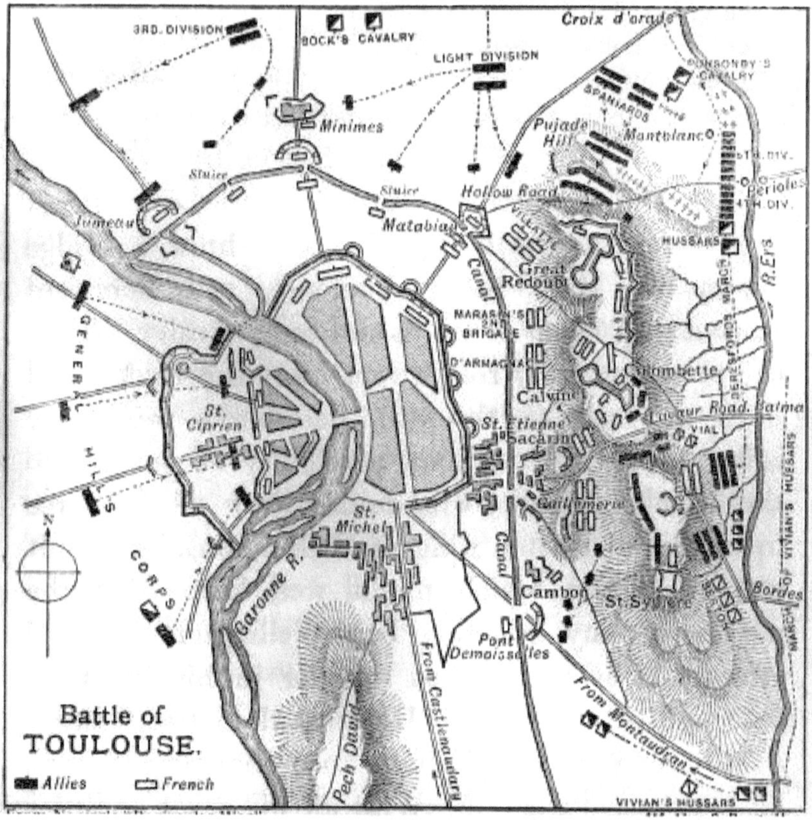
Battle of
TOULOUSE.
Allies
French
3RD. DIVISION
BOCK'S CAVALRY
LIGHT DIVISION
Croix d'orade
PONSONBY'S CAVALRY
SPANIARDS
Pujade Hill
Montblanc
5TH. DIV.
Perioles
4TH. DIV.
HUSSARS
Minimes
Sluice
Sluice
Hollow Road
Jumeau
Matabiau
Canal
Great Redoubt
MARASIN'S 2ND BRIGADE
D'ARMAGNAC
Colombette
Calvinet
St. Etienne
Sacarin
Lucaur Road
Balma
VIAL
R. Ers
BERESFORD'S MARCH
GENERAL HILL'S CORPS
St. Ciprien
Cambon
St. Sypiere
Bordes
MARCH OF VIVIAN'S HUSSARS
St. Michel
Garonne R.
Pont Demoiselles
From Castlenaudary
From Montaudran
Pech David
VIVIAN'S HUSSARS

village of Croix d'Orade, and took about 100 prisoners, and gave us possession of an important bridge over the River Ers, by which it was necessary to pass in order to attack the enemy's position. Colonel Vivian was, unfortunately, wounded upon this occasion, and I am afraid that I shall lose the benefit of his assistance for some time.

'The town of Toulouse is surrounded on three sides by the canal of Languedoc and the Garonne. On the left of that river, the suburb, which the enemy had fortified with strong field works in front of the ancient wall, formed a good *tête de pont*. They had likewise formed a *tête de pont* at each bridge of the canal, which was, besides, defended by the fire in some places of musketry, and in all of artillery from the ancient wall of the town. Beyond the canal to the eastward, and between that and the River Ers, is a height which extends as far as Montaudran, and over which pass all the approaches to the canal and town from the eastward, which it defends, and the enemy, in addition to the *têtes de pont* on the bridges of the canal, had fortified this height with five redoubts, connected by lines of entrenchments, and had, with extraordinary diligence, made every preparation for defence.

'They had likewise broken all the bridges over the Ers within our reach, by which the right of their position could be approached. The roads, however, from the Arriège to Toulouse being impracticable for cavalry or artillery, and nearly so for infantry, as reported in my despatch to Your Lordship of the 1st instant, I had no alternative, excepting to attack the enemy in this formidable position.

'It was necessary to move the pontoon bridge higher up the Garonne, in order to shorten the communication with Lieutenant-General Sir Rowland Hill's corps, as soon as the Spanish corps had passed, and this operation was not effected till so late an hour on the 9th as to induce me to defer the attack till the following morning.

'The plan, according to which I determined to attack the enemy, was for Marshal Sir William Beresford, who was on the right of the Ers with the 4th and 6th Divisions, to cross that river at the bridge of Croix d'Orade, to gain possession of Montblanc, and to march up the left of the Ers to turn the enemy's right, while Lieutenant-General Don Manuel Freyre, with the Spanish corps under his command, supported by the British cavalry, should attack the front. Lieutenant-General Sir Stapleton Cotton was to follow the Marshal's movement with Major-General Lord Edward Somerset's brigade of hussars, and Colonel Vivian's brigade, under the command of Colonel Arentschildt, was to observe the movements of the enemy's cavalry on both flanks of the Ers beyond our left.

'The 3rd and Light Divisions, under the command of Lieutenant-General Sir Thomas Picton and Major-General Charles Baron Alten, and the brigade of German cavalry, were to observe the enemy on the lower part of the canal, and to draw their attention to that quarter by threatening the *têtes de pont*, while Lieutenant-General Sir Rowland Hill was to do the same on the suburb on the left of the Garonne.

'Marshal Sir William Beresford crossed the Ers, and formed his corps in three columns of lines in the village of Croix d'Orade, the 4th Division leading, with which he immediately carried Montblanc. He then moved up the Ers in the same order, over most difficult ground, in a direction parallel to the enemy's fortified position, and as soon as he reached the point at which he turned it, he formed his lines and moved to the attack. During these operations Lieutenant-General Don Manuel Freyre moved along the left of the Ers to the front of Croix d'Orade, where he formed his corps in two lines with a reserve on a height in front of the left of the enemy's position, on which height the Portuguese artillery was placed, and Major-General Ponsonby's brigade of cavalry in reserve in the rear.

'As soon as formed, and that it was seen that Marshal Sir William Beresford was ready, Lieutenant-General Don Manuel Freyre moved forward to the attack. The troops marched in good order, under a very heavy fire of musketry and artillery, and showed great spirit, the General and all his staff being at their head; and the two lines were soon lodged under some banks immediately under the enemy's entrenchments; the reserve and Portuguese artillery, and British cavalry, continuing on the height on which the troops had first formed. The enemy, however, repulsed the movement of the right of General Freyre's line round their left flank, and having followed up their success, and turned our right by both sides of the highroad leading from Toulouse to Croix d'Orade, they soon compelled the whole corps to retire.

'It gave me great satisfaction to see that, although they suffered considerably in retiring, the troops rallied again as soon as the Light Division, which was immediately on their right, moved up, and I cannot sufficiently applaud the exertions of Lieutenant-General Don Manuel Freyre, the officers of the staff of the 4th Spanish Army, and of the officers of the General Staff, to rally and form them again.

'Lieutenant-General Mendizabal, who was in the field as a volunteer, General Ezpeleta, and several officers of the Staff and chiefs of corps, were wounded upon this occasion; but General Mendizabal continued in the field. The regiment *de Tiradores de Cantabria*, under the command of Colonel Leon de Sicilia, kept its position, under the enemy's entrenchments, until I ordered it to retire.

'In the meantime, Marshal Sir William Beresford, with the 4th Division, under the command of Lieutenant-General Sir Lowry Cole, and the 6th Division, under the command of Lieutenant-General Sir Henry Clinton, attacked and carried the heights on the enemy's right, and the redoubt which covered and protected that flank; and he lodged those troops on the same height with the enemy; who were, however, still in possession of four redoubts, and of the entrenchments and fortified houses.

'The badness of the roads had induced the marshal to leave his artillery in the village of Montblanc; and some time elapsed before it could be brought to him, and before Lieutenant-General Don Manuel Freyre's corps could be reformed and brought back to the attack. As soon as this was effected, the marshal continued his movement along the ridge, and carried, with General Pack's brigade of the 6th Division, the two principal redoubts and fortified houses in the enemy's centre.

'The enemy made a desperate effort from the canal to regain these redoubts, but they were repulsed with considerable loss; and the 6th Division continuing its movement along the ridge of the height, and the Spanish troops continuing a corresponding movement upon the front, the enemy were driven from the two redoubts and entrenchments on the left; and the whole range of heights were in our possession.

'We did not gain this advantage, however, without severe loss; particularly in the brave 6th Division. Lieutenant-Colonel Coghlan of the 61st, an officer of great merit and promise, was unfortunately killed in the attack of the heights. Major-General Pack was wounded, but was enabled to remain in the field; and Colonel Douglas, of the 8th Portuguese Regiment, lost his leg; and I am afraid that I shall be deprived for a considerable time of his assistance.

'The 36th, 42nd, 79th, and 61st, lost considerable numbers, and were highly distinguished throughout the day.

'I cannot sufficiently applaud the ability and conduct of Marshal Sir William Beresford throughout the operations of the day; nor that of Lieutenant-Generals Sir Lowry Cole, Sir Henry Clinton, Major-Generals Pack and Lambert, and the troops under their command. Marshal Sir William Beresford particularly reports the good conduct of Brigadier-General D'Urban, the Quartermaster-General, and General Brito Mozinho the Adjutant-General to the Portuguese Army.

'The 4th Division, although exposed on their march along the enemy's front to a galling fire, were not so much engaged as the 6th, and did not suffer so much; but they conducted themselves with their usual gallantry.

'I had also every reason to be satisfied with the conduct of Lieutenant-General Don Manuel Freyre, Lieutenant-General Don Gabriel Mendizabal, Mariscal de Campo Don Pedro Barcenas, Brigadier-General Don J. de Ezpeleta, Mariscal de Campo Don A. Garces de Marcilla, and the Chief of the Staff Don E. S. Salvador, and the officers of the Staff of the 4th army. The officers and troops conducted themselves well in all the attacks which they made subsequent to their being re-formed.

'The ground not having admitted of the operations of the cavalry, they had no opportunity of charging.

'While the operations above detailed were going on, on the left of the army, Lieutenant-General Sir Rowland Hill drove the enemy from their exterior works in the suburb, on the left of the Garonne, within the ancient wall.

'Lieutenant-General Sir Thomas Picton likewise, with the 3rd Division, drove the enemy within the *tête de pont* on the bridge of the canal nearest to the Garonne; but the troops having made an effort to carry it, they were repulsed, and some loss was sustained. Major-General Brisbane was wounded, but I hope not so as to deprive me for any length of time of his assistance; and Lieutenant-Colonel Forbes, of the 45th, an officer of great merit, was killed.

'The army being thus established on three sides of Toulouse, I immediately detached our light cavalry to cut off the communication by the only road practicable for carriages which remained in the country, till I should be enabled to make arrangements to establish the troops between the canal and the Garonne.

'The enemy, however, retired last night, leaving in our hands General Harispe, General Baurot, General St. Hilaire and 1,600 prisoners. One piece of cannon was taken on the field of battle, and others, and large quantities of stores of all descriptions, in the town. . .'

Return of the Killed, Wounded, and Missing of the Army under the Command of Field -Marshal the Marquis of Wellington, K.G., at the Battle of Toulouse, April 10 1814.

	Officers.	Serjeants.	Rank and File.	Total Loss of Officers, Non-commissioned Officers, and Rank and File.	British.	Spanish.	Portuguese.	Horses.
Killed	31	21	543	595	312	205	78	62
Wounded	248	123	3,675	4,046	1,795	1,722	529	59
Missing	3	—	15	18	17	1	—	2

★★★★★★★★★★

'. . . .The casualties of a British Army, after a battle, are collected, in returns, by the sergeants of companies, under the direction of, and signed by, the officers commanding them, accounting for all the men of the company thus become non-effective, absent or present. The regimental returns made from those of companies, as well as those of the brigades and divisions, are transmitted to headquarters, and from them the general return is made out and signed by the Adjutant-General and laid before the General commanding the Forces. They are transmitted to the Secretary of State, and published in the *London Gazette*, recapitulating the loss of each battalion. No officer in command of a British Army could venture to garble or alter a return. The loss so returned generally exceeds the actual loss, the officers and soldiers being interested, as their claims to pensions and rewards depend upon their names being included in the returns. . . .'

★★★★★★★★★★

Suspension of Hostilities.

To Major-General Colville.

'Toulouse,
'April 19, 1814.

'I have the honour to enclose you the copy of a convention for the suspension of hostilities, into which I have entered with Marshal the Duc de Dalmatie; and an extract of a letter from the Marshal, ratifying the convention, although not in so formal a manner as is necessary, owing to his waiting for the ratification of Marshal the Duc d'Albufera.

'I beg that on the receipt of this letter you will communicate the convention to the Governor of Bayonne, and call upon him to suspend hostilities.

'You will appoint an officer to settle with him the number of rations of provisions and forage which will be required daily by the garrison, and to settle with him the villages and towns of the country from which to be drawn; from which, of course, you will draw nothing.

'You will maintain your fortified posts in the neighbourhood of the garrison, giving at the same time free ingress to the provisions which it will be settled shall enter, and egress to whatever it may be wished to send out; and you will canton or encamp the troops in such situations as may be most convenient to you till I shall send you further orders.'

Sortie from Bayonne.

To Earl Bathurst.

'Toulouse,
'April 19, 1814.

'It gives me much concern to have to lay before Your Lordship the enclosed reports from Major-General Colville and Major-General Howard of a sortie from the citadel of Bayonne on the morning of the 14th instant, in which Lieutenant-General Sir John Hope having been unfortunately wounded, and his horse killed under him, he was made prisoner.

'I have every reason to believe that his wounds are not severe, but I cannot but regret that the satisfaction generally felt by the army upon the prospect of the honourable termination of their labours should be clouded by the misfortune and sufferings of an officer so highly esteemed and respected by all.

'I sincerely regret the fall of Major-General Hay, whose services and merits I have had frequent occasion to bring under Your Lordship's notice. . . .

'Upon the breaking up of this army, I perform a most satisfactory duty of reporting to Your Lordship my sense of the conduct and merits of Lieutenant-General William Clinton and of the troops under his command since they have been employed in the Peninsula.

'Circumstances have not enabled those troops to have so brilliant a share in the operations of the war as their brother officers and soldiers on this side of the Peninsula. But they have not been less usefully employed; their conduct when engaged with the enemy has always been meritorious, and I have had every reason to be satisfied with the general officers commanding and with them.'

Return of the Killed, Wounded, and Missing, in the Operations of the Army under the Command of Field-Marshal the Marquis of Wellington, K.G., in a Sortie made by the Garrison of Bayonne, on the Morning of April 14, 1814.

	Officers.	Sergeants.	Rank and File.	Horses.	Total Loss of Officers, Non-commissioned Officers, and Rank and File.
Killed - -	8	3	139	—	150
Wounded -	36	28	393	1	457
Missing -	6	7	223	—	236

Portuguese loss included.

PROCLAMATION.

'Toulouse,
'April 20, 1814.

'Field-Marshal the Marquis of Wellington, etc., having concluded a convention with Marshal the Duc d'Albufera for the evacuation of the strong places in Catalonia and Valencia by the French troops, and for a suspension of hostilities between the Allied Armies under the command of Field-Marshal the Marquis of Wellington, etc., and Marshal the Duc d'Albufera, respectively; and the Field-Marshal having promised the Duc d'Albufera that all French vessels in the port of Barcelona should be allowed to return to the ports of France unmolested, the Commanders of His Majesty's ships and vessels, and the Commanders of the vessels of the Allied Powers in the Mediterranean, are hereby requested to allow those vessels to pass to those ports unmolested.

'Wellington.'

GENERAL ORDER.

'Toulouse,
'April 21, 1814.

'*1.* The Commander of the Forces has the pleasure to inform the army that he has agreed upon the following Convention (of Toulouse.—W.W.), for the suspension of hostilities between the allied armies under his command and the French Armies opposed to them, and hostilities are forthwith to be suspended accordingly.

'*2.* Upon congratulating the army upon this prospect of an honourable termination of their labours, the Commander of the Forces avails himself of the opportunity of returning the general officers, officers, and troops, his best thanks for their uniform discipline and gallantry in the field, and for their conciliating conduct towards the inhabitants of the country, which, almost in an equal degree with their discipline and gallantry in the field, have produced the fortunate circumstances that now hold forth to the world the prospect of genuine and permanent peace.

'*3.* The Commander of the Forces trusts that they will continue the same good conduct while it may be necessary to detain them in this country, and that they will leave it with a lasting reputation, not less creditable to their gallantry in the field than to their regularity and good conduct in quarters and in camp.

'Wellington.'

MEMORANDUM.

To His Catholic Majesty Ferdinand VII., King of Spain.

'The Spanish nation having been engaged for six years in one of the most terrible and disastrous contests by which any nation was ever afflicted, its territory having been entirely occupied by the enemy, the country torn to pieces by internal divisions, its ancient constitution having been destroyed, and vain attempts made to establish a new one; its marine, its commerce, and revenue entirely annihilated; its colonies in a state of rebellion, and nearly lost to the mother country; it becomes a question for serious consideration what line of policy should be adopted by His Majesty upon his happy restoration to his throne and authority.

'. . . Great Britain is materially interested in the prosperity and greatness of Spain, and a good understanding and close alliance with Spain is highly important to her, and she will make sacrifices to obtain it; and there is no act of kindness which may not be expected from such an ally.

'But it cannot be expected from Great Britain that she will take any steps for the firm establishment of a Government which she shall see in the fair way of connecting itself with her rival, and of eventually becoming her enemy; like other nations, she must by prudence and foresight provide for her own interests by other modes, if circumstances should prevent His Majesty from connecting himself with Great Britain, as it appears by the reasoning in this memorandum is desirable to him.'

GENERAL ORDER.

'Bordeaux,
'June 14, 1814.

'*1.* The Commander of the Forces, being upon the point of returning to England, again takes this opportunity of congratulating the army upon the recent events which have restored peace to their country and to the world.

'*2.* The share which the British Army has had in producing these events, and the high character with which the army will quit this country, must be equally satisfactory to every individual belonging to it, as they are to the Commander of the Forces; and he trusts that the troops will continue the same good conduct to the last.

'*3.* The Commander of the Forces once more requests the army to accept his thanks.

'*4.* Although circumstances may alter the relations in which he has stood towards them, so much to his satisfaction, he assures them that he shall never cease to feel the warmest interest in their welfare and honour, and that he will be at all times happy to be of any service to those to whose conduct, discipline, and gallantry, their country is so much indebted.'

The Waterloo Campaign

Introduction

By Charles Walker Robinson

By the treaty of peace, signed at Paris on April 11th, 1814, and notified to Wellington shortly after the Battle of Toulouse, Napoleon renounced for himself, and his descendants, the throne of France, and was permitted, with a small retinue, and about a thousand of his Old Guard, to reside in the island of Elba, the nominal sovereignty of which was conceded to him.

The armies of the Allied Powers were then withdrawn beyond the boundaries of France; a British, Hanoverian, and Dutch force, under Lord Lynedoch, remained in occupation of the Netherlands; the Prussians and Germans held the territory bordering the Rhine; and a European Congress met at Vienna (September 25th, 1814) to settle many important questions connected with the re-constitution of Europe, and the future limits of the European states, which Napoleon's conquests had reduced to confusion.

At this Congress Talleyrand represented France, and Lord Castlereagh England. The progress made by the Congress was slow, it being difficult to reconcile the divergent interests of the Powers, and so by the close of the year 1814 little had been definitely settled. Balls, dinners, and conferences went on continuously; but, as Talleyrand said,

"The Congress danced, but did not move forward."

Wellington, in the meantime, after a short stay in England, had, in July 1814, been appointed Ambassador Extraordinary to the Court of France ; and it is interesting to note that in August, at the desire of the British Government, he visited the entire line of the Franco-Belgian frontier, accompanied by Colonels Carmichael Smyth, Chapman, and Pasley of the Royal Engineers, and afterwards drew up a memorandum upon its defence, (enclosed with a letter to Lord Bathurst, dated Paris, September 22nd, 1814), in which the following passage occurs touching upon the position upon which the Battle of Waterloo was subsequently fought:

> "About Nivelle, and between that and Binche, there are many advantageous positions; and the entrance of the 'Forêt de Soignies,' on the high road which leads to Brussels from Binche, Charleroi, and Namur, (it was here that the Battle of Waterloo took place), would, if worked upon, afford others."

In January, 1815, he proceeded from Paris to succeed Lord Castlereagh at the Congress of Vienna, where a deadlock had ensued.

> "The combatants, still breathless and bleeding from the struggle, (*i.e.* of the war which had been terminated by the Treaty of Paris), snarled over the prey which they had just compelled the common enemy (France) to abandon. . . . Prussia extended her clutch towards Saxony, while Russia growled over the well-mumbled bone of Poland. The western Powers—England, France, and Austria—were on the point of forming in self-defence a league against the two northern monopolists, when a common peril once more united them—Buonaparte had escaped from Elba." (*Wellington's Career*, by Sir Edward Hamley.)

The watch kept by the Powers over his movements in that island had been culpably negligent; and upon the ground that the Powers themselves were not intending to keep to the Treaty of Paris, he threw his own obligations under it to the winds. Confident that the army in France, if not the entire nation, would rally round his standard, he set sail from Elba with his Guard in a few small vessels, landed at Cannes on March 1st, 1815, and from thence proceeded to Grenoble and Lyons.

The troops sent by King Louis XVIII. to oppose him, with few exceptions welcomed him, as did also several of his former marshals,

Ney among them; on March 20th he entered Paris, and King Louis fled to Ghent.

But his appearance in France had an effect which he had not looked for. He had counted upon the dissensions among the Powers at the Congress as an element in his favour, and did not anticipate that all peaceful overtures on his part would be rejected.

For the moment he desired peace, in order, if not from any higher motives, to consolidate his position and increase his army; but his escape from Elba was felt to have been such a flagrant breach of treaty engagements, and confidence had been so entirely destroyed in his good faith, that the Powers declined to negotiate, and in a proclamation, on March 13th, 1815, declared him to be the "enemy and disturber of the world," and abandoned him to "public justice."

All Europe sprang again to arms, and on every road leading towards France troops were set in motion. The Prussians marched to co-operate with Great Britain and the King of the Netherlands in Belgium; the Austrians and Bavarians gathered on the Rhine; the Sardinians in the Apennines; the Swiss in the Alps; Spain and Portugal threatened to cross the Pyrenees; the Russians advanced from Poland; and Denmark and Sweden joined the Coalition. It was to be a struggle to the death between the Allied Powers of Europe and Napoleon, whom they had outlawed.

Wellington was at once appointed to command the "Anglo-Belgian" (or "Anglo-Allied") Army in the Netherlands, and arrived at Brussels on April 5th, 1815.

The Duke of Brunswick's Troops.

To H.S.H. the Duke of Brunswick, K.G.

'Bruxelles,
'April 6, 1815.

'It has been arranged in a treaty signed by Great Britain, Austria, Russia, and Prussia, to which all the other Powers of Europe have been called upon to accede, that the measures to be adopted, in consequence of the position in which the Powers of Europe have been placed in relation to France by Buonaparte's recent invasion of that kingdom, shall be adopted by common accord; and His Majesty's Minister will make known Your Highness's desire that your troops should be at the disposition of His Royal Highness the Prince Regent.'

Memorandum.

On the Defence of the Frontier of the Netherlands.

'Paris,
'September 22,1814.

'. . . There are good positions for an army at La Trinité and at Renaix behind Tournay; another between Tournay and Mons, on the high grounds about Blaton; there are many good positions about Mons; the course of the Haine from Binch towards Mons would afford some good ones; about Nivelle, and between that and Binch, there are many advantageous positions; and the entrance of the *forêt de* Soignies, (***where the Battle of Waterloo was fought in the following year***), by the highroad which leads to Brussels from Binch, Charleroi, and Namur, would, if worked upon, afford others . . . .'

A Mutiny and 'Poor Old Blücher.'

To the Earl of Clancarty, G.C.B.

'Bruxelles,
'May 3, 1815.

'. . . . The Saxons mutinied last night at Liege, and obliged poor old Blücher to quit the town; the cause of the mutiny was the order to divide the corps, and that the Prussian part, in which the guards were included, should take the oath of allegiance to the King of Prussia.

'We hear of Buonaparte's quitting Paris, and of the march of troops to this frontier, in order to attack us. I met Blücher at Tirlemont this day, and received from him the most satisfactory assurances of support.

'For an action in Belgium I can now put 70,000 men into the field, and Blücher 80,000, so that I hope we should give a good account even of Buonaparte. I am not satisfied with our delays.'

Buonaparte's Movements.

To Lieutenant-General Lord Hill.

'Bruxelles,
'May 9, 1815, noon.

'Matters look a little serious upon the frontier; the enemy have certainly got the greatest part of their force collected at Valenciennes and Maubeuge, and it is said that Buonaparte arrived yesterday at Condé. I was assured at Ghent on Sunday that he was to leave Paris on this day. It is certain that all communication is stopped since yesterday morning . . .

To the Right Hon. Sir Henry Wellesley.

'Bruxelles,
'May 12, 1815.

'. . . . There has been a good deal of movement upon the frontier in the last week, but I am inclined to believe it is entirely defensive, and that Buonaparte cannot venture to quit Paris. Indeed, all accounts give reason to hope that, even without the aid of the Allies, his power will not be of long duration.'

To General Lord Lynedoch, G.C.B.

'Bruxelles,
'June 13, 1815.

'. . . . There is nothing new here. We have reports of Buonaparte's joining the army and attacking us, but I have accounts from Paris of the 10th, on which day he was still there, and I judge from his speech to the Legislature that his departure was not likely to be immediate. I think we are now too strong for him here.'

Rations for Brunswick Troops.

To Commissary-General Dunmore.

'Bruxelles,
'May 13, 1815.

'I beg you will take measures to feed the Brunswick troops tomorrow, and afterwards; you will learn from the Quartermaster-General where they are, and I beg you will send somebody to their cantonments at Vilvorde in the morning at daylight. Their ration for men must be two pounds of bread, half a pound of meat and vegetables. The ration for their horses is ten pounds of hay, and one-eighth of a peck of oats. The vegetables should be: A quarter of a pound of grits, barley, or rice; or half a pound of peas, beans, vetches, or oatmeal; or one pound of potatoes, or other vegetables.'

Disposition of French Troops.

To Lieutenant-Colonel Sir Henry Hardinge, K.C.B.

'Bruxelles,
'May 16, 1815, 11 a. m.

'I enclose a memorandum which I have drawn from intelligence I have recently received, from which the marshal will see the strength and disposition of the French Army; and that with the 1st, 2nd, 3rd and 6th Corps, and the Guards, and the 3rd Division of cavalry of reserve, we have a good lot of them in our front. I should think not less than 110,000 men. . . .'

MEMORANDUM.

For the Deputy Quartermaster-General.

MOVEMENTS OF THE ARMY.

'Bruxelles,
'June 15, 1815.

'General Dornberg's brigade of cavalry, and the Cumberland Hussars, to march this night upon Vilvorde, and to bivouac on the highroad near to that town.

'The Earl of Uxbridge will be pleased to collect the cavalry this night at Ninhove, leaving the 2nd Hussars looking out between the Scheldt and the Lys.

'The 1st Division of infantry to collect this night at Ath and adjacent, and to be in readiness to move at a moment's notice.

'The 3rd Division to collect this night at Braine le Comte, and to be in readiness to move at the shortest notice.

'The 4th Division to be collected this night at Grammont, with the exception of the troops beyond the Scheldt, which are to be moved to Audenarde.

'The 5th Division, the 81st Regiment, and the Hanoverian brigade of the 6th Division, to be in readiness to march from Bruxelles at a moment's notice.

'The Duke of Brunswick's corps to collect this night on the highroad between Bruxelles and Vilvorde.

'The Nassau troops to collect at daylight tomorrow morning on the Louvain road, and to be in readiness to move at a moment's notice.

'The Hanoverian brigade of the 5th Division to collect this night at Hal, and to be in readiness at daylight tomorrow morning to move towards Bruxelles, and to halt on the highroad between Alost and Assche for further orders.

'The Prince of Orange is requested to collect at Nivelles the end and 3rd Divisions of the Army of the Low Countries; and, should that point have been attacked this day, to move the 3rd Division of British infantry upon Nivelles as soon as collected.

'This movement is not to take place until it is quite certain that the enemy's attack is upon the right of the Prussian Army, and the left of the British Army.

'Lord Hill will be so good as to order Prince Frederick of Orange to occupy Audenarde with 500 men, and to collect the 1st Division of the Army of the Low Countries, and the Indian brigade at Sotteghem, so as to be ready to march in the morning at daylight.

'The reserve artillery to be in readiness to move at daylight.

'Wellington.'

Movement of the Army.

After-Orders, 10 o'clock p.m.

'Bruxelles,
'June 15, 1815.

'The 3rd Division of infantry to continue its movement from Braine le Comte upon Nivelles.

'The 1st Division to move from Enghien upon Braine le Comte.

'The 2nd and 4th Divisions of infantry to move from Ath and Grammont, also from Audenarde, and to continue their movements upon Enghien.

'The cavalry to continue its movement from Ninhove upon Enghien.

'The above movements to take place with as little delay as possible.

'Wellington.'

Instructions for the Movement of the Army on the 16th.

The original instructions issued to Colonel de Lancey were lost with that officer's papers. These memorandums of movements have been collected from the different officers to whom they were addressed.

Signed by Colonel Sir W. De Lancey, Deputy Quartermaster-General.
To General Lord Hill.

'June 16, 1815.

'The Duke of Wellington requests that you will move the 2nd Division of infantry upon Braine le Comte immediately. The cavalry has been ordered likewise on Braine le Comte. His Grace is going to Waterloo.'

'June 16, 1815.

'Your Lordship is requested to order Prince Frederick of Orange to move, immediately upon the receipt of this order, the 1st Division of the army of the Low Countries, and the Indian brigade, from Sotteghem to Enghien, leaving 500 men, as before directed, in Audenarde.'

'Genappe,
'June 16, 1815.

'The 2nd Division of infantry to move tomorrow morning at daybreak from Nivelles to Quatre Bras. The 4th Division of infantry to move at daybreak tomorrow morning to Nivelles.'

'June 16, 1815.

'The reserve artillery to move at daybreak tomorrow morning, the 17th, to Quatre Bras, where it will receive further orders.'

To Major-General Sir J. Lambert, K.C.B.

'June 16, 1815.

'The brigade of infantry, under the command of Major-General Sir J. Lambert, to march from Assche at daybreak tomorrow morning, the 17th instant, to Genappe, on the Namur road, and to remain there until further orders.'

INSTRUCTIONS FOR THE MOVEMENT OF THE ARMY ON THE 17TH.

To General Lord Hill.

'June 17, 1815.

'The 2nd Division of British infantry to march from Nivelles on Waterloo at ten o'clock.

'The brigades of the 4th Division now at Nivelles to march from that place on Waterloo at ten o'clock. Those brigades of the 4th Division at Braine le Comte, and on the road from Braine le Comte to Nivelles, to collect and halt at Braine le Comte this day.

'All the baggage on the road from Braine le Comte to Nivelles to return immediately to Braine le Comte, and to proceed immediately from thence to Hal and Bruxelles. The spare musket ammunition to be immediately parked behind Genappe.

'The corps under the command of Prince Frederick of Orange will move from Enghien this evening, and take up a position in front of Hal, occupying Braine le Château with two battalions.

'Colonel Erstorff will fall back with his brigade on Hal, and place himself under the orders of Prince Frederick.'

FINAL WORDS.

To Major-General Colville.

'June 17, 1815.

'The army retired this day from its position at Quatre Bras to its present position in front of Waterloo.

'The brigades of the 4th Division at Braine le Comte are to retire at daylight tomorrow morning upon Hal.

'Major-General Colville must be guided by the intelligence he receives of the enemy's movements in his march to Hal, whether he moves by the direct route or by Enghien.

'Prince Frederick of Orange is to occupy with his corps the position between Hal and Enghien, and is to defend it as long as possible.

'The army will probably continue in its position in front of Waterloo tomorrow. 'Lieutenant Colonel Torrens will inform Lieutenant-General Sir C. Colville of the position and situation of the armies.'

To Sir Charles Stuart.

'Waterloo,

'June 18, 1815, 3 a.m.

'I enclose two letters, which I beg you to peruse and forward without loss of time.

'You will see in the letter to the Duc de Berri the real state of our case and the only risk we run. The Prussians will be ready again in the morning for anything.

'Pray keep the English quiet if you can.

'Let them all prepare to move, but neither be in a hurry or a fright, as all will yet turn out well.

'I have given the directions to the Governor of Antwerp to meet the crotchets which I find in the heads of the King's Governors upon every turn.

'The post-horses are embargoed in my name—I conclude, to prevent people from running away with them; but give the man orders to allow anybody to have them who goes with an order from you.'

★★★★★★★★★★

Captain William Siborne's model of the Battle of Waterloo was claimed by Siborne that the Government entrusted him with the task of making the model, but when the work was suspended in1833, owing to the change of Administration, he finished it on his own account, and at a cost to himself of more than £4,000. After suffering much disappointment in connection with the model, it was purchased from Captain Siborne by public subscription

★★★★★★★★★★

The Waterloo Despatch.

To Earl Bathurst.

'Waterloo,
'June 19, 1815.

'My Lord,

'Buonaparte, having collected the 1st, 2nd, 3rd, 4th, and 6th Corps of the French Army, and the Imperial Guards, and nearly all the cavalry, on the Sambre, and between that river and the Meuse, between the 10th and 14th of the month, advanced on the 15th and attacked the Prussian posts at Thuin and Lobbes, on the Sambre, at daylight in the morning.

'I did not hear of these events till in the evening of the 15th; and I immediately ordered the troops to prepare to march, and afterwards to march to their left, as soon as I had intelligence from other quarters to prove that the enemy's movement upon Charleroi was the real attack.

'The enemy drove the Prussian posts from the Sambre on that day; and General Ziethen, who commanded the corps which had been at Charleroi, retired upon Fleurus; and Marshal Prince Blücher concentrated the Prussian Army upon Sombref, holding the villages in front of his position of St. Amand and Ligny.

'The enemy continued his march along the road from Charleroi towards Bruxelles; and on the same evening, the 15th, attacked a brigade of the Army of the Netherlands, under the Prince de Weimar, posted at Frasne, and forced it back to the farmhouse, on the same road, called Les Quatre Bras.

'The Prince of Orange immediately reinforced this brigade with another of the same division, under General Perponcher, and, in the morning early, regained part of the ground which had been lost, so as to have the command of the communication leading from Nivelles and Bruxelles with Marshal Blücher's position.

'In the meantime, I had directed the whole army to march upon Les Quatre Bras; and the 5th Division, under Lieutenant-General Sir Thomas Picton, arrived at about half-past two in the day, followed by the corps of troops under the Duke of Brunswick, and afterwards by the contingent of Nassau.

'At this time the enemy commenced an attack upon Prince Blücher with his whole force, excepting the 1st and 2nd Corps, and a corps of cavalry under General Kellermann, with which he attacked our post at Les Quatre Bras.

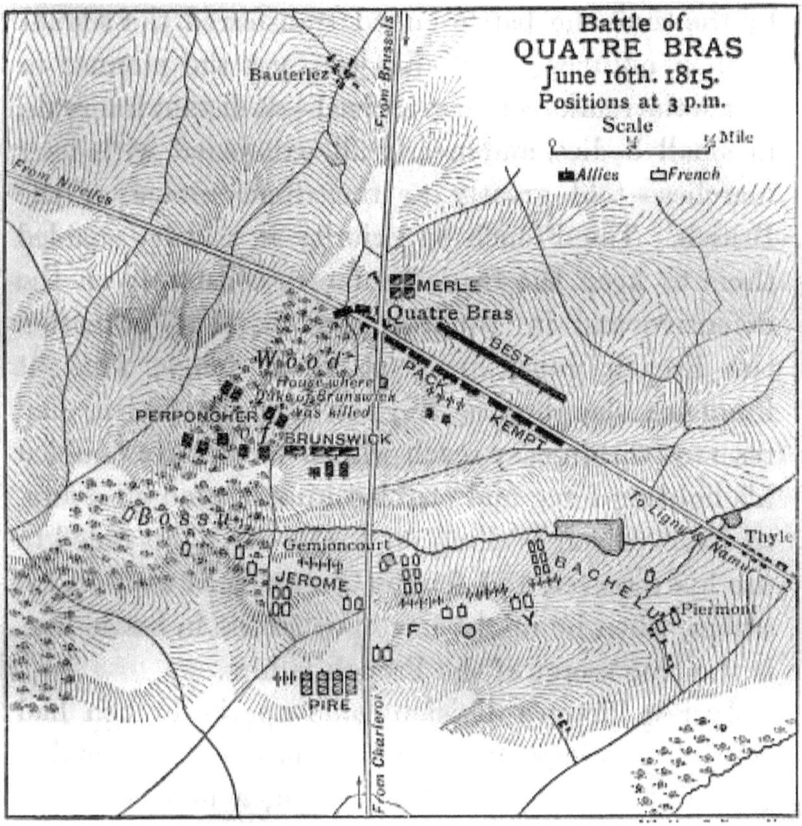
Battle of
QUATRE BRAS
June 16th. 1815.
Positions at 3 p.m.
Scale
Mile
Allies
French
Bauterlez
From Brussels
From Nivelles
MERLE
Quatre Bras
BEST
PACK
KEMPT
Wood
House where Duke of Brunswick was killed
PERPONCHER
BRUNSWICK
BOSSU
Gemioncourt
JEROME
FOY
BACHELU
Thyle
To Ligny & Namur
Piermont
PIRE
From Charleroi

'The Prussian Army maintained their position with their usual gallantry and perseverance against a great disparity of numbers, as the 4th Corps of their army, under General Billow, had not joined; and I was not able to assist them as I wished, as I was attacked myself, and the troops, the cavalry in particular, which had a long distance to march, had not arrived.

'We maintained our position also, and completely defeated and repulsed all the enemy's attempts to get possession of it. The enemy repeatedly attacked us with a large body of infantry and cavalry, supported by a numerous and powerful artillery. He made several charges with the cavalry upon our infantry, but all were repulsed in the steadiest manner.

'In this affair His Royal Highness the Prince of Orange, the Duke of Brunswick, and Lieutenant-General Sir Thomas Picton, and Major-Generals Sir James Kempt and Sir Denis Pack, who were engaged from the commencement of the enemy's attack, highly distinguished themselves, as well as Lieutenant-General Charles Baron Alten, Major-General Sir C. Halkett, Lieutenant-General Cooke, and Major-Generals Maitland and Byng, as they successively arrived. The troops of the 5th Division, and those of the Brunswick corps, were long and severely engaged, and conducted themselves with the utmost gallantry. I must particularly mention the 28th, 42nd, 79th, and 92nd Regiments, and the battalion of Hanoverians.

★★★★★★★★★★

The 28th became the 1st Battalion the Gloucestershire Regiment. The 42nd is the 1st Battalion the Black Watch (Royal Highlanders), the 79th is the Queen's Own Cameron Highlanders, and the 92nd is the 2nd Battalion the Gordon Highlanders. The pipers mustered the Highland Brigade for Waterloo to the terribly prophetic strains of 'Come to me, and I will give you flesh.'

★★★★★★★★★★

'Our loss was great, as Your Lordship will perceive by the enclosed return, and I have particularly to regret His Serene Highness the Duke of Brunswick, who fell fighting gallantly at the head of his troops.

'Although Marshal Blücher had maintained his position at Sombref, he still found himself much weakened by the severity of the contest in which he had been engaged, and, as the 4th Corps had not arrived, he determined to fall back, and to concentrate his army upon Wavre; and he marched in the night, after the action was over.

'This movement of the Marshal rendered necessary a corresponding one upon my part; and I retired from the farm of Quatre Bras upon Genappe, and thence upon Waterloo the next morning, the 17th, at ten o'clock.

'The enemy made no effort to pursue Marshal Blücher. On the contrary, a patrol which I sent to Sombref in the morning found all quiet, and the enemy's vedettes fell back as the patrol advanced. (Lieutenant-Colonel the Hon. Alexander Gordon was sent, escorted by a squadron of the 10th Hussars, to communicate, with the Prussian headquarters as to co-operation with the British Army ordered to retire to the position in front of Waterloo.) Neither did he attempt to molest our march to the rear, although made in the middle of the day, excepting by following, with a large body of cavalry brought from his right, the cavalry under the Earl of Uxbridge.

'This gave Lord Uxbridge an opportunity of charging them with the 1st Life Guards, upon their *débouché* from the village of Genappe, upon which occasion His Lordship has declared himself to be well satisfied with that regiment.

'The position which I took up in front of Waterloo crossed the highroads from Charleroi and Nivelles, and had its right thrown back to a ravine near Merke Braine, which was occupied, and its left extended to a height above the hamlet Ter la Haye, which was likewise occupied. In front of the right centre, and near the Nivelles road, we occupied the house and gardens of Hougoumont, which covered the return of that flank; and in front of the left centre we occupied the farm of La Haye Sainte. By our left we communicated with Marshal Prince Blücher at Wavre, through Ohain; and the marshal had promised me that, in case we should be attacked, he would support me with one or more corps, as might be necessary.

'The enemy collected his army, with the exception of the 3rd Corps, which had been sent to observe Marshal Blücher, on a range of heights in our front, in the course of the night of the 17th and yesterday morning, and at about ten o'clock he commenced a furious attack upon our post at Hougoumont. I had occupied that post with a detachment from General Byng's brigade of Guards, which was in position in its rear; and it was for some time under the command of Lieutenant-Colonel Macdonell, and afterwards of Colonel Home; and I am happy to add that it was maintained throughout the day with the utmost gallantry by these brave troops, notwithstanding the repeated efforts of large bodies of the enemy to obtain possession of it.

'This attack upon the right of our centre was accompanied by a very heavy cannonade upon our whole line, which was destined to support the repeated attacks of cavalry and infantry, occasionally mixed, but sometimes separate, which were made upon it. In one of these the enemy carried the farmhouse of La Haye Sainte, as the detachment of the light battalion of the German Legion, which occupied it, had expended all its ammunition; and the enemy occupied the only communication there was with them.

'The enemy repeatedly charged our infantry with his cavalry, but these attacks were uniformly unsuccessful; and they afforded opportunities to our cavalry to charge, in one of which Lord E. Somerset's brigade, consisting of the Life Guards, the Royal Horse Guards, and 1st Dragoon Guards, highly distinguished themselves, as did that of Major-General Sir William Ponsonby, having taken many prisoners and an eagle.

'These attacks were repeated till about seven in the evening, when the enemy made a desperate effort with cavalry and infantry, supported by the fire of artillery, to force our left centre, near the farm of La Haye Sainte, which after a severe contest was defeated; and, having observed that the troops retired from this attack in great confusion, and that the march of General Bülow's corps, by Frischermont upon Planchenois and La Belle Alliance, had begun to take effect, and as I could perceive the fire of his cannon, and as Marshal Prince Blücher had joined in person with a corps of his army to the left of our line by Ohain, I determined to attack the enemy, and immediately advanced the whole line of infantry, supported by the cavalry and artillery. The attack succeeded in every point: the enemy was forced from his positions on the heights, and fled in the utmost confusion, leaving behind him, as far as I could judge, 150 pieces of cannon, with their ammunition, which fell into our hands.

'I continued the pursuit till long after dark, and then discontinued it only on account of the fatigue of our troops, who had been engaged during twelve hours, and because I found myself on the same road with Marshal Blücher, who assured me of his intention to follow the enemy throughout the night. He has sent me word this morning that he had taken 60 pieces of cannon belonging to the Imperial Guard, and several carriages, baggage, etc., belonging to Buonaparte in Genappe.

'I propose to move this morning upon Nivelles, and not to discontinue my operations.

'Your Lordship will observe that such a desperate action could not

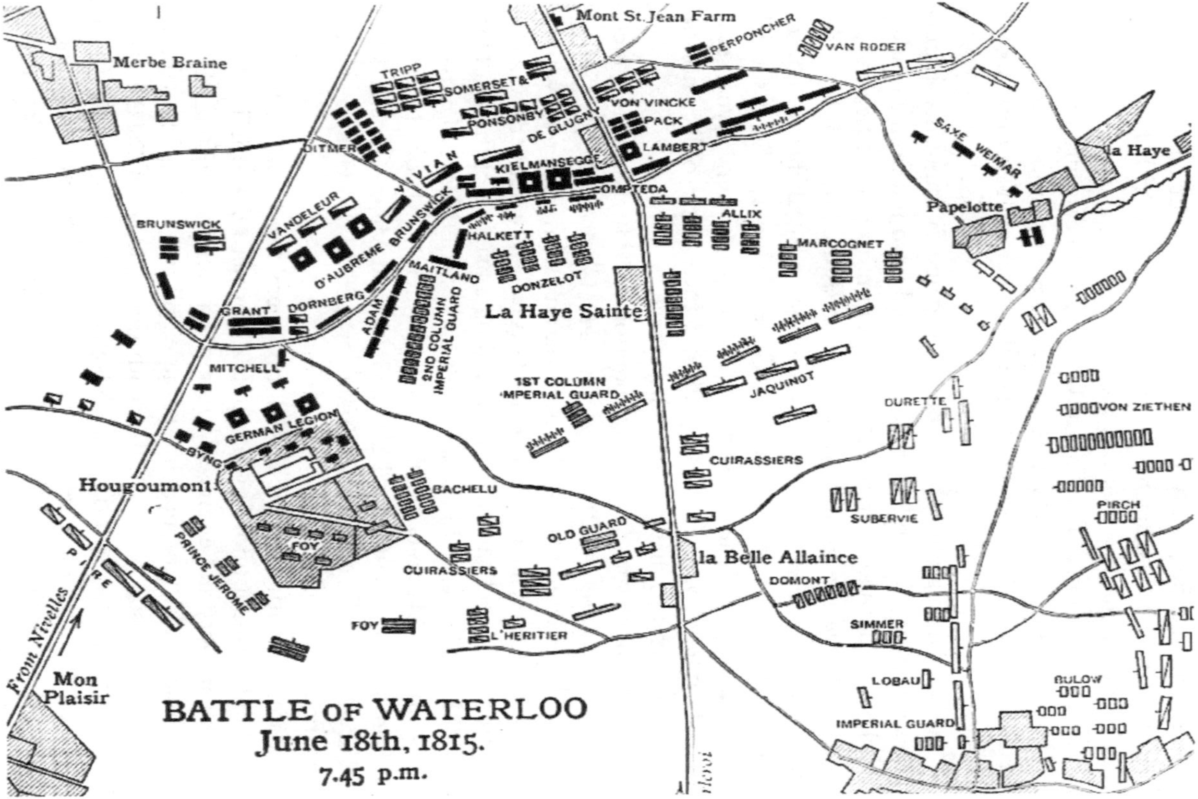

BATTLE OF WATERLOO
June 18th, 1815.
7.45 p.m.

be fought, and such advantages could not be gained, without great loss; and I am sorry to add that ours has been immense. In Lieutenant-General Sir Thomas Picton His Majesty has sustained the loss of an officer who has frequently distinguished himself in his service, and he fell gloriously leading his division to a charge with bayonets, by which one of the most serious attacks made by the enemy on our position was repulsed. The Earl of Uxbridge, after having successfully got through this arduous day, received a wound by almost the last shot fired, which will, I am afraid, deprive His Majesty for some time of his services.

'His Royal Highness the Prince of Orange distinguished himself by his gallantry and conduct, till he received a wound from a musket-ball through the shoulder, which obliged him to quit the field.

'It gives me the greatest satisfaction to assure Your Lordship that the army never upon any occasion conducted itself better. The division of Guards, under Lieutenant-General Cooke, who is severely wounded, Major-General Maitland, and Major-General Byng, set an example which was followed by all, and there is no officer nor description of troops that did not behave well.

'I must, however, particularly mention for His Royal Highness's approbation Lieutenant-General Sir H. Clinton, Major-General Adam, Lieutenant-General Charles Baron Alten (severely wounded), Major-General Sir Colin Halkett (severely wounded), Colonel Ompteda, Colonel Mitchell (commanding a brigade of the 4th Division), Major-Generals Sir James Kempt and Sir D. Pack, Major-General Lambert, Major-General Lord E. Somerset, Major-General Sir W. Ponsonby, Major-General Sir C. Grant, and Major-General Sir H. Vivian, Major-General Sir O. Vandeleur, and Major-General Count Dornberg.

'I am also particularly indebted to General Lord Hill for his assistance and conduct upon this, as upon all former occasions.

'The artillery and engineer departments were conducted much to my satisfaction by Colonel Sir George Wood and Colonel Smyth; and I had every reason to be satisfied with the conduct of the Adjutant-General, Major-General Barnes, who was wounded, and of the Quartermaster General, Colonel De Lancey, who was killed by a cannon-shot in the middle of the action. This officer is a serious loss to His Majesty's service, and to me at this moment.

'I was likewise much indebted to the assistance of Lieutenant-Colonel Lord FitzRoy Somerset, who was severely wounded, and of the officers composing my personal staff, who have suffered severely in this action. Lieutenant-Colonel the Hon. Sir Alexander Gordon, who has died of his wounds, was a most promising officer, and is a serious loss to His Majesty's service.

'General Kruse, of the Nassau service, likewise conducted himself much to my satisfaction, as did General Tripp, commanding the heavy brigade of cavalry, and General Vanhope, commanding a brigade of infantry, in the service of the King of the Netherlands.

'General Pozzo di Borgo, General Baron Vincent, General Muffling, and General Alava, were in the field during the action, and rendered me every assistance in their power. Baron Vincent is wounded, but I hope not severely, and General Vozzo di Borgo received a contusion.

'I should not do justice to my own feelings, or to Marshal Blücher and the Prussian Army, if I did not attribute the successful result of this arduous day to the cordial and timely assistance I received from them. The operation of General Bülow upon the enemy's flank was a most decisive one; and even if I had not found myself in a situation to make the attack which produced the final result, it would have forced the enemy to retire if his attacks should have failed, and would have prevented him from taking advantage of them if they should unfortunately have succeeded.

'Since writing the above, I have received a report that Major-General Sir William Ponsonby is killed, and, in announcing this intelligence to Your Lordship, I have to add the expression of my grief for the fate of an officer who had already rendered very brilliant and important services, and was an ornament to his profession.

'I send with this despatch three eagles, taken by the troops in this action, which Major Percy will have the honour of laying at the feet of His Royal Highness. I beg leave to recommend him to Your Lordship's protection.

'I have the honour to be, etc.,

'Wellington.

'Earl Bathurst.'

****

One of the eagles was taken by Sergeant Ewart, of the Scots Greys. That regiment—which became the 2nd Dragoons (Royal Scots Greys)—also bore an eagle with which is the word 'Waterloo.' The 1st (Royal) Dragoons also bear an eagle as a badge, to represent the capture of a French standard at Waterloo..

****

STRENGTH OF THE BRITISH ARMY ON THE MORNING OF THE BATTLE OF WATERLOO,

June 18, 1815.

Divisions.	Brigades.	Regiments.	Stations.	Officers.				Troop Quarter-masters and Sergeants.					Trumpeters or Drummers.					Rank and File.					
				Field Officers.	Captains.	Subalterns.	Staff.	Present.	Sick. Present.	Sick. Absent.	Command.	Total.	Present.	Sick. Present.	Sick. Absent.	Command.	Total.	Present.	Sick. Present.	Sick. Absent.	Command.	Prisoners of War and Missing.	Total Rank and File.
		Royal Artillery	Position in front of Waterloo	8	50	91	26	152	9	—	—	161	44	—	—	—	44	4,573	306	77	9	9	4,914
		Artillery, K.G.L.		2	5	12	6	20	—	—	1	21	6	—	—	—	6	520	73	—	29	—	622
		Royal Engineers		1	17	29	—	—	—	—	—	—	—	—	—	—	—	—	—	—	—	—	—
		Royal Sappers & Miners		—	—	10	—	33	—	—	2	35	19	—	—	—	19	683	10	8	17	—	718
		Royal Waggon Train		1	2	9	4	17	—	—	3	20	2	—	—	—	2	266	—	3	10	—	279
		Royal Staff Corps		1	4	11	2	9	—	—	—	9	4	—	—	—	4	238	5	—	—	—	243
Cavalry.	1st	1st Life Guards		1	3	4	4	19	—	—	3	18	4	—	—	—	4	210	10	1	7	—	228
		2nd ,,		1	4	8	3	19	—	—	2	17	3	—	1	—	4	197	—	4	30	—	231
		R. Horse Guards (Blue)		2	4	7	1	46	—	1	4	20	4	—	—	—	4	213	—	9	15	—	237
		1st Dragoon Guards		1	9	14	4	20	—	—	2	47	8	—	—	—	8	515	12	—	3	—	530
	2nd	1st Dragoons		2	5	15	6	30	—	—	—	28	6	—	—	—	6	364	7	1	22	—	394
		2nd ,,		3	6	13	6	33	1	—	—	34	6	—	—	—	6	375	1	5	10	—	391
		6th ,,		2	6	12	6	29	1	—	—	30	6	—	—	—	6	384	7	—	5	—	396
	3rd	1st Lt. Dragoons, K.G.L.		2	9	15	7	48	—	2	5	54	10	—	—	—	10	443	6	20	27	15	511
		2nd ,, ,,		4	8	14	6	30	1	9	2	41	10	—	—	—	10	433	14	37	31	13	528
		23rd Lt. Dragoons		3	7	12	6	22	—	1	3	26	4	—	2	—	6	287	—	39	16	45	387
	4th	11th ,,		2	6	14	5	34	—	—	—	34	6	—	—	1	7	368	7	1	14	—	390
		12th ,,		2	7	12	5	34	—	—	—	34	4	—	—	—	4	363	3	—	22	—	388
		16th ,,		2	6	17	6	36	—	—	—	36	5	1	—	—	6	362	5	1	25	—	393
	5th	*2nd Hussars, K.G.L.	Courtrai	3	8	17	7	49	1	—	4	53	6	—	—	—	6	493	15	17	33	—	558
		7th Hussars	Position in front of Waterloo	1	4	9	4	23	—	5	6	34	5	—	—	1	6	316	—	16	34	14	380
		15th ,,		2	7	13	6	30	—	—	—	30	6	—	—	—	6	383	3	—	6	—	392
	6th	1st Hussars, K.G.L.		2	9	17	7	44	2	—	8	53	9	1	—	—	10	498	16	6	93	—	613
		10th Hussars		3	7	11	5	31	—	—	1	32	6	—	—	—	6	389	—	—	1	—	390
		18th ,,		1	4	14	6	33	—	—	—	33	6	—	—	—	6	378	5	5	8	—	396
	7th	3rd Hussars, K.G.L.		2	10	20	5	46	2	1	14	63	11	—	—	—	11	590	26	22	149	—	787
		13th Lt. Dragoons		1	7	15	5	24	—	—	—	34	6	—	—	—	6	380	7	1	1	1	390
1st	1st British	†1st Guards, 2nd Batt.		—	4	21	4	43	—	8	5	56	21	—	1	—	22	688	—	276	12	—	976
		†1st ,, 3rd ,,		—	7	17	5	40	—	8	5	53	20	—	2	—	22	758	—	255	8	—	1,021
	2nd ,,	Colds. ,, 2nd ,,		1	5	25	5	55	3	1	6	65	15	1	—	6	22	939	49	4	11	—	1,003
		3rd ,, 2nd ,,		1	5	26	3	55	2	—	10	67	9	1	—	7	17	957	41	6	57	—	1,061
				A	B	C	D	E	F	G	H	I	J	K	L	M	N	O	P	Q	R	S	T

Division	Brigade	Regiment	Station	A	B	C	D	E	F	G	H	I	J	K	L	M	N	O	P	Q	R	S	T
2nd	3rd British	52nd Regt., 1st Batt.	Position in front of Waterloo	2	10	41	6	65	1	1	2	69	22	—	—	—	22	1,002	18	12	6	—	1,038
		71st ,, 1st ,,		3	9	32	6	61	—	—	1	62	21	—	—	—	21	798	6	4	2	—	810
		95th ,, Prov. Batt.		1	2	5	2	11	—	—	1	12	6	—	—	—	6	176	2	2	8	—	188
		95th ,, 2nd Batt.		2	6	20	6	37	1	—	3	41	17	—	—	—	17	567	10	3	5	—	585
	1st K.G.L.	1st Line Batt., K.G.L.		2	6	16	5	25	3	2	18	48	12	—	—	—	12	389	20	27	17	5	458
		2nd ,, ,,		1	6	17	5	30	1	3	16	50	12	1	1	—	14	423	25	32	13	18	511
		3rd ,, ,,		3	4	17	6	32	—	2	13	47	13	—	—	—	13	508	6	30	11	—	555
		4th ,, ,,		2	5	17	6	26	—	4	3	33	9	—	—	1	10	413	—	38	11	—	462
3rd	5th British	30th Regt., 2nd Batt.		3	5	26	6	33	—	5	5	43	14	—	—	—	14	548	—	45	9	13	615
		33rd Regt.		1	4	21	5	22	—	4	10	36	12	—	2	4	18	501	10	24	6	30	561
		69th ,, 2nd ,,		2	6	17	5	28	1	1	4	34	19	—	—	—	19	464	23	16	8	5	516
		73rd ,, 2nd ,,		2	5	12	4	32	—	5	5	42	17	—	—	1	18	496	—	102	34	—	562
	2nd K.G.L.	5th Line Batt., K.G.L.		2	4	20	5	30	—	1	16	47	16	—	—	—	16	394	32	21	10	—	457
		8th ,, ,,		2	6	18	6	31	—	—	15	46	15	—	—	1	16	436	11	3	95	—	545
		1st Light Batt. ,,		3	5	18	6	23	3	7	20	53	12	—	1	1	14	382	26	57	20	—	485
		2nd ,, ,,		1	5	19	6	24	3	4	19	50	14	—	1	—	15	332	28	59	12	—	431
4th	4th British	14th Regt., 3rd Batt.		2	8	23	5	33	1	—	2	36	11	—	—	—	11	548	9	7	7	—	572
		23rd ,, 1st ,,		3	10	25	6	35	—	—	3	38	23	—	—	—	23	639	—	5	3	—	647
		51st ,,		2	9	28	6	39	—	—	2	41	14	2	2	—	18	521	5	17	6	—	549
	6th ,,	*35th ,, 2nd ,,	Near Braine le Comte	2	5	23	6	31	—	1	2	34	16	—	2	—	18	481	6	69	14	—	570
		*54th ,, 1st ,,		2	5	29	5	38	—	3	3	44	19	—	—	—	19	497	—	37	7	—	541
		*59th ,, 2nd ,,		3	6	21	6	38	1	—	1	40	15	—	—	—	15	432	18	10	1	—	401
		*91st ,, 1st ,,		1	8	27	6	48	1	3	1	53	21	—	—	—	21	774	18	31	1	—	824
5th	8th ,,	†28th ,, 1st ,,	Position in front of Waterloo	2	8	20	5	36	1	2	1	40	27	—	1	—	28	458	—	88	9	2	557
		†32nd ,, 1st ,,		2	4	14	6	36	—	6	2	44	14	—	1	—	15	427	—	218	17	—	662
		†79th ,, 1st ,,		—	4	17	5	30	—	12	3	45	10	—	2	1	13	374	5	290	34	—	703
		†95th ,, 1st ,,		1	3	7	6	27	—	11	—	38	10	—	2	—	12	364	—	185	—	—	549
	9th ,,	†1st ,, 3rd ,,		1	5	23	7	34	—	14	—	48	17	—	3	—	20	366	—	236	2	—	604
		†42nd ,, 1st ,,		—	1	13	3	25	—	12	1	38	15	—	1	—	16	272	9	220	25	—	526
		†44th ,, 2nd ,,		2	4	18	6	39	2	2	3	46	15	—	1	—	16	396	12	32	15	—	455
		†92nd ,, 1st ,,		1	2	15	4	27	—	16	1	44	12	—	3	1	16	361	—	217	10	—	588
6th	10th ,,	4th ,, 1st ,,		1	2	20	4	36	—	2	2	40	11	1	—	—	12	596	6	55	12	—	669
		27th ,, 1st ,,		—	3	15	3	34	—	1	1	36	8	—	—	—	8	687	—	10	1	—	698
		40th ,, 1st ,,		2	9	27	5	55	—	2	1	58	17	—	—	—	17	747	—	11	3	—	761
		*81st ,, 2nd ,,	Bruxelles	2	9	22	5	26	—	1	1	28	9	2	1	—	12	406	17	16	—	—	439
7th	7th ,,	*25th ,, 2nd ,,	Antwerp	3	5	16	5	29	—	—	3	32	12	1	—	1	14	354	21	5	8	—	388
		*37th ,, 2nd ,,	,,	1	9	19	6	34	2	—	1	37	13	2	—	—	15	387	34	62	8	—	491
		*78th ,, 2nd ,,	Nieuport	2	7	19	5	22	1	—	2	25	10	—	—	—	10	313	16	5	3	—	337
		*13th R. Veteran Batt.	Ostend	1	7	19	6	27	4	—	4	35	5	—	—	—	5	649	24	—	10	—	683
		*1st Foreign ,,	Antwerp	2	6	9	5	32	2	1	—	35	12	—	—	—	12	536	40	1	18	—	595
		*2nd Garrison Batt.	Ostend	2	7	21	4	38	3	—	—	41	14	—	—	—	14	696	43	—	—	—	730
			Total	129	69	1,330	380	2,473	53	164	277	2,947	852	13	30	26	921	37,603	1,128	3,046	1,186	170	43,133

* These regiments were not at the Battle of Waterloo.

† The increase of the number included in the column 'Sick Absent' arises from these regiments having been engaged at Quatre Bras on the 16th

J. WATERS, *Lieutenant-Colonel, Assistant Adjutant-General.*

Return of the Killed, Wounded, and Missing, of the British and Hanoverian Army under the Command of Field-Marshal the Duke of Wellington, K.G., in the Battle fought at Quatre Bras on June 16, 1815.

	Officers.	Sergeants.	Rank and File.	Total Loss of Officers, Non-commissioned Officers, and Rank and File.	British.	Hanoverians.	Horses.
Killed -	29	19	302	350	316	34	19
Wounded	126	111	2,143	2,380	2,156	224	14
Missing -	4	6	171	181	32	149	1

On the Retreat from Quatre Bras to Waterloo on June 17, 1815.

	Officers.	Sergeants.	Rank and File.	Total Loss of Officers, Non-commissioned Officers, and Rank and File.	British.	Hanoverians.	Horses.
Killed -	1	1	33	35	26	9	45
Wounded	7	13	112	132	52	80	20
Missing -	4	3	64	71	30	32	33

In the Battle fought at Waterloo on June 18, 1815.

	Officers.	Sergeants.	Rank and File.	Total Loss of Officers, Non-commissioned Officers, and Rank and File.	British.	Hanoverians.	Horses.
Killed -	116	109	1,822	2,047	1,759	288	1,495
Wounded	504	364	6,148	7,016	5,892	1,124	891
Missing -	20	29	1,574	1,623	807	816	773

	Killed.	Wounded.	Missing.
Total - -	2,432	9,528	1,875

The greater number of the men returned as missing had gone to the rear with wounded officers and soldiers, and joined afterwards. The officers are supposed killed.

To the Earl of Aberdeen, K.T.

'Bruxelles,
'June 19, 1815.

'You will readily give credit to the existence of the extreme grief with which I announce to you the death of your gallant brother, in consequence of a wound received in our great battle of yesterday. He had served me most zealously and usefully for many years, and on many trying occasions; but he had never rendered himself more useful, and had never distinguished himself more, than in our late actions.

'He received the wound which occasioned his death when rallying one of the Brunswick battalions which was shaking a little, and he lived long enough to be informed by myself of the glorious result of our actions, to which he had so much contributed by his active and zealous assistance.

'I cannot express to you the regret and sorrow with which I look round me, and contemplate the loss which I have sustained, particularly in your brother. The glory resulting from such actions, so dearly bought, is no consolation to me, and I cannot suggest it as any to you and his friends; but I hope that it may be expected that this last one has been so decisive as that no doubt remains that our exertions and our individual losses will be rewarded by the early attainment of our just object. It is then that the glory of the actions in which our friends and relations have fallen will be some consolation for their loss.

'Your brother had a black horse, given to him, I believe, by Lord Ashburnham, which I will keep till I hear from you what you wish should be done with it.'

BROKEN DOWN BY LOSSES.

To the Duke of Beaufort, K.G.

'Bruxelles,
'June 19, 1815.

'I am very sorry to have to acquaint you that your brother FitzRoy is very severely wounded, and has lost his right arm. I have just seen him, and he is perfectly free from fever, and as well as anybody could be under such circumstances.

'You are aware how useful he has always been to me, and how *much* I shall feel the want of his assistance, and what a regard and affection I feel for him; and you will readily believe how much concerned I am for his misfortune. Indeed, the losses I have sustained have quite broken me down, ***(the tears ran down Wellington's cheeks as he listened***

to the surgeon's report of the losses in the battle.), and I have no feeling for the advantages we have acquired. I hope, however, that your brother will soon be able to join me again, and that he will long live to be as he is likely to become, an honour to his country, as he is a satisfaction to his family and friends.'

To Earl Bathurst.

'Bruxelles,
'June 19, 1815.

'I have to inform Your Lordship, in addition to my despatch of this morning, that we have already got here 5,000 prisoners, taken in the action of yesterday, and that there are above 2,000 more coming in tomorrow. There will probably be many more. ***(The French loss at Waterloo has been estimated at 30,000, with 200 guns. The Prussian loss was about 7,000.)*** Amongst the prisoners are the Comte de Lobau, who commanded the 6th Corps, and General Cambrone, who commanded a division of the Guards. I propose to send the whole to England, by Ostend.'

To General Doumouriez.

À Nivelles,
'ce 20 Juin, 1815.

'. . . J'avais commence cette lettre le 14, et, comme ce n'était pas jour de poste, je ne l'avais pas finie; et j'étais engagé avec Tenhemi le Vendredi, qui était jour de poste. J'ai depuis reçu votre lettre du 15, pour laquelle je vous suis bien oblige.

'Vous aurez vu ce que j'ai fait, et j'espère que vons en serez content. Jamais je n'ai vu une telle bataille que celle d'avant hier, ni n'ai remporté une telle victoire; et j'espère que c'est fini de Buonaparte . . . .'

General Order.

'Nivelles,
'June 20, 1815.

'*1.* As the army is about to enter the French territory, the troops of the nations which are at present under the command of Field-Marshal the Duke of Wellington are desired to recollect that their respective sovereigns are the Allies of His Majesty the King of France, and that France ought, therefore, to be treated as a friendly country.

'It is therefore required that nothing should be taken, either by officers or soldiers, for which payment be not made. The commissaries of the army will provide for the wants of the troops in the usual manner, and it is not permitted either to soldiers or officers to extort contributions. The commissaries will be authorised, either by the Field-Marshal or by the generals who command the troops of the respective nations, in cases where their provisions are not supplied by an English Commissary, to make the proper requisitions, for which regular receipts will be given; and it must be strictly understood that they will themselves be held responsible for whatever they obtain in way of requisition from the inhabitant of France, in the same manner in which they would be esteemed accountable for purchases made for their own Government in the several dominions to which they belong.

'2. The Field-Marshal takes this opportunity of returning to the army his thanks for their conduct in the glorious action fought on the 18th instant, and he will not fail to report his sense of their conduct in the terms which it deserves to their several sovereigns.'

PROCLAMATION.

'Je fais savoir aux Français que j'entre dans leur pays à la tête d'une armée déjà victorieuse, non en ennemi (excepté de l'usurpateur, prononcé l'ennemi du genre humain, avec lequel on ne peut avoir ni paix ni trève), mais pour ies aider a secouer le joug de fer par lequel ils sont opprimés.

'En conséquence j'ai donné les ordres ci-joints à mon armée, et je demande qu'on me fasse connaître tout infracteur.

'Les Français savent cependant que j'ai le droit d'exiger qu'ils se conduisent de manière que je puisse les protéger contre ceux qui voudraient leur faire du mal.

'Il faut done qu'ils fournissent aux réquisitions qui leur seront faites de la part des personnes autorisées à les faire, en échange pour des regus en forme et ordre; et qu'ils se tiennent chez eux paisiblement, et qu'ils n'aient aucune correspondance ou communication avec l'usurpateur ennemi, ni avec ses adhérens.

'Tous ceux qui s' absenteront de leur domicile après l'entrée en France, et tous ceux qui se trouveront absens au service de l'usurpateur, seront considérés comme ses adhérens et comme ennemis; et leurs propriétés seront affectées à la subsistance de l'armée.

'Donné au Quartier Général, à Malplaquet, ce 22 Juin, 1815.

'Wellington.'

'Declaration au Peuple Français.

'Au Palais de l'Elysée,
'le 22 Juin, 1815

'Français!

'En commençant la guerre pour soutenir l'indépendance nationale, je comp-

tais sur la réunion de tous les efforts, de toutes les volontés, et le concours de toutes les autorités nationales; j'étais fondé à en espérer le succès, et j'avais bravé toutes les déclarations des puissances contre moi.

'Les circonstances me paraissent changées. Je m'offre en sacrifice à la haine des ennemis de la France. Puissent-ils être sincères dans leurs déclarations, et n'en avoir réellement voulu qu'à ma personne.

'Ma vie politique est terminée, et je proclame mon fils sous le titre de Napoléon II,, Empereur des Français.

'Les ministres actuels formeront provisoirement le conseil de gouvernement.

'Lnté rêt que je porte à mon fils m'engage à in viter les Chambres à organiser sans délai la Régence par une loi.

'Unissez-vous tous pour le salut public et pour rester une nation indépendante.

'Napoléon.'

After the Battle.

To Earl Bathurst.

'Le Cateau,
'June 22, 1815.

'We have continued in march on the left of the Sambre since I wrote to you. Marshal Blucher crossed that river on the 19th in pursuit of the enemy, and both armies entered the French territory yesterday; the Prussian by Beaumont, and the Allied Army under my command, by Bavay.

'We have blockaded Le Quesnoi and Valenciennes; the Prussian Army Landreçy and Maubeuge. Avesnes surrendered to the latter last night.

'I expect the King of France at Mons tomorrow. I have written to urge him to come forward, as I find the people in this country well disposed to his cause, and I think it probable that he might be able to get possession of some of the fortresses.

'The remains of the French Army have retired upon Laon. All accounts agree in stating that it is in a very wretched state, and that, in addition to its losses in battle and in prisoners, it is losing vast numbers of men by desertion. The soldiers quit their regiments in parties, and return to their homes, those of the cavalry and artillery selling their horses to the people of the country.

'The 3rd Corps, which in my despatch of the 19th I informed Your Lordship had been detached to observe the Prussian Army, remained in the neighbourhood of Wavre till the 20th. It then made good its retreat by Namur and Dinant. This corps is the only one remaining entire. . .'

Napoleon's Death-blow.

To Lieutenant-General the Earl of Uxbridge, G.C.B.

'Le Cateau,
'June 23, 1815.

'. . . . I may be wrong, but my opinion is, that we have given Napoleon his death-blow; from all I hear his army is totally destroyed, the men are deserting in parties, even the generals are withdrawing from him. The infantry throw away their arms, and the cavalry and artillery sell their horses to the people of the country and desert to their homes. Allowing for much exaggeration in this account, and knowing that Buonaparte can still collect, in addition to what he has brought back with him, the 5th Corps, under Rapp, which is near Strasbourg, and the 3rd Corps, which was at Wavre during the battle, and has not suffered so much as the others, and probably some troops from La Vendee, I am still of opinion that he can make no head against us, *qu'il n'a qu'à se pendre. . . .*

'We have blockaded Le Quesnoi and Valenciennes; the Prussians, Landry and Maubeuge. Buonaparte is trying to collect his army at Laon. Avesnes has surrendered to the Prussians.'

Dissatisfaction with Inferiors.

To Earl Bathurst.

'Le Cateau,
'June 23, 1815.

'I am sorry to be obliged to report that in the recent operations I had reason to be extremely dissatisfied, not with the Commissary-General and the heads of that department, but with the inferiors, who quitted their brigades and corps without leave and without cause, to the great inconvenience and injury of the service, and were brought back from Bruxelles only by my threatening to dismiss them all. . . .'

Capture of Cambray.

To Lieutenant-General Colville.

'Le Cateau,
'June 25, 1815.

'I congratulate you, and am very much obliged to you for your success of last night. . .'

Return of the Killed and Wounded of the Allied Army, under the Command of Field-Marshal His Grace the Duke of Wellington, K.G. and G.C.B., in the Capture of Cambray, on June 24, 1815.

	Officers.	Sergeants.	Rank and File.	Horses.	Total Loss of Officers, Non-commissioned Officers, and Rank and File.
Killed -	1	—	7	—	8
Wounded -	3	1	25	—	29

A Gloomy Report.

To Earl Bathurst.

'Joncourt,
'June 25, 1815.

'I hope we are going on well, and that what we are doing will bring matters to the earliest and best conclusion, as we are in a very bad way.

'We have not one quarter of the ammunition which we ought to have, on account of the deficiency of our drivers and carriages; and I really believe that, with the exception of my old Spanish infantry, I have got not only the worst troops, but the worst equipped army, with the worst staff, that was ever brought together.

'—— knows no more of his business than a child, and I am obliged to do it for him; and, after all, I cannot get him to do what I order him. Some of the regiments (the new ones, I mean) are reduced to nothing; but I must keep them as regiments, to the great inconvenience of the service, at great expense; or I must send them home, and part with the few British soldiers I have.

'I never was so disgusted with any concern as I am with this; and I only hope that I am going the right way to bring it to an early conclusion in some way or other.

'Napoléon aux braves soldats de l'armée devant Paris,

'De La Malmaison,
'le 25 Juin, 1815.

'Soldats!

'Quand de cède à la nécessité qui me force de m'éloigner de la brave armée Française, j'emporte avec moi l'heureuse certitude qu'elle justifiera, par les services que la patrie attend d'elle, les éloges que nos ennemis eux-mêmes ne peuvent pas lui refuser.

'Soldats! je suivrai vos pas, quoique absent. Je connais tous les corps, et

aucun d'eux ne remportera aucun avantage signalé que je ne rende justice au courage qu'il aura déployé.

'Vous et moi, nous avons été calomniés. Des hommes indignes d'apprécier vos travaux ont vu dans les marques d'attachement que vous m'avez données un zèle dont j'étais le seul objet; que vos succès futurs leur apprennent que c'était la patrie par-dessus tout que vous serviez en m'obéissant, et que, si j'ai quelque part à votre affection, je le dois à mon ardent amour pour la France, notre mère commune.

'Soldats! encore quelques efforts et la coalition est dissoute. Napoléon vous reconnaîtra aux coups que vous allez porter. Sauvez l'honneur, l'indépendance des Français.

'Soyez jusqu'à la fin tels que je vous ai connus depuis vingt ans, et vous serez invincibles.

'Napoléon.'

Wellington declines to be Napoleon's Executioner.

To Sir Charles Stuart.

'Orvillé,
'June 28, 1815.

'I send you my despatches, which will make you acquainted with the state of affairs. You may show them to Talleyrand if you choose.

'General —— has been here this day to negotiate for Napoleon's passing to America, to which proposition I have answered that I have no authority.

'The Prussians think the Jacobins wish to give him over to me, believing that I will save his life. —— wishes to kill him; but I have told him that I shall remonstrate, and shall insist upon his being disposed of by common accord.

'I have likewise said that, as a private friend, I advised him to have nothing to do with so foul a transaction; that he and I had acted too distinguished parts in these transactions to become executioners; and that I was determined that if the sovereigns wished to put him to death, they should appoint an executioner, which should not be me. . . .'

The Basis of an Armistice.

To Lieutenant-General the Earl of Uxbridge.

'Gonesse,
'July 2, 1815.

'. . . . We are going on very well. We have shut the French into Paris and their lines; Blücher has crossed the Seine. Buonaparte is off,

I believe, to Havre.

'They offer an armistice; but I won't grant it unless I shall be certain it will lead to a permanent settlement. . . .'

Waterloo a Pounding Match.

To Marshal Lord Beresford.

'Gonesse,
'July 2, 1815.

'. . . . You will have heard of our battle of the 18th. Never did I see such a pounding match. Both were what the boxers call gluttons. Napoleon did not manoeuvre at all. He just moved forward in the old style, in columns, and was driven off in the old style.

'The only difference was, that he mixed cavalry with his infantry, and supported both with an enormous quantity of artillery. I had the infantry for some time in squares, and we had the French cavalry walking about us as if they had been our own. I never saw the British infantry behave so well.

'Boney is now off, I believe, to Rochefort, to go to America. The army, about 40,000 or 50,000, are in Paris. Blücher on the left of the Seine, and I with my right in front of St. Denis, and the left upon the Bois de Bondy.

'They have fortified St. Denis and Montmartre very strongly. The Canal de l'Ourcq is filled with water, and they have a parapet and batteries on the bank; so that I do not believe we can attack this line. However, I will see.'

General Order.

'Gonesse,
'July 4, 1815.

'*1.* The Field-Marshal has great satisfaction in announcing to the troops under his command that he has, in concert with Field-Marshal Prince Blücher, concluded a military convention with the Commander-in-Chief of the French Army in Paris, by which the enemy are to evacuate St. Denis, St. Ouen, Clichy, and Neuilly, this day at noon; the heights of Montmartre tomorrow at noon; and Paris the next day.

'*2.* The Field-Marshal congratulates the army upon this result of their glorious victory. He desires that the troops may employ the leisure of this day to clean their arms, clothes and appointments, as it is his intention that they should pass him in review.

'Wellington.'

Napoleon's Surrender.

To the Right Hon. Sir Henry Wellesley.

'Paris,
'July 19, 1815.

'You will have heard of our great battle in Flanders, and of its final result in the surrender of Buonaparte to the *Bellerophon*, off the Isle d'Aix; and if the Allies will only be a little moderate—that is, if they will prevent plunder by their troops, and take only what is necessary for their own security—we may hope for permanent peace.

'But I confess that I am a little afraid of them. They are all behaving exceedingly ill.'

Idle Troops.

To Earl Bathurst.

'Paris,
'July 20, 1815.

'As we keep our troops here for nothing, and it is impossible to say what may happen under the system of plunder which it is proposed to adopt, it is best that you should send us as many as you can. They had still better come by Ostend; but, as I am hereafter to occupy the country from the Seine to the frontier of the Low Countries, we shall then open our communication by Dieppe or Boulogne.'

'Pitch them to the Devil.'

To Marshal Beresford.

'Paris,
'August 7, 1815.

'I received only last night your letter of the 8th, for which I am very much obliged to you.

'The Battle of Waterloo was certainly the hardest fought that has been for many years, I believe, and has placed in the power of the Allies the most important results. We are throwing them away, however, by the infamous conduct of some of us; and I am sorry to add that our own Government also are taking up a little too much the tone of their rascally newspapers. They are shifting their objects, and, having got their cake, they want both to eat it and keep it.

'As for your Portuguese concerns, I recommend to you to resign and come away immediately. It is impossible for the British Government to maintain British officers for the Portuguese Army, at an expense even so trifling as it is, if the Portuguese Government are to refuse to give the service of the army in the cause of Europe in any manner.

'Pitch them to the devil, then, in the mode which will be most dignified for yourself, and that which will have the best effect in opening the prince's eyes to the conduct of his servants in Portugal, and let the matter work its own way. Depend upon it, the British Government must and will recall the British officers.

'I shall hold a language here that will correspond with your actions in Portugal.'

A True Account of Waterloo impossible.

To —— —— Esq.

'Paris,
'August 8, 1815.

'I have received your letter of the 2nd, regarding the Battle of Waterloo. The object which you propose to yourself is very difficult of attainment, and, if really attained, is not a little invidious. The history of a battle is not unlike the history of a ball. Some individuals may recollect all the little events of which the great result is the battle won or lost; but no individual can recollect the order in which, or the exact moment at which, they occurred, which makes all the difference as to their value or importance.

'Then the faults or the misbehaviour of some gave occasion for the distinction of others, and perhaps were the cause of material losses; and you cannot write a true history of a battle without including the faults and misbehaviour of part at least of those engaged.

'Believe me that every man you see in a military uniform is not a hero; and that, although in the account given of a general action, such as that of Waterloo, many instances of individual heroism must be passed over unrelated, it is better for the general interests to leave those parts of the story untold, than to tell the whole truth.

'If, however, you should still think it right to turn your attention to this subject, I am most ready to give you every assistance and information in my power.'

'Paris,
'August 17, 1815.

'I have received your letter of the 11th, and I regret much that I have not been able to prevail upon you to relinquish your plan.

'You may depend upon it you will never make it a satisfactory work.

'I will get you the list of the French Army, generals, etc.,

'Just to show you how little reliance can be placed, even on what are supposed the best accounts of a battle, I mention that there are some circumstances mentioned in General ——'s account which did not occur as he relates them.

'He was not on the field during the whole battle, particularly not during the latter part of it.

'The battle began, I believe, at eleven. ***(In his despatch Wellington stated that the battle began 'at about 10 o'clock.' In 1836 he said no two persons agreed as to the exact hour when it commenced.)***

'It is impossible to say when each important occurrence took place, nor in what order. We were attacked first with infantry only, then with cavalry only, lastly and principally with cavalry and infantry mixed.

'No houses were possessed by the enemy in Mont St. Jean, excepting the farm in front of the left of our centre, on the road to Genappe, can be called one.

'This they got, I think, at about two o'clock, and got it from a circumstance which is to be attributed to the neglect of the officer commanding on the spot.

'The French cavalry were on the plateau in the centre between the two highroads for nearly three-quarters of an hour, riding about among our squares of infantry, all firing having ceased on both sides. I moved our squares forward to the guns; and our cavalry, which had been detached by Lord Uxbridge to the flanks, was brought back to the centre.

'The French cavalry were then driven off. After that circumstance, repeated attacks were made along the whole front of the centre of the position by cavalry and infantry till seven at night. How many I cannot tell.

'When the enemy attacked Sir Thomas Picton I was there, and they got as far as the hedge on the cross-road, behind which the —— —— had been formed. The latter had run away, and our troops were on our side of the hedge. The French were driven off with immense loss. This was the first principal attack.

'At about two in the afternoon, as I have above said, they got possession of the farmhouse on the highroad, which defended this part of the position; and they then took possession of a small mound on the left of the highroad going from Bruxelles, immediately opposite the gate of the farm; and they were never removed from thence till I commenced the attack in the evening; but they never advanced farther on that side.

'These are answers to all your queries; but remember I recommend to you to leave the Battle of Waterloo as it is.'

Division of Spoil.

To General Comte Gneisenau.

'Paris,

'August 10, 1815.

'General Müffling, who was desired by Marshal Prince Blücher to speak to me some time ago on the subject of the guns taken at the battle of June 18 will have told him that I was ready to do anything that was agreeable to him on the subject.

'I beg you to tell him that it appears to me that it would be best to nominate an officer on each side to make the division of everything taken during and after the battle, and in Paris.'

Disgraceful Robberies.

To the Officer commanding the Brigade of Cavalry at Beauvais.

'Paris,

'September 27, 1815.

'I enclose a letter with its enclosure which I have received from the French Minister at War, from which I am sorry to observe that robberies on the highway still continue in the neighbourhood of Beauvais, committed by the British troops, and, there is every reason to believe, by the — Regiment of ——.

'This is a most disgraceful circumstance, and proves that the internal discipline of the regiment must have been so entirely neglected as that all recollection of it must be effaced. It is impossible that, if the officers and non-commissioned officers attended to and knew the character of their men, and visited their cantonments constantly, these nightly depredations upon the passengers on the highroad, and even in the towns and villages in which the troops are cantoned, could be carried on, without some discovery being made of the persons who committed them.

'I beg now to know whether any report had been made to you of these robberies, and what measures you have taken to discover the robbers, or to prevent these disgraceful proceedings in future.

'If nothing else will answer, you must have guards placed and a chain of vedettes in sight of each other, along the highroad through the whole length of your cantonments, and the rolls must be called every hour during the day and night, officers and all being present, in order to prevent the soldiers from quitting their cantonments for the purpose of highway robbery.

'I must hold you responsible that this practice shall be put a stop to without loss of time, and that the most active measures shall be taken to discover those soldiers who have disgraced the army and their country by being guilty of it.'

Provision for the Wounded.

To W. Rowcroft, Esq,

'Paris,
'September 28, 1815.

'I am very much obliged to you for your several communications on the subject of the Waterloo fund, the last of which, of the 25th instant, I have received this day. . . .

'In the provision for the wounded, I strongly recommend that the provision should be confined to those who have lost a limb, or, as soldiers, are entirely disabled from service or from work. Attention to these inquiries will place at the disposal of the Committee a larger fund for the provision for the widows and orphans of officers and soldiers, who are the really distressed.'

The Question of Promotion.

To Lieutenant-General the Marquis of Anglesey, G.C.B.

'Paris,
'October 12, 1815.

'. . . It is quite impossible to do what everybody deserves, *viz.*, to recommend him for a step of promotion. A line must be drawn somewhere, and I conceived I could not draw one that was more just towards everybody than to take an officer for promotion from each regiment. I might have gone farther, but the general officers all recommended their staff, some even who, from their standing in the service, could not be promoted; and this circumstance has rendered it necessary to leave unnoticed the claims of many meritorious individuals serving in the line of the army. . .'

Disposal of Honours.

To Major-General Sir Henry Torrens.

'Paris,
'October 14, 1815.

'I enclose a letter from Mr. Browne to Lord Stewart regarding

Lieutenant-Colonel Sir J. Browne's claim to be a Companion of the Order of the Bath.

'I will not recommend him, as I will not recommend anybody excepting for the Battle of Waterloo; but I perfectly recollect his good conduct in the battle fought by the Spanish Army near Badajoz. It was unsuccessful, and everybody behaved ill excepting Browne and Don Carlos de España, who behaved remarkably well.'

'Paris,
'October 14, 1815.

'I enclose a memorandum from Colonel Dalbiac respecting the third class of the Order of the Bath, which, as I expected, is as much looked after now as the second was last year. I do not wish to interfere in recommending him, but I must say that he is a very deserving officer. In regard to the case of Stanhope, (Lieutenant-Colonel the Hon. James Stanhope), and the others, I feel a great disinclination to do anything, though I think Stanhope in particular deserves the Order. We had better, however, adhere to the rule, as we have it, that none shall have the Order except those who actually commanded.

'My own opinion is, that the best mode of disposing of these honours is arbitrary—that is to say, without any rule excepting a sense of merit in the persons receiving them.

'But this principle excludes all rule, neither can you introduce it where there is a rule. I am perfectly aware, however, of the inconveniences, particularly in a country and in an army like ours, of disposing of honours of this description without rule; and I am now suffering them all from having disposed by selection of the orders placed at my disposition by the sovereigns without attending to any rule excepting that of taking those I thought most deserving.'

The Best Troops in the World.

To Earl Bathurst,

'Paris,
'October 33, 1815.

'. . . My opinion is that the best troops we have, probably the best in the world, are the British infantry, particularly the old infantry that has served in Spain.

'This is what we ought to keep up, and what I wish above all others to retain. . . .'

Memorandum

On the Twenty-five Millions of Francs as Prize-Money.

To Viscount Castlereagh.

'Paris,
'November 6, 1815.

'My opinion is that Government ought to give this sum to the army, to be distributed amongst them in the shape prize-money.

'It should be given to the officers and troops present in the battles of June 15, 16, 17, and 18, or present with their regiments or at their posts with the army at any period from that time till July 7, when the army entered Paris.

'According to this scheme, the officers and troops of the Armies of the King of the Netherlands, the King of Hanover, with the exception of those corps in garrison in the Netherlands, the Grand-Duke of Nassau, and the Duke of Brunswick, would be included with the British troops, with the exception of those of the latter in garrisons in the Netherlands; and the consent of the King of the Netherlands, the King of Hanover, the Grand-Duke of Nassau, and the Duke of Brunswick must be obtained. If this plan should not be adopted, the sum of 25,000,000 *francs* would be divided between the several Powers whose troops formed the army under the command of the Duke of Wellington, according to the numbers which each Power was bound to furnish for the common cause.

'Thus, then, Great Britain would receive for 150,000 men, the Netherlands for 50,000, Hanover for 10,000, Brunswick and Nassau each for 3,000. But the regiments and battalions composing the Hanoverian and Brunswick subsidiary corps, the former consisting of 16,400 men, and the latter of 4,100 men, would share with the British troops, supposing, as I imagine, that the British Government would allot its share to be divided in prize money to the army.

'It is obvious that, supposing all the Powers should agree each to give what should come to them on this account to their troops who were present in the battles and on the occasions mentioned, there would be a great difference in the amount received by the officers and soldiers of each rank in the several services; and, therefore, it would probably be the best mode to allow the whole sum to be divided according to the plan first proposed, as one mass among the officers and soldiers of the whole army.

'Wellington.'

Protests against Newspaper Statements

To —— ——.

'Paris,
'November 24, 1815.

'My name is frequently mentioned in your newspaper, and, as it is a sort of privilege of modern Englishmen to read in the daily newspapers lies respecting those who serve them, and I have been so long accustomed to be so treated, I should not have thought it necessary to trouble you on the subject if you had not thought proper to contradict, as from authority, in a late paper, certain reports which you had before published respecting differences between the Duc de Berri and me. . . .

'Other circumstances respecting me have been published in your paper, which are equally false with those to which I have above referred; but I will not trouble you upon them; nor should I have written to you at all, as I am really quite indifferent respecting what is read of me in the newspapers, if you had not given an appearance of truth to some reports by the formal contradiction which you have published of others.'

Wellington's Farewell.

General Order.

'Paris,
'November 30, 1815.

'*48.* Upon breaking up the army which the Field-Marshal has had the honour of commanding, he begs leave again to return thanks to the general officers, and the officers and troops, for their uniform good conduct.

'*49.* In the late short but memorable campaign they have given proofs to the world that they possess in an eminent degree all the good qualities of soldiers, and the Field-Marshal is happy to be able to applaud their regular good conduct in their camps and cantonments, not less than when engaged with the enemy in the field.

'*50.* Whatever may be the future destination of those brave troops, of which the Field-Marshal now takes his leave, he trusts that every individual will believe that he will ever feel the deepest interest in their honour and welfare, and will always be happy to promote either.'

www.ingramcontent.com/pod-product-compliance
Lightning Source LLC
Chambersburg PA
CBHW031559170426
43196CB00031B/164
* 9 7 8 1 9 1 7 6 6 6 5 1 0 *